MEDIEVAL EUROPE

CHRIS WICKHAM

MEDIEVAL EUROPE

YALE UNIVERSITY PRESS
NEW HAVEN AND LONDON

For information about this and other Yale University Press publications, please contact:
U.S. Office: sales.press@yale.edu   yalebooks.com
Europe Office: sales@yaleup.co.uk   yalebooks.co.uk

Typeset in Minion Pro by IDSUK (DataConnection) Ltd
Printed in Great Britain by Gomer Press Ltd, Llandysul, Ceredigion, Wales

Library of Congress Cataloging-in-Publication Data

Names: Wickham, Chris, 1950– author.
Title: Medieval Europe / Chris Wickham.
Description: New Haven : Yale University Press, 2016. | Includes bibliographical
    references.
LCCN 2016018675 | ISBN 9780300208344 (cloth : alkaline paper)
LCSH: Europe—History—476–1492. | Middle Ages. | Social change—Europe—
    History—To 1500. | Europe—Social conditions—To 1492. | BISAC: HISTORY /
    Medieval. | HISTORY / Europe / General. | HISTORY / Social History.
Classification: LCC D117 .W53 2016 | DDC 940.1—dc23
LC record available at https://lccn.loc.gov/2016018675

A catalogue record for this book is available from the British Library.

10 9 8 7 6 5 4 3 2 1

Contents

Illustrations and maps

Illustrations

Maps

Acknowledgements

My first thanks go to Heather McCallum, who suggested that I write this book and finally persuaded me; she also critiqued its drafts and was a reality check throughout. Leslie Brubaker read the whole book and made it clear what changes I could not avoid making; so did two very supportive Yale readers. Many other friends read parts of the book: Pat Geary and Mayke de Jong read Chapters 1 to 6, Lesley Abrams read Chapter 5, Chris Dyer read Chapter 7, John Arnold read Chapter 8, Robert Swanson read Chapter 10, Lyndal Roper read Chapters 10 and 12, John Watts read Chapters 11 and 12. I could not have done this without their (often highly critical) support, especially when I moved into parts of the middle ages I knew relatively little about. Several other people helped me with advice and references and to find books: Peter Coss, Lorena Fierro Díaz, Marek Jankowiak, Tom Lambert, Isabella Lazzarini, Conrad Leyser, Sophie Marnette, Giedrė Mickūnaitė, Maureen Miller, Natalia Nowakowska, Helmut Reimitz, John Sabapathy, Mark Whittow, Emily Winkler, are only some of them. I cannot even list the many people who saved me from errors in casual conversation, not knowing that I was taking mental notes; but all the speakers at the Monday-at-5 medieval seminar which I have run for eleven years at Oxford with Mark Whittow have contributed, in one way or another, to my ideas in this book. I have also to thank RAE2008 and REF2014 for their intellectual stimulus: they forced me to read significant books and articles on a wide variety of topics which I would not always have come across otherwise, and many of these are in the bibliography.

C.W.
January 2016

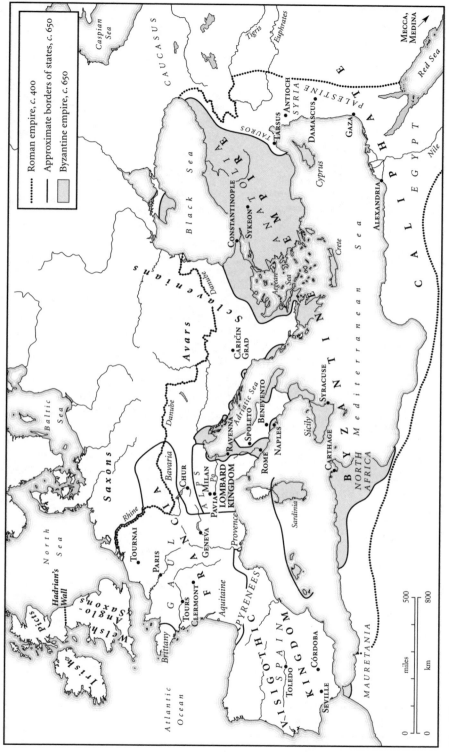

Map 1 Europe in 550.

Map 2 Western Europe in 850.

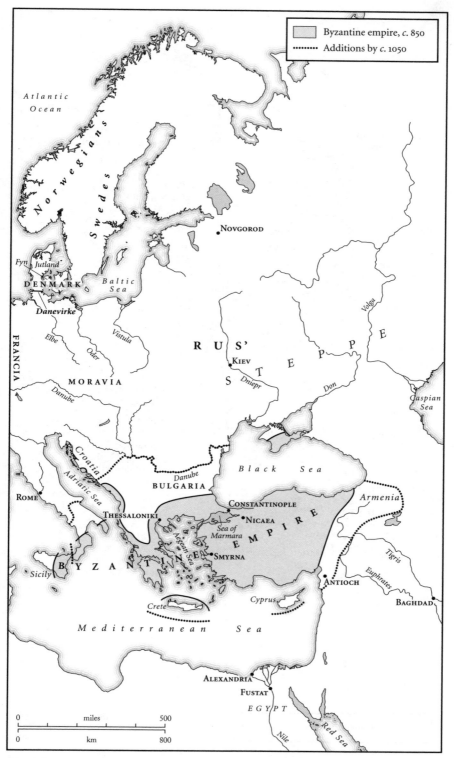

Map 3 Eastern Europe in 850.

Map 4 Western Europe in 1150.

*Atlantic
Ocean*

TRONDHEIM
NORWAY
BERGEN

SWEDEN

NOVGOROD

SUZDAL'
VLADIMIR

DENMARK
*Baltic
Sea*
Lithuanians
PRINCIPALITIES

OF RUS'

Volga

Elbe
GNIEZNO
Vistula
GERMAN
Oder
**POLISH
DUKES**
Dniepr
S

EMPIRE PRAGUE
KIEV
T

Danube
E
P

Don
P

*Caspian
Sea*

HUNGARY

Croatia
BYZANTINE
Danube

Black   Sea

ROME
Adriatic Sea
Thrace CONSTANTINOPLE
Armenia
MANZIKERT

THESSALONIKI
EMPIRE
NICAEA

**NORMAN
KINGDOM**
THEBES
Aegean Sea

SMYRNA
Tigris

Sicily
CORINTH
KONYA

Euphrates

ANTIOCH
BAGHDAD

Crete
Cyprus
TRIPOLI

M e d i t e r r a n e a n   S e a
**CRUSADER
STATES**

JERUSALEM

DAMIETTA
TINNIS
ALEXANDRIA

CAIRO
**FATIMID
CALIPHATE**
Red Sea

Nile

| 0 | miles | 500 |
| 0 | km | 800 |

Map 5 Eastern Europe in 1150.

Map 6 Western Europe in 1500.

Map 7 Eastern Europe in 1500.

CHAPTER ONE

A new look at the middle ages

This book is about change. What we call the medieval period, or the middle ages, lasted a thousand years, from 500 to 1500; and Europe, which is the subject of this book, was a very different place at the end of this period from what it had been at the beginning. The Roman empire dominated the start of the period, unifying half of Europe but dividing it sharply from the other half; a millennium later, Europe had taken the complicated shape it has kept since, with a majority of the independent states of the present recognisable in some form or other. My aim in the book is to show how this change, and many others, happened, and how far they are important. But it is not focused on outcomes. Many writers about the middle ages have been preoccupied with the origins of those 'nation'-states, or with other aspects of what they see as 'modernity', and for them it is these outcomes which give meaning to the period. This for me is seriously mistaken. History is not teleological: that is to say, historical development does not go *to*; it goes *from*. Furthermore, as far as I am concerned, the medieval period, full of energy as it was, is interesting in and for itself; it does not need to be validated by any subsequent developments. I hope that this book will make that interest clear.

This does not, however, mean that medieval European history simply consisted of swirling patterns of events, which had no structure at all except as part of some randomly selected millennium. Far from it. The middle ages had some clearly marked moments of change; it is these which give form to the period. The fall of the Roman empire in the west in the fifth century, the crisis of the eastern empire when it confronted the rise of Islam in the seventh, the forcefulness of the Carolingian experiment in very large-scale moralised government in the late eighth and ninth, the expansion of Christianity in northern and eastern Europe in (especially) the tenth, the radical decentralisation of political power in the west in the eleventh, the demographic and economic expansion of the tenth to thirteenth, the reconstruction of political and religious power in the west in the twelfth and thirteenth, the eclipse of Byzantium in the same period, the Black Death and the development of state structures in the fourteenth, and the emergence of a wider popular engagement with the public sphere in the late fourteenth and fifteenth: these are in my view those major moments of change, and they have a chapter each in this book. Linking all of these turning points was a set of structural developments: among others, the retreat and reinvention of concepts of public power, the shift in the balance of the resources of political systems from taxation to landowning and back again, the changing impact of the use of writing on political culture, and the growth in the second half of the middle ages of formalised and bounded patterns of local power and identity, which transformed the ways rulers and the people they ruled dealt with each other. These will be at the centre of this book too. A book of this length cannot delve into the microhistory of societies or cultures in any detail, nor, for that matter, provide detailed country-by-country narratives of events. This is an interpretation of the middle ages, not a textbook account – there are anyway many of the latter, many of them excellent, and they do not need to be added to.[1] I have, certainly, in every chapter set out brief accounts of political action, so as to give contexts to my arguments, especially for readers who are coming to the medieval period for the first time. But my intention is to concentrate on the moments of change and the overarching structures, to show what, in my view, most characterised the medieval period and makes it interesting; and they are the basic underpinnings of what follows.

My list of moments of change also presents a different storyline from that which appears, whether explicitly or implicitly, in all too many other accounts of the European middle ages. A very common narrative, even today, sees Europe emerging from degradation with the eleventh-century 'Gregorian reform', from ignorance with the 'twelfth-century Renaissance', from poverty with Flemish cloth-making and Venetian shipping, from political weakness with the (nation-)state-building of Henry II and Edward I in England, Philip II and Louis IX in France, Alfonso VI and Ferdinand III in Castile, to reach its apex in the 'high medieval' twelfth and thirteenth centuries with crusades, chivalry, gothic cathedrals, papal monarchy, the university of Paris and the Champagne fairs; by contrast, the post-1350 period sees a 'waning', with plague, war, schism and cultural insecurity, until humanism and radical church reform sort matters out again. That narrative will not be found in this book. It misrepresents the late middle ages, and excludes the early middle ages and Byzantium entirely; furthermore, far too much of it is a product of that desire to make the medieval period, at least after 1050, 'really' part of modernity, which I have already criticised. It is also the hidden heir of the old desire for history to provide moral lessons, periods to admire, heroes and villains, which historians say they have got beyond but often have not.

That moralism, for many, derives from the word 'medieval' itself. The word has a curious history; it was a negative word from the start, and has often remained one. From the Roman republic onwards, people regularly referred to themselves as 'modern' – *moderni* in Latin – and to forebears as *antiqui*, 'ancient'. In the fourteenth and fifteenth centuries, however, a handful of intellectuals, whom we call humanists, began to restrict the word 'ancient' to the classical writers of the Roman empire and its predecessors, whom they saw as their true forebears, with the supposedly inferior writers of the intervening millennium relegated to what was increasingly, by the seventeenth century, called the 'middle age', the *medium aevum*, hence 'medieval'. This usage was picked up above all in the nineteenth century, and it then spread to everything else: 'medieval' government, the economy, the church, and so on, to be set against the concept, also nineteenth-century, of the Renaissance, when 'modern' history supposedly started.[2] The medieval period could thus be seen as a random invention, a confidence trick perpetrated on the future by a few scholars. But it has become a powerful image, as more and more layers of 'modernity' have built up.

Once history-writing became more professionalised, from the 1880s onwards, and period specialisms developed, the medieval past began to gain a more positive image too. Some of it was somewhat defensive, as for example in the claims of scholars of different medieval centuries for 'renaissances' of their own, which might legitimate their period in the eyes of contemptuous moderns, the 'twelfth-century Renaissance' again, or the 'Carolingian Renaissance'. Some of it was very enthusiastic and sometimes fervent, as Catholic historians extolled the religious purity of the middle ages, or nationalist historians focused on the always-medieval roots of the always-superior identity of their own countries. The medieval period, a long time ago and in some places poorly documented, becomes here the imagined origin of any number of twentieth-century desires, and as fictional as the rhetoric of any humanist. But there was also a century and more of hard empirical work, which has allowed the complexity and fascination of the medieval millennium to be recognised, more and more clearly. Medieval historians often owe more to the preoccupations of nationalist historiography than they realise; it is still true that English historians are more prone to see the growth of the English state as a central theme – the first nation-state in Europe, a mark of English exceptionalism – and the Germans worry at the *Sonderweg*, the 'special path' that prevented such a state forming in their country; whereas Italian historians regard the break-up of the kingdom of Italy with equanimity, because it meant autonomy for Italy's cities, and thus the civic culture which brought with it the (to them very Italian) Renaissance.[3] But the depth and complexity of medieval scholarship by now is sufficiently great that there are also alternatives to these views, and we can get around them more easily.

That solves one problem, then; but another appears. If we no longer imagine the middle ages to be a long dark period of random violence, ignorance and superstition, then what differentiates this time from before and after? The start of the period is to an extent easier, because it is conventionally attached to the political crises which came with the fall of the western Roman empire in the fifth century, hence the rough date of 500 for the ancient–medieval divide: whether or not one sees the Roman empire as somehow 'better' than the western successor states, the latter were certainly more fragmented, structurally weaker, economically simpler. The break is complicated by the long survival of the eastern Roman empire, which we now call Byzantium; as a result, in south-eastern Europe 500 is no dividing line at all. Indeed, the break even in the west only affected a handful of today's European nations, France, Spain, Italy and southern Britain being the largest, for the Roman empire never extended to Ireland, Scandinavia, most of Germany or most of the Slavic-speaking countries. It is also complicated by the success of the last generation of historians in showing that there were strong continuities across the divide at 500, in cultural practices in particular – religious assumptions, the imagery of public power – which might make a 'late late antiquity' survive for a long time, for some to 800, for some to the eleventh century. Here the relationship between change and stability nuances the sharpness of the break when the empire broke up. But the half century either side of 500 still remains a convenient starting point, and, for me at least, a marker of strong change at too many levels to ignore.

The year 1500 (or, again, the half-century either side of it) is harder: less changed then, or, at least, the supposed markers of the beginning of the 'modern' period were not all particularly significant. The final fall of Byzantium to the Ottoman Turks in 1453 was not so world-shattering, for that once-large empire was by now reduced to small scattered provinces in what is now Greece and Turkey, and anyway the Ottomans carried on Byzantine political structures pretty effectively. The 'discovery' of America by Columbus – or, better, the conquest of its major states by Spanish adventurers in the 1520s and 1530s – was certainly catastrophic for Americans, but its effect on Europe (outside Spain) took a long time to become substantial. The humanist movement that lies at the intellectual core of the Renaissance seems increasingly medieval in style. We are left with the Protestant Reformation, again above all in the 1520s–1530s (with a Catholic Counter-Reformation later in the century), as a religious and cultural shift which split western and central Europe into two and created two often opposing blocks, each with steadily diverging political and cultural practices, which still exist. That certainly was a major, and relatively sudden, break, even if it had little effect on the Orthodox Christianity of eastern Europe. If we regard the Reformation as the marker of the end of medieval Europe, however, then we start the middle ages with a political and economic crisis in an environment of cultural and religious continuities, and we end it with a cultural and religious crisis in an environment in which politics and economics remained much the same. There is an artificiality here, in the whole definition of the middle ages, which we cannot get away from.

This recognition, however, allows us to look again at the issue of how to deal with the middle ages as a single bounded unit. It would of course be possible to look for a better date than 1500 to end a study: maybe 1700, with scientific and financial revolutions; maybe 1800, with political and industrial revolutions. These dates have been canvassed plenty of times before. But that would be to make claims that one sort of change was paramount, at the expense of others; it would be to invent new boundaries, not to relativise them. The attraction of sticking to what we have is precisely that 500–1500 is an artificial span of time, in which changes can be tracked in different ways in different places, without them having to lead teleologically to some major event at the end, whether Reformation, revolution, industrialisation, or any other sign of 'modernity'. And it must also be added, although I do not attempt the task here, that this can help wider comparison as well. Historians of Africa or India or China in our present millennium often criticise the 'medieval' label, because it seems to carry European baggage, and, most seriously, to assume a teleology of inevitable European supremacy, of a type which most historians now reject. But if its artificiality is recognised, the medieval European experience can be used comparatively, to be set against other experiences in a more neutral and thus useful way.[4]

Actually, 'Europe' is not a straightforward concept either. It is simply a peninsula of the Eurasian landmass, as Southeast Asia is.[5] To the north-east, it is separated from the great Asian states by the forests of Russia and the emptiness of Siberia, but the steppe corridor south of that linked Asia and Europe for active horsemen in all periods, as the Huns, Bulgar Turks and Mongols showed in turn, and the steppe continued westwards from Ukraine into Hungary in the heart of Europe. And, most important, southern Europe is inseparable from the Mediterranean, and from economic connections, even when not political and cultural links, to the neighbouring regions of west Asia and north Africa in all periods. While the Roman empire lasted, the Mediterranean as a united sea was far more important as an object of study than was 'Europe', split as the latter was between the Roman state to the south and an ever-changing network of 'barbarian' peoples (as the Romans called them) to the north. This did not alter soon; the Christian religion and the technologies of post-Roman government hardly extended north of the old Roman frontier until after 950. By then, the Mediterranean was anyway beginning to revive as a trade hub, and was as important as northern exchange networks for the rest of the middle ages.[6] And Europe was never a single political unit, and never has been since.

People did talk about Europe in the middle ages, certainly. The entourage of the Carolingians in the ninth century, the kings who ruled what is now France, Germany, the Low Countries and Italy, sometimes called their patrons lords of 'Europe', and so did their successors in the Ottonian Germany of the tenth century: they were posing their patrons as potential overlords of fairly vaguely characterised but wide lands, and 'Europe' was a good word for that. It survived throughout the middle ages in this rhetorical sense, alongside a basic geographical framing taken from antiquity, but it seldom – not never, but seldom – acted as the basis for any claimed identity.[7] It is true that, steadily across the central middle ages, Christianity did spread to all of what are now called the European lands (Lithuania, then much larger than its present size, was the last polity whose rulers converted, in the late fourteenth century). This did not create a common European religious culture, however, for the northward expansions of Latin-based and Greek-based Christianities were two separate processes. Furthermore, the ever-changing border between Christian- and Muslim-ruled lands – with Christian rulers pushing south in thirteenth-century Spain, and Muslim rulers (the Ottomans) pushing north into the Balkans in the fourteenth and fifteenth centuries – meant that the neatness of a 'Christian Europe' (which anyway always excludes Europe's numerous Jews) never matched reality, as it still does not. In a very general sense, as we shall see, the second half of our period does see Europe gaining some level of common development inside the framework of a variety of institutions and political practices, such as the network of bishoprics, or the use of writing in government, which linked Russia across to Portugal. This is not enough for us to see the continent as a single whole, all the same. It was too diverse. All claims to an essential European, and only European, unity are fictional even today, and in the middle ages they would have been fantastic. So: medieval Europe is simply a large differentiated space, seen across a long time period. It is also well enough documented to allow some quite nuanced study. This is not a romantic image at all, and is intended not to be. But this space and time holds some enthralling material all the same. It is my aim to give it shape.

A final warning here. There are two common approaches to the medieval centuries: to make medieval people 'just like us', only operating in a techno-logically simpler world of swords and horses and parchment and no central heating; and to make them immeasurably different from us, with value systems and categorisations of the world which are hard to grasp at all, which are often unpleasant to us, and which involve complex reconstruction to create a logic and a justification for them in their own terms. Each of these is in some ways accurate, but both, taken on their own, are traps. The first approach risks banality, or else the moralisation which results from disappointment, when medieval actors apparently fail to grasp what to us would have been obvious. The second risks moralisation too, but its alternative is too often collusion, even cuteness, with the historian-as-anthropologist focusing only on the fasci-nation of the strange, sometimes on a very small scale indeed. I would rather try to embrace them both, in a wider historicising attempt to see how medieval people made choices in the political and economic environments they really had, and with the values they really possessed, making 'their own history, but not of their own free will; not under circumstances they themselves have chosen but under the given and inherited circumstances with which they are directly confronted.'[8] Marx, whose words these are, did not think that such an analysis involved collusion, and nor do I; but it does require understanding, of the various actors in a very different but not unrecognisable world. As all history requires; although it is indeed important to recognise that the 980s were genuinely strange, with values and a political logic which we have to make an imaginative effort to reconstruct, it is equally important to remember that the same is true of the 1980s.

*   *   *

In the rest of this introductory chapter, I want to set out some basic parameters for how medieval society worked, which will themselves help to make sense of the different patterns of behaviour and political directions which we will see in the rest of this book. In this first section I will discuss politics, particu-larly in the central medieval period; then I will move on, more briefly, to the economy and to some basic aspects of medieval culture. Not that all medieval people thought and acted the same; as usual, divergences were huge; but there were some features common to a substantial proportion of them, some of which were simply consequences of basic socioeconomic patterns common to the whole period, as we shall see.

Medieval Europe was not easy to get about in. It had a network of roads inherited from the Roman empire, but these did not extend past the Roman frontier, along the Rhine and Danube; the road system in the rest of Germany and, still more, further north and east, was rudimentary for a long time, and travellers kept to water transport and river valleys as much as they could. In a world without maps, only experts could take any route-finding risks. Europe is not a continent of high mountains, apart from the Alps; what was more of a barrier was the forest cover of most of continental Europe, except Britain and some of the Mediterranean lands – some 50 per cent in what is now Germany, some 30 per cent in what is now France, more in eastern Europe. The stories of bold young tailors getting lost in the forests of the Brothers Grimm were not fantasy, at least in that respect. In 1073, the German emperor Henry IV, retreating fast from the start of the great Saxon revolt, had to take to the forest, for the Saxons were guarding the roads, and travel for three days without food before he arrived in settled lands again. And travel was anyway slow, even by road. When the same Henry, by now victorious against the Saxons, had a political showdown with Pope Gregory VII in 1075–76, the threatening messages between them, which built up quickly to mutual threats of deposition, took nearly a month to travel each way between southern Saxony and then Utrecht in the modern Netherlands, where Henry was, and Rome – and that was with fast riders, the fastest means of communication until the railways of the nineteenth century.[9] Landscape was a danger and an inconvenience; the romance and beauty of mountain ranges were seen by almost no-one – they were, rather more, the haunt of demons and (in Scandinavia) trolls.

This wildness should not be exaggerated, however. It was there as a backdrop, and sometimes forced itself into the foreground; but it did not stop some European polities from being often quite large, and stably so. The Carolingian empire, as we have already seen, stretched across over half of western Europe; the power of the princes of Kiev in the eleventh century stretched nearly as far, in what is now Russia and Ukraine, a land where, north of the open steppe, forest cover was virtually complete. People did get about. Kings were often on the move for their entire reigns – King John of England (1199–1216)* travelled an average of 20km a day, seldom staying anywhere more than a few nights.[10] Large armies regularly moved a thousand kilometres and more, as for example with the campaigns of German emperors in Italy in the tenth to thirteenth centuries, or the land marches and sea voyages of crusaders, intent on attacking Palestine or Egypt, which were, whatever else they achieved, at least logistical triumphs. More slowly, substantial populations could move, as with the German migration into large sections of eastern Europe after 1150. So: it must,

*All date spans given after rulers' names are dates of reign.

certainly, be recognised that the European world was in general very localised. Most people did indeed only know the land for a few villages in any direction, usually as far as the nearest markets. A count, i.e. the king's local representative, on the edge of a kingdom could often do pretty much what he liked for some time, without the king being able to stop him or, sometimes, even knowing what he was up to. The difficulties of communication always got in the way. But kings, if they were effective, did turn up in the end with armed men (or send other counts to take over), and counts knew they would: that curtailed at least open disloyalty. And there were other techniques of government that could extend the powers of rulers quite far, and quite solidly. We will look at them in future chapters. Here, however, let us look at some of the basic procedures of political power that operated across much of our period. I will focus on a single instance, and then discuss its implications.

In the summer of 1159, Henry II, king of England (1154–89), laid claim to the southern French county of Toulouse. Henry already held nearly half of France, duchies and counties from Normandy in the north to the Pyrenees in the south, by inheritance from both his parents and through his wife Eleanor, herself heiress to the large southern duchy of Aquitaine; Toulouse was, it could be argued, Eleanor's inheritance too, if Henry could get its count to give in. All these French lands he held from the French king, Louis VII (1137–80), to whom he had done homage and sworn fidelity, promising to defend Louis's life and person, as recently as 1158; but Louis, who directly controlled only the Paris region, had no prospect of matching Henry's military power. Henry invaded Toulouse that summer with a huge army, probably the largest he ever called together, including most of the major barons from his English and French domains, and even the king of Scotland, Malcolm IV, who had done homage to him. Louis could not allow Henry to expand his authority even further, and anyway Count Raymond V of Toulouse was his brother-in-law, so he had to try and help him, but what could he do? What Louis did was ride to Toulouse with quite a small entourage (and therefore fast), so that, when Henry arrived there with his army, the king of France was already in the city, organising its defence. Henry could probably have taken Toulouse, notwithstanding its strong fortifications – that was clearly his plan, at least – but his sworn lord was by now inside the walls. As one contemporary source said, 'he did not wish to besiege the town of Toulouse, in honour of King Louis of the French, who defended the same town against King Henry'; as another (who thought he was wrong) said, he took advice not to attack out of 'empty superstition and reverence'. That is to say, Henry was stuck. If he attacked his lord whom he had sworn to defend, what value were his barons' own oaths to him? And what would he do with a captured king who was his lord? So he did not attack, and after a summer of ravaging simply retreated. Henry, one of the two most powerful monarchs in western Europe, could not risk being seen as an oath-breaker, and preferred to lose prestige – a lot of prestige – as a failed strategist instead.[11]

The personal relationship between Henry and Louis was what mattered here. It was hedged about with ceremonial – oaths, homage (the formal recognition of personal dependence), and so on; and it was tied very closely to honour. It was also tied to assumptions about lordship: this ceremonial was part of the terms by which Henry, as a lord, held his dozen counties and duchies, with their landed resources, from the king of France, in contrast to his richest and most coherent territory, England itself, where he was fully sovereign. Here we are in the middle of the world of what is often called military feudalism: a wide élite of great aristocrats and knights did military service, and showed political loyalty, in return for gifts of office or land from kings or lesser lords, which they would lose if they were disloyal. Such men would often be called the lord's sworn *vassi*, vassals, and the conditional landholdings would be called *feoda*, fiefs, hence the words 'feudal' and 'feudo-vassalic' in modern historical terminology. Henry's French lands are often called *feoda* in contemporary sources; Henry's barons, too, above all came to Toulouse as Henry's sworn men and recipients of lands. As it happens, the terminology of 'feudalism' has often been questioned recently. Susan Reynolds has pointed out that military and political obligations, or the meanings of words like 'fief', were seldom as clearcut as this, and certainly not in twelfth-century France. Many people have also stressed that 'feudalism', not a medieval word, can mean very many different things in the hands of different modern authors, and have thus argued that the word has become so vague as to be useless. I myself think it is still useful, when carefully defined.[12] If I hardly use it in this book, it is only because I have tried here to avoid as much technical vocabulary as possible, not because it is intrinsically more problematic than any of the other terms historians employ. But, either way, the fact that Louis was Henry's sworn lord for his French lands, and that Henry's own barons had the same relationship to him, was clearly crucial for determining how Henry responded outside Toulouse. Lordship, whether you wish to call it 'feudal' or not, certainly structured this encounter.

One major reason why this was the case is that élite military service was not, for the most part, performed for a salary. Mercenaries were used in the twelfth century, and made up the bulk of infantry (including in Henry's army of 1159), but cavalry and military leaders by and large consisted of men who, even if paid in part as well, had personal obligations to either the kingdom or the person of the king, or both.[13] The Roman empire had had a fully paid army, much larger than medieval ones and permanent too, and in order to do so it also exacted heavy taxes on landholding – land being the major source of wealth by far, as we shall see. It was therefore a very coherent political structure, and the demise of its fiscal system in the west (see Chapter 2) was the major reason why early medieval successor states were much weaker. The Byzantine and Ottoman empires operated in a similar way, maintaining a continuity throughout the middle ages in south-east Europe, as discussed in Chapters 3 and 9. General taxation returned in western Europe too, even if on a smaller scale and much less efficiently, in the late middle ages; when it did, it both transformed the resources of rulers and brought new problems – notably the need for rulers to get the consent of bodies of aristocrats and townsmen who were going to have to pay for the armies (or, at least, pass on the burden to their own peasantry). We shall see in Chapters 11 and 12 how this changed the political dynamics of the late medieval west. But in the twelfth century in France, and for most of the middle ages in most of Europe, no-one was taking a land tax on more than a small scale. As a result, armies had to be constructed on the basis of the public service of landowners, or else by handing out land on which military men could live; or, when mercenaries were used, by paying them out of the landed resources of kings or counts, and from levies of money from landowners in return for not serving themselves. In this world, a substantial proportion of military service, and thus army formation, depended on personal relationships, linked to the possession of land.

This politics of land was analysed in detail by the great French historian Marc Bloch in 1940, with a subtlety that has not been matched since. (He called this land-based society 'feudal', a much wider definition of the word than one restricted to fiefs and vassals.) He argued that a land-based society implied a 'fragmentation of powers': that it tended to produce decentralised political structures, simply because (to put it much more crudely than Bloch did), in a zero-sum game, the more you granted away land, the less you had, and your landed élites in the future might obey you less if you had less to give.[14] This as we shall see was not entirely true, particularly in the early middle ages; the Carolingians in particular, who did not tax, ruled very large-scale territories indeed by any subsequent standard. But there is no denying that tax-raising states are always much more solid than those based on the gift-exchange of land for military or political loyalty. Salaried soldiers and officials are a safer bet than those who are remunerated by land gifts; the disloyal and incompetent can simply cease to be paid. A ruler whose resources are all from landowning has to tread more carefully, particularly when dealing with aristocratic army-leaders whose landed resources are hard to take away from them, if he (more rarely she) wants to achieve political success. This marked out the majority of medieval political systems.

We may seem in this discussion to have slipped from discussing political activity to discussing military service. In our period, however, there was not so much difference. Government throughout the middle ages revolved around two main structures: the organisation of law and justice, and the organisation of war. Political loyalty was inextricable from a willingness to fight; as a result, too, the landed aristocracy almost always had a military training and identity in the middle ages, which we shall see reflected throughout this book. Rulers, when praised for their military success and their justice (including their ability to get losers to concede, which covered both), were often regarded as the source of their realm's economic prosperity – and, conversely, climatic disasters were often seen as the fault of unjust rulers – but economic development was seldom seen as in their remit; poor relief was left to local communities and ecclesiastical charity; education was privately paid for, and so was medicine. The restricted remit of government in western Europe, and its close link to personal relationships, has indeed led to some influential historians arguing that it is unhelpful to use the word 'state' when we discuss medieval polities.[15] As will become clear in later chapters, this is not a view I hold; I would argue that the public authority of kings in the early middle ages, and the increasingly complex administrative systems of the thirteenth century and later, can both be usefully characterised in terms of state power. Accordingly, the word will be used in this book for most European political systems, except the very simple ones in the northern half of the continent. But their remit was restricted, however they are described.

Returning to Henry II and Louis VII: the politics of land anyway held full sway in 1159. Henry was even about to abandon the last vestiges of a land tax in England, which its kings, uniquely in Latin Europe in the period, had collected for over a century.[16] He may have done so to avoid creating opposition; conversely, he evidently reckoned that, in the zero-sum game of land grants, he was sufficiently resource-rich to be able to rely on the loyalty and gratitude of his principal aristocrats, both French and English – who were also the participants in his Easter and Christmas courts, and in the whole ceremonial culture which had built up around him and other rulers, which had its own etiquette and games-playing, and which helped to underpin loyalty.[17] And he was, for the most part, right. But even he could not risk cutting at the root element of what he got in return for his generosity, that is to say the principle of sworn loyalty, by breaking his own oath to Louis. This in itself shows that the politics of land did not have to result in the cynical manoeuvrings of lords who were just waiting for the chance to break away from weakened rulers. The obligations associated with taking land, the honour attached to fidelity, mattered too. Dishonour was indeed hard to recover from; it had to be handled with great care, and much of the political dealing of the middle ages hung on how much one could get away with before being regarded as fatally dishonourable – I will return to the point in a moment. Furthermore, in the twelfth century the rights of lords and the obligations associated with oaths of loyalty were sharpening, as both Louis and Henry knew well and used to their advantage in other contexts. Other lords in the period might and did take chances with oaths and honour, but Henry was too skilled an operator to take the risk. All the same, the power relationships inside which these games of loyalty were played were entirely constructed around the politics of land. If we understand how that worked, we can get a long way in the understanding of the political practice of the European middle ages; only the stronger state systems of Byzantium and the Ottomans, and of al-Andalus, Muslim Spain, lay outside it.

*   *   *

As to economic behaviour: the main point I want to make here, which under-pins the rest of this book, is quickly set out. Medieval political communities based their coherence and their success on the control of land, as we have just seen. The reason is simple: all pre-industrial societies are based on agricultural wealth above all. There was nothing which one could call a factory in the middle ages, or for a long time afterwards. There were craftsmen, sometimes in large numbers, in the towns of tenth-century Egypt or thirteenth-century Flanders and northern Italy, artisans who produced cloth or metalwork on a large scale for markets across Europe, but they had access to much simpler technologies than would the industries of the future, and, above all, they were a restricted proportion of the overall population; under a fifth of the total population of Europe lived in towns – often very small ones – after 1200, and rather less before. (The exact figure is guesswork, for we do not have the data, but this works as a rough guide; see Chapter 7 for further discussion.) There was also mining, for iron, and to produce the silver for the coinages of Europe after 950 or so, but the people engaged in that were a still smaller number. Most people, over four fifths of the population in the early middle ages, not much less later, were peasants: that is to say, they worked directly on the land as subsistence cultivators, on more or less fixed landholdings and in stable settle-ments (usually villages, sometimes scattered farmsteads). Agricultural prod-ucts were most of what was produced by human labour in the middle ages, and for that reason the control of these, and by extension the land that produced them, was central.

But who was it that controlled land and its produce? In some cases it was the peasants themselves, in those parts of Europe where peasant landowning was substantial – which was above all in northern and eastern Europe, particularly in the first half of the medieval millennium, although there were owner-cultivators in the south, Spain, Italy and Byzantium, too. Where states taxed, as with the Byzantines and Arabs and, in the late middle ages, many western kingdoms and city-states too – or else where rulers took tribute, less systematically, from autonomous peasantries, as with the early princes and dukes of much of eastern Europe – rulers exercised a partial control over the land, simply because they took some of its produce, even if they were not actually its owners. But much of Europe was always owned by non-peasants: landowners who lived, and were prosperous, because they took rent from peasant tenant-cultivators. (Wage labour on the land was very rare before 1200.) Such landowners made up the aristocratic élites of Europe, the militarised lords whose loyalty (or not) to kings we have just discussed, and also the great churches – lands owned by churches could be as much as a third of the total land-area of kingdoms. Kings were themselves landowners, and their resources were, too, unless they taxed, overwhelmingly from the land they owned directly. The wealth of lords – whether royal, ecclesiastical, or aristocratic – thus came from what they could extract from the peasantry. They did so by force, and by the threat of force.

It is not that every bushel of grain was extracted by violence, of course. Lords did not have the manpower to achieve such a thing, given that peasants were in the huge majority. Indeed, peasants usually agreed their rents, and lords often accepted that such agreements would regularly turn into custom, and become hard to alter. But rent-taking was always backed up by potential force, from the armed men which all lords could command; the moment of rent-taking was often accompanied by armed men watching over the proceedings (the taking of taxation, which tended to have less consent from the population, even more so). And peasant resistance, which was itself sometimes violent, for example if rents and dues were arbitrarily increased, was certainly regularly met by force. We have plenty of accounts of the often repellent things lords were capable of doing to recalcitrant peasants – destruction and expropriation of goods, beating, cutting off of limbs, torture – which in the case of torture was generally recounted in tones of disgust by our sources, but about which in the case of beating and mutilation the accounts are usually more matter-of-fact. (The sources were largely written by clerics, who did not like aristocratic bad behaviour; but they tended to like assertive peasants still less.)[18] Again: this did not happen to most people; but it could, and peasants knew it could. Violence was, that is to say, implicit throughout medieval agrarian society. Peasants did sometimes resist all the same, and sometimes even succeeded in resisting; but for the most part they were and remained subjected to lords.

Some peasants were legally free, some were not. What freedom brought, either in law or in practice (which were not the same) was by no means identical from society to society, but it was certainly supposed to allow free peasants to participate fully in the public world, for example the assemblies which were important in early medieval politics, and to have access to law courts. When such peasants were tenants, freedom often brought lower rents, too. Those who were unfree (called *servi* or *mancipia* in Latin) were even more various. '*Servus*' meant chattel slave in the ancient world: many *servi* worked on the land in slave plantations, even if these were relatively rare already by the late Roman empire, and all through the middle ages there were slave household servants in many societies. In the medieval period as a whole, however, most *servi* were tenants. They had no legal rights, as such rights were restricted to the free by definition, and they not only paid heavier rents but also often had to perform unpaid labour services, seen as demeaning; but they had similar tenures to the free, and our word 'slave' does not fit them properly – I shall call them simply 'unfree' throughout. There were quite complex pecking orders inside villages between free and unfree tenants, particularly in the early middle ages. As time went on, these lessened in much of Europe; the common experience of economic subjection became more important than strictly legal distinctions, and the free and the unfree often intermarried (even though this was for a long time strictly illegal). As landlords put more pressure on free tenants too, both groups often ended up, after 1000 or so, in a similar practical legal subjection which is often called 'serfdom' (from the French word *serf*, itself taken from *servus*). Peasant resistance in the early middle ages was frequently over whether free tenants were being pushed down over the free–unfree boundary; by the eleventh or twelfth centuries, that resistance was more often over the terms of the practical subjection which was by then more common (see below, Chapter 7), and the free–unfree divide tended to become less crucial. But it still mattered; in both England and Catalonia after 1200, for example, there were free tenants who were not 'serfs', and the end of serfdom for the legally unfree in the fifteenth century was a significant change.[19]

The dynamics of the lord–peasant relationship underlay not only all medieval economic history but all sociopolitical history too; it underpinned the sharpness of the boundaries of social stratification (see Chapter 10) and it made possible the whole politics of land as just discussed. We shall see across the rest of the book how its dynamics changed in different periods and circumstances: how autonomous peasantries were on the retreat in northern Europe in the second half of the middle ages (Chapter 5); how the nature of lordship changed in eleventh-century western Europe, bringing with it from now on many extra dues, forcefully imposed on local peasant populations (Chapter 6); what effect the economic expansion of the central middle ages had on peasant and lordly prosperity, and on how they negotiated the relationship between the two (Chapter 7); and how late medieval peasant resistance, to lords and states, operated, both successfully and unsuccessfully (Chapter 12). But what is important to keep in mind, all the way through this book, is the simple fact that wealth and political power was based on exploiting the peasant majority. The whole economic dynamic of medieval social systems, including every change which we tend to call economic 'development' – the increase in the number and size of markets, or the growth of towns and artisan craftsmanship for largely aristocratic buyers – hung on the unequal relationship between lords and peasants, and the surplus which the former managed to extract from the latter. Peasants do not appear on every page of this book, by any means; but almost everything which does was paid for by the surplus which they handed over, more or less unwillingly, in rent, and it is a mistake to forget it.

*   *   *

When we come to basic medieval cultural frameworks, it is harder to generalise, and it is also harder to select. Here, I want to set out only three aspects of medieval culture, which involved assumptions that were somewhat more widespread across Europe than others: attitudes to honour, gender, and religion. Each of them will appear in the rest of the book as well, and will be characterised in more detail later, with respect to specific regions and periods; but they need some introduction here. As we have seen, much of the force of political relationships in the central middle ages – and also, just as much, long before and long after – was based on honour. It is hard to overstate how important being seen as honourable was to all strata of medieval society, in every period and region of Europe; including the peasantry, even if others often thought that peasants were incapable of honour; including women, even if others often thought that the honour of women was really the honour of their male family. Accusations of disloyalty, or of cowardice, or of theft, or (if a female) of illicit sex, or (if a male) of being cuckolded, were all threats to honour. If you were a known thief, you risked death (theft, because it was secret, was in much of medieval Europe seen as worse than a homicide which was made publicly known); but, if not, you also risked becoming so dishonourable as to lose legal reputation, what in the later medieval west was called *fama*, which in turn might mean that you could not give evidence in court, or in some cases even swear an oath. That was in itself a serious social disadvantage, as oaths surrounded not only all politics but all judicial proceedings; thus, if you lost legal reputation, you were in many ways legally defenceless.[20]

Males defended their honour against such accusations, or against major or minor slights of other kinds, with formal oaths; but also, more directly, with violence. Violence was indeed itself respected enough for it to be a strategy in judicial proceedings: attacks on the property of others were a way of showing sufficient seriousness that you might more easily get your opponent to court; and if you did not defend your property against attack, you might be seen as having less right to it. Peasants carried knives, and used them; homicide levels in English medieval villages matched those of the most violent US cities of the twentieth century.[21] Aristocrats who were insulted in the central and later middle ages attacked each other's land and castles (the duel was less common until the very end of the middle ages and after). Revenge killing was normal, and itself honourable. It would be wrong to call most medieval cultures feuding cultures; with some clear exceptions (Iceland was one, late medieval Italian urban élite society another), most violence was one-off, and dealt with by compensation and/or judicial intervention. All the same, if men came to terms with money or gifts to end the sorts of sequences of acts of violence which we call feuds, this might itself be seen as dishonourable again – one had to be very careful, when either beginning or ending cycles of violence, not to undermine one's own honour. Even clerics, whose job was to end violence (and we have many examples of them doing just that), understood this logic. Bishop Gregory of Tours (d. 594), for example, who wrote a very detailed book of *Histories* of his own times, gives an account of an aristocrat named Chramnesind, who had accepted money to compensate for the deaths of his relatives at the hands of another aristocrat named Sichar, and went drinking with his former enemy a few years afterwards; Sichar, now drunk, remarked that Chramnesind had done well out of the deal. Chramnesind then thought (Gregory tells us): 'if I don't avenge my lost relatives, I must give up the name of man and be called a weak woman', and killed Sichar on the spot. Gregory clearly approved entirely of the sentiment, even though it was he who had brokered the compensation. Sichar's insult, essentially of profiting in a cowardly manner from his relatives' deaths, would indeed have brought death in many medieval societies; the famous Buondelmonti–Arrighi feud in thirteenth-century Florence was said to have begun in a similar way too.[22]

To repeat: it is not that the values of all medieval societies were the same. The image of the 'medieval mind' bedevils too many books, particularly those which seek to argue that medieval people did not think 'rationally' about some aspect or other of society or religion; that is yet another argument which this book is not about. Honour certainly had variants. It may have been generally not at all dishonourable for a male to have illegitimate children (even if it was a legal impediment in some places – not all – for the children themselves); but it was altogether exceptional to find, as was the case in late medieval Ireland, that it was dishonourable not to recognise anyone who appeared at the door claiming to be such an illegitimate child – lords, in particular, could accumulate many such children in Ireland, often on the basis of quite random claims.[23] But at least one can say that the violent defence of honour was quite generalised. It was very macho, too, as the Chramnesind quote tells us directly; it was about being male and not being female. It was also even more macho when men were drunk, as they very often were – in fact, many initial insults that resulted in violence occurred while people drank. (The emperor Charlemagne was claimed by his biographer Einhard not to like drinking; this claim is pretty implausible in fact, but it was certainly intended to mark him out as exceptional.) Conversely, drinking a lot of beer, mead or wine was not only a risk, but a standard element in establishing loyalty itself: if you drank together, you had obligations to each other (that was true for eating as well); if you drank in a lord's hall, you had obligations to fight for him, and you lost honour if you did not. There is a common medieval literary trope, and some actual cases, of enemies being invited to a meal to make peace, and then being killed while eating and drinking; it may have been a sensible strategy, for people's guards were down, but it was very dishonourable indeed.[24] And drinking together was itself very male; in many medieval societies, respectable women were rarities at such events, except the wife of the lord and host, who was special.

These sorts of society would not seem to have much of a space for women. And, indeed, gender roles could be sharply restricted; in peasant society, only men were supposed to plough, only women wove clothing, a norm which appears quite widely across time and space (it was a cliché in China too). In most medieval societies, women could not get away, even to a small degree, with the sort of sexual licence accepted for heterosexual men; nor was the world of violence usually theirs – men fought for them. Women sometimes had no public persona at all; in early medieval Italy and Ireland, for example, women were minors in law, with men acting for them legally all their lives, and did not inherit land easily. These constraints on women were however exceptional, and plenty of other medieval societies allowed female inheritance equally with men, or female court appearances, or even (if more rarely) female participation in public assemblies.[25] We also find women exercising political power, either for children after their husbands' deaths, or more rarely – usually in the later centuries of the middle ages – as heirs, in the absence of brothers. Some female rulers, like Margaret of Denmark or Isabella of Castile in the fifteenth century, were indeed highly successful. In the early medieval chapters that follow, we will find a number of powerful queen-mothers too.

I will return to the issue of gender roles in more detail in a later medieval context – when we can, finally, say more concrete things about more women than queens and top aristocrats – in Chapter 10. But, to anticipate, I would see the main difference between the early and the late middle ages, in much of Europe at least, to be an increase in ambiguities in female roles, as society became slowly more complicated; the legal constraints which sometimes appear quite sharp in the early period seem often to have been more mediated later on, even if female inheritance was never generous (indeed, it became in some respects harder in many places), and even if the roles for women were circumscribed in all periods. As they were also, it has to be added, for men; men who genuinely were afraid of violence, for example, which may include many of us today, had little chance of long lives if they had any military respon-sibilities at all, and little chance of much social esteem in the average village, unless they happened to be clerics and therefore to an extent absolved from violent acts. (But many clerics fought in wars with some enthusiasm, it should be added; conversely, clerics who actually were non-violent, or for that matter celibate, were often viewed with a measure of contempt for their ambivalent gender status.) As we have seen when looking at honour, the rules for male public behaviour could be as coercive, although different, as they were for women.[26] But the most circumscribed roles of all were always female. The medieval – and of course not just medieval – norm was male.

As to religion: it is banal to say that medieval people were religious, but they were, whether they were Jews, Muslims, pagans, or else members of what was by the late middle ages in Europe an overwhelming Christian majority. (If there were any atheists, they almost never expressed themselves.[27]) That banality is often associated with the 'power of the church', clerical preachers keeping the laity in line with hellfire threats of damnation, and so forth. Such preaching was, in reality, much more a feature of the early modern period, in the competing Protestant and Catholic confessions; earlier, clerics were often fairly realistic about how much they could demand of their audiences, and that is when they preached at all – for preaching, although it always existed, and developed further from the late twelfth century, was not automatic in practice by any means.[28] But it is also the case that, even though churchmen complained in every century about how little the laity followed the teachings of the church, they could rely on the fact that their flocks fully accepted the basic outlines of Christian belief. Admittedly, what the latter understood to be those outlines was not always what clerics thought they should be. Clerics reacted to this in different ways in different periods; in the early middle ages they characteristically criticised what they claimed to be 'pagan' survivals, particularly forms of ritual which seemed incompatible with Christian teachings; in later centuries complaints were more likely to be about standard forms of 'immoral' behaviour, or else, after 1000 or so, heresy – that is to say, theological beliefs which the church, whether Latin or Greek, regarded as contrary to church teachings, particularly if they involved the rejection of the church hierarchy. The laity were not always less austere in their practice than clerical moralists, it must be added; the whole monastic movement, and later on that of the friars, was a lay one (ordained clergy were usually a minority in monasteries, and, since they had to be male, did not exist at all in nunneries). Men and women in those cases autonomously chose an often extreme version of Christian practice, although this was usually legitimated by equally extreme forms of obedience to abbots/abbesses, and, through them, to the wider order of the church; it did not involve, or at least was not supposed to involve, autonomous forms of belief. We will see later, in Chapters 8, 10 and 12, what happened when lay groups actually did begin to develop their own opinions about theology and spirituality, particularly from around 1150 onwards. But what is clear is that the Christian laity, whether or not they were well informed about the details of doctrine, and whether or not they were prepared actually to follow clerical exhortations, particularly over such deeply held attitudes as those concerning honourable violence or sex, did indeed accept that religion was important, and indeed all-pervasive.

I am stressing this, not because the point is contested by anyone, but because some of its implications are not always followed through. Secular and religious motives are often separated out by historians, and put into potential, sometimes actual, opposition. When aristocrats founded monasteries or gave them large donations of land, putting their family members into them as abbots or abbesses, were they doing it for the religious motives which their charters of gift invoke (treasures on earth being exchanged for treasures in heaven, etc.), or were they doing it because such monasteries could remain controlled by their families and be a long-term landed resource, as families became too large and divided? When kings put their own chaplains and other administrators into bishoprics, were they doing so because they already knew how good these men would be as properly moral bishops, or were they trying to shore up royal authority in different parts of their kingdoms by putting reliable and loyal men into rich local power-bases? When the Frankish emperor Louis the Pious's sons forced him to do public penance in 833 (see Chapter 4), did they do so because a substantial sector of the Frankish political class had decided that his sins had become so great that they threatened the moral order of the empire, or was it because his sons wanted to neutralise him so completely that he would have to abandon his political power to them on a permanent basis? When crusaders took the cross and went off to conquer Palestine in 1096 (see Chapter 6), did they do so because they wanted, as armed pilgrims with deep commitment, to take back the holy sites in and around Jerusalem from Muslim infidels, or were they wrapping up a well-attested desire to take other people's land with a new set of religious justifications? When we face these questions, we have to answer yes to both sides in nearly every case; but, more important, we also have to realise that there were no two sides: the two motivations were inextricable, and would not have been regarded as separable in people's minds. Of course, some political actors were more unscrupulous than others, just as some were more religious-minded than others; but neither of these would have regarded what we often see as two motivations as separate either, except in the case of a few religious hardliners. The self-servingness of much medieval religious rhetoric, particularly when it was the work of the powerful, can often be only too obvious to us; but it was not hypocritical. It might, sometimes, be more palatable (to us) if it had been; but such people, in almost every case, really did believe what they were saying. We have to factor that real belief into every assessment of medieval political action, however carefully and cunningly targeted.

*   *   *

These initial observations are just starting points for understanding what will follow. The rest of this book will focus on the moments of change, and the overarching interpretative structures, which I outlined at the beginning of the chapter. Throughout the book, we will also see how these initial frameworks can, must, be nuanced at every stage by real differences: early medieval practices were very different from late medieval ones, Frankish practices were very different from Byzantine ones, and so on. It is these differences which make up much of the interest of the medieval millennium. But the parts made up the whole too. Medieval societies did indeed have parallel economic, social, political and cultural patterns, which are worth comparing, and worth explaining. I shall try to do as much as I can of that as well, inside the limits of having to analyse a thousand years in a quarter as many pages, in the rest of this book.

CHAPTER TWO

Rome and its western successors, 500–750

Why did the Roman empire fall? The short answer is that it didn't. Half of the empire, the eastern half (what is now the Balkans, Turkey, the Levant, Egypt), which was ruled from Constantinople, carried on without problems during the period of imperial breakdown and conquest by outsiders in the western half (what is now France, Spain, Italy, north Africa, Britain) in the fifth century; the eastern empire indeed survived even the massive assaults on it in the seventh century, as we shall see in the next chapter. East Rome – from then on we call it the Byzantine empire, although its inhabitants called themselves Romans until its end – continued another thousand years, until the conquest of its last remnants by the Ottoman Turks in the fifteenth century; and then the Ottomans used some of the basic fiscal and administrative structures of the Roman/Byzantine past in their own state-building, focused on their new capital in Constantinople, now Istanbul. In some senses, then, the Roman empire lasted until the First World War, when the Ottoman state collapsed.

I make this point not to conjure up the image of a past which never changes; there are always elements of the past in the present, but that does not mean that huge alterations have not taken place – they certainly did in the Byzantine empire, for example. The point is a different one. When we are faced with really big events – the end of European peace in 1914, the collapse of the Soviet Union in 1990 – historians tend to divide between those who see the catastrophe as inevitable, with structural causes, often long-term ones, which just happen to come together in a sudden shift, and those who see it as chance, the product of short-term, almost casual, political decisions; or else, when they are more nuanced, between those who, in the mélange of structural and political causes, put more weight on the former or else the latter. I tend to the structural side myself, for the most part. But when we are looking at the Roman empire in the fifth century, longer-term explanations for imperial collapse in the west do not work so well, for they so transparently do not apply to half the Roman world.

Some structural answers might still be offered: the west might have been or become more fragile than the east, or more exposed to invasion; the trend, begun already in the third century and fully established by the fifth, to rule the empire in two separate halves for logistical convenience, might itself have done harm to imperial coherence and its ability to respond to threat. Indeed, in the context of the hundreds of competing explanations for Rome's 'fall', each of these arguments has been made by someone, and has some force.[1] All the same, in this particular case, contingent choices, sometimes simple human errors, are more convincing. Our starting-point in this book is 500, the rough beginning of the middle ages, so in principle we could skip the still-Roman west in the fifth century as too early to deal with; but we have to step back a bit to begin with, to look at some of these choices at least briefly, for they had such major effects on what would happen later. All the same, one important consequence follows from this discussion as well: if there were not serious structural weaknesses in the western empire in 400, say, then many elements of the imperial structure are likely to have survived the fifth-century crisis. This was indeed the case, and we will look at this issue across the rest of the chapter.

The northern boundary of the Roman empire ran right across what is now Europe, along the rivers Rhine and Danube (plus, in Britain, Hadrian's Wall), marking a sharp north–south contrast not just in political allegiance but in culture and the economy, which outlasted the end of the western empire by centuries. The Roman world had many internal differences, but on one level it was strikingly homogeneous, held together by roads running between a network of cities with often remarkably similar public buildings, largely in stone. 'Cityness' (*civilitas*), with all the undertones of civility and civilisation which the Latin word still conveys to us, defined the élite Roman self-image; an education in classic Latin literature (Greek literature in the Greek-speaking eastern empire), and the ability to write elegantly, formed part of aristocratic status. Quite as Roman was extreme social inequality; there were still many slaves in the Roman world, and the differences between rich and poor, and the snobbery attached to those differences, were acute. All formed part of the complexity of the Roman empire, in every period. Now that the empire was Christian, which it had become, at least in terms of its governing élites, in the fourth century, Christian religious literature was added to the mix, and bishops began to rival senatorial aristocrats in influence, but not much else changed in this respect (few Christian theologians, for example, notwithstanding the egalitarian imagery of the New Testament, ever thought slavery was wrong).[2]

The contrast with what the Romans called the 'barbarian' world to the north was considerable. There, the economy was far simpler, and so was local material culture. Political groupings were much smaller and simpler too, and often indeed very fluid, with identities changing as different ruling families rose and fell. Immediately north of the Rhine and Danube, most of these groupings spoke Germanic languages, although none of them, or the Romans themselves, saw this as marking any essential homogeneity between them. (I will use the words 'barbarian' and 'Germanic' in what follows for convenience only.) Not surprisingly, 'barbarian' peoples, especially their leaders, were very interested in the wealth of Rome, and tried to get some of it, either by raiding, even invasion, or by taking paid service in the Roman army. There was a grey area along the frontier, more militarised on the Roman side, more influenced by Roman styles on the 'barbarian' side, as a result.[3] But, broadly, the boundary marked by the two great European rivers was a sharp one.

What happened in the fifth century in the western Roman empire, put succinctly, is that 'barbarian' incursions from the north, although they had been a feature of most of imperial history, this time led to political breakdown: armies which did not call themselves Roman took over the different western provinces and carved out kingdoms for themselves. In 400, none of this had started yet, except in the Balkans, where Gothic groups were trying to settle – and trying to integrate into the Roman army – after fleeing into the empire from attacks by steppe nomads, the people whom the Romans called Huns, in the 370s. By 500, the Balkans, in the eastern empire, were under Roman control again; the west, however, was very different. There, a sector of the Goths, called by us the Visigoths, controlled Gaul (modern France) south of the Loire and most of Spain; another sector, called by us the Ostrogoths, controlled Italy and the Alps; Burgundians controlled the Rhône valley; Vandals controlled north Africa (modern Tunisia and Algeria); a set of small-scale Frankish kings controlled most of northern Gaul; and south-east Britain, a province actually abandoned by the Romans already in the early fifth century, was in the hands of tiny-scale tribal communities called generically by us (and perhaps by themselves) Angles and Saxons. There were others too, in smaller areas. Territories of the former western empire which were not under the control of military élites originally from outside its borders were very few and scattered: Mauretania (roughly modern Morocco), parts of the central Alps around Chur, and western Britain, particularly Wales, plus Brittany; none of these had any link with the others, still less with the Roman empire in the east, and they lost a Roman identity fairly quickly too, except around Chur.[4]

The Roman empire had absorbed invaders before; there was a tradition of settling them in corners of the Roman world, preferably after defeating them, and then using them as army recruitment grounds, at least until they lost their non-Roman characteristics. After an alarming set of largely uncoordinated invasions in the decade of the 400s, the Roman leadership gained the upper hand and did this again: the Visigoths were originally settled around Toulouse in 418, the Burgundians near Geneva in 442, the Vandals in what is now Algeria in 435. The Visigoths, in particular, were used as mercenaries to some effect as well: against the Vandals in 417 and the Suevi in 456, both of them in Spain, and against the Huns in Gaul in 451 (the Huns were used against the Goths as well). The conquest of Italy by the Ostrogoths in 489–94 was also an imperial initiative, for they were sent by the eastern emperor Zeno from their settlement in the Balkans to remove the leader of a Roman army revolt, Odoacer, who had ruled there independently since 476; the Ostrogothic king, Theodoric, was already an imperial general of some authority. Although, as can already be seen, there was now a confusingly large number of 'barbarian' groups, many more than in previous centuries, this was not by any means a dangerous strategy in itself, as long as the Roman leadership kept control of the whole process. At the beginning of the century, for the most part they did. The problem was the Vandals, whose confederacy had entered the empire from the north across the Rhine in 407 and moved across Gaul and into Spain in the next decade; although partially crushed in 417, they were not subdued, and invaded north Africa in 429 under their new king Geiseric (d. 477). Their settlement in 435 was by no means accompanied by military defeat, and their new territory, not in itself a very fertile one, was right on the edge of the western empire's chief source of grain and olive oil, the rich lands around the great Roman city of Carthage in what is now Tunisia. Why would they not want to control that, and why would the Romans not realise it, and defend Carthage better? But Aetius (d. 454), the military and political supremo of the west at that time, did not do so, and Carthage duly fell in 439. That choice – error – was one of the major turning points in the ability of the Romans to control the terms of political change in the west. Without the wealth of Africa, the western empire began to run out of tax revenues; without tax revenues, it was harder to pay for regular troops which were ever more needed in the complex politics of the period; without regular troops, it was more and more necessary to use 'barbarian' armies as allies, but harder and harder to control them.[5]

The balancing act of using 'barbarians' but keeping the strategic upper hand was not helped by the instability of politics in the fifth-century west, with warlords ruling for ineffectual emperors and for the most part succeeding each other by violence. Political leaders seem very often to have been behind the curve, using the solutions of the previous decade to fail to solve the problems of the present one. When the empire began to run out of money, it was also complicated by a growing political separation, and rivalry, between the two major western provinces that were still largely controlled by Roman armies, Gaul and Italy. The warlord who dominated imperial politics between 457 and 472, Ricimer, was only really interested in Italy, and in those years the Burgundians (Ricimer's allies) and the Visigoths (definitely, under Euric, 466–84, acting autonomously) divided central-southern Gaul between them. Ricimer's choice was decisive here. When, in the next generation, Odoacer revolted in Italy in 476, there was little else to fight for, and Odoacer, rather than setting up another puppet emperor, simply called himself king, nominally recognising the eastern, not any western, emperor.[6]

I stress Roman choices more than 'barbarian' conquest here. There has in fact been a fierce debate in the last generation about how 'barbarian' the different Germanic peoples actually were.[7] Most of them (the major exception were the Franks) had spent some time in Roman provinces before establishing independent kingdoms; they often wore Roman military-style clothing, and had picked up other Roman characteristics too. The different sets of Goths, in particular, can plausibly be seen as rogue Roman armies, with plenty of non-Gothic members, including, doubtless, many who were Roman by descent; almost all the 'barbarian' leaders intermarried with Roman imperial families; the Roman warlords (including Ricimer and Odoacer) were often themselves of 'barbarian' origin.[8] 'Barbarian' kings were mostly bilingual, and some may have only spoken Latin. They all adopted every element of the Roman administrative system that they could. It was possible to describe them as Roman rulers in all but name, as Sidonius Apollinaris (d. *c.* 485), a Roman aristocrat and intellectual from central Gaul, did for the Visigothic king of Toulouse Theodoric II (453–66): pious (but not too much), careful in his administrative duties, a serious conversationalist, a host at sophisticated meals, 'Greek elegance, Gallic abundance, Italian quickness, . . . royal discipline'.[9] Except in the northernmost provinces, they were all Christian, or at least as Christian as the rest of the empire was (there were plenty of pagans still left in 400). Being Christian was not in itself a sign of homogeneity, it is true – the fourth and fifth centuries were a major period of religious disagreement, with different parties arguing over the nature of God, and accusing each other of heresy, Arians versus Nicaeans and Monophysites versus Chalcedonians (Nicaeans/ Chalcedonians, the eventual winners in the Roman heartlands, are from then on more often called Catholics in the west, Orthodox in the east) – but here too the 'barbarians' simply took sides. The Arian Vandals, in particular, from time to time persecuted 'heresy' – that of the Nicaean majority of Roman north Africa – as enthusiastically as any Nicaean emperor, and with the same laws.[10]

This Romanising process made accommodation easier. What happened in province after province is that Roman local élites, with ever less military support from outside, simply came to terms with their local 'barbarian' neighbours, soon to be rulers, and entered the courts of local kings (as Sidonius did with Theodoric II, although he was opposed to Euric), offering to govern for them – in, naturally, as Roman a way as possible. There was a rapprochement from the start, then, nearly everywhere, including in Vandal Africa, where, for religious reasons as we have just seen, there was greater tension than elsewhere.[11] The Roman empire had always been prey to army takeovers, from the first century AD onwards; Roman armies had long been multi-ethnic, with a strong element of provincials from frontier regions; the main thing that had changed, so far at least, was that army leaders from the frontier, or just beyond it, began to call themselves kings.

So it might be argued that what happened between 400 and 500 was not so drastic, after all. The Ostrogothic king Theodoric (474–526) ruled Italy, and northwards to the old Roman frontier on the Danube; he gained a hegemony over the Visigoths in Spain, and strong influence in both the Vandal and the Burgundian kingdoms; and he had an administration which was hardly changed from that of the Roman past. He could have easily called himself a Roman emperor, one would have thought, and our sources often treat him as if he had.[12] After he died, the eastern emperor Justinian (527–65) certainly did not see the western provinces as irrevocably lost, for he launched wars to reconquer first Vandal Africa in 533–34, and then Italy in 534–40. A revolt in Italy restored Ostrogothic kings, and it took until 554 fully to subdue the peninsula, but by then Justinian had also occupied much of the Spanish coast as well; nearly the whole of the Mediterranean was now back in Roman hands, leaving only Gaul and inland Spain as major provinces outside Roman direct rule.[13]

But, however Romanised the first century of 'barbarian' kingdoms were, some crucial things had indeed changed, and would never, as it turned out, change back. The first is that the Germanic peoples did not call themselves Roman. They clearly saw themselves as separate from the Romans they conquered and ruled, and were in this respect quite unlike any warlords and coup leaders of the past, including Ricimer and other generals in the fifth century whose 'barbarian' relatives we can track. It is true that the defeated Ostrogoths and Vandals seem to have been absorbed back into Roman provincial society, for they do not appear again in our sources – the same is true of nearly all 'barbarian' peoples which were conquered by others – but no successful Germanic élite ever came to see itself as Roman; indeed, in long-lasting kingdoms like the Visigoths in Spain and the Franks in Gaul, the reverse happened, and Romans began to see themselves as Goths and Franks. Identities changed, that is to say, and 'being Roman' was no longer the secure marker of status and culture which it had been for centuries.[14] The second shift is that the old unity of the west, everywhere from Hadrian's Wall to the Sahara, had vanished for ever. Even Justinian did not conquer the whole Mediterranean (he did not attack the coast of Gaul, and had only intermittent hegemony in Mauretania), and no-one has since. Separate political systems emerged, with separate political foci, the Paris region for the early Franks (that centrality, new in around 500, has never since gone away), Toledo in central Spain for the Visigoths, the Pavia–Milan region for the next invaders, the Lombards in Italy, who arrived in 568–69, after Justinian's reconquest.[15] All three of these central regions had been marginal for the Romans; Milan had at least been a capital in the fourth century, but Rome and Ravenna were the main centres for late Roman government in Italy.

The third major change was arguably the most important. The Roman empire was governed by a complex bureaucratic structure, paid for by a sophisticated fiscal system, which involved many taxes, but above all a complex and heavy land tax. This system worked, even if it was amazingly corrupt, unpopular, and prone to abuse; we have much legislation from emperors who were concerned that the traditional tax collectors, city councillors, were not doing their job, which might imply that tax was not effectively collected, but it was certainly carefully controlled and policed – we have, for example, records from Italy and Egypt of the systematic recording of land transfers, so that the state would be able to tax the new owner accurately, and Egyptian documents also show that even rich and powerful landowners did indeed pay their taxes. This fiscal system was largely used to pay the army, easily the Roman state's greatest expense (the civilian bureaucracy came a distant second), and this meant that money and goods regularly moved north across the Mediterranean from rich southern provinces such as Africa and Egypt, to the northern frontier regions where armies mostly were located, plus to Rome and Constantinople, capital cities which were kept large for symbolic reasons and largely fed by the state. The paid army was partially separate from the other major set of élites, the imperial (senatorial) aristocracy and the provincial and urban leadership of every part of the empire, who were landowners above all else, and also civilian.

The fiscal system thus underpinned the whole Roman state, and was not at any risk at the start of the fifth century. When, however, the empire in the west was divided into kingdoms, tax revenues ceased abruptly to be moved around, with serious effects on Rome as a city, and on many northern armies. Furthermore, the new Germanic élites had different aims from the rebellious

Roman senior officers of the past. The latter had mostly just wanted higher pay, to go with their claims for political power; but their Germanic successors wanted something different: to be landowners, like the provincial élites they were now dominating and living beside. This very Roman desire had a very un-Roman effect: it became less and less necessary to pay the now landed army. Tax régimes themselves became less necessary as a result, and since they were both disliked and complex to collect, could eventually shrivel away. 'Barbarian' kings continued to tax as long as they could, it is true. So much is clear from the Ostrogothic governmental records preserved for us in the letter collection, the *Variae*, of a long-standing senatorial official for the Gothic kings, Cassiodorus Senator (d. *c.* 580), as well as numerous other casual comments and complaints in contemporary chroniclers. But already when Justinian conquered the Vandal kingdom, and even that of the Ostrogoths, he found that re-establishing the tax system was hard and unpopular. In Frankish Gaul, tax levels had dropped precipitously by the time the historian Gregory of Tours was writing in the 580s, and kings can be seen granting tax immunities by then as a standard political privilege; by the 640s the land tax hardly existed any more in Gaul except sporadically in the Loire valley. Kings began to rely on the revenues from their own lands, which were very extensive everywhere (as imperial landowning always had been), rather than fiscal receipts, except for tolls on commerce. The whole economic basis for political action shifted, from taxation to landowning.[16] This marked a break, not just from the past, but also from the contemporary states in the eastern and southern Mediterranean, the east Romans/Byzantines and the Arabs, whom we will look at in the next chapter. The break will also underpin much of the rest of the book, for, as we saw in the last chapter, a land-based politics is less stable and normally less remunerative than a tax-based politics. We will also see in Chapter 11 that even the revived tax régimes of late medieval western Europe did not fully reverse this shift. Indeed, it was a shift that only fully changed back in the west in the very different economic world of the Industrial Revolution.

One important result of this was that the western provinces became less economically complex. Even kings were less rich (although they also had lower expenditures), with the partial exception of the Franks. Nor were the aristocracies of the early middle ages anywhere near as rich as the richest senatorial aristocrats of the Roman world, with their estates spread across the whole Mediterranean (this, with political division, was by now impossible anyway); we find, in most places, Frankish Gaul again excepted, very few landowners with estates in more than a couple of city-territories. The tax system had partially underwritten transaction costs for commerce in the later Roman empire; this had gone, which meant that interregional exchange decreased steadily, and in most of the western Mediterranean was restricted to luxury goods by 700 or so. At the same time, since aristocracies were poorer, and, since aristocratic demand fuelled much of the exchange inside regions, plus all luxury trade, commerce at all levels lessened nearly everywhere. In every western province, archaeology shows clearly that fewer goods moved about, and that élite material culture was far less ambitious. This was so also in Italy, where, even if the Ostrogothic state had had an unusually Roman form, the Justinianic reconquest was devastating. In one province where the military supply network was particularly important, Britain, the economic crisis was precipitous as soon as the army left in the early fifth century, that is to say even before the Anglo-Saxons came: cities were largely abandoned, rural villas were as well, and artisanal production beyond the village level ceased almost entirely. Nothing in Gaul or Spain or Italy matches that crisis, but each of these shows a less extreme economic simplification too. The weakening of the wealth of élites was not all negative by any means. If aristocracies had less land and wealth, even though they still had plenty of tenants (many of them unfree, as we saw in Chapter 1), landowning peasants with less, or no, dependence on aristocrats must have become more numerous, and may well have been more prosperous. But they bought fewer goods, and did not prevent the economy from simplifying. Anyone who wants to argue for continuity between the Roman and the post-Roman world must come to terms with these sharp economic changes, which are revealed so clearly in the archaeology. Whatever continuities there were (and there were many) overlay a much less complex productive and exchange system, which had become less complex as a direct result of the political break-up of the west and the move of armies to the land. These were not structural causes of the end of the western empire; but they were certainly structural results.[17]

*   *   *

The end of the western empire showed crisis, therefore, and sharp social and economic change. But not only. In the rest of this chapter, we will look at the three main successor-states to the Roman empire, as they developed after the failure of Theodoric the Ostrogoth's informal hegemony in the early sixth century: Frankish Gaul – from now on increasingly often called Francia, both then and now – Visigothic Spain, and Lombard Italy. (Britain will be left for Chapter 5.) Through a discussion of each, we will look at what survived from the Roman world, and what was new.[18] But let us begin with some general cultural and sociopolitical structures from the Roman past which continued almost without a break, and helped to define how the early medieval political systems of the west operated: the patterns of Roman provincial society and the Christian church, and the culture and values of public power.

The Roman empire had begun by being a network of largely self-governing cities, linked above all by the army. This had certainly changed by the later empire. City councils weakened and failed in the fifth and sixth century every-where, both east and west; government became more centralised after around 500 not only in the eastern empire, but, counterinituitively, in the weaker western kingdoms too. But loyalty to city-based societies survived everywhere where cities survived, which was all across the west except in Britain, north-west Spain and along the old frontier in Gaul and southern Germany.[19] Coherent collectivities of local élites existed in the cities of southern Gaul, eastern and southern Spain, Italy; they made up the surviving Roman world that the new Germanic peoples came to rule, and, as we have seen, the two sides could accommodate themselves to each other fairly fast. These city socie-ties were by now increasingly often represented, both in internal politics and with relation to royal power, by bishops. Christianisation was in effect complete in the whole of the former western empire by 500; the only major exceptions were the Jewish communities of parts of Gaul, Italy and, especially, Spain. What local populations thought Christianity actually was is another matter; as noted earlier, ecclesiastical writers, nearly all of them inflexible in their views, routinely complained about 'pagan' practices in local cults – that is to say, prac-tices which they thought were pagan, but which the populace doubtless saw as a standard part of Christian cult, new year celebrations for example, or getting drunk at church feasts.[20] But what was certainly generally accepted was that the leaders of the church were the network of bishops which the Romans had established in every one of the cities of the empire, arranged in a hierarchy, province by province, with 'metropolitan' bishops (later called archbishops) at their head, and looking to the five patriarchs of the empire, of which one covered the whole of the west, the pope in Rome. This survived the end of the western empire little changed, except that the influence of the pope was never great outside Italy for many centuries.

Bishops were important in the late empire, but it was in the early middle ages that they really became major political players. Cathedral churches became rich in land, donated by the faithful, which made any bishop more powerful as soon as he took office. Bishops gained further spiritual authority from the cult of the relics of saints, which developed in the fifth century and onwards, for they tended to be in charge of the churches which contained them. They not only controlled urban religious ceremonies, but also became increasingly accepted as local political leaders (in most cases they were from leading local families); their appointment was often the focus for rivalry.[21] And they represented their communities, to kings and other royal officials; kings took them seriously as leaders of these communities, as well as being prepared to hear the religious critiques that, as bishops, it was their task to provide. The new political prominence of bishops was partly because secular urban structures had melted away, and partly because, as a well-organised pressure group, they could make their voice heard in the weaker kingdoms of the post-Roman period better than in the imperial political system that had created them.

A good example of the activity and role of bishops is Gregory of Tours (d. 594), from an élite family in Clermont in central Gaul but with family links also in Tours, on the Loire, where he became bishop in 573. (Local rivals saw him as an outsider; he indignantly rejected this.) Gregory has left us more writing, both history and hagiography, than almost any other single author from the early middle ages, much of it about events he himself participated in: he gives us a uniquely dense, even if highly one-sided, picture of royal and local politics, society and culture for the 570s and 580s. Gregory was a bishop in the Frankish kingdoms, and, although a Roman by descent, he was loyal to the Frankish kings (there is no nostalgia for the Roman empire in his writings, and he saw his kings as Rome's legitimate successors). At that time, however, Francia was divided between three kings, brothers, then uncle and nephews; Gregory was appointed by one of the brothers, Sigibert (561–75), close to another, Guntram (561–93), and hostile to the third, Chilperic (561–84). He was thus hardly neutral as a political figure; unsurprisingly, Chilperic disliked him back, and threatened him – something which was seriously dangerous in the Francia of the period, for kings routinely killed opponents, often in imaginative ways. One of the major moments in their confrontations, in 577, is described by Gregory with an unusual care for its setting: Chilperic stood beside a little tabernacle made of branches, flanked by two bishops, with a table before them full of food, while they ranted at each other; the visual recall shown here well conveys how scared Gregory was. He much preferred Guntram, who was happy to listen to him over dinner. Gregory was a snob; his enemies were often (he tells us) people of power but low-status background, such as Chilperic's charismatic wife Fredegund, who became regent of his kingdom for their child Chlotar II (584–629). He was a great defender of his city, however, including its tax exemptions, and a systematic supporter of its local saint and his predecessor as bishop, Martin (d. 397), whose cult he promoted in a detailed account of the miracles occurring at the saint's tomb just outside the Roman city; as we saw in the last chapter, he was also a peacemaker in local rivalries. He supported other bishops if they ran into trouble with the kings, including bishops whom he did not like, and could face down even Chilperic in their defence (this is what he was doing in 577). Gregory was also a moralist; it was his job, and kings and other political figures knew that they had at least to listen to him. He was indeed, despite having no military backing (a military entourage was rare for bishops in this period, though it became common later), a power-broker whom kings needed to take seriously, for Tours was strategically important and often changed hands in the jostling for territory which these kings all engaged in. The fact that he was also a good observer (his *Histories* are fascinating in their detail) is probably a guide to his survival as a political figure as well; however often we have to calibrate for his prejudices when reading him, and however often kings did too, he clearly could deal effectively. That was what bishops were for; and he managed to do it, in often difficult circumstances, for twenty years, a long time in Frankish politics.[22]

The other inheritance of Rome which needs to be stressed was a whole conception of political legitimacy which could be called the culture of the 'public'. Under the empire, the *publicum* was taxation, imperial property, the bureaucracy, the collective good, just as the 'public sector' is today. When the *publicum* was no longer underpinned by the wealth of the tax system, this concept did not go away. Kings across the post-Roman west used the term routinely, to mean rights which belonged to them, plus their officials, law courts, the road system, and so on. The difference between the public and the private (another Roman and post-Roman word), so clearly maintained, justi-fies us considering the post-Roman kingdoms as states, even if often weak ones. Kings did not often in this period invoke the imagery of the public good when legislating; that would be for the Carolingians in the eighth and ninth centuries, as we shall see in Chapter 4. But the idea that royal power constituted the public sphere was strong; and it could be meant spatially too – justice, for example, was done *publice*, 'publicly', in the sight of all.

The sight of all mattered very greatly in the post-Roman world, in fact. Here, the *publicum* as the ex-Roman state melded with one clearly non-Roman feature of all of the early medieval kingdoms, the public assembly. Assemblies of the entire political community, national or local, were essential to legitimate royal power, royal acts, and court judgements, throughout post-Roman Europe, north of the Roman frontier and south of it alike: they were called by different names, *conventus* or *placitum*, or in Anglo-Saxon England *gemot*, or in Scandinavia *thing*, and they can be found in Celtic- and Slavic-speaking communities as much as in Germanic- and Latin-speaking ones. They seem to have derived from an early assumption, north of the border, that kings were responsible to and legitimised by all the free men (but not women) of their community, and that political practice was at its base collective. In a large post-Roman kingdom, this was impractical (doubtless it was always in part pretence), but even then kings legislated, at least nominally, 'in the presence of the whole people, in common counsel with us' (as the Lombard king Liutprand put it in 713), and the imagery of a very wide legitimising community, meeting *publice*, was a common one from 500 onwards.[23] This was not a Roman concept, then, but the attachment to it of the Roman concept of the public was a natural one, and each reinforced the other. Post-Roman kings may have been at times quite restricted in their practical power, but the public sphere was theirs to dominate, and this distinguished rulers fundamentally from alternative powers in any kingdom. We can find this pattern everywhere in the west, up to the end of the Carolingian period and beyond; and when the culture of the public weakened, along with legitimating public assemblies themselves, from the tenth century onwards, political power would sharply change in nature, as we shall see in later chapters.

The culture of the public, assembly politics, Christianity and the network of bishops, a disappearing tax system and the beginning of the politics of land, a less wealthy aristocracy and a more independent peasantry, a simpler economic system: all these features marked out the post-Roman kingdoms. So did a landed army run by no-longer-civilian aristocrats, which meant that aristocratic values became highly militarised from then on, and remained so for the rest of the middle ages and beyond; conversely, the literary education of Roman civilian élites became less important. Only the assemblies were not Roman in origin, although many were products of the division of the empire and the collapse of the fiscal system: that is to say they were very different from the Roman past, however much they developed out of it. These were, anyway, the elements that the political leaders of the post-Roman world had to play with, and the parameters of the world in which they operated. Let us see now how this worked out in the different post-Roman kingdoms.

*   *   *

The Franks were among the least Romanised of the Germanic groups that conquered a slice of the Roman world in the fifth century, and they took over a sector of the empire which had suffered particularly from the troubles of the period, northern Gaul. They were not by any means united at first, and up to the late fifth century there were several separate Frankish kingdoms, intermixed with autonomous army leaders in the Roman tradition. The king of Tournai, Clovis (481–511), however conquered all the others, plus the Alemans in the middle Rhine valley; and in 507 he moved south and defeated and killed the Visigothic king Alaric II, Euric's son, taking over south-west Gaul too. By his death he ruled from the Rhine to the Pyrenees. His sons conquered the Burgundian kingdom (in Gaul, only Brittany, and still-Visigothic Languedoc on the Mediterranean coast, remained out of Frankish hands), and they established a hegemony over wide tracts of central Germany, which had never been part of the Roman empire. By the 530s they were invading Italy too, profiting from the Roman–Gothic war, and maintained, off and on, some sort of authority over parts of the north of the peninsula for a century. This record of conquest across two generations is striking, and it established the Franks as by far the strongest power in the post-Roman west. It also rapidly exposed them to more Romanised areas of the former empire; already before his death Clovis had become a Catholic Christian (and not an Arian, unlike the Goths) and had begun to legislate in Latin. By the mid-sixth century, the Franks were less distinct from the other successful Germanic peoples than they had been, and the major difference was now probably the fact that, uniquely, they controlled lands and populations on both sides of the old Roman frontier. Clovis was also successful in establishing his own family, the Merovingian dynasty, as the sole legitimate kings of the Franks. It lasted with only one brief interval for a quarter of a millennium, up to 751; even if from the 670s onwards the Merovingian kings were usually no more than legitimising figures for powerful aristocratic supremos called *maiores*, they were still essential for that political legitimisation. Clovis divided his large kingdom between his sons, and this practice of division (one which was unusual in the post-Roman world) continued; there was only one long period of unity, 613–39, under Chlotar II and his son Dagobert, during the 150 years of strong Merovingian power, and the Carolingians continued the practice of division after their takeover in 751. All the same, Francia could frequently operate as a single power, with brothers and cousins supporting each other politically and militarily, and was regarded by outsiders as a single unit for the most part. This block of land continued to be western Europe's dominant political power until later divisions became permanent by the end of the tenth century.[24]

The late-sixth-century kings we have already seen, though the eyes of Gregory of Tours. However fractious and violent, they were hugely rich and powerful, and no opponent of theirs stayed alive for long: all aristocratic and indeed episcopal politics revolved around their courts. The power of Merovingian dynastic legitimacy meant that kings could succeed as children, and in the 580s there were two child kings, each dominated by their mother as queen regent: Fredegund, Gregory's enemy, and in Sigibert's old kingdom his widow Brunhild, Gregory's patron. Brunhild continued to dominate her grand-sons when her son died young, and even her great-grandson, until Fredegund's son Chlotar II, the only other male Merovingian by then, killed her in 613 and reunited the Frankish lands. Chlotar's grandchildren and great-grandchildren in the 640s and 650s would have similar queens regent too. Ruling queen-mothers went with strong dynasties everywhere in medieval Europe, but in this period only the Franks had such a strong dynasty in the west, so it is most visible here. It was potentially controversial, as female power always was; Gregory for example, who was certainly uneasy about it, says relatively little about his patron Brunhild as a result – if you can't be nice, be quiet, that is to say (perhaps the only time Gregory kept to this maxim) – although he does describe her, significantly, as ruling *viriliter*, 'in a manly way'.[25]

Francia was sufficiently large that not only were its kings rich and powerful, but its leading aristocrats were too. The richest of them had far more lands than the élites of anywhere else in contemporary Europe, even the eastern Roman/ Byzantine empire. Frankish aristocrats took for granted that they were not simply more powerful than anyone else, but also more virtuous; Merovingian-period saints were characteristically from aristocratic families, and the fact that bishops were increasingly from local élites fed into this imagery of sanctity as well. Leading families also founded rich monasteries, to stabilise family power and to attract donations from others, but also because the virtue of aristocratic families made such patronage a logical choice. Itta and Gertrude, founder and first abbess of Nivelles in what is now Belgium in the 640s, were for example widow and daughter of Pippin I, from one of Francia's major families, whom we call the Pippinids. The seventh-century Merovingian monastic network – patronised by kings as well as aristocrats – structured the rural political land-scape of the Frankish world until the new foundations of the central middle ages.[26] Aristocrats were also turning into political players on their own account. When Chlotar re-established Frankish unity, he only united the kingdom, not its three royal courts; and each of these, particularly the north-eastern kingdom, by now called Austrasia, and that of the north-west, by now called Neustria, became the focus for aristocratic political manoeuvring around a leading local aristocrat who acted as viceroy there, a *maior domus* or just *maior* – Pippin I was one of these, in fact.

Maiores gained further in power under the redivided kingdom of the sons of Dagobert after 639. By the mid-seventh century they were contesting the authority of queens regent when kings were children, and by now were some-times even choosing which Merovingian to make king. They were matched in their power only by a small group of really powerful bishops, many themselves aristocrats, such as Audoin of Rouen (d. *c.* 684), one of Dagobert's protégés, and Leudegar of Autun (d. 678), who was brought down and killed by the *maior* Ebroin. The last Merovingian who was a real protagonist, Childeric II, was murdered in 675, the low point in this sequence of events, and after that aristocratic families had no choice but to fight it out. The Pippinids won out at the battle of Tertry in 687, and a Pippinid *maior* was always the senior figure in Francia after that. That marked the end of the instability of the mid-century, which had, in the end, only lasted a generation. But Pippin II (d. 714), the victor at Tertry, had less power than many of his predecessors. In the period of trouble, the Franks had lost hegemony over the peoples of Germany, the Bavarians, Alemans and Thuringians, and also the dukes of Aquitaine in south-west Gaul. Even some bishops were beginning to carve out semi-autonomous territories for themselves. After Pippin's death, his family dissolved into civil war as well, in 715–19, when Pippin's widow Plectrude, regent for her own grandson as *maior*, confronted Pippin's illegitimate son Charles Martel; for a while this must have seemed like the 670s all over again. But Charles's victory showed that this was not the case; as sole *maior* (717–41), with only one court by now, he reconquered many of the newly autonomous lands, down to Provence; his sons Pippin III and Carloman I, later called Carolingians after their father, did the same with Alemannia and Aquitaine. The Frankish lands and wider hegemony could thus be reunited again, even after all the travail of the previous period, which indicates that the Frankish polity was pretty solid at its base.[27]

This solidity was partly due to the density of Frankish government. We have more evidence for Francia, particularly in the seventh century, than for other post-Roman political systems, and it is clear from that evidence that its kings were active throughout Francia, intervening a long way from their political centres and moving aristocratic officials around – Desiderius of Cahors (d. 655), for example, a major southern aristocrat, who went north to be treasurer for Chlotar II and was then sent to run Provence, before becoming bishop of his native city in 630. Merovingian government was complex and document-based, in a very Roman way; Audoin had also been Dagobert's *referendarius*, responsible for the production of formal documents for the king. This partially dropped back under Pippin II, and even under Charles Martel to an extent, but Pippin III could begin the process of re-establishing it, and by 800, under his son Charlemagne, governmental complexity was greater than it had ever been. This was certainly an important parameter, and, to repeat, one with a solid Roman (public) tradition at its back.[28] But the staying power of the Frankish political system was also the result of the constraints on aristocratic choices.

Aristocratic political strategies, however exuberant and self-interested, above all revolved around the kings (later, the *maiores*), who were even richer than they, and who provided both patronage (land and money) and legitimacy, at least for the successful. To go it alone was for long impossible, and even after the 670s only aristocrats with a formal regional command, usually dukes, could do it. Aristocrats had a local base, certainly, and we can track regional rivalries in many cases. But in most regions they did not focus on local politics except when they were dukes or bishops, again with formal offices. Indeed, they could move their lands around the Frankish kingdoms; the quantity of them was in some cases more important for political success than their location.[29] This would not change under the Carolingians either, as we shall see in Chapter 4, although, when it did change, the structures of political power would shift substantially.

The crucial point here seems to me this. The Frankish political system was the strongest in the post-Roman west; although ramshackle and often violent, it had staying power. Much of its strength came from Roman administrative traditions, as just noted. But, although the kings were unusually rich by the standards of the post-Roman world, Francia was not a tax-based political system; its armies were increasingly based on the military entourages of aristocrats, too. Kings needed to rule with the consent of these aristocrats, and rulers who did not do so, as with Childeric II in 675, and indeed Brunhild in her last years, could be killed. It was normally straightforward to obtain this consent, for aristocrats did not have an alternative political context to operate in, and royal courts were anyway rich and attractive throughout. The dice were weighted in favour of central power, that is to say. But it was necessary to seek consent; the politics of land were already in operation, and, even if authority was not yet fragile, it could become so. Assemblies came in here, for they were in the Frankish world the locus of an aristocratic as well as a royal legitimacy. Kings and other rulers routinely sought the collective agreement of assemblies, like the 300 aristocrats who were called together by Fredegund in 585 to swear to the legitimacy of her son Chlotar; conversely, when the élites of Neustria were not invited by the *maior* Ebroin to the enthronement of Theuderic III in 673, but instead were told not to come, they concluded that Ebroin was planning to rule without their involvement, and they switched their support to Theuderic's brother Childeric II.[30] This would remain a feature of the early medieval west.

Visigothic Spain faced the same problems, but dealt with them in a different way. The Visigoths had not yet gained full control of Spain when Clovis seized most of their territory in Gaul, and the next half-century was difficult for them, with a very unstable succession and separatist revolts in the great southern cities of Córdoba and, later, Seville, and even in some rural territories, plus the east Roman conquest of the Mediterranean coast. Leovigild (569–86) however united nearly all Spain by force – all except the coastal strip, which was not retaken until the 620s, and the Basque lands of the western Pyrenees. Leovigild saw himself as a unifier in all respects; he issued a law code which contained the most Roman-influenced legislation of any of the 'barbarian' kingdoms, and he tried to address the religious division between Catholics and Arians, which was less tense in Spain than in Vandal Africa but tense enough, by alternately persecuting Catholics (particularly Catholic Goths) and trying to soften Arianism to make it more palatable to Catholics. This latter procedure had parallels in the east Roman attempts to bridge the Chalcedonian–Monophysite divide (it probably copied them) and was equally unsuccessful: religious divisions over the nature of God were never resolvable by compromise. Leovigild's son Reccared (586–601) dealt with the problem by immediately becoming Catholic and, at the Third church Council of Toledo in 589, outlawing Arianism altogether: in future every Goth should be Catholic (Romans hardly appear in the council's minutes; already, in effect, nearly everyone in Spain was becoming a Goth in a political sense). The impulse to unity in Spain henceforth took on a highly religious element, as it never did in Francia or Italy, and councils of Toledo punctuated nearly every major moment of politics for the next century and more – they had reached the Eighteenth Council by 702. One result of this was that the kings began to issue laws persecuting Jews, the only substantial religious minority left, which became ever more unpleasant across the next century – these laws were easily the most extreme anti-Jewish legislation anywhere in Europe until the latest middle ages, although the forced conversion or enslavement which they envisaged probably failed, for there were plenty of Jews in Spain in the next centuries. Increasing amounts of royal legislation, however, took on the same shrill tone as the anti-Jewish laws; Ervig (680–87), for example, thought in 683 that unpaid taxes were by now so substantial that they would lead to the destruction of the world; Egica (687–702) thought in 702 that runaway slaves were hiding in every city, village and estate, and that every free man had the responsibility to report them on pain of two hundred lashes. Everything seemed so serious to the Visigoths; every failure in unity or obedience had potentially fatal consequences.[31]

The sense of doom which one finds in, in particular, late-seventh-century Gothic legislation has been taken too seriously by historians. They know that in 711 most of Spain would be conquered by Arabs and Berbers after the Visigothic king Roderic was killed in battle (see the next chapter), with different parts of the peninsula flying off in different directions, and to them Spain was already breaking up well before this point. Spanish archaeology, too, shows that the economy was becoming very localised, variable, and in many areas fairly simple; our few non-royal sources also indicate very substantial social differences between (for example) a highly urbanised Roman-style south and a rural north with some very uncomplex societies indeed.[32] As a result, the kings could not maintain their fictional homogeneity from their capital at Toledo, and their shrillness perhaps shows that they knew it. This last may be true, but it is at least as likely that the kings were simply influenced by ecclesiastical rhetoric in this very moralised world – as well as by the rhetoric of Roman imperial laws, for the Visigoths kept up a Roman governmental style to the end, with a careful attention to legal form even when the actual politics were messy. In reality, late-seventh-century Spain was very stable. After Reccared, who failed as did all Visigothic kings after 507 to establish a long-lasting dynasty, coups had returned to Spain, but were ended by the last such plotter, the elderly Chindaswinth (642–53), who executed all potential rivals. There then followed successions which, although often very tense, were at least not violent; kings henceforth died natural deaths, and rebellions failed, until just before the kingdom ended. As in Francia, the aristocracy revolved around the royal court, which was complex and more ceremonialised than elsewhere, and which, as Ervig's law shows, still collected taxes; although we do not know on what scale these were exacted – it was probably small – such taxation will have enriched the king above all, for the army was by now unpaid, here as elsewhere in the west.[33] The aristocracy was, however, as far as we can see much less rich than in Francia, and it is likely that the growing simplicity of the material culture found by archaeologists reflects this too. The rich royal court will have been all the more attractive to its members for that reason, not least because, given that succession was rarely hereditary, one might even become king oneself. So, far from showing weakness, our late-seventh-century evidence shows that, as in Francia but still more so, one could maintain a Roman-style governmental practice without the secure fiscal basis that the empire had enjoyed. These practices were further updated, too, for the Visigoths borrowed from the contemporary eastern empire as well.

Lombard Italy, finally, was somewhere in the middle. The Lombards invaded an Italy still disrupted by the Roman–Gothic war in 568–69, and one which the east Romans did not defend well thereafter, but they were a very disorganised invading force, and, after two kings in succession were assassinated in 572–74, broke up into several different political units, led by dukes. They reunited under a single ruler in 584, and their first really forceful king,

Agilulf (590–616), defeated most of his rivals and established a capital at Pavia; all the same, when peace was made in 605 with the east Romans, who had maintained themselves in the former Italian capital at Ravenna, Italy was split up into several different pieces. The Romans controlled most of the coasts, and the major cities of Ravenna, Rome and Naples, but three large blocks of Lombard territory, the central-northern kingdom of the Po plain and Tuscany, and two independent duchies in the centre-south around Spoleto north of Rome and Benevento north of Naples, divided the Roman lands from each other. This was clearly a sign of failure, both of the Lombards and of the Romans, and it lasted; Italy was never united again until 1870. Although the Lombards slowly extended their lands across the next 150 years, they never managed to take Rome or Naples, or to unify the three separate polities which regarded themselves as Lombard, even under their two most ambitious and effective kings, Liutprand (712–44) and Aistulf (749–56), who absorbed Spoleto and, briefly, Ravenna. The Lombards thus never had the military drive of a Clovis, or the urge to unity of a Reccared. Although they could hold their own against the Romans, they were in trouble when they faced the Franks, who were intermittently hegemonic over them in the late sixth century and early seventh, and who defeated the Lombard army three times in the 750s and 770s, culminating in Charlemagne's conquest of the Lombard kingdom (although not Benevento) in 773–74.[34]

This may look unimpressive, but actually the Lombard kingdom was also the most tightly governed of the three main successor-states. It was much smaller than Francia, so links between Pavia and local city-based societies were easier. It was also less regionally diverse than Spain; the economy was certainly more regionalised and simpler than under the empire, but we do not see the sharp involution of economic complexity which we see in some parts of Spain, and urbanism survived, if at a materially unassuming level, in most parts of the peninsula. What Italy consisted of was a set of small-scale but stable provincial societies, whose élites were city-dwelling almost without exception. As in Spain, there was not any aristocratic stratum rich enough to make the kings fear their opposition in any systematic way (except, as again in Spain, in the case of successful individuals, usually dukes of one of the cities, who took power by coup), and no member of that stratum would have had the ability to establish a strong local power-base, given the number of rivals there would have been in each city. The Lombard kingdom was very attached to assembly politics, as was Francia, but here the main function of both royal and local assemblies seems to have been law and justice, more than political deliberation – at least as it appears in our eighth-century sources, which are much richer than those for the previous period. People appealed to Pavia, and got royal judgements back, as we can see in texts which show the losers obeying them, as well as in a substantial set of very detailed and one-off royal laws of (in particular) Liutprand. There is an enthusiasm in some of Liutprand's problem-solving which one does not find in any other law-making of the period – as with what should the penalty be if a man stole a woman's clothes while she was bathing in the river and forced her to walk back to her house naked? (Answer: he should pay her his full *wirigild*, blood price, as if he had killed someone, for there would certainly be blood revenge taken otherwise.) This was a prag-matic, fairly low-key and cheap way of ruling, but it seems to have worked. The procedures of Lombard government were indeed borrowed from by the Franks after 774.[35]

*　*　*

We have here got a long way from the complexity, the coherence and the wealth of the later Roman empire. None of these states taxed to any serious extent by 700, and the patterns of government were much simpler as a result. The economy was far simpler too (although northern Gaul maintained more of a network of production and exchange than the others, which fitted the greater wealth of its élites); in the Mediterranean kingdoms, it probably hit its low point in the eighth century. But this was not an enclosed world – there were always interconnections, and movement, between the kingdoms, and the Lombard kings went so far as to develop a system of passports for travellers entering across the Alps at a time of political tension with the Franks.[36] And, above all, it was a governed world. All three of the post-Roman kingdoms used writing-based techniques of government, of different kinds, which had been inherited from the Roman world, together with – in Francia and Italy, rather less in Spain – a tradition of assembly politics which had not. They also devel-oped their own particular practices: in Francia, real deliberative assemblies, as well as an effective and usually regular war machine; in Spain, a tradition of strongly moralised and ceremonialised politics; in Italy, capillary government, both proactive and responsive. All these practices, largely developments of the earliest medieval centuries, would be used by the Carolingians after them, as we shall see in Chapter 4.

CHAPTER THREE

Crisis and transformation in the east, 500–850/1000

While the lands of the former western Roman empire were facing the still-uncertain prospects of the early sixth century, the eastern empire was having an economic boom. An array of well-built stone churches were being put up across the rich villages of the olive-growing region of northern Syria; irrigation was pushing agriculture out into the desert fringes of the Levant; a substantial new city was founded at Iustiniana Prima (modern Caričin Grad in the hills of southern Serbia), the birthplace of the emperor Justinian (527–65), which, as recent excavation shows, did not just have an array of state-of-the-art public buildings, but also a substantial population and a set of artisanal productions, even though it was off the beaten track then as now. Justinian also in 532–37 built the 'Great Church', Hagia Sophia in Constantinople, which was the largest roofed building to be built in Europe until the thirteenth century.[1] A network of commercial routes criss-crossed the eastern Mediterranean and Aegean, bringing Gaza wine, Syrian and Anatolian oil, Egyptian grain and papyrus, Egyptian and Syrian linen, fine pottery from the Aegean and Cyprus, to Constantinople and to other major centres. These exchanges were under-pinned by the tax system which brought food and other goods north to Constantinople and the Balkan military frontier, as well as east to the Euphrates frontier with Persia, but they went far beyond the tax routes.[2] The greatest wealth of the eastern empire was definitely located in its non-European lands, notably Egypt and the Levant, but south-eastern Europe was connected into it too, and, after Justinian's western reconquests, so were north Africa, Sicily, and the south of Italy (although not the centre-north, where most of the fighting of the Roman–Gothic war had occurred). This sixth-century exchange system would not be matched again in European history until the medieval high point of production and exchange in Flanders and Italy in the thirteenth century and onwards, in a very different economic environment (see Chapter 7). It does not seem to have been affected more than marginally by the most serious epidemic

to hit Europe and the Mediterranean before the Black Death, which affected
Constantinople and other parts of the east in 541–43 and may well have been
bubonic plague, like its more devastating successor.[3]

From the standpoint of Constantinople, then, the medieval millennium
began with prosperity; it is not surprising that it was also marked by political
protagonism. Benefiting from the secure fiscal base built up by his predecessor
Anastasius (491–518), Justinian revised the entire legal code in 528–33,
creating the corpus of texts which have been at the base of Roman law ever
since; reformed the imperial bureaucracy, legislating against the abuses of
the powerful; and fought wars not just against the Vandals and Ostrogoths
but also on his northern frontiers, and, with particular commitment, against
the Persians. He also ruthlessly repressed religious minorities who caused
any trouble at all, and many that did not. Justinian is, and was then, a controversial figure; his uncompromising toughness and his huge ambition, often
expressed in original ways – both Hagia Sophia and his legal reforms were
unprecedented in their scale – produced critics and vocal enemies. The embit-
tered retired official John Lydos attacked the emperor's chief reforming
minister, John the Cappadocian, in amazing terms, not just as the destroyer of
the administration but as physically gross, corrupt, greedy for food and drink
(his demands stripped the Black Sea and the Sea of Marmara of fish), a bisexual
predator of extraordinary cruelty, lying naked in a bedchamber covered in
excrement – all the tropes available to classical rhetoricians piled up together.
John Lydos did not attack the emperor himself, but others did, not least the
contemporary historian Prokopios, for whom Justinian was a demon and his
powerful wife Theodora a prostitute. And, indeed, the fiscal system was arguably not robust enough to fight several wars at once as well as building on a
considerable scale, and Justinian's administrative reforms did not achieve the
root-and-branch streamlining which he sought; his successors were far less
ambitious, doubtless as a result. But his reign certainly shows the possibilities
that a determined emperor could contemplate, and partially achieve.[4]

We do, however, also need to recognise that for Justinian religious conflict
was perhaps the most important issue he had to confront, or at least was
inextricable from the rest of his political activity. The Christological disputes of
the fifth century, over the nature of Christ's divinity, had produced a
Monophysite community (who held that there was no separation between the
human and the divine in his nature) at odds with the views of the capital,
but with considerable popular appeal in the eastern provinces; Justinian's
self-image as the Christian emperor par excellence meant that achieving religious unity was as important for him as it would later be for the Visigoths. He

was fully prepared to achieve this by repression, but he negotiated too (Theodora was herself a Monophysite), and in 553, in a major church council at Constantinople, he tried to create a doctrinal middle way which both sides could support. This failed, however, and the Monophysites gained an organisational coherence during his reign which made all such attempts in the future fail too; the Christian churches of Armenia, Lebanon and Egypt are still Monophysite today.[5]

The reason why the Monophysite secession mattered more than the Arian–Nicaean conflict of the fourth century had done is simply that the Christianisation of the eastern empire was by now, as in the west, effectively complete, except once again for the Jewish community. But eastern Christianity was not exactly the same as in the west. The hierarchy of bishops was as active in the east as in the west, and increasingly bishops were city leaders here as well. Bishops were less prominent players in a wider politics, however, except those of the major cities; episcopal churches may have been less rich in land, and emperors were more powerful in ecclesiastical affairs than rulers were in the west. The hierarchy of the church was also not the only basis for religious activism. Autonomous monasteries grew rapidly in number, and were not always as closely associated with aristocratic power as in the west; they were foci for some quite rough-cut popular religiosity, and monks could be fanatical religious police in places where they were numerous, as around Jerusalem and in southern Egypt. Ascetic 'spiritual athletes', even if not so many in number, were prominent too, as with Simeon the Younger (d. 592), sitting on his column for forty-four years close to the great city of Antioch, who was locally very influential, offering prophecies and religious advice even to emperors, as well as miracles. Such ascetics were also unusually effective as exorcists of demons, as with Theodore of Sykeon (d. 613) in central Anatolia, whose *Life* lists his anti-demon achievements. Local saints' cults, of martyrs of the early church, bishops, and ascetics, developed as well; such cults were focused on their relics, as in the west. Relics tended to be under the control of the church hierarchy, but there was a bottom-up religiosity in the sixth-century empire which escaped the command of any bishop, or indeed emperor.[6]

*   *   *

Wars with Persia began again after a long break in the sixth century, when the power of the shahs of the Sassanian dynasty revived, particularly under Khusrau I (531–79). Since Persia was another powerful empire with experienced troops, and since the Persian border was close to some of the Roman empire's richest lands, this was always dangerous. Justinian fought several wars, and later, in the 570s and 580s, there was near-continuous conflict; it ended only when there were two rival shahs in Persia and the emperor Maurice (582–602) backed the winner, Khusrau II, who made peace in 591. Maurice used the peace to fight in the Balkans, where a new set of invaders had appeared in Justinian's time and after, partly Slavic-speaking tribes (the Byzantines called them generically *Sklavenoi*, and I here call them Sclavenians) which were periodically given coherence and logistical back-up by an ex-nomadic Turkic people, the Avars, based just north of the Danube since the 560s. Maurice's troops, tired of winter war, revolted against him in 602 and marched on the capital, killing the emperor and replacing him with an army officer, Phocas – the first successful coup in the eastern empire for nearly 250 years, but by no means the last. Khusrau used the death of his patron Maurice as an excuse to begin the war again, on a rather larger scale. When Phocas perished in another coup, by Heraclius (610–41) son of the governor of Africa, the civil war on the Roman side allowed the Persians to break through; they occupied Syria, Palestine and Egypt, the economic powerhouses of the eastern empire, between 611 and 619. In 626, in a notable military set-piece, the Persians attacked Constantinople itself on one side and the Avars and Sclavenians on the other; but they did not take the city. That was their high point. Heraclius, who was behind Persian lines with his own army, allied with the Turks from the steppes north of the Caucasus in 627–28 and invaded the shah's political heartland of Mesopotamia, what is now Iraq; Khusrau was killed, Persian power broke down dramatically and Heraclius got back all the conquered lands by 630. This startling military success however did not even last half a decade. Both the Roman and the Persian empires were by then under attack from a new direction, Arabia. Muslim Arab armies between 634 and 642, in fast-moving campaigns and successful battles and sieges, conquered all the provinces that Khusrau had taken from the Romans, and not only: in the same short time they seized Iraq from the Persians, and in the 640s the whole of Iran – the last Sassanian shah, Yazdagird III, was killed in 651, and by then his entire empire was in Arab hands. These were conquests that were never reversed, and they affected the whole geopolitics of Europe and Asia ever after.[7]

What had happened here, and what did it mean? Let us look at this first from the Roman side and then from that of the Arabs. To the Romans, it was the greatest single military disaster which the empire had ever faced in the more than 600 years of its existence, and one that was close to incomprehensible: for the Arabs had always been until then a marginal border people, used as mercenaries at best, but no meaningful threat – there was hardly even an armed defence on the largely desert Arabian frontier. They could hope that it would be reversed, but when the first Arab civil war of 656–61 did not lead to the break-up of the coherence of the new caliphate, and Arab raiding into Anatolia increased instead, it became clearer that the new political order was here to stay. The Romans did not understand what Islam was yet – it was initially seen as a simplified form of Christianity, not a new religion – but, either way, given the way east Roman political imagery now worked, this was as much a religious catastrophe as a military one, since the victorious Arabs were certainly not Orthodox Christians. One response was to shore up Orthodox Christianity, as its internal enemies were beyond doubt the moral cause of such disaster. The 640s and 650s were marked by a reinforcement of persecution against everyone who did not accept the latest religious compromise of the Heraclian period, called Monotheletism; this time, both Monophysites and western Catholics were persecuted (and Jews too), and Pope Martin I (649–55) was arrested in Rome in 653 and, after a trial, exiled to the Crimea for rejecting the imperial line. Another was to conclude that the end of the world was this time really, after many false alarms, at hand; the so-called *Apocalypse of pseudo-Methodios*, a Syriac text soon translated into Greek and even Latin, was written in the newly hopeful years of the second Arab civil war in the 680s and widely circulated. But the end was not at hand, and apocalyptic imagery dropped back again. Interestingly, however, after the moral panic of the mid-century, so did Christological debate. Constantine IV (668–85) formally abandoned the artificiality of Monotheletism in 680, and Christological issues barely surfaced again. The new world of constant defence on all sides seems to have reduced the meaningfulness of high-level debate about the nature of God, and when religious disagreement resurfaced, in the less threatened eighth century, the issues were by then distinct, as we shall see later.[8]

In military terms, urgency did not go away. The Roman empire had lost, in eight years, two-thirds of its land-area and three-quarters of its resources, and had to defend the rest against a wealthy and active enemy. It had to change if it was going to survive, and it did. (From here on, to mark that change, I will use the new name which historians give to the still-Roman empire, 'Byzantine' – from Byzantion, the old name for Constantinople, which was used in our period only for the capital's inhabitants.)[9] The empire achieved this by organising a defence in depth behind the Tauros mountains of central Anatolia, running in a diagonal across what is now Turkey, with local army detachments settled in the military provinces (*themata*) of western Anatolia, and living off the land to supplement their reduced army pay – pay which never ceased to be paid, but was by now almost all in kind, as the coinage system had come close to collapse in the imperial heartland of the Aegean and Anatolia. Given the resistance which these detachments could put up, Arab raids, which were continuous for a century, dissipated in the poor lands of the Anatolian plateau, except for occasional organised attacks; the latter, however, could not conquer Constantinople because the city was so well-defended to the west, and was protected to the east from all but a sea invasion by the Bosporos straits, which separate it from Anatolia. The last major attack was the great Arab siege of 717–18, from both land and sea, which was announced well in advance by the Arabs and prepared for by the Byzantines, but which was as much of a failure as that of 626.[10]

The empire made it through the worst, then. It is striking and significant that it survived such onslaughts when the western empire, two centuries earlier, had failed against what were, in military terms, smaller threats. The reason is not firm leadership; in the 640s and 660s, military and political leadership was very halting and uncertain, and so was it again for a generation after Constantine IV's death. In part, it was because the organisational infrastructure of the empire, which had become well-developed in the fat years of the early sixth century, was strong enough to hold, while adapting itself quite fast (the eighth-century bureaucracy, by now entirely Greek-speaking as it had not been under Justinian, was very differently structured from that of the sixth). The landed aristocracy itself, now rather less wealthy, was absorbed into the hierarchies of the state, and aristocratic families are hardly documented again in our sources until the ninth century.[11] Most of all, though, it was because the very speed and magnitude of the disaster made it impossible to reach the local accommodations which had been so common in the west; there were no periods of relative peace in which local army leaders or provincial societies on the Byzantine side of the border could get used to local Arabs, as the west Romans had got used to Germanic military groups. Everybody knew that the alternative to radical measures was defeat. But it is also significant that one of those radical measures was not the abandonment of the land tax and the reliance on a totally landed army. The fiscal system of the Roman empire survived, in a simplified form. Indeed, in some parts of the empire – in and immediately around Constantinople itself, and in Sicily – it continued to operate in something closer to the old way, on the basis of a coinage system. This was enough to carry on with, and to revive when the situation of the empire improved, as it eventually did.

The Byzantine empire in 700 thus looked very different from that of 600. Its centre of gravity had moved westwards. Its political heartland was by now the Aegean, looking to Constantinople itself, which, although greatly reduced in size (it was no longer fed by the state), was still large and economically active as a city. The heartland had however suffered greatly. In the crisis years, the northern defence had entirely ended, and the Balkan peninsula was steadily occupied by Sclavenian tribes, some of whom got as far as what is now southern Greece; the Byzantines indeed only really controlled the eastern edge of the Greek coast, plus some isolated cities up the western side and along the Adriatic, which could be defended by sea. In 680–81, the network of small Sclavenian communities and Byzantine enclaves in the Balkans was further disrupted by the appearance of a new Turkic nomadic group, the Bulgars, who had revolted against the Avars after 626; the Byzantines were prepared (after defeat) to welcome them in, to give some stability to at least part of the Balkans, and they settled in the northern half of what is now Bulgaria, subtracting it eventually from theoretical Byzantine rule. The economy of Greece and western Anatolia simplified considerably, and most cities were abandoned except for fortified citadels – even if not all, and even if a certain level of commercial exchange never died away in the inland Aegean sea.[12]

All this gave more prominence to the western lands of the empire, the Ravenna–Rome–Naples axis, Sicily and north Africa. These were, with the exception of north Africa, much less affected by the Arab threat. Indeed, by 700 Sicily must have been the empire's most prosperous province (Africa had been finally conquered in the 690s). The network of commercial exchange around Italy's coasts matched that of the Aegean: much less complex than it had been under Justinian, that is to say, but still active.[13] It is thus less surprising than it might seem that Constans II (641–68) decided at the end of his reign to make his capital in Syracuse, the main Sicilian city, although this seemed too radical to other major players, and he was assassinated shortly after. Rome, too, kept its eastern links for a long time. The pope, not yet the formal ruler of the city but very powerful there, was still a patriarch of the imperial church, and his views counted in religious disputes; he was also a rich landowner in southern Italy and Sicily, so had substantial resources. Indeed, the importance of the pope to the emperors increased in this period. Gregory the Great (590–604), to modern eyes the most significant pope of the early middle ages, a major theologian and an active political operator, had little traction in Maurice's Constantinople, but Martin I mattered very greatly to Constans II (unluckily for him). Rome's voice mattered when Constantine IV abandoned Monotheletism, too, and from then on the popes were predominantly Greek-speaking for more than half a century, reflecting the large number of south Italian and eastern priests and monks in the city.[14] This Byzantine empire, then, was constructed on a Constantinople–Sicily axis, not on a Constantinople–Egypt one like its sixth-century predecessor. Not surprisingly, its control over the northern sea route in the Mediterranean was defended as much as possible against the Arabs.[15]

* * *

That was the Roman response to the mid-seventh-century crisis, then. That of the Arabs was quite different, of course, as they were the victors. We cannot look at the new world the Arabs created in as much detail as it deserves, in a book focused on Europe; but we need to balance it against the Roman response, so as to contextualise it; and anyway the Arab caliphates were by far the richest and strongest political systems of the Mediterranean world for the next half-millennium, with considerable effect on the European side of the sea for that reason, so deserve attention. First, Arab success: it was the product of the unification of Arabia's numerous tribes, by Muhammad (d. 632) and his successors, under the name of Islam. What form Islam took in its earliest years will never be known, although it is becoming increasingly likely that its main sacred text, the Qur'an, had reached something close to its final form already by around 650, as Muslim traditions have indeed always held. This does not, of course, at all mean that its contents were widely accepted or even known, and, as with Christianity, what early Muslims thought their religion was is likely to have been highly various.[16] But what was most important is that the Arab armies thought they were united by common religious belief, at least long enough to win their first victories and become united by common interest as well. Not that religious commitment is enough to explain their success; armies do not win battles if generals are inexperienced and discipline is weak, and the Arab armies were not initially big.[17] They were certainly well led, however; and, as with the Germanic peoples two centuries before, it is likely that many Arabs had experience in the Roman and Persian armies (even if the main Roman-federated tribe, the Ghassanids, fought on the side of Heraclius). And there can be no doubt that the stresses of the recent Roman–Persian war, in particular the destruction of armies on both sides and the exhaustion of taxpayers, cannot have helped the resilience of the two empires. This is about as far as we can go in explanation, however; our sources, although voluminous on the Arab side, are mostly late in date and do not tell us more.

What the Arabs did with their success is better documented. Muhammad's successors, the caliphs (*khalifa* means 'deputy' – that is to say, of God), ruled the richest parts of the world west of India and China; they had immense potential resources. As far as we can see, they used them. From as early as the 640s, the caliphs seem to have decided that the Arab armies would not settle on the land, as Germanic groups had done earlier, but instead were to be settled in cities and paid directly from taxation – the taxation, that is to say, which already existed in both the Roman empire and Persia, and which would still be for a long time collected and administered by traditional Roman and Persian élites. The practice of supporting the army, the ruling class and the state by a sophisticated system of taxation never failed in the Arab world.[18] This had the significant initial benefit of separating the Arabs from the local societies of non-Arabs and non-Muslims, who hugely outnumbered them, and in fact the Arabs were never absorbed by them; it was the Arabic language and Muslim religion which eventually won out, in all the areas of the caliphate except Iran. (This, too, distinguished them from most Germanic groups in the west; in Gaul, Spain and Italy, Latin-based languages survived, not Germanic ones.) Islam was a minority religion until the tenth century or so, in all the conquered lands except probably Iraq; all the same, steadily, at least from the late eighth century onwards, a new Arab and Muslim élite culture came to dominate the major centres of the Muslim world. This had some links to earlier literature and philosophy (particularly classical Greek philosophy and science), but was based by now on new styles of writing history, theology, poetry, geography, advice manuals, belles-lettres, which owed almost nothing to earlier traditions; these genres produced huge numbers of texts in the ninth and tenth centuries (far more than anywhere in Europe, possibly at any point in the middle ages), and have structured Islamic culture ever since.[19] Some of that cultural achievement, especially in medicine and philosophy, would be brought to western Europe too, by translators into Latin in the twelfth and thirteenth centuries.

The caliphate was thus kept politically operative and, for a long time, immensely rich by an effective fiscal and administrative system. This moved more slowly away from its Roman (and Persian) roots than did the fiscal structures of not only the western European kingdoms but even the Byzantine empire. In the lands of the former Roman empire, Arab-ruled Egypt and the Levant also changed less in their economy than any other region; it is indeed hard to pinpoint the moment of the Arab conquests in archaeological terms at all, and the prosperity of the sixth century, which the Byzantine provinces had lost, continued here without much change for a long time.[20] New Islamic cities, like Fustat (now part of Cairo) and after 762 Baghdad, could be huge in size. When Mediterranean-wide exchange developed again in the eleventh to thirteenth centuries, Egypt was even more dominant as a production and exchange focus than it had been under Rome. In the caliphate, that is to say, long-term cultural and religious changes were balanced, and paid for, by a much less changed economy and political structure: almost the exact reverse of the situation in Europe, east or west.

The actual politics of the caliphate were not as stable as the structure of the state. The immediate successors of Muhammad maintained a central control over army strategy and resources, which was effective, but was resented by the armies flush with success and wealth. When the caliph 'Uthman was murdered by dissident troops in 656, civil war followed, and an interruption in Arab expansion. In 661, Mu'awiya, 'Uthman's cousin, from the Umayyad family, distant relatives of Muhammad, won that war and became caliph (661–80); the Umayyads, based in Damascus in Syria, continued to rule for nearly a century. When, however, it became apparent at Mu'awiya's death that he and his successors intended to rule dynastically, revolts broke out and a second civil war followed, which was not won by the Umayyads until 'Abd al-Malik (685–705) took the holy city of Mecca in 692. 'Abd al-Malik put a much more public religious stamp on the caliphate; he built monumental mosques, as did his son al-Walid I (705–15), and he took his image off his coins, replacing it with quotes from the Qur'an. The Umayyads controlled Syria and Palestine, and never lost the loyalty of the Egyptian army until the end, but tended to be opposed in Iraq, and sometimes also in Iran. When an Iran-based salvationist revolt broke out in 747, it gained support elsewhere too; the Umayyads were defeated in 750 and almost wiped out as a family, and a new family took over the caliphal office, the 'Abbasids, who were descendants of Muhammad's uncle and thought to be much closer to Muslim religious legitimacy. (The 'Alids, descendants of Muhammad himself via his daughter Fatima, expected to be the beneficiaries of the revolt, but were not, and remained after that, for the most part, a permanently disappointed family, although with considerable religious and social prestige.) The 'Abbasid family would hold the caliphal title for centuries to come, until it was seized from them by the Ottomans in 1517, although they only kept control of effective power for 200 years, until the 940s. They based themselves in Iraq, not Syria, which was not again a major power-centre until the twelfth century; al-Mansur, their second caliph (754–75), was the founder of Baghdad, and his successors were the patrons of the Arab literary flowering of the next centuries.[21]

I cannot here pursue the history of the caliphs, or of the numerous successor dynasties to the 'Abbasids after they lost control. But it is important at least to emphasise that the lands ruled by the caliphs had by the 940s broken up into many separate states, based in Egypt, Iraq, Iran, etc., and were never part of the same polity again – only under the Ottomans were the Muslim-ruled lands of the Mediterranean plus Iraq reunited, in the sixteenth century, and they never controlled Iran. Earlier than that, the most powerful of the successor states in the Mediterranean was the independent Fatimid caliphate (969–1171), based in Egypt but extending its authority up into Syria and, at least nominally, over

Tunisia and Sicily. The Fatimids, unusually, were 'Alid by descent, or at least claimed to be; they were the most successful polity ruled through the Shi'a, rather than the Sunni, Muslim tradition during the middle ages.[22]

Arab civil wars halted the expansion of the caliphate, but their end produced new attacks on their neighbours, as a sign of renewed unity and commitment; the caliphate steadily expanded into north Africa and central Asia as a result. By the end of the seventh century, the caliphate had gained a hegemony over the Berber kingdoms of the Algerian and Moroccan coast, as well as taking over Byzantine north Africa. From here, in 711, a Berber and Arab army invaded Visigothic Spain, and had conquered nearly all of it by 718. This was as far as they got into Europe (although Sicily was conquered a century or so later); raiding into Gaul followed, but without much territorial commitment. The fact was that the caliphate had by now reached as far as, further than, it could reasonably be expected to get, stretching from the Atlantic to the border with China; it could not be maintained as a single unit on a really long-term basis, and was not, as the post-'Abbasid period shows – although holding the lands from Egypt to Samarkand together for 300 years until then was already a logistical and organisational triumph. If there was any new conquest that the caliphs really wanted after 700, it was Constantinople; but they failed in that in the same years as their Spanish victory, in 717–18. Spain was an add-on, that is to say; it was already, with much of north Africa, in revolt in 740, and after 755–56 was happy to accept the last survivor of the Umayyad dynasty, 'Abd al-Rahman I (756–88), as an independent *amir*.[23] But the amirate of al-Andalus was the one part of Europe directly transformed by the Arab conquests, and we will return to it at the end of the chapter.

As with the end of the western Roman empire, the Arab conquests have been viewed by much western scholarship through a veil of moralisation, about the failure of civilisation and the imperial project, and the triumph of barbarism. This is nonsense in both cases, but, given the sophistication of the caliphate, it is particularly egregious here. They have also been seen though the lens of Orientalism: this was the moment when the eastern and southern Mediterranean ceased to be part of a common civilisation with the northern coasts, and became an Other, full of incomprehensible intrigue and harsh and repetitive – indeed, essentially meaningless – changes of régime, under a harsh sun. This is equally nonsense, but is more insidious because it contains one grain of truth: an Arab-speaking culture was genuinely opaque to Latin- and Greek-speaking Europe, except at one or two points of contact, al-Andalus, Sicily soon, and later the great Italian trading cities, who needed to know how to deal with the rich parts of the Mediterranean. It was also only too easy for

Christian polities to see Muslim ones as existential threats, and sometimes they acted on that imagery, as, most dramatically, at the time of the crusades; and it was certainly much harder for the Christian polities to learn from the Muslim ones, even when there was much to learn. We have to recognise this difference, while not being taken in by it.

One variant of this imagery does need more comment, however: did the Arabs actually create Europe itself, by breaking the unity of the Roman and post-Roman Mediterranean and separating out the European coasts from the Asian and African ones (with some fuzziness at the margin, the Arabs in al-Andalus and the Byzantines in Anatolia being the most obvious in this period)? The great Belgian economic historian Henri Pirenne certainly thought so in the early twentieth century; for him, the Mediterranean was an economic whole until the Arab conquests broke the trading links of the Roman empire, and only then was European commerce forced northwards to what Pirenne saw as its natural focus, that is to say Belgium.[24] This is factually untrue; the western Mediterranean had already lost its economic unity before the seventh century; by the tenth century, conversely, merchants from the Islamic states were recreating a Mediterranean commercial network from al-Andalus to Egypt and Syria, which Byzantium and the Italian cities later simply plugged into.[25] But it cannot be denied that, from now onwards, the southern boundary of the Christian-ruled world was the Mediterranean Sea, and not, as it had been in 500, the Sahara. Where this seductive theory runs aground, rather, is in the evocation of 'Europe', which was a meaningless concept as yet, and never a powerful one in the middle ages, as we saw in Chapter 1; furthermore, the huge political and cultural differences between northern and southern Europe were, as yet, far greater than even the differences between the three great eighth-century western Eurasian players, Francia, Byzantium and the caliphate. This would remain the case until the latest middle ages, by which time there was also even more fuzziness at the edges, with the Ottomans by now on the border of Hungary and the Russian princes poised to break into Siberia. I would rather abandon these easy and usually complacent world-historical musings, and simply say: what the Arab conquests created was a third major player in western Eurasia, one which was more powerful than the previously dominant one, the (eastern) Roman empire, and one with which everyone would have to deal in the future. That should be enough to be getting on with.

*   *   *

After the great siege of Constantinople in 717–18, the Byzantines no longer had to operate in crisis mode, and they realised this relatively soon. The emperor who was then ruling, Leo III (717–41), the last survivor of a revolving door of army coups in the previous generation, established a solid power structure on the basis of his victory, which was inherited and carried forward by his son Constantine V (741–75). Leo legislated; Constantine rebuilt the main aqueduct system into Constantinople, a considerable undertaking, and a vital one for its water supply. He also revamped the army, establishing an expert corps of shock troops, and went on the military offensive for the first time in a century, campaigning frequently against the Bulgars and Sclavenians, re-establishing hegemony over what is now Greece and further north too, and even attacking the Arabs. Constantine had much less interest in the west of the empire, and he did little to prevent the loss of Ravenna and other central Italian territories – including Rome, where the popes established effective independence during his reign; nevertheless, in the east his military successes resonated strongly there-after. Together, Leo and Constantine created the bases for the strong Aegean-focused Byzantine empire of the central middle ages. It was still restricted in size, but coherent in fiscal and military terms; it was smaller than the other major polity in Europe, Francia, but was much more tightly organised internally, around a still-large and now, again, expanding capital, and it certainly lasted longer. A later emperor, Nikephoros I (802–11), also revised the tax system, and from his reign onwards the evidence of a revived use of coinage, and, soon, more complex economic exchange and artisanal production, increases too.[26]

We see a political confidence here which had not been properly visible since the sixth century. It was not always fully justified, as yet at least. The Bulgars regrouped under the khagan Krum (c. 800–14), and defeated and killed Nikephoros; after two more coups and a civil war, in 828 Arab forces occupied Crete, a strategically vital island, and in 827 began a long conquest of Sicily, which would take it out of Byzantine hands entirely by 902. But under Theophilos (829–42), who was, like Constantine V, a major builder in Constantinople, the empire held together, and thereafter Arab attacks dropped back. The empire was in a good position to take advantage of the first major period of 'Abbasid crisis, in the 860s, and the longer one which began in the tenth century, as we shall see in Chapter 9.[27]

This was the context, a moderately optimistic one except in the 810s and 820s, for one of the most interesting Christian conflicts of the middle ages, over the power of religious images. Alongside the cult of relics, which was long-standing, there appear from the 680s onwards references to a cult of religious images; such images had long existed too, but from now on they were regarded by many in a new way, as windows into the holy presence of the saint (or of Christ) depicted in them. This was a controversial belief, not held by all, for others believed that it was wrong to venerate what was merely paint on wood, created by humans; but it was widespread enough to have some of its elements standardised by the ecclesiastical Council in Trullo of 691/92. Why it appeared – and only in Byzantium, not in the west – seems above all to be because the late seventh century was the period when the Byzantines were adjusting to the shock of defeat; to have as direct an access as possible to the divine was attractive to many. It became mixed up immediately, however, with a felt need by the church hierarchy to control the detail of religious practices, which was in fact the main concern of the Council in Trullo – the danger of impure ritual had, in effect, replaced the danger of incorrect belief about the nature of Christ – and for many the cult of images was not just something which needed to be controlled, but was itself actively impure. The issue of whether the cult of images was a good or a bad thing also connected with a cross-cultural unease about the issue of representation in general, for this was the period in which the caliphs began to abandon the use of any human imagery at all, at least in public and religious settings. There are no grounds for arguing for a Muslim influence on Byzantine Christianity here, or indeed vice versa, but clearly the question of whether human representations were good or bad, holy or impious, resonated across political and religious boundaries.[28]

Questions of this kind help to explain the eighth-century backlash against the cult of images, which is first documented in the 720s and 730s in the actions of two Anatolian bishops. Around 750 this was taken up by Constantine V himself, who wrote two tracts against images called the *Peuseis*, and in 754 called the Council of Hiereia to condemn image veneration. A few such images in churches seem to have been destroyed and replaced by crosses, which were for Constantine fully acceptable, because symbolic, objects of veneration. (Most holy portraits were not destroyed, however, as far as we can tell today.) More important, the immediate, and uncontrolled, access to the sacred provided by religious images was to be replaced by the mediation of clerics, and by church ritual focused on the Eucharist. This is what Constantine's 'iconoclasm' consisted of (the word, it should be noted, is a modern invention, and was unknown to the Byzantines). It is hard to know how controversial this was. Constantine certainly had opponents, although we only know for sure about the popes in Rome; conversely, the army seems to have been with him, probably also the capital, and – when they got to learn about it – so were theologians in Francia, where, in a world in which images had little religious charge, Constantine's measures would have seemed fairly normal. What is clear, on the other hand, is that when Constantine and then his son Leo IV died, Leo's widow Eirene, empress regent for her son Constantine VI (780–97), was able to reverse the policy, and at the Second Council of Nicaea in 787 re-established image veneration, with a comprehensive condemnation of Constantine V and his religious views.[29] Eirene was a tough woman; she would later depose and blind her son, almost the only woman to take power by force in medieval European history, and she ruled alone until she herself fell in a coup in 802 in favour of Nikephoros I. The Second Council of Nicaea was perhaps simply a way of getting her own supporters into positions of authority instead of her father-in-law Constantine's, as well as bringing Byzantine religious practice back into line with that of Rome. Her success is also a marker of the real authority which imperial women were capable of exercising in the Byzantine world – she was part of a succession of major figures from Theodora, through the emperor-makers Sophia (Justin II's widow) in the sixth century and Martina (Heraclius' widow) in the seventh, to the empresses regnant Zoe and Theodora in the 1040s and 1050s – even if her eventual overthrow marks the fragility of female power as well.[30] But the 802 coup did not re-establish icono-clasm, which perhaps shows that there was more unhappiness, or indifference, about Constantine V's religious views than we have any evidence for earlier.

That was not the end of it. Nikephoros' death in battle alarmed the empire, and the memory of Constantine V's victories began to resonate greatly, partic-ularly inside the army; in 815, a new emperor, Leo V, returned to iconoclasm in the hope of a return to military success. But this Second Iconoclasm, as it is often called, seems to have been more of a régime and army cult, promoted with enthusiasm only by Theophilos in the 830s, and anyway the military success did not materialise. At his death, the regency council for his young son Michael III abandoned it within a year, and in 843 revived a formalised vener-ation of images which was much more thorough-going, because by now theo-logically justified in considerable detail, than it had ever been in the mid-eighth century. The veneration of sacred portraits – icons – has been an essential element of Orthodox Christianity ever since, and marked Byzantine religious culture until the empire's end. The independence of mind of some Byzantine religious writers after that may have been because, to an extent, they were starting again. The central medieval Byzantine state was the work of Constantine V, as developed by Nikephoros I and Theophilos, but the religious orthodoxy of that state was established in rejection of all three (even Nikephoros, who, although anti-iconoclast, had overthrown Eirene, the heroine of Nicaea). The Byzantine secular world in the future would have to find newer heroes.

*   *   *

Let us finish this chapter by going back to al-Andalus: not properly an 'eastern' state – in fact, it was (with Ireland) as far west as one can go in Europe – but at least heavily influenced by the political patterns which were working out in Egypt and Iraq. Al-Andalus did not include the whole of Spain; the Arabs did not take over the mountainous northern fringe of the peninsula, where small and incoherent Christian kingdoms clung on in the eighth and ninth century, becoming slightly more coherent in the tenth.[31] The Arabs also based themselves in the south, in the Roman city of Córdoba, not in the central plateau around the old capital of Toledo; Toledo and other major northern centres like Zaragoza were treated, rather, as large frontier areas, important to rule, certainly, but where central control was incomplete. The Umayyad amirate did not have an easy start; Spain was very fragmented after the conquest, with different sectors of the peninsula in different relationships with central power. It was also one of the few places the Arabs conquered which did not have a strong fiscal system already in place, and, although the Arab rulers sought to set one up as fast as they could, it was not working with the effectiveness which one would have taken for granted in the Middle East until the tenth century. Córdoba grew fast as a capital, all the same; at its height in the tenth century it may have been, briefly, the largest city in Europe. 'Abd al-Rahman I in 756 established Umayyad dynastic rule which lasted without a break until 1031, and with little by way of succession problems. This at least acted as a secure basis for a steady growth in the power of the amiral régime, which developed, notwithstanding al-Andalus's independence, largely thanks to borrowings of governmental techniques from the 'Abbasid state. This went hand in hand with the Islamisation of the ruling class and then, more slowly, of the Spanish population in general, which was notable in Córdoba by the ninth century and had probably reached a tipping point everywhere in the amirate by the early tenth.[32]

This political system nearly broke up in the first great period of civil wars, between the 880s and the 920s, when local political figures revolted across much of al-Andalus – one of them, 'Umar ibn Hafsun (d. 917), who claimed Visigothic descent, even converted to Christianity, a sure sign of flaws in Umayyad hegemony. But 'Abd al-Rahman III (912–61) reversed this rapidly, conquering almost all the new local potentates, and fully centralising his realm in fiscal terms for the first time. Facing as he did the expansionism and caliphal claims of the Fatimids, he called himself caliph in 929, and established an ambitious new court just outside Córdoba at Madinat al-Zahra', which was aimed to impress outsiders, and did. This was the century when al-Andalus reached its height, with the development of Almería as a Mediterranean port, and a complex economy and material culture developing well outside the capital. In the last years of the century, al-Mansur, the powerful chamberlain of the caliph, who ran the state in 981–1002, took war to the northern kingdoms, which had expanded during the first civil war, and sacked their major towns, León and Santiago de Compostela. Al-Andalus looked as if it might move further still, to cover the whole peninsula.[33]

This did not happen. Al-Mansur's inept heirs after 1009 allowed the state to descend into civil war over the succession; Córdoba was sacked in 1013, the caliphate was abandoned in 1031, and the state ended up fragmented between some thirty *Taifa* (literally, 'factional') kingdoms, in Toledo, Seville, Valencia, Granada and so on. We shall see in Chapter 8 that this allowed the Christian kingdoms to expand further, and to gain, for the first time, a greater military strength than the now-divided Muslim polities, as the latter found when Alfonso VI of Castile took Toledo, the first major territorial loss for al-Andalus, in 1085. This was by no means the end for Muslim Spain, however. The Taifas, long seen as a failure because of their division, were in fact often very successful and effective small kingdoms. They maintained the political and fiscal structures which were established under 'Abd al-Rahman III, and they generated a sophisticated political culture. In their wealth and intellectual activity, they recall the late medieval Italian city-states; if they were poor at defending themselves against larger armies from Christian Castile and then (invading to defend them in the late 1080s) the Almoravids of Muslim Morocco, much the same can be said for the Italian cities when they faced the French and the Germans from the 1490s onwards. The Taifas indeed produced one of the most interesting practical political treatises of medieval Europe, *The Tibyan* of 'Abd Allah al-Ziri, ruler of Granada (1073–90), who lost his kingdom to the Almoravids and wrote his text in exile in Morocco after that. 'Abd Allah's book is a mixture of Machiavelli's *The prince* and Robert Graves's *I, Claudius*: it is an autobiographical account of a failed operator whose main political success was simply to succeed to the throne, but, all the same, an operator intelligent enough to see where he had gone wrong and to reflect on his mistakes. His account of Alfonso's divide-and-rule technique, of taking protection money from rival Taifas so as to weaken them all, is justly famous ('Abd Allah learned the hard way: he refused Alfonso's first demand, but, when Alfonso was paid more by Seville, ended up himself having to pay more than the original demand); his comments on when to take advice and when not to, a common topic of statecraft literature, are unusually elegant ('I would listen to what people had to say with my ears, though not with my mind'); his account of his own fall (including an analysis of why each social group in Granada abandoned him) is a model of wisdom after the fact. It would not be until the fifteenth century, as we shall see in Chapter 12, that we would find again in a European text such practical awareness by a political player.[34]

Al-Andalus regrouped after the fall of Toledo, under Berber dynasties. They did so twice, in fact: under the Almoravids (1086–1147), as we have just seen, and then, from the late 1140s, the Almohads. Not until the Almohads were defeated by the Castilians in 1212 was al-Andalus's survival seriously at risk, and even then it took nearly 300 years more for it to vanish entirely. Much of the complexity of the Umayyad caliphate returned in the twelfth century, indeed; the intellectual and educational environment which the Almohads could pay for produced, for example, the Aristotelian philosophy and scientific treatises of Ibn Rushd (d. 1198), who, Latinised as Averroes, entranced the masters of the university of Paris in the thirteenth century.[35] This continued in the amirate of Granada later, where some of the highest-quality architecture of the whole middle ages survives in the fourteenth-century Alhambra palace.

All the same, the point about al-Andalus, which we need to end with, is not its eventual fate, however scintillating the path to it was. Rather, it is to stress that in the tenth century the Córdoba caliphate was, with Byzantium, one of the two most effective political systems of Europe, based in each case on a fiscal structure that had no equivalent elsewhere. In that century, the wealth and power of the continent lay at its south-western and south-eastern corners. The Latin Christians in the middle knew this full well. They admired Byzantium, sometimes resentfully; they feared al-Andalus; but they recognised the force of both. And al-Andalus, when it did break up, maintained the political structures of the caliphate in each of the warring kingdoms – thanks to models which had been set in place in the east in the seventh century, and developed from then on by the 'Abbasids and Fatimids. It was a rich territory when the Christian kingdoms, of Castile, Aragón and Portugal, eventually divided up the spoils.

CHAPTER FOUR

The Carolingian experiment, 750–1000

The Carolingians have fascinated a generation and more of historians for their ambition: they presided over the largest-scale attempt to rethink politics in the whole of the middle ages. On one level, it is true, largest-scale was easy: the Frankish empire of Charles 'the Great', Charlemagne (768–814), and his son Louis 'the Pious' (814–40), was substantially larger than any other political system in medieval Europe, covering as it did modern France, Germany and the Low Countries, and extending out to northern Italy, Catalonia and Austria. The political initiatives which we find in some western European polities after 1200 were not always less radical, as with the innovative political institutions of north Italian cities in the thirteenth century, or the Hussites in Bohemia in the fifteenth; but they happened piecemeal, and/or over a far smaller geographical compass. Nor were the Carolingian kings and élites fully aware of what they were doing; the mission they had was largely seen as moral, even theological, with imperatives which had old roots (they modelled themselves on biblical Israel and the Christian Roman empire), and political procedures which were often almost as old – they were just trying to do it *right*. Indeed, often they failed, for the political ambitions and assumptions of too many players, including the moralists themselves, were far too self-interested, violent, corrupt: the normal political needs of everyday life usually crowded grand theory out, as they have tended to do in most other societies too. But understanding the Carolingians is crucial for all that, as they were indeed trying to do something new, even if they did not realise it, and on bases that were quite different from those of any later political systems. They will often appear further on in this book as a point of comparison for future western European history, and we need to get them straight. They are also well documented; if we know more about the Merovingians than about any other post-Roman kingdom in the west, we know much more about the Carolingians than the Merovingians. So they justify our attention; and we will here pursue Francia past the main

Carolingian period, which ended in 887, and through into the successor states of the tenth century as well.

Let us start off with a quick narrative of the politics of the eighth and ninth centuries; then we will look at the way the Carolingians ruled, before coming to the ideological project which sought to underpin it.[1] Charles Martel, the *maior* who took over Francia in the 710s, initiated the run of conquests that mark out the eighth century in the Carolingian world, as we saw in Chapter 2. The Carolingian family was descended from him, and later medieval writers named it after him. He still nominally ruled on behalf of Merovingian kings, but they had no power at all by now, and between 737 and his death in 741 he did not even bother to create a new king. His two sons, Pippin III and Carloman I, did so when they succeeded him, but already by 751 Pippin, now sole ruler, judged it possible simply to take power as king himself. However little power the Merovingians had by now, however, the tradition of their rule was 250 years old, and the family had a sacrality which is both hard to pinpoint and impossible to dismiss; this was a coup. Pippin and his heirs spent time covering this up, and so did their historians; maybe the pope himself had agreed to it in advance; maybe the aristocracy had agreed to Pippin being anointed by Archbishop Boniface of Mainz. But it is certainly the case that Pope Stephen II (752–57), who came to Francia in 754 to seek Pippin's help against Lombard attack (it was the first time a pope had ever come north of the Alps), himself anointed Pippin king, in a gesture which had no precedent in the Frankish world – although the Visigoths had used the anointing ritual previously.[2] This set the tone for Carolingian political action ever after, for, without the support of the church, they were just another aristocratic family, even if by far the most prominent one in Francia. The commitment to an ecclesiastical vision of politics followed; already Pippin and Carloman were organising church councils in the 740s, there were more in the 750s, and there would be still more in the century to follow.

Charles Martel had had an army in the field almost every year during his rule; his sons did too, and by Pippin's death they had conquered most of the main independent regions that the Merovingians had once ruled. Charlemagne, Pippin's son, and sole ruler by 771, carried this on in grand style. He took over the Lombard kingdom of Italy rapidly in 773–74; he fought the Saxons on his northern frontier with less immediate success, for it took from 772 to 804 to subdue them and force them to convert to Christianity, but he managed it by then. (The Saxons were hard to defeat precisely because they were not a unitary people, a problem Roman emperors had found in their northern campaigns centuries before too; but they did give the Franks of the period a constant military training.) Charlemagne invaded Bavaria, the last one-time Merovingian region, in 787, and took it without a fight; Frankish raiding armies then went further east, attacking the Avar capital in what is now Hungary in 795–96, raids which did not conquer the Avars but did gain the Franks unheard-of wealth as their booty – wealth which was presumably the result of earlier Avar attacks on Byzantium. Charlemagne also moved into Spain, but that campaign, against al-Andalus, was a harder task; still, the area around Barcelona was stably under Frankish rule by 801. All in all, by the time large-scale offensive war stopped in 804, the lands ruled by the Frankish king were twice the size of those ruled by Charles Martel, and the boundaries remained firm afterwards. This was an empire, not a kingdom, by now, so it has seemed significant to modern historians that Charlemagne was crowned *imperator*, emperor, by the pope in Rome in 800; even though this seems not to have been any major turning point in reality, the title was certainly welcome to him and his successors.[3]

Charlemagne established a new palace at Aachen in the 790s, and by the time his only surviving son Louis the Pious succeeded in 814 it had become a real capital. Louis used it as his major base, for policy-making and campaign planning; by now frontier war was largely policing, but Louis established an ample buffer zone to the east, of tributary peoples, mostly Slavic-speaking, from the Baltic to the Adriatic, and he could mobilise armies fast, as in 817, when he defeated a revolt led by his nephew Bernard, subordinate king of Italy.[4] The 820s were quiet, Louis's high summer, but the 830s were not: that was when Louis faced two major uprisings in 830 and 833–34 by his three eldest sons, Lothar, Pippin and (in 833) Louis 'the German', in the second of which he temporarily lost power. This crisis for Louis is a classic case study for how Carolingian political ideology worked in practice, and we will come back to it. He recouped his power at the end of the decade, however, and passed it on without incident to his three surviving sons – Pippin, who had died, was replaced by Louis's youngest son Charles 'the Bald' – who fought a brief civil war in 841–42 and then formally divided up the Frankish lands at the treaty of Verdun in 843.

The Carolingians, like the Merovingians before them, regarded dividing the kingdom as normal, and had done so in 741 and 768; the same would have happened in 814 if Louis's brothers had not died. In 843, Lothar (840–55), as the eldest brother and already co-emperor, took the central lands around Aachen and a narrow strip of land connecting it to his political power-base in Italy; Louis (840–76) took East Francia, roughly the lands east of the Rhine; Charles (840–77) took West Francia, roughly the western two thirds of what is now France. Each of these three were divided later between sons as well. That was too many divisions, and the Carolingians were always worried about there being too many heirs; they excluded female-line heirs and illegitimate sons from the succession, and gave the latter non-royal-sounding names like Hugh and Arnulf to mark the fact. (The reason why the Carolingians have nicknames, most of which were contemporary or nearly so, is because the royal names were so few in number.) But, having done that, they ran into trouble when so many of the Carolingian cousins died without legitimate male heirs. By the late 870s, there were getting to be too few Carolingians, not too many, and a single king-emperor, Charles 'the Fat', the only legitimate adult male, inherited all of the kingdoms between 876 and 884. Charles the Fat could not, however, easily return to the centralised power of Louis the Pious's days. In the generation after 843, separate political networks had emerged for the main kingdoms (in Italy, which had had its own king almost continuously since Charlemagne's conquest, this had indeed happened well before), and it would be necessary to square each of them separately to rule effectively. Charles did not have time for that; he was toppled in 887 in a coup by his nephew Arnulf – ironically, himself an illegitimate son.[5] The different kingdoms then went their separate ways, as we shall see later in this chapter.

But they had already begun to do so. Italy was the most tightly run, especially under Lothar's son Louis II (840–75); it was relatively small, and could draw on the capillary government of the Lombard past. East Francia was the hardest to govern, as it had mostly never been Roman and had poor communications – it included the regions of Francia where the Carolingian ideological project had least traction – but it was the most powerful in military terms, as Louis the German kept his armies active with frontier wars, not least against the newly powerful kingdom of Moravia in what is now the Czech Republic. Charles the Bald's West Francia has attracted most attention, as it is the best-documented, and Charles was particularly ambitious in his political project; but it was the least successful of the three militarily, for it was the most exposed to Scandinavian Viking attacks, seaborne pirate raids (see Chapter 5), which began in the 830s and were almost continuous into the 880s.[6] Louis II could claim in a letter to the Byzantine emperor Basil I that the empire was still united, since the Carolingians were a single family,[7] and in many ways he was right; Verdun was not intended to be any more permanent than previous divisions, and Charles the Fat's succession shows it. But there was little cooperation between the brothers and cousins (against Vikings, for example); instead, and unsurprisingly, there was at least occasional war, with Louis the German trying to take West Francia in 858 and Charles the Bald attacking the East in 876. After 887, the successor kingdoms did not, for the most part, have Carolingians as kings, and the divisions became more permanent as a result.

*   *   *

It has been argued that the Carolingians ran into trouble soon after their empire stopped expanding, from aristocracies whose loyalty to the king would lessen without constant military success. That was not the case. Aristocratic rebellions against Charlemagne mark the 780s and 790s, not later, and those against Louis and his heirs were almost exclusively led by royal brothers and sons; it is very hard to link the aristocratic backing which royal rebels had to any wider disaffection with the Carolingian project as it developed.[8] Rather, the aristocracies of the Frankish world, particularly the old, land-rich, families from the royal heartland of what is now northern France, Belgium and western Germany, gained so hugely from royal largesse, both during and after the century of conquest, that their loyalty to the Carolingians, at least in general terms, was not in doubt. Anyone in favour with the king could expect gifts of both land and office, *honores* as the Franks called them (they included monastic as well as royal land, and even power over monasteries themselves). These were not necessarily permanent, or heritable, but the loyal could expect in practice to pass on royal land gifts to their sons, and local office-holding too, even if not necessarily in the same place. Aristocratic families became very widely spread indeed as a result, as with the family we call the Widonids, originating from near Mainz on the Rhine, who by the 840s included counts and dukes both at the mouth of the Loire and in central Italy a thousand kilometres away: the Widonids could present problems for Carolingian rulers, but they could not have kept this range of power without an at least partially unitary empire, and they knew it.[9]

Both king and aristocracies – secular and ecclesiastical – were very rich in land, then, as they had been in the Merovingian period, but by now still more so. This was also the context for a considerable activity in the economy of the Frankish lands, particularly in the northern parts between the Rhine and the Seine, the Frankish heartland. (It is much less evident in Carolingian Italy, where the evidence also indicates that élites were not so wealthy.) This may have had partially wider roots; there are signs that the ninth century was the period in which the population of Europe as a whole started, slowly, to rise, although such a rise was only significant in later centuries, as we shall see in Chapter 7. But it was also the result of a greater intensity of agrarian exploitation. The ninth century was a period of particularly active estate management by some major landowners, particularly monasteries in the north, which is documented in detailed registers of land and rents called polyptychs – more detailed than any others we have for Europe until the thirteenth century. Church owners, at least, and the kings as well, were concerned to get resources out of their properties as systematically as they could. They sold the surplus too, and this must have been to buy things: we have written sources showing a network of markets in ninth-century Francia, and wine and cloth moving substantial distances. This is confirmed by archaeology, for coins and well-made pottery were widely distributed, as were more specialised products like glass, and basalt quernstones from the Rhineland.[10] On the Rhine, cities like Cologne continued to be important commercial centres, and some, like Mainz, show new activity; and, not least, a network of ports on the Frankish coast reached their height, such as Dorestad in the Rhine delta near modern Utrecht, which show that this active exchange had an international dimension – there were equivalent ports in England and Denmark.[11] (These were the routes the Vikings came down.) In this period, economic activity is above all a guide to élite demand, and thus élite wealth, but this was clearly considerable if as much activity as this was generated in northern Francia. It gave a further bounce to the political protagonism of the period.

Every lay aristocrat or senior cleric who wanted to be recognised as a political player came to the king's great assemblies. Those who did not might be seen as enemies; worse, they risked being thought to be nobodies. They were expected to bring gifts, which were so numerous that, in Charlemagne's time, horses given in gift had to have labels to make it clear who gave them. The assembly politics of the Merovingian period was at least as important under the Carolingians, and perhaps even more so; major affairs of state were decided at the *placitum generale*, the standard name for the usually twice-yearly assembly, meeting in different places in the Frankish heartland (as also, separately, in Italy), which united the principal secular and ecclesiastical lords. The political conflicts of each reign were worked out in these public spaces too, as when Louis the Pious chose to do public penance at the 822 Attigny assembly for the blinding and subsequent death of Bernard of Italy after his rebellion, so as to draw a line under a controversial act. These assemblies were thus not just a place for the Frankish élites to seek the favour of the king, but were necessary for royal legitimacy too – they were still, as in previous centuries, the places where royal power and royal actions (of which a good example is Louis's Attigny penance itself) were presented in public to the *populus*, even if that was a highly élite subset of 'the people', to gain its consent.[12] The use of the word 'public' here reflects the texts, for the Carolingians used the word *publicus* often, referring (among other things) to penance, the *placitum*, and, more generally, the *res publica*, meaning something close to what we call the state. Kings and their senior ministers worked hard to ensure that the debate at such assemblies was controlled, and did not get out of hand; but it is important to recognise that there was indeed debate, and people did express unpopular opinions, as when Archbishop Agobard of Lyon (d. 840), always an outspoken man, made a speech against lay occupation of church land which went down badly at the same Attigny assembly. Indeed, in smaller versions of the general *placitum*, meetings of the closest royal *fideles*, there could be a lot of argument. But kings had the last word; when they did not, as we shall see happened to Louis in 833, they were in serious trouble.[13]

It needs to be stressed again that aristocrats also found themselves in what we could call the royal sphere because the alternatives to it were not as attractive as they would be in later centuries. As with the Merovingian period, we do not find any good evidence for local lordships under the Carolingians: territories dominated by a single landowner, in which he was lord and others were his followers, which could operate as autonomous power-bases. None of the three Widonid political centres, for example, counted as such – even the march of Spoleto in central Italy, which they controlled for a long time, for their tenure of it still depended on royal appointment, which could be reversed. As earlier in Francia, the political foci of aristocrats could move around, as a man in royal favour might pick up land in unexpected extra places – and, after 843 when rival kings wanted more exclusive loyalty from followers, as he might lose it elsewhere too. So, for example, in the showdown between Louis the German and Charles the Bald in 858, some members of the Welf family, related to Louis the Pious's second wife Judith and ancestors of one of the major families of central medieval Europe, chose Charles and lost their East Frankish *honores*; the family split in two as a result.[14] Every aristocrat (or, by now, abbot or bishop) had a military retinue, with men who had sworn loyalty to him as their lord (*senior*); Carolingian armies were above all made up of such private retinues. Personal relations of dependence were fundamental to this world. But every free man had also sworn an oath of loyalty to the king – Charlemagne made such oaths very elaborate in 802 – and the king indeed regarded such men as his, as much as or more than the men of their personal *senior*; when, for example, Bishop Hincmar of Laon removed lands from insufficiently loyal followers in the 860s, they complained directly to Charles the Bald.[15] And men of military standing, the most prosperous free men in any locality, could have a variety of different patrons. Einhard (d. 840), the biographer of Charlemagne and a major figure in Louis's court after him, who had a wide patronage network, wrote to Archbishop Hraban Maur of Mainz in the 830s about one of

Hraban's men, Gundhart, who had been called to the army by the local count, probably in the Rhön region of central Germany; but the count was in feud with him, and fighting under him would be close to a death sentence. Gundhart planned not to go, and instead to pay the fine for neglect of military service; Einhard was asking Hraban to agree to him doing this. Gundhart thus had obligations to the king, via the count; to his personal lord, Hraban; to his kin-group (hence the feud); but also had an entirely separate patron in Einhard.[16]

This sort of multiple network was common in the Frankish lands, and it substantially inhibited the construction of a local power-base by any lord. It can be added that the system of public law courts continued in the Carolingian world, courts to which even peasants had some access; we have several cases in which they took on lords, and fragmentary evidence which shows that in some circumstances, if they got to the king, or perhaps when they had the patronage of others, they too might win.[17] This local public activity made private authority harder too. Recent high-quality studies of parts of the Carolingian and imme-diately post-Carolingian world show local societies with considerable complex-ities of social practice, which single lords could not easily dominate.[18] Of course, we are dealing here with militarised aristocrats, and therefore with men with a considerable commitment to oppression and violence in their own interest. Great landowners, both lay and ecclesiastical, had by now extended their properties substantially and often illegally at the expense of the land-owning peasantry; this process had become generalised in the seventh century, and was being finished off in the ninth, as Carolingian legislation often complained.[19] One area of particularly clear dispossession and subjugation of the peasantry in this period was Saxony, where after the Frankish conquest both Saxon aristocrats and incoming Frankish secular and ecclesiastical lords rapidly extended their power over the landowning peasants of much of the region; during the civil war period of 841–42, this led to the Stellinga move-ment, the most substantial peasants' revolt in the whole of the middle ages until the late thirteenth century, which was put down in 843 by Louis the German very violently.[20] Although this was an extreme, there were doubtless plenty of areas where, for most of the time, individual aristocrats commanded in practice. But they were not power-bases they could fully rely on, and, if they ever had to try, it would be because they were political losers. They needed the royal courts, and were willing participants in royal policy-making, of all kinds.

*   *   *

It is under Charlemagne that we first have good evidence of how the Frankish kings tried, in practical terms, to keep their vast empire under control; the evidence swells under Louis, and continues under his sons. One method was what one could call a flexible uniformity: every district had a count, an aristocrat often sent from elsewhere, who ran justice and the army (to repeat, the two basic elements of government); marches, more militarised territories, were created on the frontiers; local judicial assemblies (also called *placita*) came very widely to have men called *scabini*, members of local élites, who ran the court for the count. These were not exactly innovations, as such men had existed everywhere before, but they were regularisations. Counts were clearly seen as agents of royal power: a poem from 834, which seeks to praise Louis the German, does it through praise of the judicial activity of a local count in Bavaria called Timo, 'your count and legate, glorious king, rendering justice to the good, . . . hated by thieves and detested by robbers, he abhorred conflicts and extended justice'.[21] Bishops, too, were used as judicial figures, and as checks on counts, including in regions such as Italy where they had not been prominent in secular affairs before. And under Charlemagne and his successors royal representatives called *missi*, usually a count and a bishop working in a pair, were routinely used as roving legal authorities, sent to hear appeals against local counts and also running their own hearings; after 802 in much of the empire they had defined districts in which they moved. Other local figures were also asked, often with written instructions, to do one-off tasks for kings, as letter collections show. These overlapping roles, as Jennifer Davis calls them, were not arranged in a precise hierarchy, but they amounted to a network of controls over corruption and the abuse of power, abuses which were sometimes remedied; and they pointed back to the king, as final arbiter in the case of any dispute. We even have a set of written replies from Charlemagne to a *missus*, who is asking for royal advice over a set of legal issues, such as social status and illicit tolls (read the law, one of the replies says in irritated tones, and only bring the issue to the *placitum generale* if you can't find an answer there). Counts certainly could be corrupt – there is much complaint in our sources about a culture of gift-giving for favourable judgements (what we would call bribery), for example. So could *missi* be, for that matter; other *missi* are sometimes recorded reversing the abuses of their predecessors, and there are hints of collusion between different sets of officials as well. Counts were rarely dismissed on these grounds, too – such dismissals were, rather, usually for participation in rebellion and the like.[22] But the fact that in the Carolingian world there were always men being sent out to check on other men was another, substantial, corrective to any tendency for officials to go too far in illegal activity – or to create local power-bases, even on the edges of empire, which were by now a long way from the centre. Eventually, someone would find out and, however delayed, a reaction would follow.

This was linked to written law. The Carolingians issued many laws and regulations, called capitularies as they are divided into *capitula*, chapters, plus the acts of church councils which partially overlap, reaching their height in the years 800–35. They vary considerably in type, from agendas for assemblies and one-off instructions to *missi* which cannot be thought of as legislation, through formal revisions of the traditional laws of the peoples of the empire, to high-flown statements about morality and the liturgy. Some only survive in single copies, but many have multiple manuscripts, and it is evident from some that they were systematically sent around the empire – one manuscript of a capitulary of 803 states that all the magnates in the assembly of the city of Paris signed it. They do not show us that their very detailed regulations were obeyed, or even necessarily known about, but their frequency shows that writing was seen as a natural part of government, and Charlemagne's comments about law cited in the last paragraph show that he assumed it too. Counts were not necessarily literate, but very many were, and collections of capitularies and other laws, prepared for lay officials, survive or are referred to in wills. The written word, in Rosamond McKitterick's influential formulation, was important in Carolingian government; there are many references not only to written instructions going out from the court, but also to demands for written replies. It was not as important as oral communication (as we will see later, it never was in the medieval world, or for long after), but it structured the whole way that the Carolingians saw the task of controlling the huge and highly diverse realm that they ruled.[23] Overall, although this governmental practice was imperfect, it was the densest which was as yet possible in a polity without the complex administrative system which the Byzantines and Arabs took for granted, and denser than any other in western Europe for a long time – until England in the late eleventh century, Italy in the mid-twelfth, France in the thirteenth.

Which brings us to the religious side of the Carolingian project, which was, indeed, seen as indissoluble from the task of governing as just described. This was certainly for the most part new in the Frankish world; as implied at the start of the chapter, it must have largely stemmed from the structural relation between the Carolingians and the church, which began with the coup of 751 and even before. But, however it derived, it was fully visible by the 780s, and made up a major part of political rhetoric, and even political practice, for a century. Charlemagne and his successors were aiming at nothing less than the creation of a collective moral framework for the salvation of the entire Frankish people, and they assumed that their actions were consistently being monitored by God. This is particularly clear in a remarkable capitulary, the *General admonition* of 789, in which the king legislated about clerical morality, the episcopal hierarchy, the need for peace and concord, the general avoidance of sin, and much else along these lines: the stuff of church councils, normally (and largely borrowed from canon-law texts), but here issued exclusively under the name of the king, and addressed to all. This imagery was mixed together with more secular regulations in many subsequent texts.[24] We have seen that east Roman/Byzantine rulers regarded correct Christian belief and practice as fundamental to their political mission, and so did the Visigoths (the Franks indeed had access to texts of Spanish church councils); nor would any later medieval ruler have denied it, if asked. But in no later polity, except perhaps the France of Louis IX, and again Hussite Bohemia, was the question of moral reform – *correctio*, 'correction', as the Carolingians called it – as prominent and urgent. Everyone (or, at least everyone among the empire's élites) should engage in it, as immediately as possible. This urgency came from the king, rather than from the church, even if Frankish bishops were keen participators in it; notably, the pope in Rome had much less connection to it, and some popes, such as Paschal I (817–24), were competitive with, perhaps indeed hostile to, it. Only later in the ninth century did Nicholas I (858–67) and John VIII (872–82) realise that the Frankish interest in religious legitimacy would allow them to make interventions in politics north of the Alps.[25]

Royal enactments were here backed up by a clearly structured programme of education. A letter of Charlemagne to his senior clergy of *c.* 784 stresses that education was essential for anyone who wished to please God (or indeed the king), and from then on we find systematic references to schools: there was a palace school for aristocrats at Aachen, in particular, and royal monasteries, such as St-Martin in Tours in the west or Fulda in the east, became particularly active in educating both monks and lay aristocrats. This was one major reason why the kings could assume that counts and *missi* would – could – read their instructions and laws; and the signs are that, although certainly with exceptions, this assumption was justified. The monasteries also created libraries by copying large numbers of earlier texts, of all kinds: much classical Latin literature, such as Caesar, Horace and much of Cicero, only survives because of Carolingian copies. And this educative programme went with another new feature of Charlemagne's court, followed by those of his heirs: the considerable space there for intellectuals, coming from all over Francia and the conquered lands (and England and Ireland), brought there by the remuneration the kings offered (they almost all ended up rich), and by the simple attraction of being part of such a large-scale project. These included Alcuin from Northumbria (a plausible partial drafter of both the 784 letter and the *General admonition*), Theodulf from Spain, soon Einhard from East Francia; and in later generations

Charles the Bald's main advisor Archbishop Hincmar of Reims, the Irish theologian John Scotus, and major Frankish aristocrats like Hraban Maur, among many others. They were royal advisors and, often, serious political players; and they created a critical mass of new writing (biblical commentary, theology, poetry, history), debate and intellectual excitement. This is already visible in our sources by 790, and it carried on for three generations. The huge scale of some of the tracts which came out of court circles, like Theodulf's *Opus Caroli* of 790–93, written against the anti-iconoclast proceedings of the Second Council of Nicaea, or the lengthy responses by Hincmar and others in the 850s to the views on predestination of the Fulda monk Gottschalk, are further signs of that commitment. Such intellectuals were expected to 'admonish' kings as well as advise them, just as Charlemagne admonished the whole kingdom in 789, and we have plenty of texts in which they did just that; Hincmar was a master of it, for example.[26]

A key point is that this was not exclusively an affair of ecclesiastics. Einhard was a layman, from a minor élite family too, made influential by intellectual skill; a generation later, Count Eccard of Mâcon (d. *c.* 877), whose will lists several law-books, histories and the works of major Christian fathers, was just as committed to the Carolingian project. That went for the royal family as well: Louis the Pious was steeped in it, and so were his sisters. Perhaps the most significant example of this was Dhuoda (d. *c.* 843), wife of Bernard of Septimania (Louis the Pious's chamberlain and a highly controversial figure in the crisis years around 830), who wrote a *Handbook* for her son William full of advice and admonition from the Bible and Christian Latin literature: for if Dhuoda had been educated as fully as this, almost certainly at Aachen, then her male aristocratic counterparts would definitely have been.[27] We can conclude, therefore, that at least some aristocrats bought into the Carolingian project as much as Charlemagne and Louis, and their religious theorists, hoped. As we saw in Chapter 2, Frankish élites had long assumed that they were by definition more virtuous than everybody else; but Charlemagne's and Louis's court, and schools, certainly gave them new reasons for believing it.

This is relevant for understanding the whole tenor of Carolingian politics, in which, particularly from the 810s onwards, every major political manoeuvre was expressed in terms of an emphatically religious and moral discourse, expressed in programmatic writing which is at times daunting to read. We can see such writing as the dressing up of low politics in the new-style rhetoric of the court, but all the signs are that the major players, at least, fully accepted this style of argument; indeed, given the density of biblical commentary in these texts, many of them must have known the Bible pretty well. So, for example, minor military defeats in Spain in 827 had led to the dismissal of two counts, who were (doubtless not coincidentally) both close to Louis the Pious's eldest son Lothar; but the defeats were also seen in Aachen as signs of very serious divine displeasure, and generated a moral panic. In 828 Louis not only did not call a summer *placitum generale*, but even, at the end of the year, stopped hunting – real signs that something was going wrong in the body politic. Instead, in a smaller winter assembly, Louis's advisors planned four great penitential church councils for 829, and at least two of his most senior *fideles*, Wala (Louis's cousin) and Einhard, presented memoranda which made statements about what had gone wrong. Einhard claimed, in a baroque detail, that his criticisms had been generated in two sets, in a vision from the archangel Gabriel and via a demon called Wiggo who had possessed a girl and spoke through her. Both Wala and Einhard thought that the reasons for the crisis lay in sin: perjury, pride, hatred, the neglect of Sunday as a rest day, and (in Wala's case) the usurpation of church property. Clearly the Franks needed to repent, and the 829 church councils duly took this up. Collective penance was necessary, from top to bottom, and not least in the royal court itself, the moral centre of the Frankish universe. The Spanish defeats, which might have been hardly noticeable in a less quiet decade, had thus spiralled, to engulf the whole of political society.[28]

This religious tension was also the setting for the two revolts of Louis's sons in the immediately following years. One of the new accusations at the time of the 830 revolt was the claim that Louis's wife Judith – the stepmother of the sons in revolt – was sleeping with Bernard of Septimania. The claim was very unlikely, but reflected tightly the importance of keeping the court morally immaculate. The imagined sexual misdeeds of queens punctuated Carolingian politics for that reason, and several after Judith – Lothar II's wife Theutberga in the 850s–860s, Charles the Fat's wife Richgard in the 880s, Arnulf's wife Uota in the 890s – faced high-profile accusations and court proceedings as a result. Carolingian queens were never regents, unlike in the sixth and seventh centuries and again in the tenth, but their importance to ruling, both in practice (they were major patrons and agents of government) and in moralising theory, is shown clearly in their exposure to sexual accusations of this kind. Carolingian politics was moralised not only in religious but also in gender terms. If Louis could not keep his court sexually pure, his enemies thought, he was not fit to rule.[29]

Louis faced out his sons in 830, but they were not really reconciled, and revolted again in 833. This time they won, for, when Louis with an army confronted that of his sons near Colmar in Alsace, at what came to be called the Field of Lies, Louis's army melted away and joined the opposing side; the emperor was imprisoned and replaced by his son Lothar. We cannot really tell why Louis's support vanished; the narratives of the occasion are detailed, but are no more than manifestos for each side. What we do know, however, is that in the Compiègne assembly that October, the magnates and bishops of the kingdom determined that Louis was not only deposed, but also that he should do public penance for his ill-doing. We have the texts written by the bishops involved; Louis's sins included assembling an army during Lent, and requiring contradictory (and thus perjured) oaths, as well as more ordinary offences such as exiling opponents and having Bernard of Italy killed. But was this penance, which Louis subsequently performed at Soissons, voluntary and thus just, or forced and thus – even if shameful – invalid? The ritual could be, and was, capable of several different readings, and our texts reflect that. When Louis's sons fell out the next year, enabling his return to power, the invalidity of the penance was of course stressed most, and assemblies in 834–35 vehemently underlined that. By now, the whole period of the uprisings was simply the work of the devil.[30]

It would be easy to rewrite the last couple of pages in purely secular terms, and historians have frequently done so; Louis can be seen falling out with and mishandling adult sons, who were anxious to succeed and worried about his second wife and her own growing son, a situation exacerbated by the lasting hostility of lesser political players, both counts and bishops, who had fallen out of favour and ended up in Lothar's camp, such as Agobard of Lyon (who wrote some of the 833 texts). And that was of course a major context for the events of these years as well; self-interest was a key element here. But this does not mean that the players regarded the moral/religious framing of the events, which is stressed by all our sources, as a sham. The insistence at Compiègne on the penance, like the panic that led to the councils of 829, would hardly have been needed if so. The key issue was that everything in Carolingian high politics was by now so tied up with the validation of divine approval that resolutions of political problems by means of penitential and other ecclesiastical ritual were seen by every player as entirely appropriate procedures. This religious under-standing was not exactly practical (indeed, the panic of 828–29 could easily be seen as a huge waste of everyone's time), but that was not the point. Even in crisis, the Carolingian political world was ambitious beyond ordinary levels, for they assumed that everything they did, including when they did it badly, was crucial to God.

We can find a similar degree of dense moral imagery used to describe and frame many of the political manoeuvres (some of them very dubious) of the Carolingian cousins into the 870s. It was weakening in the 880s; even though it had not gone away, Charles the Fat showed less commitment to it. All the same, that Charles was very interested in his Carolingian heritage: at his request, between 885 and 887, Notker of St. Gallen wrote his *Deeds of Charlemagne*, a set of mostly imaginary stories about an already semi-mythical, and certainly allegorical, emperor. Notker imagined that Charlemagne, whom he calls 'most vigilant', had the windows of his palace specially built so that 'he could see everything, whatever was being done by people coming and going, as if in hiding ... nothing could be hidden from the eyes of the most clear-sighted Charles'.[31] The fact that the image of Charlemagne had, seventy years after his death, become encapsulated in this idea of vigilance and surveillance, fits what we have seen so far in this chapter. The Carolingian imperial system relied on knowledge and communication, and on the belief that the emperor could potentially see everything. But God's vigilant surveillance over the palace, and the empire, was equally complete.

∗   ∗   ∗

In 887, things certainly changed. Arnulf's coup only brought him to power in East Francia, and the early death of both him and his sons forced the East Frankish magnates in 911 to elect a non-Carolingian, Conrad I, a duke in central Germany, and another in 919, Henry I, duke of Saxony in the north. In Italy, two non-Carolingian families had already fought it out in contested elections in 888–89. Berengar I (888–924), marquis of Friuli in north-east Italy, survived five rivals in the end, and even made himself emperor in 915, a title which, by now, went with the kingship of Italy only; but after his murder that kingship went to three more families in turn. The Rhône valley became two independent kingdoms, of Burgundy and Provence, with other former aristocrats as kings. West Francia saw the count of Paris, Odo (888–98), become king, but opposed by a surviving Carolingian, Charles 'the Simple' (898–923), who succeeded him as king after a peace agreement; Odo's brother Robert I (922–23) later revolted against Charles, and the two families continued to be rivals after that. All in all, across the century after 887, nine Frankish aristocratic families became king of somewhere in the former Frankish empire; some of them had Carolingian female-line descent, but most did not. A contemporary chronicler called them *reguli*, 'kinglets'. For a generation and more after Charles the Fat's deposition, that is to say, the political structures of each kingdom were of uncertain legitimacy and highly unstable – the only one which was not unstable was the small kingdom of Burgundy, around Lake Geneva, which kept a single dynasty under four long-lived kings up to 1032, and absorbed Provence in the 930s. Under these circumstances, it is not so surprising that the Carolingian moral-political project faded away across the same period; Henry I's family, whom we call the Ottonians, by far the most successful of this set, revived some of it later in the century as we shall see in a moment, but never to the same extent. Education and politically orientated religious writing, both of which continued, became more the province of the church by now, and the sort of programmatic admonition of kings which had continued late into the ninth century was far less common in the tenth – with the exception of the highly Carolingian-influenced kingdom of England, as we shall see in the next chapter.[32]

As in the ninth century, but even more so, West Francia was the most troubled of the kingdoms. At least Scandinavian attacks finally ended when Charles the Simple gave the Seine Vikings a separate county, the core of what became Normandy, in 911; but the king only had any real authority north of the Loire, and that was itself a territory in which he had to compete with rival powers, Odo's and Robert's 'Robertine' family being only one of them – and the Normans, always hard to keep quiet, were by now another. By the 930s, Charles's son Louis IV (936–54) controlled only a few counties directly, fewer than the Robertines. The West Frankish lands became a patchwork of duchies and counties, with only nominal links to the kings in the north. Nor did this change when the Robertine duke Hugh Capet definitively took the throne away from the Carolingians in 987, for the group of counties which the Capetian family (as we call them from now on) had long controlled around Paris had by now broken up as well.[33]

Henry I for some time had little control over most of the East Frankish lands either, and his power-base was far away from the traditional Carolingian heartland, based as it was on the east Saxon military frontier. But this at least gave him a fighting force, which trained by attacking and enslaving the Slavic-speaking peoples to the east (see Chapter 5); this allowed him to conquer the territory around Aachen, called Lotharingia by now, which had much royal land in it, and to defend East Francia from the attacks of the newest nomadic people to enter Europe, the Magyars, known to their neighbours, then as now, as Hungarians. This gave him sufficient status throughout the kingdom for there to be no opposition to the succession of his son Otto I (936–72). Otto faced out rebellions twice in his reign, which allowed him to replace most of the dukes of the major East Frankish duchies with his own relatives, at least for long enough to bring their power structures more under his control; he was hegemonic in the old Frankish heartland, and even the West Frankish kings recognised his role of senior Frankish ruler – his sister the queen-mother Gerberga and his brother Archbishop Brun of Cologne were the effective regents of West Francia in the late 950s. He took this further by invading Italy twice, and making himself both king and emperor in 962; the kingdom of Italy was thereafter part of the Frankish empire again, and Otto, his son Otto II and grandson Otto III (983–1002), henceforth ruled stably over more than half of Charlemagne's old realm, with no rivals of remotely the same level of power among the other kingdoms. This stability by no means diminished in the thirteen years when Otto III was a child (he died at the age of twenty-two), during which the kingdom returned, with no unease, to queen-mothers and even queen-grandmothers, Otto II's wife, the Byzantine princess Theophanu (d. 991) and Otto I's wife Adelaide (d. 999) – these female rulers indeed faced less hostility then their Merovingian predecessors.[34]

Ottonian power, particularly after 962, is thus easily the best comparator to that of the Carolingians, and the way it worked allows us to see what had by now changed. The Ottonians still ruled through assemblies, for a start; lay and ecclesiastical magnates now came to Saxony rather than the Frankish heart-land, but they certainly came. The kings were closely connected to the church; their court chaplains routinely became bishops, and they presided over church councils just as Louis the German and his sons had, councils whose acts often cited Carolingian conciliar decisions. They went so far as to depose popes in Rome and to appoint their own, which the Carolingians, however much they may have been tempted, never did. Their army was the largest in the west, by far. The Ottonians were also wealthy: they had access to the old Carolingian royal lands around Aachen and around Frankfurt, to which they added those around Milan and Pavia when they took Italy, and the Ottonian family power-block in south-east Saxony – and also the profits from the rich silver mines found south of Goslar in their Saxon heartland in the 960s, which furnished silver for the coins of the whole of the west. They had the capacity to attract loyalty and service, therefore, and they did. But they did not rule with the density of the Carolingian kings. After all, they were based in the old East Francia, the kingdom which was already less tied into the Carolingian project under Louis the German; the Carolingian heartland around Aachen was by now just another duchy. It is significant that they moved around their kingdom much more than the Carolingians had needed to, simply to make their pres-ence felt directly, to the extent that, when Otto I spent some years in Italy in the 960s to gain control of it properly, there were hostile reactions back in Saxony. Conversely, they shifted aristocrats around far less, except Ottonian family members, and the local societies of the great duchies in Italy and Francia by now had relatively few interconnections.[35]

This fits with the fact that, as already noted, the Ottonians did not fully revive the Carolingian moral project. They patronised intellectuals; the

mathematician and polymath Gerbert of Aurillac (d. 1003) was one, and
Otto III actually made him pope, as Silvester II, in 999. But Gerbert's letters do
not show that he, even, had any commitment to admonition, unlike Agobard
or Hincmar. The Ottonians hardly legislated, even if their church councils did.
The court in Saxony had courtiers who wrote history, poetry and even (in the
work of the nun Hrotsvitha in the royal monastery of Gandersheim) plays,
which show considerable sophistication and classical inspiration (Sallust and
Terence among others), but not political theology.[36] This is quite a lot in itself;
the Ottonians deserve a respectable place in the history of intellectual culture.
But no kingdom, by now, could simply resurrect the ambition of the early ninth
century; too much had happened since. The next time a religious revival had
political overtones, under Pope Gregory VII and his successors, it was by no
means closely associated with kingdoms, and indeed it became increasingly
hostile to kings taking on the religious leadership role of rulers like Charlemagne
at all.

One thing had not changed in the tenth century, however: public political
culture. Defined territories dominated by local lordship, based on personal ties
of loyalty and dependence, hardly existed in East Francia and Italy, and were
only beginning in West Francia. East Francia was certainly decentralised; all
the same, as in earlier centuries, Ottonian politics revolved around assemblies,
national and regional/local, and the manoeuvres that were possible inside
them. Much work has been done on the way these manoeuvres worked: in
particular, on how formalised public behaviour in the Ottonian period and
after created the appearance of concord, which both resolved disagreement
and covered it up when it continued. Its Carolingian antecedents have not
always been recognised, because by now, even when such public acts used
ecclesiastical ritual, they were not attached to the penitential imagery of the
ninth century; but they represent a continuation of the public world which we
have seen operating in Francia since the sixth, and which derived from the
powerful governmental structures of the Roman empire before it.[37] This is
important. It marks a fundamental difference between the political systems of
the early middle ages and those of later centuries, in which the public sphere
had to be recreated, and always coexisted with a cellular structure of locally
based powers, as we shall see in later chapters.

Slowly, however, the sense of the public did become weaker in the Frankish
world. This development happened first in parts of West Francia, where the
force of the public power was hollowed out from inside in a much more fragmented political world, and local lordships became much more important as a
result. The decades around 1000 have often been posed as a tipping point here;

although this date (and the tipping point itself) has been hotly debated, and anyway varied from region to region, the rough timescale still works for me. Thereafter, in the eleventh century, the political world of the tenth (let alone the Carolingians) seemed to many by now almost meaningless, for the parameters of politics had changed so fast, and it was quickly forgotten; even if Carolingian theological debates were remembered and reused, their political context was lost.[38] In Italy, local lordships were beginning by 1000 too, but the culture of the public survived much better in the network of cities, where large and well-organised judicial assemblies still met, until an abrupt crisis in the civil wars of the later eleventh century. In East Francia, assemblies and a collective commitment continued longest, even if only in the regions where kings held on to substantial powers; here, however, the public world was also backed up by a continuing relative incoherence of local power-structures, and would not be fully undermined until that changed, sometimes as the eleventh century moved into the twelfth, sometimes later still. These processes were not universal, but they were quite generalised. Some of them, indeed, had roots in the Carolingian experiment itself, for the Carolingians were interested in making rules for everything, and the boundedness of local societies under the control of lords, which was in general a very eleventh-century development, had a relationship with these rules.[39] But the end of the public and collective legitimacy which the Merovingians, Carolingians and Ottonians all took for granted, and which the Carolingian urge for grand moral solutions elevated for a while into a political art form, marked a radical change for all that. How that worked out we shall see in Chapter 6.

CHAPTER FIVE

The expansion of Christian Europe, 500–1100

The Christianisation of northern Europe transforms what we can say about the continent. In 500, the border of the Roman empire divided the known from the unknown in Europe. North of that border, what we have is archaeology, which tells us about many things but by no means all – plus the views of Roman observers looking northwards, which were not only usually ill-informed, but in most cases were not even trying to give accurate reportage, but, rather, using the 'barbarians' as a mirror to reflect critiques of Roman society itself. In 800, for all the events that had happened in between, the situation was not markedly different. The Franks by now controlled most of Germany north of the Roman frontier, even if it was not yet fully integrated into the Frankish political system; we can say a substantial amount about Ireland, and also Anglo-Saxon England, technically a former Roman province but very different in its social structure by now; but elsewhere we are still looking northwards from the Rhine and Danube with the help only of archaeology and inaccurate external documentary sources. In 1100, however, all is changed, for by now we have at least some written evidence for most places, and we can see much better how societies worked in the northern half of Europe. When we do, we find that nearly everywhere in the north we can also track political structures which were rather more complex than they had been in Charlemagne's time.

Christianity did not do that by itself, of course. When different polities in the north went Christian, mostly what this meant was the conversion of kings and their entourages – the rest of the population followed after, often long after – and that conversion, however genuine, usually only slowly affected the range of values and practices which each society regarded as normal, meritorious and moral, for these values were now defined as Christian as well, whether or not they resembled those of the New Testament.[1] But Christianity brought with it the structures of the church, and with them a commitment to the written word (vital in order to read the Bible), and to record-keeping (which was the normal

1. Consular diptych for Manlius Boethius, 487. It was very common for late Roman aristocrats to commission commemorative ivory diptychs (pictures in two halves) such as this one, for special occasions – in this case Boethius' appointment as consul and prefect of Rome. On the right he holds the signal for the start of chariot racing, for these offices involved the patronage of expensive games. The consul was probably the father of the major philosopher, also called Boethius, executed for treason by Theoderic, king of Italy, in 524.

2. The baptistery at Poitiers, sixth century. Very little survives of Merovingian monumental architecture, but this is a good example, in a major city of southern Gaul. All the fabric visible here is original except the modern buttresses, put there to stop it falling down the hill. How much of it dates from the late Roman period, before the Frankish conquest in 507, is a matter of dispute, but the building certainly shows that the Merovingians built – or rebuilt – in a classic Roman style.

3. The votive crown of Recceswinth, 660s. Several crowns given to a church, including those of two Visigothic kings, were found in a treasure hoard in 1858 at Huertas de Guarrazar near Toledo, the Visigothic capital. This one is in gold set with jewels, with the name of the king in pendants hanging below. It is unlikely that it was ever worn. Giving such crowns was a Byzantine practice, imitated by the Visigoths.

4. Hagia Sophia, Constantinople (now Istanbul), 530s. The Great Church of the Byzantine capital was built by the emperor Justinian in 532–37 on a huge scale, larger than any other known roofed building from the Roman empire, and larger than any European successor until Seville cathedral, built between the thirteenth and sixteenth centuries. The roof fell in in 557 and was rebuilt by 562. Only the Ottoman minarets are more recent.

5. The Birmingham Qur'an, *c.* 640s–650s. The parchment of these pages of the Qur'an, discovered in the University of Birmingham library in 2013, have been carbon-dated to before 645 with 95 per cent accuracy. The text would thus have been written later – normally not all that much later. This date plausibly fits the caliphate of 'Uthman (644–56), who is credited in Islamic tradition with the compilation of the Muslim holy book in its present form. This plausibility, however, has not prevented arguments about Qur'anic dating from continuing.

6. The reconstructed reception hall of the Umayyad caliphs of Córdoba at Madinat al-Zahra',
950s. 'Abd al-Rahman III built this palace, which was destroyed around 1010; it was excavated in
the twentieth century, and reconstructed in the twentieth and twenty-first centuries. Its stucco
decoration is of very high quality, and we have narrative accounts of how much it impressed envoys
from abroad.

7. Charlemagne's palace chapel at Aachen, interior, *c.* 800. Charlemagne's new capital at Aachen had a large chapel attached, which was consecrated by Pope Leo III in 805. It was built to the richest specifications, with marble veneer walling (taken from Rome and Ravenna, according to Einhard, Charlemagne's biographer), bronze work and now-lost frescoes.

8. A Frankish legal handbook from the 850s–870s. This book, surviving in Wolfenbüttel in Germany, is a ninth-century compilation of Frankish law, from the sixth-century *Lex Salica* (its opening page is pictured) to the capitularies of Charlemagne's time, up to the 810s. There are dozens of such collections surviving from the period, and they show the importance to Carolingian political leaders of having such handbooks of legal materials.

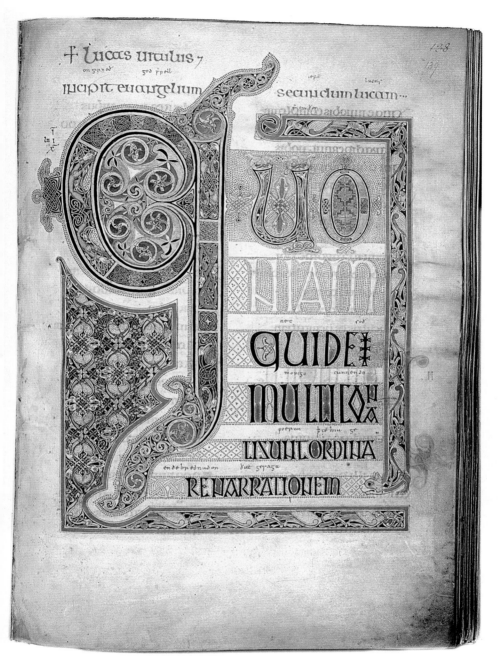

9. The Lindisfarne gospels, early eighth century. These gospels are among the most sumptuously illustrated of the whole medieval period. They were probably written and illustrated at the monastery of Lindisfarne in Northumberland, and are similar to several other gospel books of the same period in England and Ireland, regions which specialised in such decoration. This page opens the Gospel of Luke.

10. The stave church of Heddal, Norway, thirteenth century. Medieval Norway specialised in a highly innovative style for churches made of wood. This, at Heddal in southern Norway, is the largest, although it was enlarged in the 1890s.

11. The bronze doors of Gniezno cathedral, late twelfth century. Poland's earliest cathedral was rebuilt in the fourteenth century, but these doors survive. They show scenes from the life of the missionary Adalbert of Prague, killed by pagan Prussians in 997, whose body was later bought by the Poles and buried in the cathedral; the scene above the right-hand doorknob shows his death. Their style is that of the German-French borderlands, but the workmen could have come to Poland to make them.

12. Rocca San Silvestro, Tuscany, thirteenth century. Perhaps the best-preserved abandoned medieval village anywhere, Rocca San Silvestro was a silver- and copper-mining village on the Tuscan coast until the metal ran out; its high point, and the date of the present buildings, was the twelfth and thirteenth centuries. The castle at the top was the lord's; the rest was the housing of ordinary villagers, in very good quality stonework. The lord controlled the mining very closely, but the miners seem to have been prosperous too.

13. The apse mosaic of San Clemente, Rome, c. 1118. This spectacular and expensive mosaic, commissioned by a cardinal close to Pope Paschal II, consists of a vine-scroll representing the Christian Church, and is full of images of humans, some of them doing domestic tasks. It shows how the papal leadership wished to display the symbolism of their power and wealth, at a time when they struggled to control Rome itself.

14. Pisa cathedral, late eleventh and early twelfth century. This building is the most innovative Italian church of its time, and clearly shows the ambition of the Pisans. Much of the cost of the building was paid for from booty taken from naval attacks on rich Muslim cities, some of which are commemorated in inscriptions on its façade.

15. The castle of Ghent, late twelfth century. The core of the castle of the counts of Flanders at Ghent (including the gateway on the right) is original, although the building was substantially rebuilt in the nineteenth century. It was one of the major centres of the power of the counts, inside what became the largest town in Flanders. Ghent's success as a manufacturing centre started with the castle, but the town became the count's most serious opponent as it became larger and richer.

means which churches used to protect their lands, newly donated by kings – almost all early documentary records concern the church, everywhere in northern Europe). Historical narratives soon appeared too, usually in Latin but also in local languages (in particular in Irish, Norse and Russian), to justify royal and clerical actions.[2] And more followed, for Christianisation was also a means for kings to introduce at least some of the techniques of ruling which were used by the two great European powers of the early middle ages, Francia and Byzantium; indeed, in some cases the possibility of a greater openness to southern European influence and political procedures was virtually the only reason why rulers changed religion, and virtually the only change which Christianity brought. All the same, Christianity did not in itself produce a more homogeneous Europe; just a Europe in which there was a rather more widespread interest in more ambitious, but still-distinct, forms of political power. How the new religion affected each region in the north operates, above all, as a sort of barium meal, which in each case shows us, not homogeneity, but difference.

Christianity spread across northern Europe more or less from west to east, slowly, but with greater speed after 950 or so. Ireland was first, in the fifth and sixth centuries; there followed Pictish Scotland, England and central Germany in the seventh century, Saxony – by force as we have seen – after Charlemagne's conquests in the eighth, Bulgaria, Croatia and Moravia in the ninth, Bohemia in the tenth, Poland, Rus' (covering parts of European Russia and Ukraine) and Denmark in the late tenth, Norway, Iceland and Hungary in the years around 1000, Sweden more slowly across the eleventh century.[3] Only the far north-east of Europe was left out of this, the Baltic- and Finnish-speaking lands, the former of which would eventually, in the thirteenth century, turn into the only large and powerful pagan polity in medieval Europe, Lithuania, before its grand dukes went Christian as late as 1386–87. We cannot look at all these in detail, and our information, even after conversion, is as yet too sketchy for too many of them, for a survey to be interesting. Here I shall focus in particular on Ireland, England, Denmark, Norway and Poland, in that order, as illustrations of the distinct ways in which the new Christian religion was absorbed into, and illuminates, different sorts of society in the period up to 1100. Bulgaria and Rus' will be added later, in Chapter 9, as the process of conversion northwards from Byzantium was in some ways separate; and I will survey all the other European polities, as they appeared in the last quarter of the middle ages, in Chapter 11, so what happened to them eventually will appear there. In this chapter, we will also look at some of the major developments in the north which did not relate to Christianity at all, notably the expansion of the peoples which ended up speaking Slavic languages, and the appearance of Scandinavian Vikings in Ireland, Britain and Francia.

Before we do that, however, let us look at some of the common elements in the societies of northern Europe before they converted, as far as we can tell from our scanty sources, and from what we can read back from later evidence. What was not in common was language; the northern Europeans spoke nearly every one of the language groups of modern Europe. Nor was religion; the paganism of the north was at least as variegated as that of the Roman empire, with – as it seems – pantheons of gods in some places, single high gods in others, more generalised nature cults or shamanism elsewhere, probably over-lapping; and also ritual run by specialist priesthoods in some places, and by local political leaders in others.[4] But two basic features do seem to be common to every northern society: the relative weakness of rulership, and the relative independence of peasantries. As to the first: northern political units were in general very small indeed, and unstable, for a long time. Ireland had up to 150 kingdoms in 800; Anglo-Saxon England had, as it seems, dozens before some consolidation can be seen around 600, and even then over ten; Norway prob-ably one political unit per valley up to the tenth century; in what is now Poland, or the Sclavenian areas of the Balkans, Frankish and Byzantine sources of the seventh to tenth centuries list large numbers of ill-defined peoples. Even what to call such units is hard, for, although some had rulers, titled in different ways, whom we might call 'kings', others did not have clearly defined or permanent rulership at all. 'Kingdom' is therefore not a word we can easily use for some of these small units. We could use 'tribe', and I shall do so sometimes, while rejecting the idea that this implies that such groups are in some way 'primitive'; but 'peoples' and 'polities' are probably the most usefully vague terms when generalising over the whole of the north. Assembly politics was a crucial feature of most of them, as we have seen for the post-Roman kingdoms of the west; kings where they existed deferred to assemblies quite often (here our clearest evidence is from Sweden and Norway); and in some places, as with Iceland, newly settled from Norway in the decades around 900, and the Slavic-speaking Liutizi of the Oder valley around 1000, all political decisions were taken by assemblies, and no single person dominated, at least in theory.[5] When such peoples did have rulers, then, there is rarely any sign that they had unmediated power. Such rulers certainly had armed entourages, and used them for small-scale domination as well as inter-community warfare, but it is hard to find many early examples of detailed top-down political interventions, and it is likely that most rulers had to collaborate and consult with smaller or larger collective groups in each community.

This was linked to the fact that the northern half of Europe appears to have had a largely independent peasantry, that is to say a peasantry who did not have to deal, to a major extent, with landlords. This does not mean that society was egalitarian; unfree people existed everywhere, working for élites in largish numbers, and in ones and twos even for some peasant families, as household and farm servants. There were also everywhere, as just implied, élites, who were richer and/or of higher status; rulers normally came from élite strata too. But these strata did not directly control more than restricted quantities of land; even in later periods, by which time élite landowning (not least by churches) had substantially increased, we have in some cases – particularly in Scandinavia – evidence that such landowning was not always dominant. This means that non-élites, i.e. peasants, must have controlled the rest; and in general the economy of most of the north is likely to have followed the logic of peasant, not aristocratic, choices and needs for a long time. This is supported by the rarity of large concentrations of wealth in the early medieval archaeology of the north, with the significant exception of Denmark, until the Viking period, which we will come back to. The power of élite individuals was probably some-times unstable, making them what anthropologists call 'big men', who might move back into the peasantry in a later generation if they were not effective local dealers, or if they had too many children and had to divide their wealth. Conversely, however, their position was sometimes buttressed, as in Ireland, by quite elaborate legal hierarchies, and sometimes, as in Scandinavia, they had local religious and political roles which were inherited.[6]

Which means: although peasantries were in economic terms largely inde-pendent, we need to recognise that they had to deal with élites everywhere. They did so in many different ways. In Ireland, they engaged in elaborate rela-tionships of clientship with aristocrats, based on gifts of cattle by a lord (not – unlike in most of Europe – land), in return for hospitality and political and military services. In England up to the eighth century, kings and aristocrats seem to have dominated large defined tracts of land on which peasantries lived, but they did not do so as landowners; peasants owed small-scale tributes to lords, perhaps on an occasional basis, rather than paying rent (except for the unfree, who can be seen already as subject tenants).[7] In Iceland, and perhaps the rest of Scandinavia, free peasants were all part of the followings of local leaders at assemblies, and paid a fee if they did not go; later, local leaders also benefited from controlling church tithes. In what became Poland, more-or-less independent peasants owed tribute to local rulers as in England, but, as it seems, without defined territories. In the wide forested lands that became Russia, peasant agriculturalists and fur-trappers owed similar tribute to often quite distant lords, such as the khagans of the Bulgars on the Volga, and, later, the Scandinavian (Rus') princes of Kiev and Novgorod; the political systems of Russia were very large in geographical area, and more clearly based on domination by rulers and armed entourages than elsewhere, but local control was not intense for centuries, and tribute may have been for long intermittent – the peasantry of Russia did not fully lose its landowning autonomy until the early modern period.[8] These different political and economic patterns each contained potential levers which élites could use to increase their power and wealth, but this did not as yet by any means automatically happen: it did in England but not in Ireland, it did in Denmark but not in Sweden, and so on. Indeed, as late as 1100 aristocratic and royal control was only fully developed, among these northern peoples, in England. How that was we shall see later in the chapter.

*   *   *

It was, then, a set of small-scale polities, without elaborate socioeconomic hierarchies, which slowly went Christian across six centuries. But, as I said earlier, the consequences of Christianisation were very different from place to place. Ireland was the first. There, the conversion process began already in the fifth century, when the Roman world was still in place; it was associated from early on with one important missionary, Patrick, a British Christian who had spent some time in Ireland as a slave captive and knew it well, as his own writings show. Patrick and other missionaries had to go from kingdom to kingdom in order to preach, and had to face out a strong trans-kingdom specialist priesthood, the druids, in order to do so. We do not know how they succeeded (all we can say is that the process took at least a century), or what kings thought Christianity could bring them – perhaps some version of Roman power? But if so, the timing was wrong, for the western empire was collapsing, and nowhere more so than in the closest Roman province, Britain, which had seen an extreme socioeconomic breakdown when the Romans left: in Wales and the rest of western Britain, the part of the province not conquered by Germanic-speaking Anglo-Saxon political groupings in the fifth and early sixth centuries, a dozen kingdoms and more were crystallising.[9] In Ireland, far from the new Christian church acting as a basis for political aggregation, its episcopal and monastic hierarchies (for monasteries were important in Ireland from early on) were as fragmented as was the secular political structure; in effect, clerics had simply replaced the druids as a specialist order. The interest in writing which the new religion brought extended to another older specialist order, the lawyers; hence the existence in Ireland, not just of chronicles and records of church synods, and prose epics later, but also very elaborate legal handbooks. All of these allow us to see the degree to which the next centuries simply consisted of small-scale wars between very small tribal kingdoms, which were at most arranged in hierarchies, in particular around two very large family groupings covering several kingdoms each, the Úi Néill of the centre-north and the Eóganachta of the south-west. The kings were all Christian by now, but their authority was highly ritualised and bounded by taboos, which doubtless had pre-Christian roots. It would be hard, in fact, to say what changes Christianity had made here at all, except for the addition to the political landscape of influential churches which had some limited connections to the rest of Europe.[10]

Viking attacks in the ninth century had more of an effect on Ireland than Christianity did. There were never many Scandinavians in rural Ireland – they mostly settled in coastal trading towns, above all Dublin, which they had founded; but their raiding forced a greater measure of political aggregation in order to resist them. We begin from here on to find kings who claimed wider hegemonies, and even the title of 'king of Ireland', notably Máel Sechnaill mac Máele Ruanaid (d. 862) and Brian Bóruma (d. 1014); and by the eleventh century such paramount kings, now sometimes from different dynasties from before, ruled wider areas than they had done in the past, and had slightly wider powers within them.[11] But that was as far as political aggregation went; the economic resources which kings had were too restricted, and their infrastructures too simple, to establish more on a permanent basis. English invasion under Henry II after 1169–70, and a partial conquest which brought Henry's son John the title of 'lord of Ireland' by 1177, introduced a set of Anglo-Norman lordships which came to resemble contemporary Irish kingdoms as much as the lordships of England and the continent. The Irish church had, already from the 1110s, adopted a more continental-style structure, it is true, and Irish kings (as they were called in Irish-language texts up to 1400 and beyond) recognised their at least nominal subjection to the English government in Dublin. All the same, the 'Gaelic' lordships of the late middle ages, and some of the English ones, still had many of the social and cultural characteristics of the kings of 500 and more years before, and, where they did not, the new developments were mostly internal ones, rather than imposed from outside. There was now a dialectic between English political power and these lordships, but apart from that Ireland was less changed than almost any other part of Europe at the end of the middle ages.[12]

*   *   *

England was dramatically different from this. As we have seen, early Anglo-Saxon polities were often tiny, as far as we can tell from placenames, inferences from later written evidence and archaeology. Even after some aggregation, there were still ten to fifteen kingdoms when missionaries appeared from Rome, Francia and Ireland in the early seventh century. As in Ireland, they were converted one by one across three generations; but here it is much more obvious that the kings concerned were interested in the cultural and political connections which Christianity could bring them – to the popes in Rome, and above all to the kings in Francia, their neighbours just over the Channel, who were richer and more powerful by up to two orders of magnitude. The kings of Kent, the kingdom closest physically and politically to Francia, converted first, after 597, thanks to a mission from Rome; the kings of Wessex (i.e. Hampshire and Berkshire) were converted by a missionary from Francia in the 630s. The Northumbrian kings in the north were finally converted from Ireland in the 630s, but adopted the continental calculation for Easter at a church council at Whitby in 664, and after that were more closely linked to Rome and Francia. The most ambitious kings, those looking for wide hegemonies, were associated with conversion, with the major exception of Penda of Mercia (d. 655); but, after Penda was killed in battle with the Northumbrians, Mercian kings went Christian too. After 670, a new archbishop of Canterbury, Theodore of Tarsus (d. 690), a Byzantine appointed by the pope, did something which no Irish church leader could dream of yet, and united the bishops of all the Anglo-Saxon kingdoms into a single hierarchy. The Anglo-Saxon church was, from then on, fully integrated into that of the rest of western Europe, and increasingly resembled it.[13]

It cannot be said that seventh-century kings in England resembled their continental counterparts as yet. They could be personally rich, as royal graves show (the best-known is Sutton Hoo, deposited around 625), but kings otherwise had limited resources and very simple governmental powers, based as elsewhere on assemblies; they seem to have focused their activity, as in Ireland, on small-scale wars fought by kings and their military entourages. Gradually, however, they picked up other responsibilities. Some of them legislated, with law codes resembling those of the continent (although here they were written in Old English). By the end of the century, they established trading connections with Francia via a set of ports, Ipswich, London, Hamwic in modern Southampton, which paralleled those on the coast of the continent such as Dorestad.[14] And in the eighth century, a run of powerful Mercian kings, Æthelbald (716–57), Offa (757–96) and Cenwulf (796–821), had close links to the first Carolingians. Offa not only had a hegemony over southern England but also absorbed most of its kingdoms into Mercia itself, something again with few parallels in Ireland – by his death, there were only four kingdoms left, the others being Northumbria, a by-now larger Wessex, and East Anglia. He had much more of a visible organisational infrastructure. It was less systematic than that of the Carolingians, and used the written word rather less, but it included a control over manpower which allowed Offa to build fortifications in a number of Mercian towns, and also a 100km-long earthwork, Offa's Dyke, which still exists: the largest-scale European construction since Hadrian's Wall, which delimited the kingdom with relation to the Welsh. In the 760s, he instituted a new coinage which imitated that of Pippin III a few years earlier (the latter itself perhaps influenced by earlier English coinage developments); and after 742 we have documentation for a steady sequence of Mercian church councils, resembling those of the Franks, which lasted until the 830s.[15]

Clearly, by 800 England (or at least Mercia) was much more like Francia than it had been in 600, or even 700. This was a result partially of borrowing, and partially of developments which had their own internal logic. Both were facilitated, even though not always caused, by Christianisation. This was backed up by what was perhaps the most significant socioeconomic change in the English kingdoms, which probably began under the Mercian hegemony and moved further on in the ninth century: the slow development of private landowning, by kings and aristocrats, out of the large tribute-rendering territories of the past. It was more or less complete in the mid-tenth century, as it seems, and, when it was, it transformed the English economic environment; for, from here onwards, village structures crystallised in half the country, peasant autonomy ended virtually everywhere, and kings, who took over the largest landholdings, became even more dominant than before – including over an aristocracy which stayed close to the kings, for it benefited from this development almost as much.[16]

Mercia did not hold on to its eighth-century dominance. In and after the 820s, it faced civil wars, and Wessex took over many of the former kingdoms of the south, such as Kent. None of the kingdoms were, however, prepared for the attacks of Viking raiders and then armies, which began to be serious in the 850s and which turned, after these armies realised how vulnerable all the English kingdoms were, into a war of conquest in 865–78. Scandinavian rulers occupied eastern England, ending all the kingdoms except Wessex; they nearly took over Wessex too, but its king, Alfred (871–99), after initial defeat, regrouped and won against the Vikings in 878, exacting a peace treaty, which more or less held. Alfred reorganised his people on a war footing, fortified the major West Saxon towns, and occupied the non-Scandinavian-controlled southern half of Mercia. This was a basis for his son Edward 'the Elder' and daughter Æthelflæd (who ruled Mercia) to conquer the Scandinavian kingdoms of southern England in the 910s, and for his grandsons, notably Æthelstan (924–39), to push north as well; by 954 Northumbria was in their hands, except for the autonomous earldom of Bamburgh in the far north, which had survived the Viking takeover. This West Saxon conquest unified, indeed created, England for the first time; already Alfred called himself 'king of the Anglo-Saxons', and the term 'England' began, although slowly, to be used from now on.[17]

Alfred, Æthelstan and, later, the latter's nephew Edgar (957–75) were thus the real successors of Mercia, and more so, for there is no sign that Offa had contemplated taking over the whole of England. To run it, they borrowed heavily from the Franks. Alfred, himself well-educated, had a Frankish intellectual at his court, Grimbald of St-Bertin, and he sponsored a translation movement of Christian classics, translating some into English himself; the collective oath which his laws required from all free men matches that of Charlemagne. Later laws in the tenth century resemble, and even quote from, Carolingian capitularies, and we know there was at least one copy of these available in England – by the tenth century the Carolingian project was no longer very active on the continent, as we have seen, so its imagery was above all available to the English in books. Archbishop Wulfstan of York (d. 1023), who owned the capitulary text, wrote admonitory tracts and moralising law codes which owed much to Carolingian imagery, and the royal-sponsored monastic reform movement of Edgar's reign was visibly influenced by that of Louis the Pious. The army-muster and assembly politics of the Anglo-Saxon past continued to be of crucial importance in tenth-century England, but there were innovations here too: the appearance of a hierarchy of judicial assemblies for shires and hundreds, obeying royal instructions, parallels Frankish procedures. The tenth-century kings furthermore married into the Ottonian and Carolingian families, and intervened in West Frankish politics. These trends reached their height with Edgar and his son Æthelred II (978–1016); these two were the effective creators of the strength of the late Anglo-Saxon state, together with their close aristocratic and ecclesiastical collaborators, which included Edgar's grandmother Eadgifu and Æthelred's mother Ælfthryth – for both kings succeeded young, as did most tenth-century English kings, and queen-mothers were major players. By 1000, England was the most obvious heir of the whole Carolingian project – an irony which Charlemagne could never have imagined – and by now, helped by the fact that it was small, also the most coherent kingdom in the Latin west. Æthelred even instituted a land tax, the first in the west, as we shall see in the next chapter. The roots of this strength were of course not only Carolingian; they had much to do with the changes in landowning already mentioned, and also with the fact that the West Saxon aristocracy, which gained so much from the conquests, stuck together as an oligarchy, running the kingdom with the queens when kings were children, until Æthelred unwisely brought many of them down. But the ability of the kings to use Carolingian models clearly helped the sense of confidence which we get from our tenth-century evidence, and this points up the degree to which the bet made by seventh-century kings to go Christian, and to enter the world of continental politics in so doing, had paid off.[18]

*   *   *

England was thus the part of northern Europe in which the changes that began with Christianisation were most total – together with Saxony, which was forced to Christianise by the Franks. It helped that it was, thanks to the sea crossing, safe from Frankish attack; adopting the Frankish religion could thus be seen only as advantageous. Other polities, when they could choose, were more cautious. One of these was Denmark, where the final conversion moment came much later, in the 960s; but to understand what happened there we will have to go back in time somewhat. Denmark is good farmland, unlike the rest of Scandinavia, and can sustain a denser population. Already by the fifth century, some of its rulers were rich; Gudme, a political centre on the island of Fyn, is striking for its gold finds, and it was not the only such centre. It is likely that Danish rulers benefited from the booty taken from the western Roman empire in its century of crisis, but it at least shows that such rulers were strong enough to accumulate it. Denmark at that time may have had four or five polities in its land-area (which included what is now southern Sweden), inside which local élites, although probably not landowners on any scale, nonetheless had polit- ical hegemonies. By the eighth century, however, when Denmark gets more consistently into Frankish sources, it had fewer kingdoms. Godofrid, a king based in southern Jutland (c. 804–10), and later his son Horic I (c. 827–54) were the dominant kings in Denmark, and may perhaps have ruled all of it; they certainly had a hegemony which extended into Norway and southwards into what is now north-east Germany, and they had the sort of infrastructure which, like that of Offa but on a smaller scale, allowed the building of major earthworks, including one to mark the border with Saxony, the Danevirke. Godofrid fought off attacks from Charlemagne, and even attacked back; he and his son controlled and patronised major trading ports, Ribe and Hedeby, which attracted Frankish goods. This all happened without any input from outside, and that includes religion; one of the competing kings of the 810s and 820s, Harald Klak, accepted Christianity in Louis the Pious's court in 826, but his hold on a

Danish throne did not last a year. Horic I and Horic II (d. after 864) allowed Frankish missionaries into Denmark, but did not themselves convert. It is likely that for all these kings Christian conversion was closely connected with acceptance of Frankish hegemony, which was mostly not part of their plan.[19]

Denmark was thus unusually centralised by Scandinavian and wider north European standards, already by 800, and it would stay so throughout the middle ages. That did not prevent Godofrid's kingdom from collapse after the 860s, however, and one cause was probably Vikings. Scandinavian ships were by the eighth century of high quality, and from the 790s sea-raids began in Francia and England, with Ireland soon after; they escalated in the 830s and grew in seriousness from then on. Vikings (the word means 'pirates') came from both Denmark and Norway, and they seem to have been merchants, used to the North Sea trade routes, who seized the opportunities given by unde-fended coastlines; plus late adolescents who were taking advantage of ship technology to enjoy themselves freebooting and to accumulate wealth before they settled down – with the addition, in Denmark at least, of exiles from an increasingly hegemonic royal court, who often acted as leaders. They were paralleled by another example of merchants seizing opportunities when they appeared, the successful implantation of Swedish fur-traders as Rus' princes in Kiev and other cities in the river systems of eastern Europe in the ninth century, whose later history we will look at in Chapter 9. Viking attacks lessened (while not yet ending) in the tenth century, after the establishment of diaspora king-doms in England in the later ninth and, on a smaller scale, Ireland, the northern isles of Scotland, and then the duchy of Normandy in the early tenth century. The Vikings were also sidetracked by the settlement of Iceland in the period c. 870–930. All the same, for three generations they showed that even the unstructured polities of the north could have a major effect on established kingdoms elsewhere. They brought serious wealth back, too, as the archae-ology of the trading towns of Scandinavia shows, but they also brought insta-bility; rival Norwegian kings into the eleventh century were usually returning Vikings, and the failure of the ninth-century kingdom of Denmark, although undocumented, is most likely to fit with this too.[20]

It was not until the second quarter of the tenth century that we find a king ruling a substantial sector of Denmark again, probably from an new family, Gorm (d. 958); his son Harald 'Bluetooth' (958–c. 986) was the first clearly Christian ruler of the kingdom. Harald was a contemporary of Otto I, whose power-base was markedly nearer to Denmark than Charlemagne's had been, and he was converted before 965 by a German missionary who was close to Otto's brother Brun. It is very likely indeed that Harald was trying to get closer to Otto, to use him as a political model and to neutralise him as a threat. The interesting thing, however, is that, although Danish bishops are documented from now on, Harald's own rule owed little to them. He established his power over the whole of Denmark by force, and around 980 built a network of circular military camps which archaeologists have identified; this seems to be linked to the stabilisation of his conquest, as well as to a systematic regularisation of the army and navy. These, plus a long-lasting assembly politics, were the bases for Danish royal power, not the church. They were sufficient for his son Svein and grandson Cnut (1014–35) to conquer England in the 1010s, and to establish intermittent hegemony in Norway too. Cnut brought English, rather than German, bishops into Denmark, and made a well-publicised pilgrimage to Rome in 1027 to coincide with the coronation of the German emperor Conrad II; he was certainly by now using his place in the Christian European community for political ends. Even if this wider hegemony soon broke down, Danish royal power was from now on internally solid – by 1100 more solid, indeed, than in much of the Frankish lands.[21] Denmark was, at the end of the period covered by this chapter, the most powerful kingdom in the north after England and probably Hungary, and had by the 1070s obtained a standard episcopal structure; a network of parish churches would soon follow, many of which survive. It had an aristocracy that more and more conformed to continental modes of behaviour (although private castles were rare), and we can by now track, in documents, large-scale landowning by both aristocrats and ecclesiastics (as well as peasant owners).[22] Its subsequent history (kings vs. bishops vs. aristocrats) can be assimilated to some quite standard European models. But here, unlike in England, the core of Danish political power owed little to Christianisation; the church was an add-on, even if an important one, to social and political developments that were occurring anyway.

✳   ✳   ✳

Norway was unified late and unevenly. It seems, given the archaeology, to have consisted of a network of kingdoms without much hierarchy, separated by mountains, forests and tracts of upland plateau, across the early middle ages. The first attempts to conquer the whole are associated with the semi-mythical Harald 'Finehair' (d. c. 932), one of the local kings, and his sons and grandsons. Their success was incomplete, however. For the tenth century, we still see in our Norse-language narrative sources – which are late, thirteenth-century, but which are structured by poetry from a much earlier, often contemporary, date – a network of local societies, focused on assemblies (*thingar*), which were made up of autonomous peasantries, even if they tended to be dominated by local aristocrats, called earls (*jarlar*) or 'landed men'. The next two kings who tried to establish some level of wider power were Olaf Tryggvason (*c.* 995–1000) and Olaf Haraldsson (1015–28). Both had become Christian while fighting abroad, and their expansionism was associated with a deliberate process of more or less forced conversion of the Norwegian regions, *thing* by *thing*, as well as a courting of aristocrats with gifts and local administrative positions. So, according to the later historian Snorri Sturluson, the free men of the Rogaland *thing* elected their three most eloquent men to counter the 'fine words' of Olaf Tryggvason, but different speech defects prevented them from saying a word on the day, so they all were baptised; at the Gulathing the king bought off an influential local aristocrat by marrying his sister to the aristocrat's kinsman, and then at the *thing* both local leaders pushed for Christianity and 'no-one dared oppose it'. At the Frostathing the local community – forewarned, one would suppose, by these events – arrived fully armed, as if for a campaigning *thing*, and King Olaf therefore did not use threats, but instead acceded to their demands that he make sacrifice at their festival at midsummer; when he came there, the king said he would indeed make a sacrifice, but it would be of the leading men of the community, and faced with this coup de théâtre the latter backed down. These are literary images, obviously, and they do not tell us how successful the king really was, but they give a clear sense of how kings might be seen to negotiate with *thingar*, and how much negotiating there was indeed to do. Neither Olaf succeeded for long; both were, as Harald Finehair's family had been in the 970s, brought down by Danish intervention, although Olaf Haraldsson's general high-handedness also, when he attempted a return to power, resulted in an uprising of both peasants and aristocrats, and his death in battle at Stiklarstaðir in 1030. It is striking that later sources are quite sympathetic to the uprising, even though Olaf was regarded as a martyred saint almost immediately after the battle; but it is equally significant that Olaf's sanctity was important to the risings against Danish rule which restored his son Magnus to power in 1035, and to the more stable rulership of Olaf's half-brother, another fighter from abroad, Harald 'Hard-ruler' (1047–66) and his heirs. Harald developed an aristocrat-led army which he used to suppress opposition, and a Norwegian church which he kept firmly under his control.[23]

A simple political narrative of the eleventh century may make it appear that Norway had by now become much like Denmark; but this was not the case, as we find out if we pursue Norwegian history past 1100. When civil wars between royal heirs started in the 1130s, they began, as such wars often did, as confrontations between rival kings supported by the armies of groups of regional aristocrats; but these armies were as much the reflection of regional as of royal loyalties, and they increasingly chose their own kings. The most successful army, around King Sverre (1177–1202), was not even aristocratic, but originally a largely peasant army from the far east and then the north, the 'Birchlegs', which ended up confronting an army from the south-east, the 'Croziers', led by bishops (Sverre defied Innocent III, and died excommunicate) – a compromise peace was not made until the 1220s.[24] The fact is that Norway was neither fully united under kings like Harald Hard-ruler, nor fully dominated by kings and aristocracy. The politics of regional assemblies continued to be powerful here later, and peasant participation in them lasted a long time too; the rule of the kings was never strong, and was contested if it was ambitious. Inside this decentralised political system, on the other hand, the process of conversion under the Olafs, and the organisation of the church from the 1030s onwards, were important tools for kings to use in asserting what authority they could. They had more of a structural role in the underpinning of royal power than did Christianity in Denmark, even if that power was weaker. Norwegian Christianisation, unlike that of England, Denmark or, as we shall see next, Poland, owed little to the Franks; but the organised church of the mid-eleventh century and onwards was more continental in form than anything else in the kingdom, and only a king as charismatic as Sverre could dispense with it.[25]

*   *   *

Poland is my last example, and here, as with Denmark, we have to go back some centuries to understand what Christianisation, which began in the 960s as in Denmark, really meant. The sixth and seventh centuries saw, right across east-central Europe (what is now Poland, the Czech Republic, Slovakia, Hungary) as in the Balkans, the appearance of communities marked archaeologically by small villages with sunken-floored houses and a very simple material culture, plus, usually, cremation cemeteries. These were very small-scale communities indeed, initially without significant hierarchies; it is striking, given this, that they managed to expand so consistently, both to the west and to the south, and it is doubtless a marker of the weakness of all politics in eastern Europe in the sixth century that they could do so. The people living in them were called, as we saw in Chapter 3, *Sklavenoi* by the Byzantines – in the Latin of the Franks, *Sclaveni* – but we cannot automatically assume they spoke Slavic languages, and many of them certainly did not. Only by the ninth century can we be fairly sure that in east-central Europe they generally did so, and from then on we can confidently call them 'Slavs', but only on linguistic grounds; they had no unity of identity, and were divided up into very many, and probably ever-changing, different tribal peoples. From around 600 on, however, their neighbours were not always politically weak, and in the case of the Franks were potentially highly menacing. The Franks never sought seriously to conquer them, but they did raid, from the seventh century to the tenth, above all for slaves; by the ninth century *sclavus* began to mean 'slave' in Latin, and it eventually became the standard word for chattel slave in most western languages. The Franks also bought slaves from the Slavs themselves (tenth-century Prague had a slave market), and so did other neighbours of these communities, the Venetians to the south, the Scandinavians in the Baltic and Russia, Arab merchants coming in from the east; the armies and bureaucracy of al-Andalus contained a large contingent of *Saqaliba*, Slavs, who were originally slaves. An entire economy developed around the slave trade, which is mostly only visible archaeologically, either through the distribution of iron manacles or through the presence of Iranian coins in eastern Europe – the latter of which, by the tenth century, are found in very large numbers. It was as a reaction to this set of dangers that we first find, in the eighth and ninth centuries, larger fortified settlements in much of east-central Europe, strongholds for some sort of political leaders, who were doubtless both protecting themselves from attack and providing slaves for attackers. One network of particularly rich strongholds was the basis for the Moravian kingdom of the ninth century, until incoming Hungarians destroyed it in the 890s. Hungarian raids added one more danger for the tribal communities around them.[26]

It is in this context that in the early tenth century, in the centre of what is now Poland, a new set of uniform fortifications are attested archaeologically, while many others were destroyed: a new Slav power was crystallising. It may not have been called 'Polonia' (the Latin term) yet, but it was by 1000. German written sources first notice it in the 960s, when its ruler, Mieszko I (d. 992), first appears fighting Saxon armies. He established in 965 a marriage-alliance with the neighbouring dukes of Bohemia, whose power had crystallised a generation earlier and were already Christian; in 966, Mieszko went Christian too, and in 967 he appears at Otto I's Saxon court, referred to as 'the emperor's friend' in a contemporary source. It is fairly clear what Mieszko was doing: like Harald of Denmark, but with a much newer and more fragile political base, he was trying to get accepted as part of the Christian family of rulers – they were usually called 'dukes' in Latin sources in the case of both the Poles and the Bohemians, for the German emperors were cautious about recognising them with a stable royal title as yet. This would be a protection against generic raiding and slaving (though certainly not against more organised wars). It is also significant that 'Polonia' was surrounded by numerous other smaller Slav peoples, who resisted Christianity; they both protected it from Saxon attack and could be a resource for Mieszko's Piast family for slaving raids on its own behalf, for the slave trade seems to have been at its height in this period. Christianisation could also potentially, as we have seen elsewhere, offer the Piasts an organisational infrastructure which they so far lacked: early Piast power seems to have consisted more or less exclusively of the duke plus his warband, who exacted army-service and tribute from surrounding peasant communities. (An assembly politics is less visible in the Piast realm, unlike in its smaller neighbours.) And, indeed, for a time things went smoothly; bishops arrived, mostly from Bohemia; and in 1000 Otto III himself came to Poland, as we can now call it, and established an archbishopric, and thus a theoretically autonomous church, in the heartland fortified settlement of Gniezno. Mieszko's son Bolesław I 'the Brave' (992–1025) built on that, expanding his rule in all directions, up to the Baltic, in wars against the Germans, and even conquering Bohemia for a year in 1003–04. Poland began to look like a successful new polity.[27]

This did not, however, last. After Bolesław's death, his hegemony fell apart; not only did much of his territory slip out of Piast control, but pagan revolts destroyed the episcopal infrastructure, which had to be built up again under Kazimierz I (1039–58) and his successors.[28] The fact was that as yet the Polish dukes had no political organisation which was capable of holding onto large tracts of land for more than a few years; the limits to early Piast dynastic activism here perhaps show parallels more clearly with Ireland than with any other polities we have looked at so far in this chapter, and Christianisation, even if this meant attachment to more clearly established church hierarchies, had not helped with developing that. This did not immediately change. Polish borders became more stable from now on, and continued to move steadily outwards again, at a slower and safer speed than they had under Bolesław I; but the pattern of a king and immediate entourage, of aristocratic officials and governors and slightly less privileged knightly warriors, simply collecting tribute, remained the basic model for some time.

Shifts began to occur in this pattern from the late eleventh and twelfth centuries. The warrior élite began to be assigned territories in which they could extract tribute directly; and, slowly, as in England, these developed into landed estates, which, when held by the emerging aristocracy, could be large. The church did the same. Peasants became tenants, more and more legally constrained, although the final subjection of the Polish peasantry was not until after the Black Death. German settlement, which was protected by German law, had the same effect from the late twelfth century onwards. But, unlike in

England, the Piast dukes did not keep on top of this process. Wars between brothers occupied them in the century after Kazimierz I; and, at the death of Bolesław III in 1138, Poland was split up between his four sons, whose heirs continued to fight, and also divide up power further, for a century and a half. In this context, too, the fact that we are now in a period in which the western church was claiming independence from secular authority, as we shall see in the next chapter, had an effect as well; bishops claimed autonomous rights that dukes could not easily prevent. By now, Poland was certainly, in many ways, moving in the direction of western European political patterns (particularly those of Germany), but not to any form of strong government; and the church remained of little help to the dukes. The episcopal hierarchy at least prevented the concept of a common Polish territory from disintegrating, but, unlike in Norway, it was not a resource for any form of large-scale political power. Indeed, although by 1150 local powers – sovereign dukes, churchmen and aristocrats – were far stronger than they had been in 950, the geographical scale of the individual political structures of the Polish lands had changed back to those of two centuries earlier.[29]

*   *   *

Thus we see, in these five different regions, five very different instances of the effect of Christianisation – and, above all, the introduction of the hierarchies of the church – on a region of Europe. In Ireland, the church adapted quickly to the decentralised structure of the Irish kingdoms and simply added one more complicating element to their interplay. In England, the church was an integrating element from early on, and contributed powerfully to the absorption of the Mercian and then West Saxon kings into a common western European (that is to say, Frankish) political and even moral-political framework. In Denmark, the church contributed much less to a political system that was already developing in the same direction. In Norway, it contributed substantially to the hegemony, even if a weak one, of kings over isolated and often unwilling regions. In Poland, even though communications were much easier on the flat land of the North European Plain, the structures of the church did not have much of an integrating effect, and royal hegemony broke apart. There were, therefore, few common patterns here. If we added more north European regions to this list we would find greater variability still; although Bohemia might go with Denmark, Hungary partly with Denmark and partly with England (see Chapter 8), Sweden partly with Poland and partly with Norway, Scotland first with Ireland then (incompletely) with England,[30] these are very broad categorisations, and the differences between them all were quite as great.

Are there common trends in these regions at all, though? And here the answer has to be yes; in fact there were several. One was, as noted at the start of the chapter, a great increase in our information, with the introduction of a more systematic writing habit along with Christianisation into every one of these political systems. Poland is at the extreme here: we know nothing at all about it, except via archaeology, until three years before Mieszko converted to Christianity, and after that we do, consistently; but the same is true for all the others, if more slowly. This does not, it is important to stress, mean that Christianisation meant an 'entry into history'; we have seen some major historical developments prior to religious change even in this brief survey, the Slavicisation of eastern Europe, or the establishment of Scandinavian kingdoms from Dublin to Kiev. But we can say less about these, and, even though the western Scandinavian diaspora kingdoms are sometimes reasonably well documented, it was always outsiders who described them, until they went Christian themselves. A second trend, less linked to Christianity and the church, was the steady weakening of peasant autonomy all over the northern lands; even where political power was fragmented, as in Poland and Ireland, peasants were increasingly subjected to local lords. This was not a uniform process by any means; in England it was pretty much complete by 1000, but in Norway (still more so Sweden) there were plenty of autonomous peasants into the end of the middle ages and beyond; but it was generalised. This is one of the major changes of the whole of the middle ages in the north. One consequence was an increase in concentrations of surplus available to élites, and with that the extension of trading connections. More of England became integrated into the trading networks of the west after 900. The Baltic, too, developed steadily as a trade route. Networks of coastal ports appeared along the coast of modern Poland from the eighth century onwards, and seem to have related at the start to the fortified settlements of the interior, acting as craft centres and probably slave entrepôts, helped later by the Scandinavian connections to the North Sea and down the major Russian rivers to Byzantium and the caliphate; but, as élites became richer, the ports were increasingly foci for exchange of all kinds, and they would become part of the Hanseatic league in the late middle ages.[31]

The other general trend, however, was a cultural one, and it was connected quite directly with the other consequence of Christianisation. This was the gradual opening of each polity which adopted the new religion (even Ireland and Norway) to the Frankish and post-Frankish world of western Europe and its political-cultural practices, including a trend towards common assumptions about political action. Robert Bartlett has stressed naming practices, the introduction of saints' names like John and Franco-German names like Henry all across the north, alongside, and sometimes supplanting, older and more local names like Brian and Æthelred and Olaf and Bolesław; and also the increasingly generalised use of charters as documentation and coins as a means of exchange.[32] In the arena of aristocratic behaviour, too, northern élites slowly began to adopt Franco-German practices like seals, the ritual of homage, castles (except in Scandinavia), and, later, coats of arms and the imagery and literature of chivalry. There were Cistercian monasteries everywhere by 1200. Latin Europe had expanded to the Arctic circle and the edge of what is now Russia, and, east of that, Greek Europe, in a parallel set of trends, had done the same (see Chapter 9). Some of the same pressures were shared by each region, too, such as the impact of the claims of the international papacy (see Chapter 8) or, later, the new political claims of parliaments (see Chapter 12). It is tempting to see this as a generalised homogenisation: it might, that is, be seen as the creation of a common European history, with only differences in detail between the different polities of the continent. This would, however, be an illusion; the very distinct histories sketched out here continued to underlie distinct developments for the rest of the middle ages and well beyond. Above all, in northern Europe (here the major exceptions are England and Hungary) the fiscal systems of the later medieval centuries were much weaker than in western and south-eastern Europe, which reflected long-standing differences in the infrastructure of royal power, and which meant that, however much kings and aristocrats wished to behave like those in France, they in fact did not have the wealth to do so. This we will look at in more detail in Chapter 11.

CHAPTER SIX

Reshaping western Europe, 1000–1150

At the end of Chapter 4, I proposed that there was a major difference between the public political world of the early middle ages in western Europe and a smaller-scale, more personalised, lordship-based politics which marked later centuries. The latter came in slowly from around 1000 onwards, starting in West Francia; by 1100 it dominated in many places. Although larger-scale political systems returned after that, local lordships did not go away; their presence is one of the key elements which mark out the second half of the middle ages in the west as different from the first half. How that new politics developed is the main theme of this chapter. For an idea of what I mean by it, however, let us start with a text, which gives us a sense of what the new political parameters of the period could look like.

In the 1020s, Hugh, lord of Lusignan in western France, had a long memorial written, which listed all the injustices done to him by his *senior* (lord), William V, count of Poitou and duke of Aquitaine. William promised him wives which he then did not allow him to marry; he did not let Hugh inherit lands he was entitled to; he acted without Hugh's advice; he did not help Hugh when others sought to take his lands (Hugh said to William 'I never lose except because of my fidelity to you'; William was unsympathetic: 'You are mine to do my will'); he did not stop castles being built to Hugh's detriment; he had Hugh's new castles burnt down. Hugh complained at every stage, and William promised his support at every stage, but never kept his promises. In the end Hugh 'defied the count, in the hearing of all, except for his city and his own person', and they fought a small war; only then did the count-duke agree to come to terms and give Hugh part of his withheld inheritance, in return for very solemn oaths, and Hugh's oath of fidelity. We do not know how long it lasted, but at least Hugh was reassured enough to have his plangent text stop there.[1]

Hugh poses himself as a victim in this memorial, but in reality was far from that; he was one of William's most powerful and potentially dangerous aristocratic dependants, and there will have been another side to this story. But it is striking how far his whole text revolves around a personal bond, posed as one of trust and betrayal. It indeed resembles French verse epics of the twelfth century, such as that of the emblematically bad lord Raoul de Cambrai, who burned down a nunnery with his faithful vassal Bernier's mother in it, and then in the end hit Bernier with a spear-shaft, before Bernier could bear formally to break his bond of fidelity.[2] This was, then, a political structure dependent on personal relationships. It was also a very localised one, all taking place in Poitou, with other counts (such as the count of Anjou, 100km to the north) mentioned almost as foreign powers. William was in fact one of the most successful regional rulers of early-eleventh-century France, as Hugh's memorial reluctantly testifies; but his territory was a network of the castles of others, even if he was active enough in trying to bring as many of them as possible under his control. And, although he claimed full power over his aristocratic dependants, when he did make peace with them he had to make promises back to them as well. Personal relationships of this kind had old roots, but they had never before characterised the whole of politics.[3] Whatever this world was, it was not the world of Charlemagne or Otto I.

Western and southern Europe in 1000 had a fairly clear hierarchy of states. Al-Andalus and Byzantium were, as we saw in Chapter 3, easily the most powerful political systems, at the south-west and south-east corners of the continent, particularly as the force of the Francia of Charlemagne had become substantially diminished. Francia was by now indeed permanently divided; although nothing which we could call national consciousness existed in its two main successor-states, East and West Francia, we can by now call them Germany and France for convenience, and I shall do so henceforth.[4] Of the two, Germany was clearly dominant, with king-emperors who ruled Germany and Italy; the French kings were by contrast very weak, and the only other polity in Latin Europe with a real political solidity was England, a kingdom not much larger than a German duchy. This hierarchy might have looked stable enough, but was far from that, as the next century showed. Already by 1030 al-Andalus had, after a twenty-year civil war, broken up into about thirty successor-states; in 1071, the large armies of the Seljuq Turks defeated the Byzantines, and the latter permanently lost control over the eastern third of the Byzantine empire, modern central Turkey. After 1077 the German empire, too, lapsed into civil war and Italy, in particular, went its separate way. England maintained its coherence, but had to face two violent conquests. The French kings did not become any more powerful, but France was a cockpit of ambitious and prickly lords like Hugh of Lusignan, and some of them, in particular those from Normandy, acting as mercenaries and freelance fighters, managed in the second half of the eleventh century to conquer southern Italy from its previous rulers, and by 1100 even Palestine, at the end of the First Crusade. Elsewhere in Europe, new kingdoms emerged from nowhere as strong political powers, notably Hungary and Castile. And, on top of all this, the western church, led by the popes of Rome for the first time, was beginning to pose itself as an independent moral authority to rival that of the traditional secular powers. These political developments, and their causes and contexts, frame the major social changes we need to discuss. What happened to Byzantium we will see later, in Chapter 9; Hungary and Castile will appear in Chapter 8. In this chapter we will look at what happened in what had been Carolingian or Carolingian-influenced western Europe, Germany, Italy, France and England in particular, with a political narrative first and a structural discussion after, before ending with the changes in the western church and the Normans in the Mediterranean.

Germany was in 1000 by far the largest and militarily strongest western power, even if it was never as internally coherent as its Carolingian predecessor, let alone the tax-based states of the south. (Now that I am using modern country names, it is worth adding that the 'German kingdom/empire' continued to include, throughout the middle ages, what we would now call the Low Countries, Switzerland and Austria.) The Ottonian king-emperors of the tenth century, based in Saxony in the German north, were rich as we have seen, with lands and silver-mining in Saxony, and landed bases also in the Rhineland and in northern Italy. Germany was hard to control in depth, given its forests and its few roads – the only real north–south route was along the Rhine – but these three linked the north and the south of the power of the Ottonians, at least. After 1024 they were succeeded by female-line heirs, the Salians, an aristo-cratic family from the Rhineland, and that area was further strengthened as a political focus for the king-emperors; they moved around Germany much as the Ottonians had, but by now went rarely either to Italy (except to be crowned emperor) or to most of Saxony. Italy stayed more or less loyal, although its powerful cities henceforth showed a greater tendency to revolt; Saxony, however, now that it was less of a royal power-centre, felt its distance from the rest of the kingdom and became more and more resistant to the tight royal control of the silver-mine area; by 1073 it too was in open revolt.[5]

The first two Salian king-emperors, Conrad II and Henry III (1037–56), managed to keep their German hegemony solid. They did so by focusing its aristocracy on the great ceremonial assemblies around the king, by being generous with land-giving as far as they could, and by moving militarily to bring down disloyal dukes when necessary, all traditional procedures. But after 1056 Henry III's heir Henry IV (his long reign lasted until 1106) was a child, and royal hegemony weakened fast. Henry IV as an adult, after 1065, moved quickly to revive it, but he was a heavy-handed operator, with an interest in innovation – as with the development (alongside other lords) of new methods of keeping control over his lands, which were increasingly entrusted to *ministeriales*, local figures of knightly but technically unfree status who would find it harder to break away. Not only the Saxons, but also the southern dukes, became opposed to him. When Henry fell out with Pope Gregory VII in 1075–76, the pope threatened Henry with deposition. Henry moved quickly to Italy, and in one of the famous images of the middle ages stood three days and nights in the snow outside the castle of Canossa in January 1077 until the pope, who was inside, accepted his penance; but the German dukes were not reconciled, and deposed him anyway in 1077, electing a rival. Civil war in Germany lasted for twenty years; after 1080, when relations with Gregory had finally broken down again, it began in Italy too. Henry won in Germany, where he was fighting rival claimants to kingship. In Italy, where he was fighting pro-papal cities and lords (notably the powerful marquise of Tuscany, Matilda, one of whose main castles was Canossa), there was more of a stand-off, and the result was that by 1100 there was no effective imperial presence at all; here the hegemony of the king-emperors, which had lasted even though they were so seldom south of the Alps, had virtually ended, and the cities began to fend for themselves, as we will see later. Under Henry's weaker successors, Germany began to be more regionalised too, although imperial protagonism was still recognised, and under Frederick I 'Barbarossa' (1152–90) could be temporarily revived.[6]

On one level, France had a less difficult history in the eleventh and twelfth centuries, for it had a single line of uncontested kings, the Capetians, who ruled in unbroken father-to-son succession from 987 to 1316 – and even after that, it managed a sequence of male-line heirs who provided kings until 1848, a unique achievement for Europe, and only surpassed in the world by the succession in Japan. But these kings, in this period, were reduced to a royal heartland which stretched 120km from Paris to Orléans on the Loire, plus the rights of appointment over bishops in a wider area of northern France. The rest of the kingdom was in effect autonomous, with dukes and counts, such as William V of Aquitaine whom we met at the start of this chapter, establishing their own rule with almost no reference to the king. Twelfth-century kings could occasionally call out an army from nearly the whole kingdom, as Louis VI (1108–37) did against a threatened German invasion in 1124, or else be recognised as judges well outside their power-base, as Louis VII (d. 1180) did in his well-attended

royal court of 1155. The bonds of loyalty to the king were steadily being recognised as stronger again by the twelfth century, which, as we saw in Chapter 1,
Louis VII exploited with great effect against Henry II of England, by now ruler
of much of France by marriage and inheritance, in Toulouse in 1159. But it
would not be until the wealth of fast-expanding Paris became a real royal
resource in the late twelfth century, that Louis VII's son Philip II 'Augustus'
could move against Henry II's son John and conquer the core of his French
lands in 1202–04, which established the king of France as the major player in his
own kingdom for the first time in nearly 300 years. The history of France in the
period of this chapter is thus the separate histories of its duchies and counties.
Some of these – such as Flanders, Normandy, Anjou and Toulouse, joined by
the royal heartland in the twelfth century – remained relatively coherent
political units: their rulers were sufficiently fearsome, and managed to keep
strategic control of enough castles and lands, to remain at the centre of the
system of landed rewards. As a result, lesser lords like Hugh of Lusignan were
kept, however unwillingly, onside. Others – Champagne, Burgundy, and, after
William V, much of Aquitaine too – fragmented, sometimes quite rapidly at the
start of the eleventh century, into steadily smaller and smaller territories, ending
up in some cases as no more than clusters of autonomous lordships ruled by
lords who had a handful of castles each.[7]

Only England kept its coherence in this period. Renewed Scandinavian
attacks between 990 and the 1010s did, it is true, lead to the temporary expulsion of King Æthelred II (d. 1016), another king who was heavy-handed in
unpopular and often unsuccessful ways, and some social breakdown; but by
1016 the Danish kings had conquered the country outright, creating a
combined English and Danish kingdom under Cnut (d. 1035), as we saw in the
last chapter. Cnut established himself as an effective English-style king in
England, creating his own aristocracy out of a mix of English and Danish families. After 1042, there was a return to tradition under Edward 'the Confessor',
Æthelred's son, but he had to fight his corner against Cnut's aristocrats, and at
his death in 1066 one of them succeeded him as Harold II. The tension around
that allowed William 'the Bastard', duke of Normandy, who had no serious
claim to the throne at all, to invade and defeat Harold at Hastings later in the
same year. William, by now 'the Conqueror' to historians (d. 1087), after the
end of the 1060s dispossessed almost the entire English aristocracy, replacing
them with French families: perhaps the most complete destruction of a ruling
class there has ever been in Europe, up to 1917.[8]

The interesting thing is, however, that throughout all this the English state
remained organised and the king hegemonic. William I inherited what was by

western standards a tight political system, based on large-scale royal land-owning, and a land tax (originally instituted by Æthelred to pay off the Danes, and carried on by Cnut), which William re-established. As its ruling class became French in genealogy, language and values, state effectiveness was not changed; William indeed engaged in some very specific and demonstrative political acts, not least the huge Domesday survey of 1085–86, again without parallel in Latin Europe, to record the agricultural and landholding detail of nearly the whole country, which impressed and appalled contemporaries and has absorbed historians ever since. Royal wealth and ruthlessness during two generations of Norman kings, and the fragmentation of royal grants to the new aristocracy (which meant that few of them had a single local power-base), plus the coherence of a county-based system which still involved local judicial assemblies in an early medieval tradition, allowed the state also to remain effective during a civil war between two grandchildren of William I in the 1140s. The heir of one of them, Henry II, count of Anjou (1154–89), emerged victorious; he ruled England, and a large collection of French duchies and counties as we have seen, fairly tightly for thirty-five years, an achievement not lessened by our knowledge that his son would lose half of them only fifteen years later.[9]

*   *   *

This is, for the most part, a history of political breakdown. The power of French historiography in the second half of the twentieth century meant that the French experience was taken very widely to be normal. Although, as this brief survey shows, it was not, there has as a result been a substantial debate since 1990 as to the significance of that French experience. This has been seen by many as the 'feudal revolution', with a sharp increase in violence and a privatisation of political power, and by a few even as the real end of the ancient world; but such views have been attacked by a second group of historians, who argue that the changes around 1000 (or at later dates in the eleventh century) were a marginal shift, since the basic structures of political power remained the same, even though on a smaller scale, as also did aristocratic values such as loyalty to lords and honour, which hardly changed across the early and central middle ages.[10]

The second group has brought much-needed nuance to our understanding of what really changed in the eleventh century; all the same, I remain, broadly, with the first. Smaller-scale political structures, especially if they are based on militarised foci such as castles, do tend to produce more capillary violence everywhere, even if it is (as it usually was) quite carefully targeted. The heavily personalised political relationships shown in the complaint of Hugh of Lusignan are also only possible when power is so localised that every actor is known to every other, as was far from the case in the Carolingian world, even if (as we saw earlier) personal relationships – and also violence – certainly existed then too. The sort of political power shown by our eleventh-century sources for France, even when exercised by dukes and counts directly, was heavily based on the establishment of sets of increasingly specific aristocratic rights over small territories, including powers of justice, and rights to tolls and dues of all kinds, which are called by French historians the '*seigneurie banale*'; these were under their private control and could even be bought and sold separately, as well as fought over. Their holders were frequently small-scale lords, called in our sources *milites*, 'knights', who held one or two castles each: very unlike the great aristocrats of the Carolingian period, who could have dozens of estates. And, as an overarching and crucial development, this power, as its parameters became more local, became more clearly bounded and formalised. From now on, it mattered where the edge of a lordship was, for outside it a lord could not so easily claim dues, or rights to judge; and the rights involved in lordship themselves became more defined. For the same reason, if a lord claimed lordship over a village, it increasingly mattered how far the territory of that village extended; village territories, and also parishes, thus became more clearly marked out on the ground too. Castles, which were more common by the eleventh century, became the new points of power in a landscape, of a type which no Carolingian aristocrat had needed, for he had so many estates and so seldom used them as a local power-base – as opposed, that is, to using their rents to allow him to pay for political action at a regional or royal level. The French peasantry were increasingly caged inside the cellular structure of local power, and subjected, on top of rents, to lordly exactions which were often heavy, sometimes arbitrary, and always designed to underpin direct domination. Such exactions could also increase, as the agricultural economy produced more surplus in an age of population increase and the clearance of land: at least until peasants resisted this collectively, as we shall see in the next chapter.[11]

These were major changes, for they all privileged the local. Up to the eleventh century, kings – and also regional rulers, dukes, counts and bishops – could rule from the top down, using the old Roman imagery of public power and the early medieval collective legitimation which was assembly politics, without considering in a very organised way what was going on locally, unless it involved disloyalty, or an injustice which was so clamorous that it actually reached their ears. The small-scale lordships of the late eleventh and twelfth centuries in France could not afford to be so detached; exactly whom they controlled, and how, mattered much more. It is important to recognise that this shift was the result of two separate processes, for the weakening of the public world of kings and assemblies, and the growth of local lordships, had distinct histories. On the other hand, each of course affected the other: the slow development of local power structures meant that the public world was not the only possible location for political action, which especially mattered if rulers faced difficulties; conversely, the weakening of the public framing for politics forced local powers to become better defined, creating the cellular structure of the future. And both of these developments fit what Marc Bloch meant by the 'fragmentation of powers': they were an always-possible consequence of the politics of land, in a world where the state was not separately supported by taxation.[12] A localised world was far from an inevitable consequence of the politics of land; but the possibilities were always there if rulers were not secure, and watchful. Although its development was very variable in both dating and intensity – here, as elsewhere in this book, we cannot deal with all its complexities – a cellular structure for politics can henceforth be tracked even in relatively strong regional units in France such as the counties of Toulouse and Flanders, or again with William V of Aquitaine in his dealings with Hugh of Lusignan; rulers of all kinds had to recognise lordships as the building blocks of their political authority.

This was the French pattern, which we can easily see as an extreme; but how far did it extend elsewhere? Some of it did. There were castles all over western Europe by 1100, for example – although not Byzantium, which had a very different development. They were rare until the end of the ninth century (Merovingian and Carolingian aristocratic residences were mostly unfortified), but from then on the fortification habit spread slowly and steadily everywhere, even, particularly after 1066, in perennially strong polities such as England: initially as the foci for royal power for the most part (as with the well-excavated Ottonian palace site of Tilleda), but increasingly as the must-have for every local lord, large or small, in Germany, Italy, Christian Spain, as in France.[13] But the breakdown of political power elsewhere did not happen as it did in France. In England, as also in twelfth-century Castile, castle-holding lords remained fully part of a king-centred political structure, for kings were so rich that cutting oneself off from their patronage remained a losing option, even if one survived royal wrath and armed attack. There, either private *seigneuries* were internally divided and interspersed with the lands of the king (as in Castile), or they did not develop at all. This was above all the case in England, where, apart from during the civil wars of the 1140s, kings kept control of justice over the free, and left lords to claim judicial rights only over the unfree – even if that left them with substantial powers, for the unfree were numerous in England, and became more numerous in the late twelfth century as the free–unfree boundary moved.[14] England, indeed, kept most of the Carolingian-style public political structure it had developed in the later tenth century, with greater success than anywhere else, although royal assemblies were no longer the legitimating venues they had been before the Norman conquest.

Germany did not develop quite as France did, either. The king-emperors were, for a start, powerful at least some of the time and in some parts of the country, up to the 1240s, and had to be reckoned with, for their army remained substantial; an assembly politics centred on the kings also persisted, and assemblies were major loci for political acts of all kinds. They had a relatively restricted administrative infrastructure beyond that; but German dukes were not, as far as we can see, much better-rooted in their large duchies, and, under them, counts in many cases did not have unitary counties, but, rather, fragmented sets of rights. For the most part, then, neither dukes nor counts could have easily constructed strong territorial power-bases in the absence of kings in the way William V of Aquitaine did. Nor were other aristocratic and ecclesiastical landowners any more focused; they usually had widely scattered lands. When the power of kings faltered, as at the beginning and then the end of Henry IV's reign, or in the 1140s, or above all from the 1240s onwards, local powers took some time to consolidate; and when they did, they tended not to develop territorialised *seigneuries banales* of a French type. We find instead intersecting accumulations of hereditary land (perhaps focused on a family monastery), royal castles held in fief, rights to take market tolls, and – a German speciality – strong local power derived from holding the 'advocacy' over ecclesiastical land, the right to run justice on these properties, which German bishops and abbots routinely ceded to hereditary lay advocates.[15] A well-studied example is the Zähringen power network which took shape in the twelfth century around the Black Forest and in what is now northern Switzerland; it was an ad hoc collection of rights by a local lordly family (including the title of duke), but it was solid, right up to 1218, when the Zähringen family died out.[16] Already-existing dukes and counts were beginning to do the same themselves. All the same, developments such as this certainly represented political localisation. There has been little work comparing Germany and France, but there are more parallels between the two than are always recognised.[17] German local power consisted of more of a network of overlapping authorities, from the ever more distant king down to local lords and advocates, rather than the relative boundedness of many French lordships, but the effect was otherwise similar. In the late middle ages, German local lordship became more bounded too, and then we find hundreds of autonomous rural (and also urban) powers inside the confines of the overarching and increasingly theoretical kingdom of Germany.

Northern Italy, finally, was partially different again. Local lordships slowly developed there too, in the eleventh century in particular, inside the Lombard and Carolingian network of counties, and marches such as Tuscany (which maintained a political structure of a Carolingian type without a break right up to the wars of the 1080s and 1090s); such lordships were based on collections of private property (including castles), hereditary fiefs, and rights to take the tithes of rural parishes. It was not until those wars, however, that public power went into crisis, and, in reaction, such lordships began to turn themselves into coherent and bounded territories, based on judicial rights over all the inhabitants, owners and tenants alike, which were called in Latin *dominatus loci*, 'domination over a locality', and which were a close Italian equivalent to the French *seigneurie banale*. This happened up to a century after their appearance in France, but the similarity of development is here clear, even if such lordships tended to be weaker and to make lighter demands than in France.[18] What made Italy different was that cities were here large and powerful, because most rural lords lived inside their walls – which in itself lessened substantially the autonomy of lordships; from 1100 urban centres were also expanding because the economy was rapidly becoming more complex. When the kingdom of Italy lost its force, it was above all the cities which took over local ruling.

Autonomous Italian cities developed their own forms of collective and deliberative assembly. These were different from the judicial assemblies of the Carolingian and post-Carolingian past, but they made the same assumptions about the close link between political legitimacy and large gatherings of people. In the early twelfth century we find, more and more, that these assemblies, and cities as a whole, were being ruled over by annually changing collectives of ruling officials called 'consuls': in Genoa and Pisa by 1110, in Milan and the other cities of Lombardy by the 1130s, in the Veneto by the 1140s. Such men came from the richest civic élites, of landowners and sometimes merchants, usually including some castle-owning lords; they were not a new social group. But their collective activity was new, and by the mid-twelfth century they called themselves 'communes', a word which explicitly marks that collectivity. Such communes claimed powers over the old Carolingian county network, which in Italy was city-based, and by 1200 most of them had re-established their power over the rural lordships of their territory. Only a handful of rural lords stood out, in less urbanised areas. These communes look very different from the rural lordships of France or Germany or, indeed, Italy itself, and they certainly came to feel they were; by the 1130s they were beginning to use the word 'public' to describe their power, and they were beginning to legislate on their own behalf. But it is worth also stressing that they were, like any rural lordship, the result of an initially highly ad hoc and informal, indeed insecure and uneasy, localisation of power, which became more formalised in the context of royal weakness, and that their growing concern for judicial rights located inside political boundaries (which they were keen to fight over, often bloodily) matched that of *seigneuries banales* as well.[19]

So western Europe was not all like France; but, equally, it can be seen that, across a long eleventh century, everywhere except England experienced a set of developments which at least parallel those of France. Why did it happen then? As I have argued, the crisis of public power itself made local solutions more attractive; but it is also the case that they were by now in themselves more stable. In part, this is simply because the checks and balances of the Carolingian world were now less in evidence, and local power-bases could be created more easily. But there were also by now social changes within the aristocratic strata which made ever-smaller lordships possible. In the Carolingian world, 'real' aristocratic status was regarded as belonging to a relative few, essentially the families which might be appointed as counts; smaller-scale military figures would probably hold a couple of estates and have a local prosperity, but their status was tightly bound up with their membership of comital or episcopal entourages, and they had no chance of going it alone. By the eleventh century, however, if you had a castle you did have a local military status which was largely your own. Your ancestors were very often members of Carolingian entourages, and occasionally even rich peasants made good more recently; the social group which we can call 'aristocratic' had widened as a result. Your own lord, a count or a duke, could still hope to dominate you, but had to deal with you, as with William V and Hugh of Lusignan. Indeed, if your lord was insufficiently feared or insufficiently successful, you might well start to act increasingly autonomously, to go for your own local power, however small-scale: to create your own local lordship, that is to say, with its own rules and demands. This was new; there had been plenty of periods of weak or chaotic rule in earlier centuries without autonomous lordships developing, to more than a small extent. Nor did they always do so now; a determined count or duke, and indeed king, could hold this process off, or reverse it – William the Bastard managed it for example after the civil wars which marked his accession as a child in Normandy in 1035,[20] and in England the 1140s civil war could also be recovered from, quite easily in fact. But from now on this process was a *possible* development; a weak ruler, or a civil war, could set it off anywhere, and there were a good few of these. When this happened, the process was very often not reversed, and formalised units of local power appeared as a result, making up a cellular structure which later rulers would have to deal with in new ways, if they wished to rebuild their own polities.

*   *   *

Local concerns and creative power-building also marked out two of the particular novelties of the eleventh century, which go beyond the country-by-country sociopolitical discussions which this chapter has focused on up to now; both fit well into, and add to, the general picture which I have just set out. They are the ecclesiastical 'reform' movement and the Norman/French expansion into southern Italy and Palestine. Let us look at them in turn.

The history of Christian Europe has been studded with religious reform movements; they, so to speak, come with the territory of a religion based on an extremely long sacred text, the Bible, some of whose sections advocate moral values opposed to those of any political system or religious structure which has ever existed, and which attentive readers can discover and rediscover at any time. (The Qur'an has had a similar effect, forceful but intermittent, in the Muslim world.) In the Carolingian world, as we saw in Chapter 4, religious and political 'reform' – as we call it, although medieval theorists did not, hence the inverted commas for the noun – was important; it was in the hands of emperors and kings, acting with and often directing collectivities of bishops and abbots, and indeed lay aristocrats. As political power became more localised in the tenth century, however, bishops began to look for a legitimacy which was not all focused on royal power (they often found it in Gregory the Great's work[21]); councils of bishops from now on more often met without royal involvement, too. And from then on, particularly in the eleventh century, reforming groups became more locally diverse and did not always look to central powers either, even if their preoccupations – ascetic monasticism, the sexual purity of the clergy, the spiritual education of the laity, or the evil of simony, that is to say giving money in exchange for ecclesiastical office – were rarely all that new. That localisation of religious action did have results, however, which were rather different from those of previous centuries. Let us look at some examples, region by region, ending with the activity of the popes in late-eleventh-century Rome, which, at least at the outset, was as localised as any of the others, although soon it changed the parameters of religious action much more generally.

In the 960s, a monastic 'reform' movement took off in England, aiming to introduce a more rigorous monastic life. It was heavily patronised, and indeed effectively controlled, by the king of England, Edgar, and his immediate entou-rage, and was thus (and intentionally) the heir to the centralised monastic reorganisation initiated by Louis the Pious in Francia 150 years before. But the English movement did not just focus on monasteries: it was also substan-tially involved with the 'reform' of cathedral churches, whose canons became monks and whose bishops were often monks themselves. This gave the English church a monastic flavour that had little or no parallel elsewhere in Europe, and which certainly did not look to the Carolingians; the English thought it up for themselves.[22]

An example of a quite different development was the independent status of Cluny, a monastery founded in 910 on the edge of Burgundy by William 'the Pious', duke of Aquitaine, but subjected, not to the dukes, but to the pope in Rome. Cluny, a monastery with a famously demanding monastic practice, has often had the reputation of being a forerunner of the wholly autonomous inter-national church of the later middle ages, but its abbots, while usually not from major aristocratic families and also not closely connected to any local political power (it helped that Cluny lay geographically in something of a power vacuum), had very close links with some of the other lay rulers of the age, beginning with Alberic, prince of Rome (d. 954), patron of Abbot Odo in the 930s. Cluny's own landholdings indeed swelled prodigiously through pious gifts from lay families everywhere, and the monastery was built and rebuilt on a huge scale as a result. Cluny's real novelty was that it came to be the mother house for monasteries across half of western Europe, whose main loyalties were to Cluny, and not to any local figure, whether bishop or count; it created an international network of identity and elaborate liturgical ritual which cut across all traditional political boundaries, and which would be the model for plenty of monastic orders later as well.[23]

Between these two examples, of close association with lay authority in England and a certain degree of autonomy from it in Burgundy, was the church of Upper Lotharingia (now Lorraine), on the western edge of the German kingdom. Here bishops, of Metz or Toul, were independent protagonists, acting to reform local monasteries like Gorze outside Metz or Saint-Èvre in Toul without any lay intermediary; but these bishops were themselves personally linked to the German imperial court. Bruno of Toul, for example (bishop from 1026 to 1051), revived Saint-Èvre and nearby Moyenmoutier; but Bruno was of the highest local aristocracy, related to the king-emperor Conrad II (who appointed him bishop), to the dukes of Upper Lotharingia, and to the bishop of nearby Metz, and would never have thought of himself as separate from impe-rial authority.[24] His world was a reforming one, for sure, again focused on monastic rigour, but in a specific Lotharingian context, which, like England and Burgundy, was developing its own protocols and assumptions.

Councils or synods of bishops still existed everywhere; but now, frequently, they were not only called independently of secular authorities, but also more critical of those authorities. One well-known example of this was the Peace of God assemblies of central and southern France in the late tenth century and early eleventh. These were essentially local church councils, called by bishops, with a strong lay participation as well. Their surviving proceedings lay a good deal of weight on the depredations of local lords (especially against church land), which they sought to limit by the swearing of oaths, by the establishment of rules which extended church sanctuary, and, later, by restricting lay warfare to certain days of the week. It has been easy to fit these assemblies into the narrative of the 'feudal revolution', although there has, once again, been a retreat from this more recently: the peace movement was by no means hostile to lords, who were involved with it throughout; the attacks on lay violence can easily be seen as standard rhetoric (although this does not mean that such violence did not occur). The same is the case for their role in the narrative of church 'reform'; certainly, bishops were here giving autonomous guidance to lay society, in an unusual way, but counts and indeed kings could appropriate the practice as well, and did so quite quickly. More important here, is that they were a specifically regional response to perceived social problems, for the assemblies hardly extended outside central-southern France. In a sense, in fact, the Peace of God assemblies were imitations of Carolingian *placitum* assemblies, but this time called by local powers: a Carolingian tradition was here in effect reinvented, from below, and only in one region.[25]

This bottom-up moralistic protagonism could even be pursued by people without formal office. The Pataria in Milan in the years between 1057 and 1075 is a good example. This was a popular purist religious movement, led by both (lesser) clergy and laymen, which was violently opposed to clerical marriage and to simony in the Milanese church; it was one of the first of such movements to be largely run by the laity. It split the city, for married clerics were a long-standing feature of the very elaborate ecclesiastical traditions of Milan, and were as fiercely defended as they were attacked; the accusations of simony against Archbishop Guido da Velate (d. 1071) were also somewhat artificial, although the movement managed to expel him from the city. It is nonetheless evident that in Milan, the fear of simony, as an act which not only menaced but polluted the church, was strongly rooted in popular values; Milan, by far the largest city in northern Italy and by now commercially active, knew how sales worked, and some of its inhabitants by now saw simony, often defended as an exchange of favours, to be a sale of goods and thus inappropriate for a pure church. Simony and clerical marriage, as noted earlier, were not recent preoccupations, at least of clerical reformers; the Milanesi were not voicing new fears. But the moral panic attached to them was much more intense by now; and the Pataria was also new in that it was a popular movement, with, again, a specifically local base. There were similar movements in some Italian cities, but in others the laity were indifferent or hostile, and even in Milan a counterattack by traditionalist aristocrats in 1075 resulted in the death of the lay Patarene leader Erlembaldo and the eclipse of the movement.[26] It can be added that, although the Pataria was strongly supported by the papacy in the 1060s and 1070s, its largely lay focus brought its own dangers: what if lay people began to make their own decisions about, for example, doctrine? When they did in the eleventh century, it was more likely that they would be considered heretics, rather than in the moral vanguard of the church: as at Arras in France in 1024 or Monforte in north-west Italy in 1028, when lay people decided that baptism (in the former case), or papal supremacy (in the latter), was unnecessary, and bishops condemned them for it.[27] We will come back to the implications of this tendency, which became much more widespread in the west after 1150, in Chapter 8; but it is worth adding here that, when it did, 'Patarene' became a synonym for heretic too. Although Pope Urban II made Erlembaldo a saint in 1095, there was an undercurrent of danger about the Patarene moment which was not forgotten.

My last and longest example is Rome itself, another localised development which had, however, more substantial implications. In 1046, the papacy faced one of its recurrent crises over who was the legitimate pope, with, less usually, three rivals at the same time. The German king Henry III deposed two of them and forced a third, Gregory VI, to resign at the Synod of Sutri, held as he was coming to Rome to be crowned emperor, and appointed his own pope, a German, as Clement II. German kings had deposed popes before, several times since Otto I first did so in 963; appointing non-Roman popes was less common, although Otto III had done it in 996 and 999. Henry, however, ensured the appointment of five Germans in succession, and from now on native Roman popes were a rarity until late in the twelfth century; by the 1050s, the college of cardinals was changing fast as well, as they too became overwhelmingly non-Roman from now on. The third of Henry's popes, the longest-lived and most effective, was Bishop Bruno of Toul, who became Pope Leo IX (1049–54). He was, as we have seen, close to the imperial court, but was also an active opponent of simony, and he used his new papal office to hold a series of synods across Europe, from Rome to Reims in France, in which simony was at the top of his agenda. At Reims in 1049, where there was no lay participation (the king of France refused to come), Leo had all the bishops and abbots who attended state at the start that they had not paid money for their office: a coup de théâtre which forced several to confess that they had, and some were removed from office as a result.[28]

Reims inaugurated a new period of church 'reform', one in which, for the first time, papal participation was important, under Leo, Alexander II (1061–73), and Gregory VII (1073–85), the former Archdeacon Hildebrand, whose charisma, ambition and lack of compromise have led to the whole 'reform' movement being called 'Gregorian' by many. It was wider than that, however; what characterised this period was the degree to which reformers of all kinds converged on Rome: Lotharingians in the entourage of Leo, such as the anti-simoniac extremist Humbert of Moyenmoutier; north Italians like the monastic founder Pier Damiani (both became cardinals); and reform-minded members of the Roman clergy itself, notably Hildebrand. What held them together was the belief that the church had become polluted by simony, which, as we have already seen, was the moral panic of the age, as well as by clerical sexuality, which particularly preoccupied Pier Damiani – for him in particular, clerical sex was equivalent to incest, and he wrote at length about its dangers, including a long and strikingly detailed tract against homosexual acts, which was too extreme for Leo IX.[29] The problem was: what actually *was* simony? Buying church office was its obvious meaning, but even then Gregory VI, who was forced to resign for buying the papacy from Benedict IX, saw himself as a reformer (Hildebrand was his protégé), and seems to have thought of it rather as paying off a disreputable predecessor. Others did indeed see such payments as part of the gift exchange of favours, which was part of all medieval (and not just medieval) politics. Conversely, on the purist side, some thought that the pollution of simony could extend to any lay involvement in ecclesiastical elections – which was considerable, for emperors and kings routinely chose bishops and indeed popes, as we have just seen, and always had done; and they also participated in church rituals of consecration and investiture. Humbert of Moyenmoutier argued that lay investiture of clerics was simoniac in the 1050s, for example, although his views were not picked up by anyone else for some time. Gregory VII did so in the end, in 1078, with a decree against lay investiture at his spring synod of that year, but only after his troubles with Henry IV had already begun;[30] because of this eventual choice by Gregory, the contest between emperor and pope has often been seen as a struggle over who should control the ritual of investiture. But that in reality was only a minor element in a wider set of issues about the spiritual distinctiveness, authority and autonomy of the clergy, which, it became steadily clearer, was what the panic over simony (and also clerical sex) was really about. Although arguments about investiture heightened the temperature of debate very greatly at the end of the century, it is significant that it could be compromised over when a measure of peace was established, in 1122.

The imperial-backed 'reforms' of Leo IX could be seen as part of a tradition that went back into the Carolingian period. When Henry III died in 1056, however, the reformers began to divide. Some were comfortable with a move-ment that continued to look to the imperial court; others saw reforming protagonism as being the responsibility of clerics alone. The latter group, led by Hildebrand/Gregory, eventually won out, although with difficulty. After Gregory fell out definitively with Henry IV (initially over the crisis in Milan, not any theological issue), Henry took Rome in 1084 and had his own pope, Clement III (1080–1100), consecrated, with a good deal of church support. The lay élites of Rome had mostly backed Gregory, but when the latter's allies, the Normans of southern Italy, burned down parts of the city in order to allow him to escape, the majority of Romans changed sides, and Clement held Rome against his rivals for most of the time until his death.[31] Gregory's second successor Urban II (1088–99) had almost no Roman base at all. If his side won widespread support in the end, enough to take over Rome again in the last year of both rival popes, it was because of a further novelty in his practice, one with parallels to Leo IX (and for that matter to the Peace assemblies) but in a very different political situation: the holding of church councils, with substantial lay participation but emphatically under clerical direction, in a number of places across northern Italy and France. These included that triumph of charismatic leadership (but also careful planning), the Council of Clermont of 1095, where Urban preached the First Crusade.[32] After 1100, resistance to the Gregory – Urban faction receded quite quickly. By the time we reach the twelfth century, in fact, the autonomy of the clergy from secular powers was more and more taken for granted, and married clergy slowly became less common in most of western Europe as well.[33] (By contrast, in Byzantium, which was not affected by these events, they remained normal.) The clerical–lay spiritual divide was henceforth far more marked, and the supremacy of the pope over the ecclesi-astical hierarchy of western Europe was also increasingly accepted – in theory, at least. The moralised royal political initiatives of Charlemagne and Louis the Pious were henceforth much rarer in this new environment; popes, from now on, thought that such initiatives ought to come from them, and that kings, although they should certainly obey popes, could now be seen as having a more specifically secular role than they had ever had before.

Even today, a surprising number of historians turn their accounts of the church 'reform' period of the later eleventh century into a triumphal narrative, with goodies and baddies – even, remarkably, historians writing in the Protestant tradition, a tradition which regards clerical marriage and lay participation in the choice of ecclesiastics as actively virtuous. This is not, or should not be, the point; rather, we need to understand how come, and in what framework, the Gregorian side of the 'reform' movement won. And here we need to come back to the localisation of politics. 'Reform', of whatever type, was in the mind of every ambitious ecclesiastic of the eleventh century (as, indeed, in most periods); but its impetus, as we have seen, was by now not necessarily connected with any central authority – neither emperor nor pope, indeed. Because practical politics of every kind had moved towards the local, 'reform' had its own local logics and dynamics, as well as different local foci, as we have seen with monasticism, the Peace of God and the Pataria, and now papal Rome itself. And that continued. Councils of bishops were called everywhere; monasteries were reformed and new purist monastic orders were founded everywhere; individual bishops and dioceses could also pursue their own agendas of spiritual 'reform' and pastoral care (a well-studied example is Verona); these processes carried on autonomously, and also slightly differently everywhere.[34] And this meant that no-one could easily stop them, too. Henry IV and his allies could keep popes in the Gregorian tradition out of Rome, but they could not prevent Gregory, and still more Urban, from linking themselves to the local 'reform' initiatives of the rest of the west. Conversely, however, the real challenge these popes faced was to be taken seriously outside Rome as players even when they faced papal rivals (England, among others, remained neutral for much of the civil war period). There was a tradition of invoking the power of papal confirmations and judgements which they could draw on, one which Gregory strongly developed; but that was fine only as long as they were accepted as the legitimate popes.

For the first time, then, papal legitimacy was put to the test of local (élite) opinion, Europe-wide.[35] Urban, who was French and also a Cluniac monk, was however popular in France, a popularity which the excitement of the Clermont council only extended. France, added to Christian Spain (whose interest in what German emperors did was always limited), plus at least half of north-central Italy and the Normans in southern Italy, was enough to balance, and more than balance, the strong support for Clement III in most of Germany and some of Italy. However, once the Gregory – Urban succession won out, with Paschal II (1099–1118), a far less adept dealer but one who had no rivals after 1105, the problem for him and his successors was that church 'reform' would still continue along local lines, often without looking more than nominally to popes. The twelfth-century international church indeed shows us some major political operators, most notably Bernard of Clairvaux (d. 1153), whose religious legitimacy did not come from the papal tradition at all. Bernard, a monk and monastic founder from the austere Cistercian movement in France, established his moral authority on the back of the rapid success of Cistercian monasticism in the early twelfth century, his own extensive writings, his public asceticism, and a charismatic and very uncompromising personality. He dominated the church politics of northern France for twenty-five years without needing any support from the popes – indeed, in the next wave of papal turmoil, in the 1130s–1140s, it was popes themselves who needed Bernard, not vice versa.[36] The authority of Bernard shows up as well as anything the degree to which the church was as localised as was secular politics in this period. It is true that such a local base was not at all new for charismatic religious figures; it is also true that the way Bernard leveraged it into influence across much of France and Italy shows that even informal ecclesiastical authority was beginning to be transnational in its potential. But his was still a bottom-up achievement. In later centuries, future Bernards would run into much more trouble from popes.

The 'papal monarchy' of the twelfth century (a phrase of modern historians, not a contemporary one) was, then, in some respects like that of the king of France, who was recognised throughout his kingdom but without much chance of controlling what went on in it. At the level of local religiosity, papal power would never be determinant, either: the tension between centralisation and local diversity marked the rest of the middle ages and beyond. But it turned out to be possible for the papacy to come to establish a considerable element of control for all that, just as the king of France eventually would. How that happened we shall see later.

*   *   *

One of the most intriguing developments of the eleventh century was the Norman conquest of southern Italy and Sicily, from a series of different powers: the Byzantine provincial government of Puglia and Calabria, the Arab *amir*s of Sicily, and the dukes and princes of six autonomous states on the Italian mainland, looking to old Lombard or Byzantine capitals in Benevento, Salerno, Naples and others. It is often linked to the Norman conquest of England, but in fact was its opposite: the English conquest was an organised military operation by the Norman duke and his army, hanging on a single battle and complete in under five years; that in Italy was the work of a set of soldiers of fortune from the lesser Norman nobility and it took two generations of casual violence to achieve. It is a thus a marker of the possibilities of the localised politics which we have amply seen develop across much of western Europe in this chapter.

There is at least no doubt that the division of southern Italy between so many powers was older than this: it dated to the ninth century, in fact, when civil war broke up the old Lombard principality of Benevento, and urban leaders in Naples and neighbouring towns grabbed their own independence from Byzantium as well. What happened is that Normans and other northern French began to be recruited as mercenaries in the continuous desultory wars between these powers in the early decades of the eleventh century, and realised that there were opportunities in establishing their own lordships. The first of these was at Aversa north of Naples in 1030, which the duke of Naples still theoretically controlled; by the 1040s, however, different Norman groups were aiming at conquest, in all areas of the mainland south. In 1053 they defeated Leo IX at the head of a papal army aiming to push them out, and by the end of the decade most of the mainland was under Norman control. This was not, however, anything resembling a unified structure. Different lords established their own lordships, both large and small, on a great variety of bases. Sometimes these simply replaced the political structures of their prede- cessors; sometimes they resembled northern *seigneuries banales*, based on both expropriated land and localised judicial rights; sometimes – in the ex-Byzantine and, later, ex-Arab lands – the new rulers partitioned the taxation rights which had been the fiscal basis of the previous régime, and their lordships were based on that rather than on landholding. In the 1060s to 1080s they conquered Sicily as well, in a slightly more organised way, and Sicily was ruled centrally there- after, largely through an Arab and (above all) Greek official class. Apart from there, however, the next generation simply replaced the fighting of the conquest with clashes between the Normans themselves.[37]

Around 1100, then, the Norman south was a miscellany of highly localised political units. If they looked to a few superior lords, the prince of Capua or the duke of Puglia, who were often related to each other (the two most powerful Norman rulers in the 1080s, Robert Guiscard in Puglia and Salerno and Roger I in Sicily, were brothers from the Hauteville family), they were far from closely controlled by them. The Normans made little attempt at state-building here, as yet. It is indeed hard to avoid the impression that most of the time they were simply having fun: they had a reputation for oppression and imaginative brutality which they strove to live up to (people surrendered more easily),[38] and doing it in the sun of southern Italy was also probably more fun than doing it in Hauteville, one of Normandy's more miserable villages. But once again a localisation of politics, an even greater one than southern Italy had previously had, was the result. The Normans managed to impose that transnationally, across the frontiers which there had previously been, the strong state system of the former Byzantine provinces merging into the land-based system of the Lombard polities: all of them simply became Norman lordships. It is in this respect that the history of southern Italy has interesting parallels with the history of the western European church: in both cases sharply changing local practices came to be linked across traditional boundaries, and, even if remaining localised, were all the stronger for that transnational linkage.

Strongly regional and local practices were, in fact, exportable still further. European division did not by any means undermine the capacity of European powers of all kinds to extend themselves well outside their regions of origin. The First Crusade, above all, linking the church with excited and unscrupulous secular powers, pushed outward very fast. After a request for help from the Byzantine emperor Alexios I (see Chapter 9), Urban II preached it in 1095–96 at Clermont and elsewhere, linking the image of religious pilgrimage to a long-standing rhetorical desire to 'liberate' Jerusalem from Muslim rule. Even Urban must have been surprised at the speed with which this was taken up, for recruitment began among the counts and castle lords of France at once, extending also to Germany (where a millenarian peasant contingent was also numerous) and, slightly later, Italy. Armies set off as early as the following spring, and continued to do so for several years more. Few got very far – Hungary and what is now Turkey saw most come to grief – but the largest contingent, leaving in August 1096, mostly French, made it through a very cautious Byzantine empire and eventually, against the odds, took Antioch and then Jerusalem in 1098–99.[39] The story of this success has been told often, in varying tones of enthusiasm, notwithstanding the massacres of the communities of Rhineland Jews which accompanied it in 1096, and of Muslim and Jewish inhabitants of Jerusalem in 1099; although the damage European adventurism can do to the Middle East is by now rather better known, given the history of the grim decades since the Second World War, this knowledge has had only a minority effect on crusades historiography.[40] What is important here, however, is that the First Crusade was not at all led by kings, but rather by dukes and counts (of Toulouse, Normandy, Flanders among others, as well as Guiscard's son Bohemond), bishops and lesser lords, plus Italian city leaders: by, that is, the local lay power brokers discussed in this chapter. Notwithstanding their genuine religious fervour, they bickered throughout the journey, and some of them left early; a few, like Bohemond (who ended up ruler of Antioch), were as interested in land-taking as in actually getting to Jerusalem. But those who made it were then able to impose in the east just the sort of cellular political structure they knew in France or Italy, bringing fractious colonial-style lordships to Syria and Palestine which matched anything experienced in southern Italy, for the century of their power up to Saladin's nearly complete reconquest in 1187–88.[41]

*   *   *

To summarise. In the eleventh century, political power became more localised, and more carefully bounded. Its holders were often smaller figures than any Carolingian aristocrat would have recognised as an equal. Lords could be creative in its construction, as indeed could cities, grabbing rights in a way that was initially illegal, but, once accepted, defined a new legality. This power structure was new; it maintained plenty of continuities with the past (particularly in a network of aristocratic values which hardly changed), but from now on this sort of practical power depended on a knowledge of, and a concern for, detailed rights and relationships on the ground. Powerful kingship would, certainly, be reconstructed, and often quite soon: by Roger II of Sicily in the 1120s–1140s, by Henry II of England in the 1150s–1160s, by Frederick Barbarossa in Germany and (with less success) in northern Italy in the 1150s–1170s, by popes from Innocent II to Innocent III across the second half of the same century, and then by Philip II of France in the 1200s–1210s. But when that power was reconstructed by such rulers, and others, it would be based on this cellular structure of de facto powers, and not – or only to a small extent – on the practices and royal ideologies of the past.[42] The public world which the Carolingians and Ottonians had inherited from the Roman empire was gone almost everywhere, and had to be rebuilt, on different bases. This is why this set of developments mark a turning point, in western Europe at least: later medieval political processes all presupposed it. How that reconstruction took place we shall look at in Chapter 8.

CHAPTER SEVEN

The long economic boom, 950–1300

Here is what we know about the economic expansion of the central middle ages, in a nutshell. Across the period 950–1300, the population of Europe multiplied by up to three times; there was an extensive process of land clearance, with woodland and rough pasture converted to arable to feed those new mouths; towns greatly expanded in size and number throughout the continent, making goods (above all clothing and metalwork) with an artisanal professionalism that had been much rarer earlier, and selling them far more widely; the use of coins (in this period, overwhelmingly in silver except in Byzantium) became much more common in daily exchange; agricultural specialisms began to develop; the movement of goods and people became, over all, far more extensive, particularly after 1150 or so; and the exchange complexity of western and southern Europe began to extend to the north as well. By medieval standards, this was an economic boom. A much larger population can simply mean that everyone gets poorer; not in this period, however, when there is no doubt that Europe's economy was much more complex at the end of it than at the beginning, although there are signs, as we shall see, of some regions reaching a population ceiling in the early fourteenth century.[1]

Here, however, is what we don't know: why that demographic expansion actually began (and when); how it really related to the economic changes of the period;[2] when long-distance exchanges of products became important (Italian merchants could be found in Flanders by the 1120s, but when did their presence become economically significant?); how much any region in Europe really gained from such exchanges, apart from the two great urban epicentres, Flanders and northern Italy; which social groups gained most from the growth in economic complexity, and whether that changed; how far production depended on peasant (i.e. large-scale) rather than aristocratic (i.e. restricted) demand; or the relative importance of agricultural products as against manufactured goods in the European 'market', seen as a whole. We do not even really know such crucial basic details as what goods were actually made in twelfth-century Latin Europe's largest city, Milan, and where they were sold, before Genoese commercial records (which capture only a small part of them) begin to be dense around 1190;[3] when it was that English wool became the basic raw material for the Flemish cloth towns, let alone how and why; or why it is that the development of silver mines – in this period, a literal licence to print money – can so curiously seldom be seen to have had much of an effect on the prosperity of the wider region in which the silver was.

Our lack of knowledge here has several causes. It is of course the result of problems of evidence, for these are things our sources very seldom tell us directly about, at least before 1300; we will never get the full picture here, in fact, although future archaeological work will certainly help with some of it. But other causes derive from the failings of historians. One is the decline in fashionability of the large-scale serial work on medieval archive sets, which is the only way to get at patterns of development reliably (many current accounts present as 'fact' claims that go back to speculations made by pioneers in economic history in the 1960s and often well before, which have never been seriously tested).[4] Another, an important one, is the fact that few people, except in some very localised contexts, have ever seriously tried to create an economic model of how the medieval world worked and fitted together.[5] In most cases, instead, they have borrowed models from the industrialised or industrialising world and applied them to a historical period where things worked very differently, with at best discussions of how particular medieval socioeconomic structures or political policies 'blocked' a development which – supposedly – might otherwise have been more similar to that in, say, 1750.

These are problems that cannot be solved here, obviously. But they have to be borne in mind as we proceed. For the *fact* of this economic expansion is of essential importance if we want to understand the whole dynamic of medieval society in these central centuries and indeed later; but when it is explored here it must be recognised how far basic data and interpretations are missing. Some general points are clear: the fact that Paris and the Paris basin became unusually economically active in the twelfth century, for example, is a basic context for the growth of the Paris schools and, later, university (for there was no point attracting students if there was no infrastructure to feed them), as well as for the capacity of Philip II of France, with only a restricted territory under his direct control, to match the resources of John of England in their wars in the early thirteenth century, and also for the concentration of resources which produced the striking density of very expensive new Gothic cathedrals in every city of northern France. But, having said that, we must be honest and admit that we do not really understand how the economy of the Paris region worked in this period.[6] At every stage we have to see that economic changes had important consequences, while recognising that we often cannot tell exactly how. That will be the tension underlying this whole chapter. But it is still better than trying to characterise the social, political, cultural shifts in Europe, particularly after 1150, without taking that economic context into consideration at all.

Demographic expansion, then: at least there is no doubt it happened, for a sense of there being steadily more people pervades our documentary records. The scale of it cannot be tracked exactly, however. The only half-reliable figures come from the English Domesday survey of 1086, and then from the English poll tax records of 1377, which come from after the Black Death, the plague which killed between a third and a half of Europeans between 1347 and 1352, and came back in waves later – the European economy was certainly different after that, and we will look at the post-1350 period separately, in Chapter 11. England seems to have had a population of around or above 2 million in 1086 and slightly more in 1377, so clearly had much more before the Black Death. How much more depends on much less complete and more locally based data, but around 5 million (an eleventh of what it is today) is a rough estimate for around 1300, the likely moment of peak population, and 1.5 million is conceivable for the tenth century, when the period of demographic expansion may have started; hence the calculation of a threefold multiplication. Rougher guesses for elsewhere in Europe fit this too; and the estate surveys of the Carolingian period give hints that in Francia the process may perhaps have already begun in the ninth century. The demographic rise probably reached its peak between 1150 and 1300.[7]

If a population triples in size, even if over 300 years, then peasants – always, as we have seen, the huge majority of the population – have to react. They can do so by limiting births (late marriage, stringent rules around sex, abortion, child abandonment), although evidently did not do so, or not enough, in this period. They can farm the land more efficiently, with more systematic crop rotations, better ploughs (which were available, but expensive), and more careful plantings of crops or pasturing of animals on soils which suit them best, even if this means having to exchange your wheat for someone else's barley or sheep. They can clear nearby woodlands and moorlands and add to the arable fields at their disposal. Or they can move to towns, or even emigrate, to regions where there is more empty space (in Europe, this usually meant clearing woodland again). European peasants visibly did all these things between 950 and 1300. Peasants tend not to choose work-intensive farming methods, even where they are available, unless they have to, but this was a period when they did have to (they had more manpower, too, precisely because families were bigger). Organised three-field crop rotation, for example, slowly spread across north-west Europe, just as irrigation spread across al-Andalus and Arab-ruled Sicily, and, later, northern Italy.[8] This intensification developed even more as time went on; not only irrigation in the south but also the introduction of new crops in the north made fallow years unnecessary in a few areas, such as parts of Norfolk and Flanders. There is also widespread evidence for small-scale clearance in already-settled land, as new village- and field-names referring to former woodland show throughout Europe, plus good evidence for land recla-mation in marshy areas such as the deltas of the Rhine and the Po.[9] And urban expansion is well documented throughout Europe in this period, as we shall see, which always means immigration, as no town before the modern period had more births than deaths (they were always unhealthy places – almost none of them had even rudimentary sewage systems, for example – and they were also home to the destitute, immigrants who had not been lucky, who died sooner); although moving to towns simply meant that peasants somewhere else had to grow the crops to sell to feed the new urban inhabitants.

What came rather slower was long-distance emigration. Peasants are highly averse to risk, and going off to seek one's fortune in unknown countries has seldom appealed to them, before the great nineteenth-century colonisations. But the extension of the European political network eastwards, through the conquest and/or Christianisation of the Slav and Hungarian lands (see above, Chapter 5), themselves often underpopulated, made it possible to see that a future in what is now Poland, for example, was less like stepping off the edge of the map. Indeed, once people began to move east (after around 1150, which in itself shows that it was slow to start), they were actively trawled for across Germany and the Low Countries by professional middlemen, employed by lords for that purpose; in return for a leading role in the subsequent settlement, their task was to collect up new settlers, offering them low rents and a stable village environment. The Germanisation of large portions of eastern Europe followed, only reversed in the forced population movements of the late 1940s. The settlers largely cleared land that had been forest before, but frequently expropriated previous inhabitants' land as well, often with the active support of local powers, who were indeed by this point often themselves German. That is to say, this was not at all the colonisation of wholly virgin soil. (Still less were the other major colonial movements of the period, in Spain and Syria/Palestine – quite heavily populated regions.) But nonetheless, it did lead to a further gradual extension of the arable land of Europe.[10]

One wonders whether, once European peasants realised that to maintain their living conditions in an age of population increase they would have to intensify their labour and extend their fields, there was ever a moment in which they were ahead of the game, and were actually better off. The answers are uncertain and contradictory. Clearing local woodland, for example, was not wholly beneficial; if one cleared it all, one would run short of firewood and building materials, not to speak of resources of wood and waste like swine-pasture and fruits/nuts; a grain monoculture made for a more monotonous and less healthy diet for a thirteenth-century peasant family than had been normal in, say, 900.[11] It is at least the case, however – it is clear in the archaeology – that villages became more coherently planned and houses became better made across this period in many parts of Europe; in much of Italy in the twelfth century they moved from wood to stone, for example, and, although this was rarer in the north (where wood is so widely available and easy to use), stone foundations became slowly more common, as did more sophisticated wood construction techniques such as timber framing: all of these are signs of greater local expertise, and the resources to pay for it, that is to say village-level prosperity.[12] By the thirteenth century, too, excavation shows that peasants more often possessed relatively standardised metalwork such as knives, and indeed dress ornaments (as also good-quality pottery jugs and bowls, although that was an older trend; note that archaeology tells us less about cloth), which indicates a greater access to markets which were themselves more numerous.

I will come back to markets later. They are not, however, only signs of peasant prosperity, for the steady commercialisation of society can be accompanied by increased landlordly pressure, and indeed often is. And this last remark also shifts the focus for us. The last three paragraphs have said little about lords; but most peasants, at least in the densely settled lands of the west and south, had landlords. In western Europe, only Italy and Spain had large numbers of free landowning peasants, although there were smaller regions where the same was true, such as the Alps, or the coastal regions of the Netherlands and northern Germany. As we saw in Chapter 5, there were certainly more in northern Europe, but the trend in nearly every part of the north in this period was towards the greater power of large landowners too. Lords were indeed in many cases swift to react to the possibilities of taking more from peasants, if peasants became capable of growing more; and the pressure on peasants from the rise in population was everywhere less immediate, perhaps indeed less visible, than the ever-present pressure on them from lordly exactions. It might indeed be argued that the pressure of the latter was more important for the Europe-wide agricultural expansion, commercialisation and growth in productivity than was population growth on its own. I do not think so for these centuries, for we can also track this expansion in regions of Europe (such as parts of Italy) where rents and dues did not yet increase significantly. But demography, the pressure of lords and the increase in agrarian productivity and commercialisation all worked on each other to produce a more complex economy in nearly every region of Europe.

The trends in the pressure of lords on peasants did not all move in the same direction in this central medieval period, all the same. Carolingian estate management frequently focused on the establishment of bipartite estates or manors, with peasants both paying rent and doing regular labour service on a demesne which was run entirely for the benefit of the lord: manors were never universal, but they represented a state-of-the-art management of an estate for profit.[13] Early medieval estates also had often large numbers of unfree people on them with no legal rights, who owed high rents and most of the labour, and who were sharply differentiated from free peasants who had lighter burdens (see above, Chapter 1). These two patterns became steadily less important across our period, and by the thirteenth century they were only really common in England, where indeed they had seen a revival at the end of the twelfth. Elsewhere in Europe, manors had either never existed (in Spain or Scandinavia or the east) or else were losing coherence rapidly (already in the tenth century in Italy, by the twelfth in France) in favour of more flexible patterns of exploitation – surviving demesnes in France in the thirteenth century, for example, were largely cultivated by wage labour. Agricultural labour service, even in small quantities, still tended to mark unfree legal status, but both dropped back substantially in much of Europe across the period, even if neither had entirely ended before the Black Death. Rent-paying was the overwhelmingly dominant form of tenant obligations thereafter.[14]

Conversely, the development of political rights over the peasantry, the *seigneurie banale* (see Chapter 6) – rights to take dues for justice, pasturing and wood rights and the use of the mill, and rights to require labour for transport, castle-building and castle guard, as well as extra ad hoc and sometimes large exactions (in France, where these were particularly common, they were called *taille*, a 'cut') – could build up to substantial extra demands on top of rent, and could be exacted by some lords not just from direct tenants but also from free landowning peasants in the territory of a castle. France, western Germany, northern Spain and Italy were the main regions where these patterns could be found. Peasants subjected to all of this were sometimes so dependent that, as also in England, they were called by the old Latin word for slave, *servus, serf* in French. Whether or not legally free in origin, they had drifted back into a practical unfreedom, often in the twelfth century; this development was further sharpened by the greater local use of written law, which often reintroduced or reinforced older conceptions of unfreedom. With all the dues available in a seigneurial régime, manorial labour service was hardly necessary any more; and such dues (in particular *taille* and its equivalents) were also easier to increase than rents, which tended quickly to become fixed.[15]

Historians writing on the medieval peasantry until recently saw this set of developments as proof that peasants for the most part paid all their surplus, beyond bare subsistence, to lords, and remained close to destitution as a result. It is now rather less clear that this was always the case, even if we set aside the growing scale of the colonised areas of Europe, where settlers had much lower rents. Even in England, with its high and expanding indices of real unfreedom, rents were not in the thirteenth century at all as high as they could have been, given what we know of grain yields and subletting.[16] And in Italy, Spain and France, one important trend of the twelfth century and early thirteenth was for peasant communities to band together to obtain franchise charters, documents in which the lord agreed to abandon unpredictable demands, and set out levels of exaction which were much more restricted. We can only reconstruct the context of such agreements from the outside; the texts tend to give us very sententious reasons, the good will of the lord and suchlike, for their enactment. A grandiloquent example is the agreement of 1207 made by the lord of Tintinnano, a small fortified village in southern Tuscany, to stabilise rents there:

> Since Rome, which was once ruler and capital of the entire world, reached so far by holding to these three: equity, justice and liberty . . . so I, Guido Medico, . . . rector for the affairs of Tintinnano, considering the state of the castle and of the lords and faithful men who live there [which had gone] from good to bad and from bad to worse, because of inequity, injustice and servitude, and was by now reduced to nothing . . . I proposed to bring the situation back to its earlier good state and to improve it if I could. And I saw that there was no other way to fulfil this process unless the customary services, which the men of the place were accustomed and obliged to pay to their lords, were turned into rents, . . . so that the lords would not dare to require from the abovenamed men anything more against their will . . . This must contribute to the growth and improvement of the castle of Tintinnano, which, if it had a large population, would be so very flourishing among the castles of Italy . . .

In reality, despite these fine words, the peasants of Tintinnano, now Rocca d'Orcia, a couple of miles off the main pilgrim road from France to Rome (whence perhaps also some of Guido Medico's more resonant phrases), were threatening to abandon the village altogether if their lord did not make some concessions to them. It is also very likely that the charter was given out in return for money from the peasants, who would have been prepared to pay a one-off sum to obtain the detailed rules for rent-paying and peasant rights which make up the rest of the text: documents like this do often admit that, even if not in this case. This mixture of struggle and pay-offs was replicated, with different emphases in each case, throughout Europe in the development of village franchises.[17]

What franchises show in every case, however, is a community which managed to gain a level of economic stability, and greater local institutional strength as well, by collective action. We have seen that medieval politics was often collective; Carolingian and northern European assemblies show it, and so do Italian city communes. This worked in villages as well, throughout Europe.[18] Even English villages, where franchises were rare, had collectively established customs. Village communities, which before 1000 were as far as we can see strong only in Spain and probably Denmark, across the central middle ages gained strength everywhere in Europe; they became protagonists, and their leaders gained institutional recognition, indeed calling themselves consuls in parts of Italy and southern France, on the model of cities. These were members of the richest local families in nearly every case; peasant élites always gained most from political and economic autonomy from lords. But such élites needed the backing of a wider community, and that community gained too. Parishes and thus local religious activity were more and more village-based as well; and villages more and more had a serious economic role too, to run open fields in northern Europe, irrigation in the south, common pasture everywhere.[19] This sort of collective protagonism, seldom in this period moving into outright revolt, is one reason why lords indeed did not exact as much from their peasants as they might have. It shows that peasants were not always victims in these social developments. It also gives some context to the archaeology of village prosperity. Although it is never yet possible to be entirely sure whether this prosperity (such as it was) preceded or succeeded the crystal-lisation of village communities and the obtaining of franchises, it does show, as the protagonism of communities also shows, that peasants could take some advantage from the economic expansion of these centuries, and perhaps some-times even keep it.

One steady trend, when seigneurial rights were added to rents, and even to an extent when they were not, was for the exactions by lords from peasants to be more often in money, as the eleventh century moved into the twelfth and thirteenth. The reasons are simple: there was more silver around, so it was actually possible to expect that peasants might have access to it; and lords increasingly preferred money rent, as it was easier to use it to buy goods. When taxation restarted, usually in the thirteenth century, as we shall see in the next chapter, it was almost always in money too. The great mines of Goslar in Saxony from the 960s, Meissen in Saxony from the 1160s, Friesach in Austria from the 1190s, Jihlava in Bohemia from the 1220s, Kutná Hora in Bohemia from the 1290s, and (the exception to this central European set) Iglesias in Sardinia from the 1250s, each lasted a century or so. These, plus a host of smaller mines, in central-northern Italy and again central Europe, provided enough silver to be coined and recoined for all this period, although there were serious low points around 1100 and then again later around and after 1400.[20] We have a substantial amount of evidence for the coins that resulted, for they survive, in hoards and excavations, and are also constantly referred to in narratives and documents. On archaeological sites, they are commonest from the early to mid-thirteenth century onwards, but written evidence shows they had already become by 1000 the point of reference for at least larger transactions throughout most of Europe. When lords switched to rents in money rather than produce, they had to have been confident that peasants could at least – so to speak – buy the coins they needed for rent by selling goods in local markets.

It is often still thought that an active exchange economy needs coins. This is not true; credit is enormously important in most exchange systems, then as now, and debt-credit agreements can be complicated without any physical money changing hands at all. The medieval economy worked on credit to a very large extent, indeed. We can assume it did in markets when peasants were buying or selling on too small a scale for coins to be useful (in twelfth-century England, a whole sheep went for four pennies, the smallest standard coin, before the price inflation at the end of the century); and certainly it did back at home, when grain was needed in advance of harvests, or goods had to be got together for a dowry, or when an extra field needed to be added to a peasant tenure to feed a growing family, but could not be paid for at once.[21] The documents which show these sorts of transaction, which were ever more common in the most active local economies, show debts being totted up in coins, but these were never necessarily needed to pay debts back. All the same, coins steadily spread into all types of transaction, and by the thirteenth century their availability in western and southern Europe, at least, seems to have been taken for granted. Once peasants were forced into market exchange by the need to pay rents in money, coins became steadily more normal in the countryside, which in turn facilitated the next (and more important) change, the growing practice of buying artisanal products rather than making them oneself. This was one essential backdrop to the other side of the economic transformations of this period, the growth of towns.

*   *   *

Overall, the weight of urbanism in the central middle ages was not huge. In Domesday-Book England, where our earliest relatively good data come from, some 10 per cent of the population lived in towns (with, across Europe in 1050, a regionally varying range from maybe 2 per cent in Scandinavia to maybe 15 per cent in Italy). It is likely that all these proportions doubled by 1300. But we are still not talking of anything near to an urban dominance of the overall economy, except probably inside the close-packed network of medium-sized towns in Flanders and northern Italy, and in particular around the very largest towns in Europe: Paris and Milan at maybe 200,000 inhabitants in 1300; Constantinople (well down from its height a century earlier), Genoa, Venice and Florence at maybe 100,000; London at less, maybe 80,000, but acting as the undisputed centre of a coherent state.[22] Only in Italy did towns rule the countryside politically, because independent Italian communes were all urban, although it must be recognised that the Flemish towns were locally hegemonic in practice too, under the ruling counts of Flanders, and spent much of the fourteenth century (and to a lesser extent both before and after) in revolt against their rulers. Outside these two networks, towns operated in an economic and political landscape dominated by rural powers; they cannot be seen separately from the aristocratic world that surrounded them and bought their products. (The old phrase of the British economic historian Michael Postan that towns were 'non-feudal islands in the feudal seas' is wholly inaccurate, then;[23] indeed, urban leaders also held values identical to those of more traditional aristocrats, such as the need to defend one's honour by violence, and were often hard to distinguish from them.) It is not surprising, in fact, that after a generation of excited work in the mid-twentieth century on the supposed proto-capitalist potential of medieval urban economies, the best work of the next generation focused on the agricultural sector, although more recently good studies have been made again of both Flemish and English urbanism. To see how urban growth actually worked on the ground, however, let us look at examples. Here I will briefly describe three very different towns, Pisa, Ghent and Stratford-upon-Avon, and then consider wider questions on the basis of that.

Pisa, like almost all major Italian towns, was an old Roman city, with a continuity of settlement and political activity from the Roman empire to the present day. Around 1100, it had an archbishop and a viscount, plus the beginnings of a city commune. It lay in the marshy delta of the River Arno, and, south of the city, the *portus Pisanus* was the best port on the western side of Italy between Genoa and Naples; Pisa always looked to the sea, and after 950 or so was increasingly active as a maritime centre. Archaeological evidence shows that from then on – as under the Roman empire, but rather less in between – Pisa was the funnel for imports of goods into Tuscany from the rest of the Mediterranean, particularly high-quality decorated glazed pottery from Tunisia and Sicily (for pottery always shows up best on archaeological sites). It is not clear who brought them, whether in Pisan or Tunisian/Sicilian ships, but it is at least certain that a Pisan fleet did exist by the eleventh century, for Pisans had some form of commercial connection with the *amir*s of Denia in al-Andalus, and they were also developing a tradition of violently sacking rich Muslim-ruled Mediterranean cities (such as Palermo in 1064 and Palma de Mallorca in 1115) and taking their treasure. Pisa's remarkable late-eleventh-century cathedral, still standing almost unchanged, was largely built with that treasure, as inscriptions on its façade boast. Eleventh-century trade routes in the Mediterranean were overwhelmingly those of the Muslim world; the Pisans were, in effect, forcing their way into full participation in these networks by violence, much as the Vikings had in the North Sea two centuries earlier. By the early twelfth century, after their successful contribution to the First Crusade (Archbishop Daiberto of Pisa became Latin patriarch of Jerusalem), the Pisans could establish commercial treaties with Byzantium in 1111, Cairo in 1154, Tunis in 1157; by then, together with the Genoese and Venetians, they were major players in the growing networks of Mediterranean exchange. The urban élites of Pisa were not all obviously merchants – many were landowners of a classic medieval type, and the merchants all had some land too – but some had a clear commercial interest, and there were by now Pisans abroad from Constantinople to Sicily. We do not have the remarkable early notarial registers for Pisa that we have for Genoa, its sister city and rival, from the 1150s onwards, which show the complexity of the contracts which ship-owners made by now, and the density of funding of sea commerce engaged in by traditional élite families, stretching again, very visibly, all over the Mediterranean. But the more prosaic and traditional land documents we do have for Pisa show, all the same, that the city's richest figures were similarly active.[24]

On the basis of this, Pisa expanded rapidly, in the twelfth century in particular. By 1100, its market area was already stretching outside its old Roman walls; in the 1150s, the city commune built a new wall circuit, which included six times the land-area of the old city, both north and south of the Arno. By then, Pisa was full of the stone and brick tower houses of the aristocracy – some of them survive today – as well as the one- and two-storeyed houses of more ordinary citizens. In 1228, a collective oath of all the city's adult males shows us that Pisa had around 25,000 inhabitants. Many of them were artisans, in well over a hundred trades, in particular bakers, shoemakers, smiths and textile workers, plus the ever-present *mercatores*, merchants of differing levels of importance.[25] This looks impressive at first sight; but the city had probably by now passed its peak. Its pattern of trades was typical of any medieval town of any size after 1100 or so, and by 1228 the city was in fact beginning to be left behind by Genoa. Its prosperity was as a commercial centre, bringing goods from one region to another, not as a manufacturing centre specialising in goods that would be sold widely by others. And the people who needed to buy goods via Pisa in particular were limited. The inland towns of Tuscany, Lucca, Siena and the rising Florence, certainly did; but Pisa did not have the advantage Genoa had, with its fast roads to Milan and the Alpine passes. Genoa a few decades later would be four times the size of Pisa, and in 1284 in a great sea battle off the mouth of the Arno, the Genoese destroyed the Pisan fleet; the city never regained its former prominence.

We can set that history against that of an equally active north European town, Ghent in Flanders, which is situated at the confluence of the rivers Scheldt and Leie near the coast – here, too, a marshy delta area in our period. Ghent was hardly settled before the seventh century, when a monastery was founded there. By the ninth century there was a river port beside the monastery, but Vikings destroyed both in 879. They were replaced slightly later by a new settlement on the other side of the Leie beneath the modern town centre, fortified by a ditch; by the mid-tenth century this was set against a castle of the count of Flanders, initially made of wood, but rebuilt in stone in the mid-eleventh century. Ghent steadily expanded in the direction of the count's castle, beside which the town's major markets were located, showing the importance of the demand of the castle-dwellers for the early development of the town. By the early twelfth century, a sizeable settlement of some eighty hectares, about half the size of Pisa's walled space in the 1150s, had developed here, from a more or less standing start in 900 or so. By the late thirteenth century, indeed, Ghent probably had over 60,000 inhabitants, far more than Pisa by then, and more than any other town in Flanders, although Bruges and Ypres, each only 50km from Ghent, had over half that. As at Pisa, some twelfth-century élite housing was already in stone, as was at least one market hall, and there were tower houses here too in some cases. Some of these houses also had substantial warehouses; they were commercial establishments. Ghent's élites were rich and autonomous, operating in a commune (*communio*) with aldermen, by 1128, and doubtless the town already had a merchant's guild – such guilds are attested, with elaborate statutes, for two nearby towns in the late eleventh century, Saint-Omer and Valenciennes, even if not yet for Ghent itself. This autonomy continued, under an oligarchy that by the thirteenth century was called the Thirty-Nine, although successive counts of Flanders could and did contest it. In the fourteenth-century wars with the count, the leaders of the Flemish cities were very often from Ghent; Jacob van Artevelde in the 1340s and his son Philip in the early 1380s were briefly in effect rulers of the whole of Flanders.[26]

Unlike in Pisa, these élites were not primarily landowners; although they bought land as time went on, their wealth was urban-based in every period. They were merchants, as in Pisa; but here the wider urban economy was quite different, for the town was a cloth-producing centre above all. Flanders developed its own wool production, directed into its towns to be made into cloth, in the eleventh century; by the 1110s at the latest, however, it was importing wool from England, and English wool was henceforth the basic source for the Flemish cloth industry until after the Black Death. In the thirteenth century, around half of Ghent's population were textile workers, a concentration only matched in Ypres and Milan and, later, Florence, although two dozen towns in Flanders and Italy (and also the Flemish countryside) had similar specialisations on a smaller scale. Ghent and its neighbours exported this cloth across most of Europe: Ypres merchants are documented in Novgorod in the 1130s. Flemish cloth, indeed, dominated even Florentine manufacturing until the thirteenth century, which was up till then focused on dying and finishing woven cloth from Ghent, Ypres and the others. Merchants from all over also came to Flanders' five cloth fairs, which had an annual sequence by 1200. Ghent thus depended for its prosperity on a Europe-wide distribution; it also depended for its food on an exchange network which stretched almost as wide, as Flanders could not supply all those towns itself. This was an élite market; Flemish cloth for export was too high-quality for mass consumption, which was still highly localised and hardly commercialised as yet. But there were enough élites across Europe to make its producers numerous and its owners rich. Class conflict followed: the largest-scale popular revolts before the Black Death, among the most effective of the whole middle ages, linked clothworkers and peasants in Flanders in 1297–1304 and 1323–28. They defeated the king of France himself in a pitched battle at Courtrai in 1302.[27]

Pisa and Ghent were very large towns which depended on an international exchange network. Most towns were however much smaller, and served much more local markets. In England, where there has been the most systematic work on this subject, there were between 500 and 600 boroughs (settlements with an urban charter) in 1300, of which only 112 are recorded in Domesday Book, implying that most were new foundations; the great majority of these had fewer than a thousand inhabitants each.[28] Such centres at best served a 25km-radius surrounding area, a day's travel there and back. One well-studied example is Stratford-upon-Avon in Warwickshire, which was a village in Domesday Book, but was given a market charter by King Richard I for its owner the bishop of Worcester in 1196, and was then laid out in uniform plots by the bishop, for standard rents.[29] Stratford survived and prospered, and indeed the bishop's plots are sometimes still visible in the layout of the modern town (one is the modern Shakespeare Hotel). By the 1250s, it had some 1000-plus inhabitants, so the town had grown fast by English standards; the families were almost all from places inside the same 25km radius. The town had a coherence by now, which was emphasised by the appearance in the 1260s of a local religious fraternity to which even some poorer Stratfordians belonged, plus incoming traders. The town's inhabitants were largely artisans, in leather, cloth, metal, wood, and food preparation: that is to say in the standard trades in any medieval town, without any particular specialisation. This is however important. Stratford was well located. It lay between two well-defined economic areas, the rich arable land of the Avon valley plus the rolling Felden plain to its south, set against the Arden woodlands to its north with a more pastoral economy; it was also on a Roman road which ran over the Avon bridge, west to the salt-producing centre of Droitwich. It was thus a good centre for regional exchange across south Warwickshire, and its market allowed people to come from each of these directions to buy and sell goods. But its artisans point at something else: the beginning of a small-town-based productive network with a potentially peasant market, the 10,000 or so people in its immediate hinter-land. For who else would go to Stratford? The local rich, bishops, earls or gentry, would go (or send) to the nearest really big towns, Coventry or Bristol, two of the five largest in England, and neither of them so very far away. The appearance of artisans here – and in very many other small towns, which in this respect are the most significant markers of the process – is thus a sign of the next major shift in the exchange economy: the beginnings of urban produc-tion for the mass of the population, and not only for élites, and, conversely, the beginning of the habit by peasants to buy their cloth (cloth being the most important of all these products) and not make it for themselves. Although, as I said at the start of this chapter, we have as yet only the beginnings of an under-standing of how far that commercialisation process had reached in the rural economy as a whole, the success of a small town like Stratford does lie at those beginnings.[30]

Thus towns operated at two different economic and geographical levels. One was the simple exchange between rural and urban. Town-dwellers for the most part did not grow their own food; they made and sold things, and got the coin to buy food from the countryside from that. Sometimes, when towns were large and/or dense, that exchange went very far into the countryside; London's demand affected markets as far out as Dover, Oxford and even Peterborough; and Sicily from 1200 or so onwards became a bread basket for half the great central-northern Italian cities.[31] But essentially this was a local exchange process.

The other level was the long-distance trade which connected Flanders to Italy, and both of them to far further afield. This became very elaborate. There had long been two major maritime networks around the edge of Europe, the Mediterranean and the North Sea. They had different ups and downs (in the early middle ages, the low point for the North Sea was the sixth century, in the Mediterranean the eighth[32]), but both were expanding in the scale and density of shipping by the eleventh. There were by now important entrepôts in Constantinople, Alexandria (and Cairo further inland), Palermo, Almería and Venice for the Mediterranean; London, Bruges, plus inland Rhine ports such as Cologne for the North Sea. Venice, joined by Genoa and (more briefly) Pisa, later developed whole commercial and colonial empires in the eastern Mediterranean, in the wake of the Crusades. The routes by now expanded outwards, too, notably across the Baltic, hopping from port to port in what is now Germany and Poland – the towns which would in the fourteenth century league together as the Hanse – and then going along the great Russian rivers via Novgorod and Kiev to Constantinople again. And the rapid urbanisation of Flanders and northern Italy encouraged a network of more direct land routes too, even, remarkably, across the Alps. By the twelfth century, Italian and Flemish merchants met roughly halfway, in Champagne, where a series of six great annual fairs, set up entrepreneurially by the local counts, became in the thirteenth century an additional entrepôt on a European scale.[33]

Products from both Europe and beyond were exchanged in the Champagne fairs and elsewhere along these routes: silks from Byzantium and Syria; linen and sugar from Egypt; pepper and other spices from across the Indian ocean; the best woollen cloth from Flanders and Italy; arms from Milan; furs from Rus'. As exchange systems became ever more complex, long-distance credit agreements, made in Champagne and elsewhere, developed into organised banking, in which the Tuscan towns, Lucca and Florence at the forefront, became specialists. By the end of the thirteenth century, the greatest banks became so large that they were themselves international-level middlemen (the Bardi and Peruzzi banks of Florence ran much of England's wool export to Flanders) and by now lent not only to merchants but to kings, who needed instant money for wars and were prepared to pay high interest in return. As in 2008, that ambition did not end well for many, for kings, when they defaulted, did so on such a scale that whole banks collapsed: Edward I of England destroyed the Riccardi bank of Lucca in this way when he confiscated their assets in 1294 (they went under in the next decade); the Frescobaldi of Florence fell when Edward II ran into trouble in 1311; and the Bardi and Peruzzi, by now overextended, in part with loans to Edward III, fell in their turn in 1343–46.[34] But by now it was possible for families to gain great wealth, and successful career paths over several generations, and major social and political prominence in their home towns (Giotto painted the Bardi and Peruzzi family chapels in Santa Croce in Florence), simply out of the financial and commercial market, that is to say mercantile capitalism – something which had never been possible in European history before, even under the Roman empire.

   This pattern of development, especially when painted in romantic colours as it often is, has seemed so compelling to historians that it sometimes looks like 'the' medieval economic development par excellence, the proof that, if something had not gone wrong (perhaps the Black Death, perhaps the restrictive policies of medieval guilds, perhaps, although less likely, the Hundred Years' War, or the early fifteenth-century silver famine), medieval Europe might have achieved the industrial capitalist breakthrough centuries earlier than it did. In fact, however, European international exchange was not the most important part of the economic boom at all. For a start, Europe was not at the centre, but rather on the edge, of this exchange network; it stretched eastwards from there through Egypt to the Indian Ocean, extending as far as China, where, in the thirteenth century, the Yangzi valley was the most economically complex region in the world. As far as Mediterranean trade was concerned, its real powerhouse until at least the fourteenth century was Egypt, focused on Cairo, which was (after Constantinople's post-1204 decline, for which see Chapter 9) the Mediterranean's largest city, double the size of Paris and Milan. Egypt also had specialist cloth-making factory towns like Tinnis and Damietta; its production of linen, as also sugar, was industrial in scale.[35] The banking sophistication of Italian cities in the thirteenth century was largely borrowed from the merchant entrepreneurs of Cairo and Alexandria. Many of these were Jewish, which helps us to know about them, for a huge cache of medieval Jewish documents, the *geniza*, survives from Cairo, and these tell us a substantial amount about the complex commercial and financial practices of merchants in the Islamic world from the eleventh century to the thirteenth. (In Europe, by contrast, Jews were restricted to rather smaller-scale and more socially unpopular moneylending than the Italian bankers managed.)[36] Genoa and Venice, in particular, largely depended on Egypt for their success as middlemen, and, although the Flemish and inland Italian cloth towns did not, Egypt outmatched them for a long time.

Secondly, the international commercial system, for all its glamour, was less significant in overall economic terms than the first level of the urban economy, the small-scale exchange of primary products and low-quality cloth and iron-work between towns and the countryside. The international system was above all a luxury system, focused on expensive items which would be sold to kings, aristocrats, senior clergy, urban patricians, and their clientèles. Banking went further than that, for it financed wars, and thus the distinctly less luxurious aspects of military logistics, but the arena remained that of high politics. Only the need for consistent food and fuel supplies in every great town, for élites and workers alike, plus that for raw materials such as wool, linked this international network to the peasant majority. (Peasant sales did not always dominate this supply, too: in much of Italy, lords moved away from money rents in the twelfth and thirteenth centuries, for they realised what profits could be made from their own sales of grain and wine to towns.)[37] It was small towns and small-scale exchange that, very slowly and haltingly, introduced lower-cost manufac-tured products to a mass market, which would have been – and, eventually, was – a far more secure basis for the sort of industrialisation which took place 500 years later. We shall look again at the way the countryside became more commercialised at the end of the middle ages, in Chapter 11; even then, no part of Europe was on any sort of path to industrial transformation. But that path, when it began in the end, would be waymarked with low-value products for rural buyers, not the argosies full of silk and spices which docked at Venice.

One commercial development of the twelfth and thirteenth centuries which was genuinely important, however, and which indeed linked the rural and urban parts of this chapter in lasting ways, was the tendency towards agricul-tural specialisms. As we saw earlier, one way peasants can cope with the pres-sure on land is to grow the crops which flourish best on that sort of land and to specialise in them, selling them outwards in return for crops which grow better on land elsewhere. They will probably not do this completely – rural commu-nities living entirely on cash cropping, and thus buying, rather than producing, most of their food, were rare before the twentieth century. But we can track such specialisations, first at the local level and then more widely. In Italy, for example, already by the eleventh century we find that hillsides were often much more clearly specialising in vineyards than in previous centuries, and that the plains grew more grain; clearly, that sort of difference assumed exchange between the two. In England, the same happened between pastoral and agricultural areas, as there were each side of Stratford.

Slowly, however, entire regions began to specialise for export too. Grain could be grown almost everywhere, but rich areas which were close to rivers and the sea could export to grain-poor regions, as Sicily, as we have seen, did to the hyper-urbanised parts of north-central Italy; Polish grain would have a similar role by the end of the middle ages for much of northern Europe. Wine-producers in France started off by specialising at the northern margin of vine cultivation, regions such as the Paris basin and Champagne, which were closest to those where wine could not be grown, but whose élites might want to drink it. But actually the vineyards on that margin were less productive and produced poorer wine than those further south (the famous and expensive bubbly Champagne did not develop until the eighteenth and nineteenth centuries); once transport infrastructures improved, large-scale production for export switched to Bordeaux and Burgundy, where the most lasting specialised viticulture developed. Wool production became intensive and export-led in England by the twelfth century; in central Spain and southern Italy, similar developments came later, in the thirteenth and fourteenth. Timber became a specialised production too, in the great woodlands that survived clearance and were close enough to convenient water courses, like the Black Forest beside the Rhine in Germany and the limitless coastal forests of southern Norway. Even dried fish became such a commodity; northern Norway's very existence as a settled area largely depended on being able to sell stockfish via Bergen to England and further south still.[38] These interlinkages, once established, survived. A product of the need to rationalise agriculture in a period of rising population and urban demand, they continued to provide exchange outlets even when the population dropped rapidly, in town and countryside, in the late fourteenth century. Indeed, those population drops fuelled a further move to pasture, that is to say to wool production, in many places in Europe, which would continue to be the basis for cheap woollen cloth in future centuries.

All the changes described in this chapter came on the back of a rising population. As I have implied several times, this would come to an abrupt halt when the Black Death hit Europe in and after 1347–52. What happened then we will look at in Chapter 11. But it is not quite the case that Europe was expanding its economy in all respects, right up to the eve of the great plague. Peasant populations can only do so much to cope with long-term population rises, without radical new technologies and cultivation methods. Those available to thirteenth-century peasants reached full capacity by the end of the century, and, from then on, as population grew, famines begin to be attested more and more in our sources. Previously, in years of bad harvests, rural communities could just about survive, but now, at the limits of demographic growth, this might not happen any longer. In 1315–17, often extending later, hard winters and wet summers exhausted the resources of the whole of northern Europe, and even the interconnected relationships we have seen developing were not enough to avert famine, after the first year at least. Grain and wine yields dropped dramatically, sheep epidemics reduced the wool supply to Flanders, even salt production suffered.[39] The death toll, although hard to calculate exactly, was great; and famines on a smaller scale studded the next decades too, including in Italy by now. It was here that demographic expansion came to a halt, and peasant populations had to face how to limit births more radically than they had managed before. This can be seen in very catastrophist terms, and indeed used to be, when the whole of the late middle ages was seen as a period of depression and crisis. Interpretations are more nuanced now, and the post-Black Death period can be seen as one of increasingly capillary commercialisation. This interpretation is by now often extended to the period 1300–50 as well, with a steadily rising curve of economic integration proposed.[40] But it would be hard not to say that the decades just before 1350 were tough for Europe's peasants, at least in regions where there was little room by now to expand, Italy, northern France, the Low Countries, much of England. For them, however brutal it is to say it, the plague brought some relief. But we shall look at this in greater detail later.

*   *   *

What, finally, did the long boom bring to Europe's social and political frameworks which was not available before? A sense of movement, for sure. It had never been impossible to get about in Europe; but with Flemings in England, Italians in Flanders, the French in Italy, for trading purposes, but also increasingly, on the back of trade routes, for education or political career paths, links were created which could be complex – even if they were never fast, for it was no quicker to get from England to Italy in 1300 and indeed in 1500 than it had been in 800. Social mobility was also on the rise; urban expansion achieved this on its own, for life in towns was very unlike that in villages, and a small percentage of the lucky could prosper in this new world – even if it was mostly rural élites who made it in the urban environment, and not the poorest of all. Inside villages, too, economic opportunities meant that richer peasants prospered more than their poorer neighbours, whom they sometimes, by now, employed as part-time wage labourers: social mobility thus also increased social differentiation. Expertise was more accessible; with the new craft foci developing in Europe's towns, it was easier than it had been before to get state-of-the-art knowledge if one had enough money. The multilingual cathedral construction sites of Europe, together with the steady spread of expertise in the new Gothic building techniques from northern France to England, Germany, southern Spain, Italy, Bohemia, were a sign of this everywhere in the thirteenth century.[41] For rulers, the wider availability of money, and the general (if harder to pin down) extension of prosperity at all levels, gave opportunities for taxation, which was already important for John in England and Philip II in France in the 1200s, but which their late-thirteenth-century successors, Edward I and Philip IV, took even fuller advantage of, as we shall see in the next chapter. That in itself allowed them to create more ambitious state structures, which had their own effects on social mobility (new strata of officials, in particular, with their own training and expertise) and social constraints. It also allowed them to fight bigger wars, which introduced an element of adventurism into fourteenth-century European politics that had not been seen to such an extent before; the greater social and political flexibility created by the long boom was not all positive, that is to say. Overall, however, even if one is not romantic about the centuries of expansion, one can at least see that they had major effects on European practices, at every social level. When set against the effects of the localisation of politics described in the last chapter, they underpinned most of the developments analysed in the rest of this book.

CHAPTER EIGHT

The ambiguities of political reconstruction, 1150–1300

When in 1093 King William II of England appointed a new archbishop of Canterbury, Anselm of Bec, he invested him as archbishop with the staff of office, as kings had traditionally done. Anselm soon fell out with William and left the country, arriving in Rome in 1098. Here, however, he discovered that, as we saw earlier, popes had been condemning lay investiture since 1078; so, when he returned to England after William's death in 1100, he duly informed the new king Henry I that such rituals were invalid. This caused renewed trouble, and peace was made between king and archbishop only in 1107. Anselm was not much given to compromise – hence the trouble – but he was no provincial: he was Italian, he had been abbot of a major Norman monastery, and he was an innovative and respected theologian. That someone as connected as Anselm could have been unaware of one of the major elements of the conflict between popes and emperor tells us something about the lack of density in political communication in the years around 1100.[1]

Contrast the Fourth Lateran Council, held in Rome a century later, in November 1215. This, the largest of medieval church councils, was called by Pope Innocent III in April 1213, and was attended by a huge number of bishops and abbots, over twelve hundred senior clerics from all Europe and even the east. The canons (decrees) of the council covered every angle of church practice as it had by then developed, including elections, the running of church courts, excommunication, judicial ordeal (the council prohibited it), heresy, attitudes to Jews, crusading, and – not least – the development of pastoral care and preaching. Subsequently, they were made available across the whole of Latin Europe, systematically, through the dissemination of the text of the council, and the expectation (partly realised) that bishops would instruct their own parish clergy about it. If these decrees did not result in instant 'reform' in most places, as historians point out, that is hardly surprising, although in the longer term many of them did have an effect. Nor were they wholly new, although they were newly ambitious in their aim for uniformity. But more important is that they became a new basis for current practice everywhere.[2] This difference marks more than one change. First, it shows how much more powerful popes were in 1215 than they had been in 1100, as is simply shown by Innocent's capacity to get everyone to come to Rome, and to take home the decrees of a council which were above all papal in inspiration. But it also shows how much communications had developed. Innocent could by now get all these people together, using networks of messengers riding along all the roads of Europe – and not all roads were good, as for example in Germany or Poland, not to speak of having to travel across the sea to Ireland, Scotland, England or Scandinavia, all of which sent prelates. People were indeed ready to come, and this too shows that the density of political contact had increased substantially. Power, communications and the use of texts were thus all changing in this period, and would continue to do so across the rest of the thirteenth century. What some of the implications of this are will be the theme of this chapter.

The twelfth and thirteenth centuries saw political systems become larger-scale and/or more powerful almost everywhere in Latin Europe, after the contraction in scale which we looked at for the eleventh century in Chapter 6. Not in Poland or Sweden, as we also saw earlier; after the 1240s, famously not in Germany, as we shall see; but more or less everywhere else. We shall begin by rapidly running through how this worked in, in turn, France, England, Castile, Hungary, Italy, the western church, and finally Germany, to get a sense of the different but often convergent ways it happened. But the core arguments of the chapter will focus on the implications this process had for communication and control. A greater use of writing, the growth of concepts of accountability, the growing complexity of law, and a slow increase in ideas of problem-solving were all important developments in this period, and all had an effect on how political practices worked. These developments link as well to the concurrent development of a much more complex environment of intellectual enquiry, and to new forms of local religious practice, which were challenging to the growing centralisation of ecclesiastical legitimacy. How such a complicated mix worked, and could be controlled, was at the centre of the problems of power in this period; we shall look at each of these aspects in turn.

France once again provides a textbook example, this time of political unification. We saw in Chapter 1 how Louis VII (1137–80) could use his residual powers as judge and lord, turning back even Henry II of England at Toulouse in 1159, but this did not change the fact that the territory under his direct control hardly extended beyond the Paris basin, and that the lands of the English king covered nearly half the area of the kingdom of France. His son Philip II Augustus (1180–1223) moved on from there, however, to considerable effect. As we have also seen, the Paris basin was rich, and Philip could take considerable resources from it, so he was strategically in a stronger position than might appear. Henry II's son John made a set of tactical missteps in 1201–02 over an apparently small issue: he married Isabella of Angoulême, the fiancée of one of his French counts, another Hugh of Lusignan, and then refused to come to Paris when Hugh appealed to Philip as John's own lord for his French lands. In response, however, Philip took the remarkable step of declaring John's lands forfeit and invading them. John lost the war of 1202–04 and most of his French lands; he only kept his southern Aquitainian (Gascon) territories around Bordeaux, which remained under English control for another 250 years. Philip nearly doubled his resources and quadrupled the area he ruled directly, and from that basis royal power moved ever further afield. The Albigensian Crusade of 1208–29 (discussed later in this chapter), although initially undertaken by armies not under his control, increasingly came under the generalship of his son Louis VIII, and eventually resulted in the extension of effective royal power as far as the Mediterranean coast.

This political network held together, including in the uncertain years of the minority of Philip's grandson Louis IX (1226–70) in the 1220s and 1230s, and in the equally uncertain years when Louis IX went on crusade, to Egypt and Tunisia (in each case with total lack of success). This was largely because in most of the steadily extending lands of the royal domain the kings did not hand back local power to hereditary counts or dukes, but instead sent lesser-ranking and temporary officials, called seneschals or *baillis*, who were paid salaries by the 1220s, to run each territory for the king. In the reign of Philip IV (1285– 1314), royal authority was solid in most of the kingdom, with by now rather fewer great lordships left, above all Flanders, Burgundy, Brittany, and of course English Gascony – large, autonomous and for the most part rich, it is true, but next door to royal lands which were ever more tightly governed. The network of officials Philip had during his reign is well documented, and was dense and loyal – we can follow the careers of some of them, as we shall see. Philip had the clout to pull off some remarkable coups, including the coordinated destruction of the military order of the Templars, and the seizure of its lands, through show trials in 1307–14; as well as the sending of a small force into Italy to arrest Pope Boniface VIII in Anagni, east of Rome, in 1303, after the pope had denounced him and claimed authority over him. By now the king of France was the strongest power in Europe, only a century after the fall of John.[3]

France was unusual in moving so fast from fragmentation to autocracy; most other polities had rather more to work with. But they show parallel developments all the same. We saw in Chapter 6 that England was almost alone in western Europe in avoiding the localisation of political power in the eleventh century. The cohesion of the kingdom remained second to none in the next centuries too. When John (1199–1216), an able administrator but a terrible politician in almost all fields, failed to reconquer his French lands, this did not result in the weakening of central power, but, instead, in the uprising of half of his aristocracy in 1215 and the imposition of a comprehensive charter of liberties, Magna Carta: this laid out royal obligations to his people (above all his aristocracy) in the framework of a more just, but still complex, government. Magna Carta did not hold in 1215 (it was, among other things, condemned at the Lateran Council), but its reissues during the minority of John's son Henry III (1216–72) did. The point about England is that leading aristocrats, far from seeking to establish autonomous local powers, felt that the government of the country was as much their right and responsibility as the king's. This sense of a collective oligarchy went back to the unification of England in the tenth century, and had survived both the total change in personnel after the Norman Conquest and the periods of untrammelled power of forceful twelfth-century kings like Henry I and Henry II – who had, indeed, reinforced the trend against autonomous powers by ensuring that local authority was largely in the hands of temporary royal officials, here sheriffs and travelling judges ('justices in eyre'), much as in France later.

English government continued to develop in sophistication in the thirteenth century, but the transactional power of the aristocracy increased too. This was in particular because renewed tax-collecting by kings came to be seen as dependent on the assent of royal assemblies of barons and knights (and, by the end of the century, representatives of towns), which by the 1230s were called parliaments. Under Henry III, this culminated at the Oxford parliament of 1258 in the attempted takeover of royal authority itself by leading barons, led by the earl of Leicester, Simon de Montfort, who sought to bypass the royal control of government and to set up local commissioners to investigate administrative abuses at all levels. They failed (civil war ensued, and the barons were defeated in 1265), but the momentum of governmental rethinking continued. Edward I (1272–1307) incorporated it into his own political practice, with a run of far-reaching statutes in the 1270s and 1280s which lay, together with Magna Carta, at the back of English common law as it subsequently developed. Edward was also a conqueror, putting Wales permanently under English rule and English governmental structures in the 1280s, and in the later 1290s absorbing Scotland temporarily into his kingdom too. (Ireland was already partially under English control, although society was very different indeed there: see Chapter 5.) War however was expensive, and taxation essential. In 1297, with war in France as well and taxation rising, the baronial leadership of parliament forced Edward to agree to measures to restrict arbitrary tax demands. If aristocratic collectivities could defy even Edward I, they could certainly do so with weaker kings, and did so from here on. The dialogue between kings and parliamentary assemblies, not least over tax, marked the political particularity of England ever after, as we will see in later chapters.[4]

Castile had a different starting point. None of the tiny kingdoms of northern Spain in the early eleventh century had a very developed infrastructure, even the largest of them, León, which became the kingdom of León–Castile when Ferdinand I (1035–65), ruler of the newly established kingdom of Castile, took over his larger neighbour in 1037–38. This was however the generation in which al-Andalus broke up into successor kingdoms, the Taifas; by Ferdinand's death he and his Christian neighbours were taking substantial protection money from them, and became rich. In 1085, as we saw in Chapter 3, his son Alfonso VI (1065–1109) conquered one of the main Taifa kingdoms, Toledo, the old Visigothic capital and the key to central Spain; he and some of his successors took the title of emperor. So began, according to an older historiography, the *reconquista* of Muslim Spain. The reality was far from that, for the Muslims regrouped after 1086 under a new Moroccan dynasty, the Almoravids; inconclusive wars with them and equally inconclusive wars between and inside the Christian kingdoms marked the next century and more. The fact was that few people in Christian Spain saw Muslim conquest as their main aim, even if a succession of popes, and also French volunteers, introduced crusading imagery into at least some Christian–Muslim wars in the peninsula. More important to Alfonso VI's successors was the prevention of the break-up of Castile itself. Attempts to unite with Aragón failed, and Portugal spun off between 1109 and 1140 to become a separate kingdom, its identity legitimated by the conquest of Lisbon in 1147 with the help of passing northern knights on their way to the Second Crusade. León temporarily became a separate kingdom again in 1157 too; if we add tiny Navarre, there were by now five kings in Christian Spain. But Castile never disintegrated into the counties and castellanies of France; the permanent war on frontiers, both Christian and Muslim, helped the kingdom to stay solid, and the aristocracy remained focused on the Castilian court, ready to receive rewards in the form of land and rights of local government in a very Carolingian way (they were sometimes even called the same, *honores*). When these *honores* or *tenencias* began, as elsewhere, to be undermined by castle-based private lordships, plus the powerful towns of the frontier region, the kingdom skipped two centuries of trans-Pyrenean history: its kings henceforth developed local government and justice based, as in France and England, on more temporary officials, here often called *merinos*.[5]

It was this system that was extended to the south when Alfonso VIII of Castile did make a breakthrough against the Muslims, at the battle of Las Navas de Tolosa in 1212, and then when Ferdinand III (1217–52) occupied nearly the whole of al-Andalus in the next generation – only the *amirs* of Granada remained independent. The kings of Castile thereafter dominated thirteenth-century Spain. The huge patronage available after these conquests, backed up by more substantial taxation from the start of the thirteenth century, kept the kings at the centre of attention of every ambitious local power in Spain for over a century. Even the flawed politics of the intellectual and lawgiver Alfonso X (1252–84) did not shift that; what Alfonso tried to do, among other things, was to undermine the local laws which underlay private lordships, and the successful resistance of his aristocrats in the 1270s and later marked the (temporary) failure of an aggressive, not a defensive, kingship.[6]

Hungary was another kingdom whose history was converging with those of its neighbours. It had settled down considerably after its origins as a raiding nomadic power in the tenth century. Stephen I (997–1038) had adopted Christianity, and it was also he who began to borrow infrastucture from the Frankish world – not only bishoprics, but counties – to turn his dynastic hegemony over an ex-nomad ruling class into something more organised. Still more than in England, the king managed to establish himself as the over-whelmingly dominant landowner, which made his patronage crucial for all local powers. There was still the risk that counts would appropriate that land (and they did), but the king kept the strategic edge, despite frequent wars of succession. Twelfth-century kings fought aggressive external wars, in Croatia and Russia, and that momentum, plus the wealth from silver mines, allowed Béla III (1172–96) to reorganise government, borrowing from German and probably Byzantine examples; a chance surviving document shows him with very considerable wealth by twelfth-century standards, probably greater than that of the kings of England or France, from land, silver, and tolls on exchange. It is true that Andrew II (1205–35) chose a different political path, ceding substantial lands to favoured aristocrats; a failed crusade and revolts against his landed policies forced him to agree the Golden Bull of 1222, which protected (as in England, but still more so), the rights of different strata of the aristocracy from the king. His son Béla IV (1235–70) tried to reverse this, but the Mongol invasion of 1241–42, which nearly destroyed the kingdom until the attackers withdrew, showed all Hungarians that defence in depth was crucial, and the resultant new system of castles was above all aristocrat-controlled. All the same, residual royal power remained strong, and, as we shall see in Chapter 11, could be turned around again after 1300. The Hungarian state was less organised internally than England or even Castile, even if often rich; but the increasing explicitness of the balance between royal power and collective action by aristocrats links the last three kingdoms we have looked at.[7]

Italy also showed the sharpening of political power. It did so on the largest scale in the south, where Roger II of Sicily (1105–54) unified all the Norman principalities in wars between 1127 and 1144, and was recognised as king by Pope Anacletus II in 1130. The Norman kingdom was tightly governed from then on for the most part, with a rich capital at Palermo and an elaborate Greek–Arab–Latin administration, linked to the provinces by royal-appointed justiciars. This structure survived conquest by the German emperor Henry VI in 1194 and the long minority of his infant son Frederick II (1197–1250). The adult Frederick would indeed be among the most centralising of rulers in his Sicilian and south Italian kingdom; his Roman-influenced legislation, his relatively heavy taxation and his careful undermining of the private lordships of his aristocrats all mark it, and, unlike some of the more ambitious thirteenth-century kings elsewhere, he did so with very little resistance. This continued even when the kingdom was conquered again, this time by Louis IX's brother Charles of Anjou, in 1266.[8]

The situation in northern and central Italy was very different, but there were parallels here too. Here the fifty-plus city communes gained coherence in their governing structures from the early twelfth century onwards, under the rule in nearly every case of consuls, as we saw in Chapter 6; this was just in time to confront the attempt by the German emperor Frederick I Barbarossa (1152–90), the most successful emperor of the Staufen family, to re-establish his power in the north, between 1158 and 1177. Frederick's claims to imperial authority were based by now on Roman law, and they were not at all implausible, as city leaders knew; but they were tougher in practice than the communes could tolerate, and, one by one, the cities revolted and grouped themselves against him, and he was decisively defeated at Legnano in 1176. The Italian cities had to face several attempts to take them over across the next centuries (not least by Frederick II after 1235), but fought them all off, up to 1500. Communal government, then, meant the opposite of the steadily extending powers of a king of France or Castile or Sicily. Furthermore, it was not even stable; rule by consular collectives did not manage to overcome the tendency for each city's substantial military élite to divide into factions and fight internally. The next centuries show the cities developing a continuous series of new institutional measures to overcome this: first, from 1190 or so, salaried annual *podestà*, who were from outside the city so neutral between rivals, supposedly; then, after 1250 or so, *capitani del popolo*, who represented the cities' lesser élites, less prone to faction-alising than the magnates, supposedly; then, increasingly after 1300 (all these dates are very variable), *signori*, autocrats who soon became hereditary. This might not seem very impressive as Europe's main alternative to monarchical rule, and some still hankered after that (one example was Dante Alighieri, as we shall see in Chapter 12). But nonetheless, throughout all these changes, city governments steadily gained in coherence, with ever-more-developed judicial and fiscal systems (some became more elaborate than those anywhere else in Latin Europe), and ever-clearer structures of control over their territories. Even the fragmented pattern of north Italian urban power, then, matched most of the developments of the most successful kingdoms of the thirteenth century.[9]

The popes were also based in Italy, but they had powers extending over all the clergy of Latin Europe, taking advantage of the clerical autonomy from lay authority which was increasingly recognised by the early twelfth century. We saw in Chapter 6 that early-twelfth-century popes did not by any means have an unchallenged hegemony over church affairs. Each kingdom had potentially different practices, and its bishops would not necessarily appreciate or even recognise papal direction; local charismatic leaders like Bernard of Clairvaux could well have more force than distant Rome. What changed this was legal procedure. Early medieval legal systems were complex, but it was rare for appeals, whether lay or clerical, to go beyond the judicial tribunals of single kingdoms. In the twelfth century, however, it became more and more normal for clerics throughout Europe to petition the pope to resolve their disputes – and the laity too, in areas, such as marriage disputes, which the church was by now making part of canon law. This appeals system developed rapidly under Innocent II (1130–43), and still more so later in the century. It was not a full centralisation process, for most church government and dispute-settlement remained the task of bishops, and was dealt with inside dioceses. Dioceses, often still divergently organised into the thirteenth century and beyond, thus represented a cellular ecclesiastical structure, which closely paralleled the patterns of secular power. But canon law slowly became more standardised across Europe, and the possibility of appeal linked diocesan politics more and more to that of Rome. There was a dialectic here: the cases soon overwhelmed the papal Curia, and already under Innocent II it became normal to delegate justice back down again to local bishops and abbots; but their decisions could be – and were – appealed back to the Curia again, often over and over. This legal system made large amounts of money for the papal administration (the Curia was very expensive in bribes), and a substantial bureaucracy could be paid on the back of it, which was then available for more focused efforts to deal with local issues. The capillary network of papal intervention in local affairs thus became steadily stronger, right up to the late fourteenth century. In strategic terms, the papacy in the later twelfth century was not yet well situated, for trouble with Frederick Barbarossa and with the city of Rome itself, which had revolted against the pope in 1143 and established a city commune independent of him, meant that the popes were usually travelling. But in 1188 Clement III made peace with the city and returned, and fifty years of popes from Rome's own élites followed, who could use the international judicial network of their predecessors ever more stably and forcefully, as the impact of the Fourth Lateran Council showed.[10]

Innocent III (1198–1216) was the most charismatic of these Roman popes. He certainly equalled the kings of Europe in his capacity for targeted political action: against John of England for his support of the wrong archbishop of Canterbury; against Philip II of France for his marriage problems; against each of two rival kings of Germany in turn. Innocent and his thirteenth-century successors, up to Boniface VIII (1294–1303), were major players in Europe, with intermittent claims to authority over every secular power. Appeals to Rome, still the basis of this power, were ever more regularised and bureaucratised; the right of popes to choose bishops throughout Europe, and thus to have more (if still incomplete) control over dioceses, was becoming well developed too. We have seen that claims that were too uncompromising brought Boniface himself down, but his rhetoric was matched by several of his predecessors, and indeed his successors. Intercutting with the growing power of kings, that is to say, and often in competition with them, was Europe's first major international power, with an infrastructure by now as coherent as that of any kingdom, and, importantly, an authority which was for the most part not lessened because it was not backed up by battalions: communications, legal precedent, bureaucratic machinery, could do it without arms. We shall come back to this.[11]

So why, then, did this move to more clearly characterised and more centralised power not happen in Germany? For it is certainly the case that the revived power of Frederick Barbarossa, who could intervene throughout Germany, including in 1180 bringing down his greatest aristocrat, Henry 'the Lion', duke of both Bavaria and Saxony, did not outlast the early death of Barbarossa's son Henry VI in 1197. Frederick II was a child in Sicily, and succession was disputed between Henry VI's brother Philip and Henry the Lion's son Otto IV.

Innocent III in the end, in 1211, set Frederick, already king of Sicily, up against the survivor, Otto, and Frederick did indeed succeed in establishing his rule in the 1210s, but the cohesion of the kingdom had gone. After that, Frederick was seldom in Germany, and a series of formal privileges to the German princes in 1213 (under Otto), 1220 and 1231 gave them the same sorts of powers that the Golden Bull did in Hungary, with the difference that the king-emperor was mostly not physically present. When Frederick fell out definitively with the pope of the period, Innocent IV, in 1245, civil war followed, and after the death of Frederick in 1250 and his son Conrad IV in 1254, there was a power vacuum in Germany, with no widely accepted ruler until 1273. The king-emperors of the end of the century and the centuries following, from new families, the Habsburgs of (eventually) Austria, the Luxemburgs of (eventually) Bohemia, the Wittelsbachs of Bavaria, had no pretensions to direct rule over the German lands as a whole, and nor did any successor before 1866.[12]

All the same, to ask why Germany failed to develop as an effective polity is to ask the wrong question.[13] It is not a question we ask when we look at northern Italy, where a parallel process had already taken place. The fact is that the sharpening of political power indeed occurred, but at a different level from that of the kingdom: in the duchies, counties, smaller lordships, bishoprics, and autonomous cities (as in Italy, there were many of these) stretching across the wide lands from the Baltic Sea to the Alps, and from Antwerp to Prague and Vienna, on the basis of the increasingly coherent localised power structures which we saw developing in Chapter 6. This was already the case in Barbarossa's time; he established his own direct rule in his upper Rhine power-base above all, with law-giving in 'land-peaces' (the image was borrowed from the Peace of God) and a tight network of dependent *ministeriales*, but intervened in the German principalities above all from the outside – some of them had been 'far from the king', in Peter Moraw's phrase, for two centuries before 1273, if not more, for no king-emperor had ever ruled all Germany in equal depth.[14] When Barbarossa brought down Henry the Lion, for example, he nonetheless recognised Henry's family land as still his, and this was enough to be the basis of a lasting principality in the north around Braunschweig (Brunswick) and Lüneburg – which, although divided between heirs at different times, still remained in the hands of Henry's descendant George of Hanover when he became George I of Great Britain in 1714. Later, after Frederick II's death, the Rhineland base of the Staufen king-emperors fragmented, often into remarkably small units in fact, but many other principalities carried on. Local rulers, whether in old territories like the duchy of Bavaria or the march of Meissen, or in newer ones based on family property like the Zähringen lands or

Braunschweig, or on ex-royal property and church advocacy as with many small *ministerialis*-based lordships, established powers of justice, control over local churches and monasteries, fiscal powers, their own land-peaces, just as kings did. They varied in their coherence, from the tightly run march of Meissen to the baggy and feud-focused duchy of Austria made emblematic by Otto Brunner, but it was here that power was crystallising, everywhere.[15] What marked Germany's particularity was less the fact that the king-emperor was weak than that, in this network of local polities, he remained recognised at all – for he was; he was always a significant point of reference in every period, respected as a distant lord by all and sometimes appealed to for neutral justice. Indeed, as we shall see later, the sense that Germans had of being part of a single cultural and, in a loose sense, political community was in some ways stronger in the late middle ages than it had been in 1200.

*   *   *

This set of sketches of political narratives shows some common themes. One is that war and justice, the core elements of medieval governance up to this period, had been added to by now, in particular by a greater attention to fiscal rights. Kings had their own lands, and, for most of the middle ages, most kings based themselves largely on the resources from them, but taxation became slowly more important. It developed in England first, with Æthelred II's Danegeld around 1000, but in the later twelfth century it was beginning to appear in polities of all kinds, from Catalonia, through Philip II's French royal heartland, to the Italian cities fighting Frederick Barbarossa.[16] As war became more expensive in the thirteenth century – for it was based increasingly on a stratum of professional soldiers who needed to be paid, more than on the levies and personal followings of the past – taxation steadily increased in importance, in order to fund it. The kings of Sicily depended on it most fully; Frederick II probably, and Charles of Anjou certainly, were the richest kings in Europe.[17] In England, although taxation dropped back in the twelfth century, it was revived on different bases in the thirteenth, precisely to help pay for war. Crusades by now needed taxes, as Louis IX found, and from 1294 onwards the taxation of the French clergy to help finance a war with England was one of the underpinnings of the trouble between Philip IV and Boniface VIII.[18] This taxation was by no means as heavy as it had been under the Roman empire, and still was in Byzantium and the Islamic states: it was, and remained, inconsistently collected, including in Sicily, where, although the kingdom was fiscally precocious, the expertise of the recent Islamic past had already been lost – we will return to the point in the next chapter. It was also not until the Hundred

Years' War that taxation became a fundamental feature of English or French budgets; we will therefore look at the issue in more detail for the kingdoms of the post-1350 period in Chapter 11. But for western rulers, even outside Sicily, it was already adding to the flexibility of their resources before 1300; and, not least, both taxation and land-based revenues increasingly also allowed the funding of paid officials in large numbers, who could, as under the Roman empire, substantially increase the effectiveness of strong states, in local justice and administration above all.

This is indeed the second common theme we have seen: that nearly every polity came to rely, even for local government, on career officials, rather than on the high-status regional representatives, dukes and counts and hereditary castellans, of the past. Not all of these were salaried as yet (France, England and Italy were the pathbreakers here), but they were moved around, thus inhibiting hereditary rights, and they were anyway generally of less high status – perhaps petty aristocrats, perhaps townsmen, in Germany even technically unfree – which further inhibited their ability to establish autonomous power, as indeed rulers intended. This official stratum tended to be corrupt, as their successors have mostly been since as well (people wanted to build up the personal wealth that would match the power they were routinely wielding for others), but it also tended to be loyal, for its members had little chance of exercising power except as royal representatives; the better the job they did, the more power they might keep. And, more and more as the twelfth century moved into the thirteenth, they tended to be trained, sometimes in theology in the case of clerics, sometimes in the notarial tradition in the case of the laity, regularly in law in the case of both. Non-élite lay advisers and officials were not an invention of this period; as we saw in Chapter 4, Einhard had been one for Charlemagne, an educated and intelligent man from nowhere much in central Germany who rose socially because of that education and intelligence, and indeed, unusually, managed to avoid the snobbish hostility of traditional aristocrats in so doing. Rulers had also systematically used clerics, whether from the élite or not, as administrators, from the Merovingians onwards, partly because they were more likely to have writing skills, but also partly because they, too, were less likely to establish local family traditions of office. A standard path instead was for successful clerical courtiers to end up as bishops, as kings from Dagobert I in the seventh century, through Otto I in the tenth, to Henry I and II of England in the twelfth, would routinely ensure. But more and more, after 1150 or 1200, we can see an entire career structure for an official stratum appearing, and a group identity in some cases; these things were new. Let us look at a couple of examples of such official careers, before we see how the procedures of government itself changed, which was both a cause and a consequence of the growing professionalism of its administrators.

Walter of Merton (c. 1205–77) is an example of a clerical career in England: from a middling family in Hampshire, he gained a training in legal practice from the priory of Merton in Surrey. After King Henry III happened to come there in 1236, the year Walter seems to have become a priest, he began a career in the office of the chancellor, who was then one of the two chief ministers of the kingdom. In 1240 he was surveying royal lands in south-east England; in the 1240s he was working in Durham in the north; by 1258 he was deputising for the chancellor. In 1261–63 he became chancellor himself, in the middle of the baronial revolt, and then again in 1272–74, for Edward I. Like plenty of his predecessors, he became a bishop in the end (of Rochester, 1274–77), but that was when he was nearly seventy, and it was by now a retirement perk rather than the culmination of a career. He did well out of that career. From the 1240s onwards, he accumulated more and more lands by careful and well-documented dealing, and by the 1260s was very prosperous indeed; he used his lands to found Merton college in Oxford in 1264, as a training ground for the next generation of clerks, not least his numerous nephews.[19]

For a lay career, a good example is Guillaume de Nogaret (c. 1260–1313): born in the countryside east of Toulouse, again from a non-élite family, he became a Roman lawyer, and by 1287 he was a member of the law faculty at the university of Montpellier in the far south of France. This brought him to royal attention, and in 1293 he was dealing locally for Philip IV and was appointed a royal judge at Beaucaire on the edge of Provence. So far, this was a normal career of local preferment, but it was accelerated abruptly when in 1295 he joined the royal court in Paris. Between then and his death, he was never far from the king's interest: he was a royal commissioner in Champagne, a member of the (largely judicial) *parlement* of Paris and the king's council, and then, in 1307–13, keeper of the seals, France's rough equivalent to the English chancellor. Guillaume was a hyper-loyalist, involved in Philip's most questionable actions: it was he who arrested Boniface VIII in 1303 (in a notably audacious operation, and one which earned him the enmity of the next popes as well – he was not absolved until 1311), and he also set up the expulsion of the Jews from France in 1306, and the show trials of the Templars after 1307. He did well out of it, too, as Walter of Merton did; not excessively (he was feared and hated, but never accused of systematic theft), but all the same he ended up locally powerful between Montpellier and Beaucaire, whether by using Philip's substantial cash gifts or though direct royal grants. This early version of Thomas Cromwell depended for his remarkable career not just on royal patronage and his own political skill, but also on an extensive training in Roman law, for it was this which gave him the expertise necessary to deal as he did.[20]

Royal (and, in Italy, urban) government increasingly needed expertise, simply because it was getting more complicated. We can most usefully explore that complexity through discussions of writing, accountability, law and problem-solving, and we shall look at each of them. In England, the pioneer here since at least the time of Domesday Book, the numbers of written documents increased rapidly across the late twelfth and thirteenth centuries, including still-surviving serial records of government finances on long parchment rolls, beginning in the 1130s and extending to judicial and administrative acts by the 1200s. That might be a sign of obsession rather than complexity, for there is little sign that these rolls were regularly consulted; but Michael Clanchy's much-cited calculation that the amount of sealing wax used in the English chancery multiplied by a factor of nearly ten between the late 1220s and the late 1260s, from 3.6 to 31.9 pounds per week, is a guide to the significance of this increase in documentation, for the wax was used to seal letters which were actually sent to people from that office.[21] The papal chancery, whose registers survive almost continuously from Innocent III onwards, shows a similar spiralling of activity. So do the surviving archives of Italian cities, where public serial records begin to survive in different places in the thirteenth century, as with the registers of criminal justice of Bologna and Perugia starting in 1226 and 1258 respectively, or the Biccherna fiscal registers, balancing incomings and outgoings, of Siena, which also start in 1226.[22] The simple fact that such registers began to be produced is a marker of scale, and inside them the number of records once again steadily grows.

It is important to stress that this growth in written documentation is not yet, in itself, a sign of increasing literacy, however that is to be defined (I mean by it here the ability to read, and/or familiarity with the written word); that trend was more a late medieval one. Indeed, the Carolingians, as we saw, had a mostly literate aristocracy, probably more than was the case by 1200; they did not depend exclusively on the clergy for writing skills, and dealt with writing in a range of ways, both inside government and outside;[23] but they nonetheless produced fewer documents than many of the governments of far smaller territories by 1200. Rather, what had come to be common, and increasingly normal, was the use of documents as part of everyday political communication at quite mundane levels of business, including with people in the countryside whose literate skills were by no means up to receiving them. In the ninth century, Louis the Pious would have sent a messenger to tell a local assembly of his will (even if that messenger often had a written text as well, as we saw earlier); in the thirteenth, Edward I sent a short sealed writ, with specific addressees and specific instructions, and kept a copy. Communications were much tighter as a result. Information was also exchanged like this; governments increasingly used writing to disseminate news, and got responses as well, at least in the form of petitions.

This is not to say that kings and their advisers only, or even principally, relied on this form of communication. (This is a good moment to add that the increased use of writing was also only a technical tool; it did not change anyone's ability to express themselves, still less to think in different ways, as has sometimes been claimed by historians and social theorists.) Oral communication was as important, just as it is today. Indeed, one frequently has the sense that all those travellers from courts, whose updated political gossip is the main meat of many a monastic chronicle, had been sent with that precise purpose in mind, as a form of orally transmitted news-management, and news-gathering (that is, spying) as well. But this, too, involved a much denser network of travellers on official business than previous centuries had at their disposal – a network which the commercial changes of the period, discussed in the previous chapter, made more normal too, as also did the growth of the Cistercian and other monastic networks, and, soon, those of the friars, as we shall see later. The letters of Abbot Lupus of Ferrières in West Francia in the 850s and 860s sometimes show an anxious uncertainty about where the king even is; this information was systematically broadcast in England by the early twelfth century – unless, of course, the king wished to keep it a secret.[24] So: governments had more personnel; officials travelled and discussed state affairs more systematically; they sent out documents far more frequently; they provided local justice more often; and they took tax more systematically too, which both paid for this increase in personnel and also – because of the need for accurate assessment, even if this was frequently done by the taxpayers themselves – increased the capillary presence of the state in the towns and villages of each kingdom, principality, city territory of Europe. Italy and England followed this path first; France (and its most governmentally elaborate principality, Flanders) and Aragón soon after; Castile, Hungary and one or two of the German principalities slightly later; the rest of northern and eastern Europe much more slowly. But the direction was the same everywhere, and it was one towards an ever-greater density in communication, between government and communities and back again, as well as a greater level of control.

To repeat: officials were normally loyal, but were also frequently corrupt. How could one ensure that that corruption stayed within reasonable bounds? The Carolingians faced this problem by demanding elaborate oaths to the king, by sending *missi* out on a regular basis to enquire whether justice was being done by counts and other local representatives, and, more grandly, by organising collective penitence. The Carolingian tradition of a highly moralised royal politics had gone everywhere by the early eleventh century, and it was only really carried on later, as we have seen, as one of the elements which came together, by now independently of secular powers, in the eleventh-century church 'reform' movement. But the idea of sending out central-government inspectors, commissioners, enquirers, was an easy one to revive, if it had ever really vanished. Twelfth-century English justices in eyre were one example, papal legates and judges-delegate another. And, more and more, we find specific and targeted 'inquests' of local officials in England and France: the Inquest of Sheriffs of 1170 in England, the root-and-branch commissions initiated by the English barons in 1258–59, or the equally elaborate national *enquêtes* set up by Louis IX in France in and after 1247–48, all of which uncovered local abuses and dealt with them on a considerable scale.[25]

On top of this, we find developing ideas of accountability which became routinised, indeed often bureaucratic. England again shows an early example, in place by the mid-twelfth century: the annual presentation of a county's accounts by its sheriff to the Exchequer, so named because a chequerboard was used as an abacus by the royal treasurer to check the figures while the sheriff watched – he was doubtless both puzzled and scared, and our best source for it, Richard fitzNigel's *Dialogue of the Exchequer* of the years around 1180, is explicit that the theatricality of the occasion matched what he called a 'conflict and struggle' between the sheriff and the treasurer. Louis IX also ordained, his biographer Joinville tells us, that *baillis* and other officials should stay in their circumscription for forty days after their term of office ended so that complaints could be heard against them – a different form of accountability (the Exchequer did not check for local bad behaviour, only debt and fraud) but nearly as organised. This was further elaborated in Italy, by the 1210s in cities such as Siena, later in the thirteenth century in others, in the annual process known as *sindacatio*, in which the outgoing *podestà* and other officials of each city remained for a specific period until enquiries about their office had been completed, which concerned both complaints against their justice and honesty and a check on their economic management.[26]

This sort of process was a logical one to develop, especially once officials started to handle a lot of money, as tax-raising régimes would increasingly need. The 'Abbasid caliphate, for example, by the end of the ninth century had already developed a coercive version of it called *musadara*, in which outgoing vizirs were systematically shaken down and often tortured, to extract from them their illegal gains while in office.[27] Like inquests, it was also a natural consequence of the very old idea – far older than the Carolingians – that ruling should be just in religious terms, which was policed not only by God, but also by sensible humans who wished to avoid the sort of collective punishments (natural disasters, losing wars) that the divinity might require from unjust political systems. To this was added a more recent assumption that officials could not be trusted, and that, in kingdoms, royal justice had to be at least periodically visible on the ground without mediation. Counts and other high-status representatives in the past had got away with far more, because to second-guess them except in extreme circumstances was a breach of honour; lower-ranking officials were the object of more careful scrutiny from the start. But the development of a growing concern for exactness in the assessment of governmental activity in the thirteenth century in Europe was, as in the caliphate, a particular result of the growing complexity of institutions.

Such concerns were also a product of the increasingly explicit reliance on elaborate legal systems and legal writings in these states. The word 'inquisitio' (hence inquest, enquête, enquiry, and also inquisition) itself comes from classical Roman law, and contains the assumption that judges will in some circumstances call witnesses independently from those offered by the accuser and the accused; the Carolingians made such judicial inquisitiones, and the process subsequently remained in use – and in this period was increasingly used – in legal investigations. One of the most interesting features of the century and more after 1150, however, is the increasing interest in Roman law itself, throughout Europe, even in places where its remit did not actually run – which was most of Europe, in fact, for classical Roman law was the basic law only in the Byzantine empire, and in some Italian cities. Most regions had fairly substantial corpora of written law in 1150, in particular ex-Lombard Italy, ex-Visigothic Spain and ex-Anglo-Saxon England (each of them using essentially early medieval compilations), and also in Ireland – although less so the Frankish lands, France and Germany, by now. Icelanders, Norwegians and Hungarians hurried to catch up as well.[28] But Roman law dwarfed them all; in its definitive written form, codified by Justinian in the 530s (see above, Chapter 3), it was enormous in scale and elaboration, enough for a lifetime's happy work for any lawyer who wished to get inside its interstices, and such lawyers began to be active and influential in more and more of Europe.

Given the existence of these other, more indigenous and therefore more relevant, legal systems, all of them regularly updated in local custom and practice, exactly why pre-sixth-century Roman rules seemed so useful in the late twelfth and thirteenth is not always obvious. But their intellectual principles were more explicit, which helped analysis, and their very elaboration allowed lawyers to get a sense of just how detailed and subtle legal arguments could be – both of which also provided something formal to be trained in, increasingly often at universities, at Bologna and Montpellier. The impact of Roman law is anyway evident everywhere, including in England, where its systematising influenced the great treatise on contemporary common law called 'Bracton' in (probably) the 1230s; in Castile, where Alfonso X commissioned a comprehensive Spanish-language legal code, the *Siete partidas*, based largely on Justinian; and in Philip IV's northern France, where southern Roman lawyers were much in demand – Guillaume de Nogaret was by no means the only one. Bits of Roman law were increasingly borrowed to fill in the cracks of local practices; whole sectors of it – judicial torture being one of the most obvious – were brought into those local practices as signs of up-to-the-minute legal expertise; justifications for political claims could be newly couched in Romanist terms, as Frederick Barbarossa did in Italy; local custom could be newly codified along Roman lines too, as Oberto dall'Orto (d. 1175), a ruling consul from Milan, did for the law of fiefs.[29] And Roman law also heavily influenced the only other legal system which matched it in elaboration, the canon law of the church, also taught at universities (sometimes by the same teachers), which – unlike most other legal systems of this period – was constantly updated by new written laws, derived from church councils and the legal decisions of popes, frequently enough in a Romanist direction.

This network of developments had a further consequence. Given the number of people involved in government by now who were formally trained (including in universities, where disputation was a standard teaching method), given the disjunction between local laws and the elaborate legal-moral systems which both Roman and canon law involved, and given the trend to detailed accounting and inquest which accompanied office-holding, the idea that governmental practices might be made to run better slowly gained ground as well. Of course, once again, versions of this were old. The Carolingians, for example, systematised government quite consciously, as part of *correctio* (see Chapter 4), and streamlined much of it: *missi*, and also the continual issuing of capitularies, are examples of the novelties which were generated as a result. But that was in the context of a very high-flown need to reshape the whole Latin Christian world under the eyes of God, and much of the streamlining seems almost an accidental by-product of that wider ambition. Rulers (including popes) and their advisers were less conscious later for a long time, and tended to see governmental 'reform' as either a return to a supposedly more perfect past, or else an attempted alignment of their realms with those of their more powerful neighbours, as with the newly Christianised kingdoms of the north and east. Even real transformations, such as the appearance of consular-run communes in Italy, were posed in the most traditionalist of terms by their authors, when the changes were recognised at all. It would indeed not only have been hard, but damning, to boast of novelty here, given the fragile legitimacy which consuls felt they had, with their elections by their peers and inferiors rather than a stable placement inside older hierarchies; only a second generation, as with the uprising which produced the commune of Rome in 1143–44, could sometimes claim to innovate, as we shall see in a moment.[30] The past was invoked by reformers in the thirteenth century as well: the English barons of 1215 simply referred to the supposedly more just kingship of the past when demanding changes in the present, and so, later, did the opponents of Alfonso X, and of Philip IV at the end of his life. Change, which occurred in this period as much as any other, was usually ad hoc, a response to immediate problems, unintended to be a guide for the future for the most part, even when it came to serve as the template for the next changes a generation later: the growth in the role of parliament across the thirteenth century in England, both before and after the quasi-coup of 1258, or the growth of the papal inquisition from the 1230s, being good examples of this.

Slowly, however, from the mid-twelfth century onwards, we can find rulers or (usually) their ministers beginning to tinker with governing structures, much more deliberately. There are a number of examples from England of ministers experimenting with different kinds of record-keeping, for example, and then sometimes abandoning them if they did not work.[31] The appearance of *podestà* in Italian cities, too, could be quite a conscious decision: as the official Genoese Annals for 1190 put it, 'because of the envy of many men who excessively desire to possess the office of the consulate of the commune, many civil discords and odious conspiracies and divisions have greatly risen up in the city. So it happened that the wise men and the counsellors of the city met together and determined by common counsel that the consulate of the city would cease in the following year, and almost [note that 'almost'] everyone was in agreement about having a *podestà*'. This was clearly seen as an emergency measure in hard times, but it was new for all that (even if not as instant as it sounds – consuls and *podestà* alternated in Genoa until 1217). So, less defensively, was the proud foundation of the 'sacred Roman senate', the commune of Rome of 1143–44, which was even used in dating clauses for communal documents thereafter, or the formal adoption of Roman law in Pisa on 31 December 1160, after a five-year period in which Pisa's new law codes were researched and written by *constitutores*.[32] These examples of conscious innovation were as yet relatively few, but they extended the range of what was possible in government. When, in the fourteenth century, we find for the first time a few theorists of ideal rule who were not deriving it entirely from the theological environment in which discussions about moral rulership had traditionally been placed, such as Bartolo of Sassoferrato in Italy, they were not totally isolated from a real practical context; and that practical context would have more space for conscious problem-solving, as well as innovative suggestions by government critics, than it had done in the past. We will return to this later.

The final point that needs to be made here, picking up on arguments earlier in this book, is that the processes of centralisation and the ever-growing density of political power, which began above all in the period 1150–1300, were differently based from that which had been taken for granted in, say, 800. The classic early medieval combination (above all visible with the Carolingians) of ex-Roman conceptions of public power and authority and north European assembly politics, together with the assumption in the latter that legitimacy (including, not least, justice) derived from collective presence and activity, had gone, except in the England of long-lasting shire and hundred law courts. State-building was by now based on different, cellular, units: the newly legal, although of course highly exploitative, local lordships, large or small, of the eleventh century – to which we can now add the urban and rural communities of the twelfth, which gained their own autonomy, where they could, inside and against these lordships; and also dioceses, the cells of the international papal network. We have seen all of these at work here and in the previous two chapters.[33] In Italy and Germany, the point is obvious, for the powers of kings were retreating fast, and principalities and city collectivities occupied the terrain instead. The French kings for their part united their kingdom brick by brick, and each brick was one such lordship, either conquered directly or coerced into making its theoretical loyalty to the crown real; conversely, the relations of seigneurial domination (and opposition to it) inside each remained, sometimes for centuries – the last 'feudal' rights only going in 1790. The counts of Catalonia – who were one of the most successful princely families of the twelfth century, and who took over the kingdom of Aragón as well in 1137 – did the same, but faced a collectivity of lords who in 1202 established the right to mistreat their own dependent peasants without royal intervention, later generalised as the *ius maltractandi*.[34] (Even in England lords kept that right, as long as their peasants were legally unfree.) In Castile, kings were almost always hegemonic, but by 1200 they too presided over a patchwork of urban jurisdictions (*concejos*) and lordships (*señoríos*). The latter gained their own typologies in royal texts: royal, monastic, lay, and collective (i.e. where many co-lords split the seigneurial takings). Their lords, even though keen to asso-ciate themselves with the royal court, Carolingian-style, thus had structured local power-bases which few great Carolingian aristocrats ever had.[35]

Assembly politics related to power differently too. Whereas Carolingian assemblies had been, at least in theory, gatherings of the free male population of the kingdom, legitimating royal authority from the outside, the royal assem-blies of 1200 in France, Castile, Aragón, England, were by now simply the king's own court writ large. They would come to claim a wider legitimating role: the phrase 'community of the realm' appears in England in 1258, France in 1314, and (reacting against English aggression) Scotland in 1320, in the Declaration of Arbroath. But, although general ideas of kingdom-based communities might have been old, these particular versions of it were recon-structions of collective power, now based on the counterposing of the local rights of lords to a newly assertive royal authority. We shall see in Chapter 12 how this developed further in later centuries.[36]

In the period of this chapter, in fact, what legitimated royal power was first and foremost the personal loyalty of these lords. This was buttressed more and more by rituals, notably the ceremony of homage, to make it more imposing and convincing to the lords who swore it (and to their own men in their own lordships, who did the same). 'Feudo-vassalic' relations (see Chapter 1) were indeed developed in large part simply to make that loyalty more formalised and ritualised, and – kings and lords hoped – harder to break. Royal courts became vastly more elaborate stage sets for aristocratic life in general, with new forms of etiquette, including the norms of 'chivalric' behaviour, which began in the mid-twelfth century and were steadily refined for four centuries to come (see Chapter 10). Such elaboration made them all the more alluring for aristo-crats to be part of, indeed to learn to be part of, and in each case this strength-ened royal authority, for the direction of this stage was royal, and was punctuated by alarming shows of royal anger, carefully choreographed (even if often only too real), and, if necessary, reconciliation. Walter Map in his book of courtiers' stories even likened the court of Henry II of England to hell, such was the potential for disorientation and danger in it, but the whole book shows its allure. Such public choreography had older roots once again, as Gerd Althoff has shown, but it too gained steadily in complexity.[37] The new claims to royal authority which Roman law made possible and which fiscal needs often made necessary, and the new practices of local control, were simply superimposed on top of this. So were religious forms of royal legitimation, such as the trend for each kingdom to have at least one king who was made a saint, thus sanctifying his office too: in the kingdoms focused on in this chapter, Stephen I in Hungary in 1083, Henry II in Germany in 1147, Edward the Confessor in England in 1163, Louis IX in France in 1297, and – most implausibly of all – Charlemagne himself in 1165.[38] This new composite legitimation soon became very strong, particularly where kings themselves were strong – even if it did not prevent unpopular or inept kings from trouble, even deposition, as with Edward II of England in 1327, the accusation against whom stated that 'he abandoned his kingdom and left it without government', his royal role being now separable from his person.[39] But its underpinnings had at their core the cellular structure of local power.

*   *   *

We have in this chapter been looking at politics and political culture, but that must be set against wider cultural trends as well. I will look here at two: the development of what became universities, and the varying fortunes of lay religious commitment. Both fit into the picture of the interplay between the localised patterning of political practice and the trends towards centralisation that have been the focus of the foregoing, although in rather different ways.

The cathedrals and monasteries of Latin Europe had long educated not just clerics but also the local laity, usually but not only aristocrats, in basic literacy, plus, at a second level, grammar and rhetoric. Notaries organised their own secular training in Italy, and at least informal law schools existed there by the eleventh century too, at Pavia in particular. It the same period, some cathedral schools, such as that of Bishop Fulbert (d. 1028) in Chartres, had enough students that a critical mass of intellectual discussion was reached and arguments multiplied very interestingly, much as the Aachen court school had managed in the early ninth century. But it was the twelfth century which saw the development of a new phenomenon, towns which attracted large numbers of students, sometimes from many countries, to learn from masters whose success was based on their teaching and debating ability, independent of external ratification. Such students hoped for positions in secular government and the church as a result, even if not all succeeded – the myth of the impoverished scholar begins here, in twelfth-century Latin letters and poetry.[40]

Paris (for theology, from the 1090s) and Bologna (for law, from the 1120s) were the main centres here, although Montpellier, Oxford, Padua, Salamanca and others eventually joined them at a second level. Their development was inseparable from the development of urban economies and a money-based economy that allowed masters to earn a living and their students to be fed, as discussed in the last chapter; but it moved fast in the early twelfth century. By the 1150s, Bologna's main canon-law text, Gratian's *Concordance of discordant canons*, was structuring the legal disputes of more and more churches in Italy and (soon) the entire papal appeals network, and Bologna's Roman lawyers were advising Frederick Barbarossa. The *studium* of Bologna, and the usually short-lasting rival *studia* which followed it after 1150 or so, became the major training ground for Italy's urban leadership thereafter. As for Paris, which reached the critical mass that generates new ideas by 1100 at the latest, it became the focus of some highly charismatic intellectuals. The best known of these was Peter Abelard (d. 1142), whose innovative logic and theology, vigorous and arrogant debating skills, and romantically tragic private life (he had an intense affair with a student, Héloïse, herself a serious intellectual figure, and was castrated by her guardian) fascinated contemporaries, as it fascinates historians still. Abelard became the *bête noire* of Bernard of Clairvaux, the most powerful religious figure in northern Europe, and was condemned for heresy (for a second time) as a direct result, but scholars influenced by him and his extensive writings became important in the church, and in secular government as well. It was Abelard's style of logic-based theological enquiry which made Bernard, a theologian himself but of a more interior-directed, contemplative type, so angry, but it was the Abelardian style, toned down, which would have a future in Paris, and the basic medieval theological text-book, Peter Lombard's *Sentences* of the 1150s, owed much to him.[41]

The early-twelfth-century Paris schools may have been fun, but they did not offer a stable career structure; all the major figures in them ended up as bishops, or in monasteries, as they got older. If masters wanted to stay in Paris, they had to group together, in effect in a craft guild (*universitas*, a word used in Paris by 1208, meant 'guild', or indeed 'commune'), to organise curricula united by shared values rather than competition, and they did so. By the early thirteenth century they had statutes regulating them; they had also gained privileges to protect them against Parisian secular and church authorities, from the king of France in 1200 and the pope in 1208–09. In 1229 they fell out with the regent of France, Louis IX's mother Blanche of Castile, and abandoned Paris en masse, until Pope Gregory IX moved rapidly to arbitrate and got the schools reopened by 1231, issuing a bull to back this up.[42] This bull is much more than a standard papal legal decision or privilege; it is a full-blown mission statement for what we can, by now, call the university, as a key location for learning, including an element which was by the thirteenth century crucial in church activism, learning how to preach. Gregory's involvement here is interesting, for it might not be obvious that the health and success of the university of Paris would be the concern of a pope, to the extent of him reissuing its statutes and intervening in its curriculum, often in some detail. But the intellectual coherence of the newly unified church was increasingly associated with what was taught in Paris. Innocent III himself had been trained there, and into the thirteenth century a high proportion of bishops and other church leaders had an education from Paris (or from other theology-focused universities, such as Oxford or Salamanca); a substantial percentage of the main religious intellectuals of thirteenth-century Europe taught there too, culminating in the south Italian aristocrat Thomas Aquinas (d. 1274), whose strikingly intelligent and systematic works are still points of reference for western theology.

An important aspect of these developments is, of course, that they are another example of the growing institutionalisation of power across the period 1150–1300. This was partly the simple routinisation of the charismatic figures of the start of the twelfth century, whose role could not realistically have been maintained; indeed, the masters already stand out less from our sources after 1150, until the major scholars of the mid-thirteenth century and onwards. But it is partly, as with government, a sign of a greater felt need for control. In fact, it never was possible fully to control what went on in universities; every master had his own view on all issues. This was ever more visible once public disputations began to be recorded in the thirteenth century, with questions to the master on all manner of subjects and his replies; these were called 'quodlibets', and they were often distributed widely. But this carried its own risks, not least the danger of disseminating heresy, and for this reason popes and other powers, both external and internal to universities, found themselves trying to micromanage: both the content of what was taught (as with, for example, how much Aristotle and Averroes could be taught, given that these authors were not Christian) and who could teach it (as with the perennial debate from the 1250s onwards about the role of friars in the university of Paris). Popes, and also secular rulers, indeed have kept an eye on universities ever after; as potential powerhouses both of élite education and intellectual critique, they have been too important to let hold of entirely. But all the institutionalisation and external control of universities that could be put in place did not alter the fact that they were essentially cellular intellectual structures whose legitimacy sprang from the success of the individual masters who made them up.

*   *   *

Lay religious culture was even more localised, and it presented very different challenges to central authorities. In the eleventh century, as we saw in Chapter 6, some lay groups began to formulate their own, locally varying, versions of Christian values and practice, and to come up with answers which sometimes fitted those of clerical reformers, but sometimes could be labelled as heresy.

After 1150 or so this was much more common; the growing availability of Biblical texts which could be read independently by lay men and women, who were either literate or had access to what Brian Stock has called 'textual communities' of readers and listeners, allowed religious involvement to take a variety of forms – not least because Europe was so politically fragmented.[43] Sometimes this resulted in new monastic or canonical foundations, as in previous centuries – the Premonstratensians, the Gilbertines and so on, and, in the crusader states and later in the west too, the military orders of the Templars and the Hospitallers – which, whether successful or not, at least fitted standard models of hierarchical religious commitment. Sometimes, however, activists remained in their own communities, and preached their own version of Christian purism. One such, Valdes, a layman from Lyon, sought preaching rights for his followers from Pope Alexander III in 1179, at the Third Lateran Council; these were granted only if the local church allowed however, and the new archbishop of Lyon refused, expelling them. The 'Waldensians' did not give up preaching, and so were increasingly lumped together with other heretics and sporadically persecuted, although surviving in the valleys of the Alps until they were absorbed into sixteenth-century Protestantism.[44] Another group, the female ascetics of the Low Countries known as Beguines (a founding figure was Mary of Oignies, d. 1213), who lived by weaving in large part, stayed somewhat on the margins of local ecclesiastical structures and faced intermittent suspicion, although they were certainly absorbed into the religious life of at least the Flemish towns.[45] Luckier was Francis of Assisi (d. 1226), a convert to total poverty in 1205 in the face of his merchant father, and a charismatic leader of friars, literally 'brothers' – matched by their female counterparts the 'Poor Clares', founded by Francis's associate Chiara of Assisi (d. 1253) – who were not allowed to touch money and whose preaching was funded by alms. Francis, who always fully accepted ecclesiastical authority, impressed Innocent III, who allowed his friars to preach in 1209. Francis's personal ascetic practice was so extreme that there was a constant tension after his death (even before, indeed) between followers who wished to maintain his practice entirely and other followers who thought it needed to be adapted to the ongoing needs of real life. Whether the first group, the 'Spiritual Franciscans', was potentially heretical was an issue by the end of the thirteenth century. Conversely, the main body of Franciscan friars eventually did well by doing good, and their giant and expensive hall-churches are still one of the notable features of late medieval architecture on the edges of many a city (not least Assisi) today; the Franciscans remained suspended between power and marginality in interesting ways.[46]

Where the 'Cathars' came from and what they believed is more of a problem. It was obscure then, and there is a considerable debate about it now. Were they dualists, believing that the world was created by an evil God and that procreation should be abandoned, and linked institutionally to the dualist Bogomil church of Bulgaria? Or is this picture the invention of the church's own inquisitors, over-influenced by a knowledge of ancient heresies, and prone to 'persuade' the unfortunate men and women who were pulled into their net to confess heretical beliefs which were really only in the inquisitors' own minds, much as witchcraft confessions were secured in the early modern period? It has been pointed out that the most complex accounts of their beliefs come precisely from inquisition records, which furthermore do not become dense until the 1240s, by which time the movement was increasingly in hiding from persecution everywhere. This debate has led to a notable sharpening of the sophistication of textual analysis in historians' studies of 'Cathar' beliefs and heresy in general. On balance, it seems most probable that a dualist theology was indeed a feature of committed believers, who often had some form of organisational structure too, but that only some of the most active 'Cathars' necessarily knew or cared much about it.[47] What is not in dispute, however, and it is more important for us here, is that by the mid- to late twelfth century, in the cities of communal Italy and in both cities and countryside in Languedoc and the Toulousain in France, there were numerous groups of celibate laity called 'good men' and 'good women' (only in Italy were they regularly called 'Cathars', and only by opponents, although I use the label here for convenience), who preached the good religious life autonomously of the church; they sometimes lived as artisans, and were often vegan. They denied the spiritual validity of the church hierarchy, unlike the Beguines and Franciscans, and sometimes also major church rites such as baptism. The main rite they practised was the *consolamentum*, the formal entry into their own ranks, which ordinary laity tended to take on at their deathbeds. As with the Waldensians and others, such lay religiosity and autonomous local ritual had clear antecedents in the previous century and more, but here it was moving in rather more original directions. Anyway, whatever the detailed beliefs of the good men and women, their rejection of the church hierarchy was clearly heretical by the orthodox standards of the age, even though, to the ordinary lay Christians of Italy and southern France, their personal virtue seems to have been their most important characteristic (there are examples in Italy of recognised saints who were later condemned as heretics, sometimes with little effect on their local cult[48]). Their difference from the friars, in particular, may not have seemed very great, except when friars were the inquisitors.

There were rumbles in church councils about the 'Cathars' by the mid-twelfth century, and sporadic attempts to oppose them on a local level. Later, increasing pressure was put on Count Raymond VI of Toulouse (1194–1222) to deal with them in his territories (interestingly, similar pressure was never put systematically on the Italian cities), which Raymond resisted; but, when Innocent III's legate in the Toulousain was murdered in 1208, the pope called a crusade against the count and the 'heretics', the notorious Albigensian Crusade. North French knights poured into Languedoc and the Toulousain under the leadership of Simon de Montfort (father of the baronial rebel in England in 1258–65) and laid it waste for a decade and more, massacring its inhabitants on occasion too.[49] We have seen that this led to north-French rule in the south, eventually at least. But it also led to a notable extension of the practice of inquisition, and soon to its theorisation as well, as inquisitors' handbooks were written and rules for how hearings should be held were laid down – which, however little we identify with inquisitors, was better than heretic-finders destroying lives at random, as had been a feature of several early anti-heresy campaigns. One prominent figure in Languedoc after 1206 was the Castilian ascetic Dominic of Caleruega (d. 1221), who believed that in order to confront the 'Cathars' one should adopt the same sort of vows of poverty as the good men and women; his order of friars was given preaching rights by the pope in 1217. The Dominicans were thus in the front line of anti-'Cathar' activity from the start, and, when inquisition became more regularised, from the 1230s on, both they and the Franciscans, as the two main orders of lay preachers, were its mainstay. This was steadily extended across France and Italy; eventually 'Catharism' lost ground, and was rare by 1300. This did not affect the wider spread of autonomous lay religious activism, however, which remained extensive in the late middle ages, as we shall see later.

The stress on preaching in the Fourth Lateran Council in 1215 and in Gregory IX's bull for Paris university in 1231 was partly related to the perceived need to combat heresy, and to help establish church authority as a result. Both Dominicans and Franciscans moved very swiftly into teaching at Paris, as part of their preaching training – indeed, they provided many of the most prominent intellectuals of the century (Aquinas was a Dominican, for example). But the sense that there should be a major push to develop preaching was a wider feature of the church in the thirteenth century in particular, and it came to be seen as a major element in the presence of the church on the ground; preaching had, certainly, been seen as part of church ritual since the early middle ages, but from now on, explaining the nature of the faith to the laity was ever more important.[50] This meant trying to get parish priests to preach more (not always successfully), and handbooks for them became more common now; but the friars fitted into this as well, and their constant travelling, even if usually focused on towns rather than the countryside, extended preaching further. This had to mean that more and more laity would know about the details of the Christian faith, and this was indeed the church's precise aim. Religious enthusiasm could hit the laity on a large scale, as with the Alleluia of 1233, preached by friars, which excited citizens of a number of Italian cities from Parma to Verona and resulted in mass revival meetings.[51] This, as usual, had its risks, for it is certainly true that, as with 'Cathars' and Waldensians fifty years before, a better-informed laity, or at least its religious-minded minority, could end up with the 'wrong' beliefs; but that was a danger which existed anyway. More important by now was that lay religiosity, now that it was more formally recognised, could and should be channelled by church direction, as for example in the rapid growth of religious confraternities after 1250, which became an important part of late medieval collective activism, linking craft guilds to parish communities.[52] The dialectic between church direction and lay ingenuity in finding new forms of religious commitment would continue thereafter.

The move by popes to combat heresy has more or less exactly the same pacing as the growth of papal government through the appeals process, and on one level it has the same root: overall, popes and other church leaders were centralising the church, and wished to control all aspects not only of religious practice, but also belief. Whether or not one sympathises with their aims or (still less) methods, one can scarcely say that helping humans to what they saw as salvation was not their proper role. But since full control of belief was not possible – it still is not, of course, even with modern technologies – religious leaders overreached. Jews, in particular, found their lives increasingly circumscribed in many parts of Europe, largely because of church pressure, as we shall see in Chapter 10. Bob Moore and John Boswell have argued that lepers and homosexuals faced greater exclusion and persecution too: all out-groups, that is to say, were more visible and faced more trouble, in this would-be homogeneous Latin European society.[53] The intolerant and coercive pursuit of homogeneity would continue in later centuries too; it would be developed even more systematically in the charged religious atmosphere of the sixteenth century.

*   *   *

In this chapter, I have been arguing that late-twelfth- and thirteenth-century western Europe was reconstructed as (in most cases) a set of more centralised powers, on top of a new basis, the cellular politics of the eleventh century. Law gave a stronger framework for control, and techniques of communication and accountability made control more operative in practice, but the cells, that is to say local lordships and urban or rural communities, were for the most part left in place. When we come to the increasing centralisation of belief, the same basic techniques were used: record-keeping, manuals, checks on bad behaviour by officials (friars who went too far in the inquisition could be investigated and sometimes brought down),[54] a legislative backing in the form of papal decrees. It is harder to say that there was a formalised pattern of communities of belief underpinning that; popes and other ecclesiastical theorists would certainly have disagreed – they claimed an equal power over all individuals, in a way that kings did not. But belief communities were at least divided up institutionally by the cellular structure of dioceses; and, above all, the practical differences in beliefs which did in reality exist, from region to region, town to town, village to village, as expressed (among other things) in the forms of lay religiosity we have looked at, acted as a similar kind of brake on this newly ambitious ecclesiastical vision. Every time we read the accounts of what inquisitors actually found in the rural neighbourhoods of southern France, and then Italy, and then, a century or two later, in England and Spain, we find societies which had made their own minds up about what was important and how things worked, in the spiritual as much as the temporal world.[55] As with magnifying glasses in the sun, the inquisitors' vision burned, badly, those upon whom it focused, but no-one could reach everywhere, and certainly in the medieval period no-one tried. There were plenty of local, sometimes downright strange, beliefs left, for later outsiders to uncover, if they ever did.

CHAPTER NINE

1204: the failure of alternatives

The western European kingdoms, which we have just looked at, were riding high by the thirteenth century, but until then they were not the only powerful Christian states in Europe, or indeed the most powerful. In 1025, at the death of the emperor Basil II, his empire – we call it 'Byzantine', but, as we saw earlier, he and his subjects called it Roman, as Augustus and Justinian had – was beyond doubt the strongest political system of the continent. It stretched from the Danube to Antioch, and from Bari in southern Italy to what are now the borders of Iran. That is to say, the Balkans, Greece, Anatolia (what is now Turkey) and the south Italian mainland were all governed by a single and cohesive political structure, with a complex fiscal system which was unmatched by that of any medieval Latin power, and ruled from a capital, Constantinople, which was then, at probably well over a quarter of a million inhabitants, the largest city that ever existed in medieval Europe.[1] Indeed, until the last years of the twelfth century, Byzantine wealth and power, although by now reduced territorially, was still greater than that of any western polity. All the same, a few decades later, that empire had vanished. Turks controlled the Anatolian plateau; the Balkans were in the hands of Serbian and Bulgarian rulers. Constantinople itself had fallen in 1204 to the French and Italian troops of the Fourth Crusade, which had notoriously been diverted from its initial aim of attacking Muslim Egypt, and instead had destroyed a Christian political system. Confronting the small new Latin empire of Constantinople, and a Venetian takeover of the Greek islands, were not one Byzantine government in exile but three, based at Nicaea (modern İznik), Trebizond (modern Trabzon) and Arta in north-west Greece, together with smaller lordships elsewhere in Greece. Although Latin-ruled Constantinople fell in its turn to the Nicaean emperor Michael VIII Palaiologos in 1261, united Byzantine power was never re-established. The Byzantine imperial system was a genuine alternative pattern for European development to that lived through by the western powers, but after 1204 it was, quite simply, lost.

Why does this matter? In part, because the break-up of the Byzantine empire is, in itself, as large a political event as the similar break-up of the western Roman empire, and is as complex to explain. In practice, less analysis has been devoted to it than to the fate of the western empire, partly because the Fourth Crusade itself, although it was only part of the process, has seemed fairly straightforward to explain (crusader greed, Venetian cynicism, imperial ineptness); but it deserves attention in a book such as this. In part, also, because if we are to understand how medieval European history took the directions it did, we need also to get a sense of some of the opportunities that were forfeited. The Byzantine empire at its height was a major medieval success story, a key point of reference, and Europeans outside its remit knew it, not least the Carolingians and the Ottonians.[2] It was a model for governance elsewhere, from the Rus' of the tenth century to the Sicily and the Hungary of the twelfth. When it failed, its techniques of government were no longer available to Latin Europe, and had to be reinvented, which took a long time. The heirs of the Byzantines, and the re-establishers, in the century after 1350, of the scale of empire which Basil II had controlled (and eventually still more), were instead the Ottoman Turks, whose Muslim religion meant that they were, like the earlier caliphates, never likely models for the rest of Europe. But by 1204 Byzantium was no longer a model either; hence, indeed, the ease with which it could be destroyed. We need to get an idea of why.

As we saw in Chapter 3, the Byzantine crisis of the early middle ages was over by the mid-ninth century. Basil I (867–86), a usurper of apparently peasant origin, then established the Macedonian dynasty which lasted nearly two centuries, to 1056. Its existence did not prevent others seizing power – the dynastic principle was never strong in Byzantium – but the family maintained a legitimacy, and were constantly returned to, until they died out. During Basil's reign, the coherence of the 'Abbasid caliphate began to slip, with a period of crisis in the 860s followed by two decades of civil wars; Basil took advantage of this and began to attack eastwards over the Tauros mountains in central Anatolia, which had been the effective Byzantine–Arab boundary for two centuries, as well as conquering half of southern Italy, which partly made up for the war being lost in Sicily. When the 'Abbasids faced their final crisis, in the 930s and onwards, Byzantine armies returned to attacking eastwards, and began to conquer here as well. Between the 930s and the 960s they occupied the upper Euphrates valley, stably, as well as capturing the main Arab-controlled islands in the eastern Mediterranean, Crete and Cyprus, and by 969 had moved into Syria, taking Antioch. From this secure Anatolian and Aegean base they then moved westwards, taking over Bulgaria in 971; this did not hold, and a restored Bulgarian empire, led by Samuel (997–1014), had to be fought and defeated in thirty years of campaigning, but after 1018 the whole of the Balkans was under stable Byzantine control too. This was the work of a series of notably able aristocratic generals, some of whom seized power as emperors (the most effective was Nikephoros II Phokas, the conqueror of the 950s and 960s, who ruled in 963–69); but the Macedonian heir Basil II (976–1025) was his own general, and was the architect of the Bulgarian campaigns, as well as extending his authority even further east, into Armenia.[3]

There were two sides to this century and a half of successful aggression. The first was a paid and professional army. The Byzantines had survived in the seventh century by organising defence in depth, based on the military provinces of the empire, the *themata*; although semi-professional thematic armies remained at the basis of military engagement, emperors increasingly relied on permanent paid and trained units, who were the shock troops of the conquest period. The Byzantines were proud of their military system, and even theorised its organisation; the Macedonian period saw the writing of several military handbooks, some of them the works of emperors themselves, notably the *Taktika* of Leo VI (886–912).[4] The second side was that a paid army also required a fiscal system which was robust enough to pay for it, year after year – for the Byzantines were almost permanently at war in this period, especially from the 950s to the 1010s. No western state of the period could have managed this, but, as we saw in Chapter 3, the Byzantines had never abandoned, and never would abandon, a land tax, which by the mid-ninth century was collected in both money (the Byzantines minted coin on a large scale) and, in campaigning areas, supplies. Basil II's state was indeed sufficiently organised that he managed to build up a very large fiscal surplus in coin by the end of his reign, despite fighting campaigns so regularly; underground tunnels were said to have been built to house the money, a long-standing literary image of wealth and avarice.[5] A western state would have expected its aristocrats to run its armies, and Byzantium was, by now, no different; from the ninth century, a military aristocracy developed, with lands largely on the Anatolian plateau, and with military command inherited from father to son in some cases (the Phokas family is a particularly good example). But the armies were separate from them; they had careers *in* the army, rather than providing the army themselves, and there were always generals whose family backgrounds were highly obscure. The Byzantine aristocracy was also never, before the twelfth century at the earliest, locally dominant in most of the empire, except probably its central Anatolian heartland; Byzantium had a substantial independent peasantry, which made up thematic militias, as well as – and above all – being the major source of tax receipts. Aristocrats could not easily go it alone under these circumstances, and opposition to imperial power tended to be in the form of attempted usurpations, not provincial separatism.[6]

This fiscal system needed people to run it, and Constantinople had a very substantial bureaucracy of officials, who ran every sector of government in complex hierarchies – as it had under the Roman empire, although they were by now substantially reconfigured. The capital itself was so large that it required officials to run it too, headed by the eparch, the direct heir of the urban prefect of the sixth century. The latter had organised the state-run grain supply for the late Roman city, which had ended with the Persian conquest of Egypt in 618; but the city, expanding again in its population from the eighth century, became, as we have seen, very large by the eleventh, and emperors could not risk it running out of food – they could and did fall if the urban populace turned against them. The task of managing a food supply which, although by now supplied by private landowners and merchants, had to come from all over the empire, was substantial, and the surviving regulations in the Book of the eparch show that, by 900, eparchs fixed prices or regulated the terms of trading for every major foodstuff.[7] The imperial aristocracy was important in the civilian administration too, and it was as well paid as the army. (It used to be thought that a civil and a military aristocracy were opposed to each other, but this is not true – there was no structural difference between them, and generals could be bureaucrats at other times, as well as having career bureaucrats as brothers.) The western diplomat Liutprand of Cremona (d. 972) records the Easter ritual of paying officials as he saw it in 950: the emperor himself handed out heavy bags of gold coins to his senior officials in order of status, across a three-day period, and then the head of the imperial bedchamber paid lesser officials across the next week. This was part of the highly elaborate ceremonial of the empire, which was expressed also, at least in Constantinople, in an extensive network of processions, criss-crossing the capital but usually focused on the great church of Hagia Sophia at the eastern end of the city; these were arranged according to the liturgical cycle of the church, but also included complex rules for imperial entry and triumphs after successful war. The population of the capital was involved in this processional practice, and it was an important part of imperial presence and legitimacy in the city.[8]

Court culture in Constantinople was dense and complicated too. All the Byzantine élite were literate, in a way that the post-Carolingian west would not match for centuries; career soldiers could write books (Nikephoros Phokas provided at least the notes for a military handbook; Kekaumenos in the 1070s produced an advice manual for statecraft); rural landowners could have substantial libraries, as with the eighty books left in his will by Eustathios Boilas in 1059, including Christian religious classics and secular romances.[9] In the capital, however, leading bureaucrats were highly educated in theology and literature, from Homer onwards, and many of them were writers – as also were emperors, not only Leo VI: his son Constantine VII (913–20, 945–59) wrote an analysis of the empire's neighbours, and at least some of the *Book of ceremonies*, the long basic handbook of the processions of the capital, in which he associates them explicitly with the 'order and dignity' of power.[10] Intellectuals could write elaborate poetry and prose for emperors, often in very difficult, by then archaic, Greek; a literary world was kept in play (and documented for us) by an extensive formalised letter-writing culture. This world claimed to be very traditional – literary accomplishment was supposed simply to imitate the classical past – but in reality it was innovative both in genres and in content: Constantinople after 850, like Aachen after 800 and Paris after 1100, had enough resources to train enough intellectuals to establish a critical mass of new thinking. There is significant theological writing from career officials, from the official-turned-patriarch Photios (d. *c.* 893) onwards; and the legal knowledge necessary to translate Justinian's whole legal corpus into Greek in the years around 900 and reorder it as the *Basilika*, turning it into a functioning law code for the empire, was very considerable.[11] Later, Michael Psellos (d. *c.* 1078), a courtier of and sometimes a senior minister for seven emperors (he survived even though they were often highly opposed to each other), and author of one of the most significant and complex historical accounts of the eleventh century, the *Chronographia*, as well as letters, rhetoric, philosophy and scientific treatises, saw himself in effect as a new Plato, and commanded a remarkable range of neo-Platonist writing as well as the standard run of classical and Christian authors.[12]

Byzantium expanded its influence culturally as well. The Bulgarian khaganate which had stabilised itself inside imperial borders in the late seventh century, when it faced more effective aggression from Constantinople in the mid-ninth century than it had before, recognised the need to adopt Byzantine styles of ruling to survive, and accepted Christianity in 865, much as the Poles did a century later, as we have seen. By 913, the Constantinople-educated Symeon (893–927) was recognised by the Byzantines as emperor, tsar in Slavic (the Slavic component in Bulgarian culture was from now on dominant), and Bulgarian government became highly Byzantine in inspiration. This worked, in that it was the direct reason why the Byzantine conquest of Bulgaria was such a long-drawn-out process.[13] From Bulgaria, Byzantine-style Christianity could also be exported to other Slavic groups, and in the late ninth century there developed a Slavic-language, 'Slavonic', liturgy, based on a newly invented Cyrillic alphabet which had a long future. The next people to follow Bulgaria's lead were the Ryurikid princes of Kiev, of Scandinavian origin but ruling a Slavic-language people; these were by now called the Rus', a word originally meaning 'Scandinavian' but by now firmly attached to the Slavic-speakers under Kiev's rule, in the core lands of what would later be called Russia. The ruling princess Ol'ga (c. 945–65) converted personally in Constantinople in c. 955; her grandson Vladimir (972–1015), Basil II's ally, formally declared Rus' to be a Christian polity around 988.[14]

The Rus' did not face the same dangers from Byzantium that the Bulgars did. Kiev lay on the edge of the forests beyond the steppe corridor, which was in general a land of Turkic-speaking nomads, as the Bulgars had been once; the steppe was currently ruled by the Khazar khaganate, which had adopted Judaism as a religion, the only realm in medieval history ever to do so. The rulers of Rus' were indeed often enough also called khagans, Turkic-style, and developed a system of tribute influenced by Turkic models. For the Rus' as for the Danes of the same period, Byzantine Christianity was simply a useful extra, which brought with it an ecclesiastical organisation headed by a metropolitan bishop, artisans to build the largest Byzantine church still surviving from the eleventh century, St Sophia in Kiev, and also a culture of writing which would be important for government as it developed. As with Bulgaria, however, what it also brought was Slavicisation. Kiev was fully Slavic already, and indeed Vladimir and his father Svyatoslav already had Slavic names; but it is significant that their other major political centre, Novgorod in the far north, founded by Scandinavians in a Baltic-speaking area, was almost wholly Slavic-writing and Cyrillic-using by the time of the first birchbark documents found there – these survive in many hundreds, starting in the 1030s, in waterlogged excavations, and are still being found.[15]

Rus' was a huge area, the size of Germany, and almost entirely forested; communications by river were good, but the area could not be controlled in depth with tenth-century technologies, and would not be for centuries. The fur-trappers, and then, increasingly, peasant agricultural settlements in the midst of the forests, simply handed over tribute to the princes and their *druzhina* or military entourage, via a network of trading towns. As Russian ruling princes tended to have many sons, the towns were divided up between them. Vladimir himself had started in Novgorod, and only reunited Rus' in 978. His son Yaroslav (1015–54) did the same, becoming prince of Kiev and sole ruler in 1036. None of Yaroslav's sons or descendants ever united Kievan Rus' again, however, before the fifteenth century. Kiev remained the senior principality, but by 1100 there were a dozen princes, all related and each with his own *druzhina*, fighting it out. Three areas were particularly important, Kiev itself, Novgorod, and increasingly a fringe area to the north-east around the towns of Suzdal' and Vladimir, which, once it was cleared of forest, was fertile land. By the late twelfth century, this was for the most part the dominant principality. But the Ryurikids were still fighting when the Mongols appeared in 1237–40, to sack Russian towns and to reduce the princes to tribute-paying subjects. The Mongols were almost entirely a negative force, with their tendency to mass killing and brutal exploitation nearly everywhere they attacked; even their very brief appearance in Hungary did that kingdom serious damage, as we have seen. But, from now on, the steppe corridor, regularly so dangerous to early medieval European states, was above all dangerous to the Russian principalities.

*   *   *

Basil II was a highly charismatic emperor, even if in a humourless and unmerciful mould. His successors were less so, and were also not as long-lived: the longest continuous reign between 1025 and 1081 was thirteen years, and policy-making was less continuous in this period. Until the 1060s these were decades of peace for the most part, with the empire not seriously under threat, but a bad sign was the Norman takeover of most of Byzantine Italy in the 1050s, for imperial armies were hardly able to confront it at all. Given the peace, fears of usurpation and financial problems led to military pay arrears and a decrease in the size of the army, and the thematic troops, a basically defensive force, largely disbanded. This did not help matters when the empire came to face a military danger on a scale not matched since the ninth century, the Seljuq Turks, who had, from their central Asian base, conquered half the Muslim world since the 1030s; they were moving into Armenia by the 1050s and into Anatolia shortly after. In 1071 Romanos IV faced them in a pitched battle near the eastern border at Manzikert, and lost; the Byzantine army melted away, and, although the Seljuq rulers did not move systematically into Anatolia, ad hoc Turkish groups, plus rebel Byzantine mercenaries, turned the plateau into a political vacuum. Civil war made things worse, and a long-ruling Byzantine emperor did not reappear until Alexios I Komnenos (1081–1118). By then, however, the Turks had moved far to the west and were attacking the Aegean; they soon established themselves in some of the major cities in Constantinople's immediate hinterland, such as Nicaea and Smyrna (modern İzmir). Alexios also faced attacks in the Balkans from the Normans, after the latter had wrapped up Byzantine Italy, and from Turkic semi-nomadic groups directly from the steppes; he defeated them by 1091, and stabilised his Balkan power. But he had lost control of most of Anatolia, and the situation worsened in the early 1090s.[16]

This was when Alexios asked for western support, and Urban II preached the First Crusade in 1095 as a result. The main crusader contingent reached Constantinople in 1097, and was indeed able to retake Nicaea for Alexios, allowing him to regain power in the eastern Aegean as well. By the time the crusaders finally took Antioch and Jerusalem a year later, however, relations with Alexios had broken down (historians still argue as to whose fault this was), and the rest of the crusade did not bring any returns for the Byzantines, but, instead, a set of unstable and often resentful Latin principalities in Syria and Palestine, to add to the Turkish amirates which slowly crystallised in central Anatolia, notably the Seljuqs of Rum, based in Konya. This was from now on the new geopolitics. Alexios had retaken western Anatolia, and his son John II and grandson Manuel I (1143–80) re-established Byzantine power along the south coast too, but henceforth Byzantium, unlike in the eighth to tenth centuries, was far more a European power than an Asian one, and the emperors not only did not retake the Anatolian plateau, but barely tried to: the only serious attempt, in 1176, was a disastrous failure.[17]

This looks menacing on a map, but in fact was not. Central Anatolia became Turkish for ever, but Byzantium was not again threatened from the east until the very different world of the fourteenth century. What the Byzantines lost was their aristocratic heartland, and many of the great families of the tenth and eleventh century had lost their power by the twelfth as a result; what was left was essentially nostalgia, as for example in the great verse romance *Digenis Akritis*, a twelfth-century evocation of border warfare on the plateau, with a hero of mixed Arab and Greek birth.[18] The main survivors were the Komnenoi themselves, and the closely related Doukai, whose power-base moved to government, for Alexios and his successors put family members into high position everywhere, inventing new titles for them as they did. Alexios indeed used his mother Anna Dalassene in effect as his finance minister, bringing into government the gender roles of the family economy. The culture of coups ended for a century, and government stabilised without otherwise having to change much – certainly the taxation system did not change, and we have more evidence of a densely organised judicial system. The army maintained its structure as a paid and professional force, although here there was a greater tendency than in previous periods to recruit from abroad, and there are by now examples of military men being given land or local tax rights, *pronoia*, in lieu of pay. This was complained about by the early thirteenth-century chronicler Niketas Choniates, keen to find the internal roots of imperial collapse around 1200, and stressed by modern historians, keen to find parallels to western military feudalism, but not yet significant.[19]

The high Komnenian period in fact was in most respects as stable as the empire of Basil II. Constantinople was at least as large and rich as before, and helped in that by a clear economic upswing in the twelfth century in the Aegean. This was fuelled, as in the west, by demographic growth, and added to by the fact that the period shows a expansion of large landowning, both ecclesiastical and lay, at the expense of peasants. By this time in most of western Europe, such an expansion was complete, but in Byzantium, as we have seen, an independent peasantry had always been numerous, and private wealth came from official salaries paid by tax-receipts, as much as or more than from rent-collecting from family lands. From now on, however, as large landowning developed, peasants often had to face paying both tax and rent at once. That renewed exploitation provided more élite buying power, and thus more exchange. Wine specialisations were beginning to appear on the Greek islands, and olive specialisations in the Peloponnesos; mulberry production for silk was focused in several areas, with significant silk-weaving at Thebes and Corinth in central Greece, and exports not only to the capital but westwards as well. Excavations show that major towns such as Corinth had diversified productions, glass, pottery and metal as well as silk; other towns had significant markets. In the capital, the *Book of the eparch* gives clear evidence for trade guilds already by 900, and production was certainly strongest of all there.[20] Overall, Byzantine economic growth may not have equalled that of northern Italy or Flanders, but it at least matched that of most other parts of the west. This prosperity – for some – further funded the fiscal system and thus the armies of the state; and it allowed the intellectual life which is so visible in the tenth and eleventh centuries to continue as well. The same array of literary interests among political actors is documented, indeed in greater density (not least Alexios's daughter Anna Komnene and her husband Nikephoros Bryennios, both of whom wrote histories), and there were novelties as well, such as satire. As part of that, we begin to find the kind of literary complaints about the unfairness of poverty, if one is educated, which Paris shows in the same period – that is to say, here too, people were buying education in hopes for social mobility, and not always being successful.[21]

That wealth and that cultural bounce had its counterpart in politics. Byzantium by now had more structured relationships with the west than ever before, given that western links to the crusader states – and the crusades themselves – passed across Byzantine-controlled sea and land routes. Indeed, Italian ships, from Venice, Pisa and Genoa, from now on carried much of Byzantium's sea traffic, and had commercial quarters in Constantinople just as they did in the Levant and Egypt. Conversely, Manuel, in particular, intervened westwards in ways that emperors had not attempted since Basil I, both diplomatically, with marriage and other alliances (he was most influential in Hungary), and militarily: although, unlike Basil, he never managed to establish his rule in Italy, it is significant that he tried, with an invasion of formerly Byzantine Puglia in 1155–56. Manuel wanted to be taken seriously in the west as a player, and in part he was, thanks in particular to his money, in the swirl of ever-changing alliances between pope, Sicilian king, Italian cities and German emperor.[22]

Greater western familiarity with the Byzantines did not, however, lead to a greater understanding between the two cultures, and this became a crucial issue as time went on. Manuel may have tried to further it, but not many other people did. It may have been too obvious that many Byzantines thought of westerners simply as greedy barbarians (it was widely believed that westerners ate carrion, as well as there being genuine religious differences which seemed horrible to Byzantines, such as demanding the celibacy of priests and eating unleavened bread at the Eucharist).[23] It was certainly too obvious that the Byzantines had little sympathy with the crusader states, which always enjoyed a warm glow of religious frontline commitment in the minds of western observers. Western political players were anyway becoming surer of their own identity and cultural superiority, and had begun to close themselves off more to alternative values and practices. The western view that Greeks were ungrateful cowards, as well as over-clever theological logic-choppers, which had been a cliché since the Roman republic, and a subtext of some defensive western rhetoric across the earlier middle ages, became much stronger in the twelfth century. The tone of genuine impressedness at Constantinople's grandeur, wealth and sophistication, which is visible, partly against his will, in Liutprand of Cremona in the 950s–960s, is by now heard much less often in western sources, except in the form of a semi-mythical city of wonders, like the exotic images of Arab wealth which had long existed – Byzantium, that is to say, was becoming orientalised, in Edward Said's terms.[24] And that Byzantium's effective and wealthy fiscal system might have been a useful model for generally cash-poor western government is not heard at all.

This was the context of the period after 1180, when, after Manuel's death with only a child heir, the Byzantine state faced a new round of coups and unstable, indeed incompetent, rulers. The fact that all the rivals were Komnenoi by now did not help; they behaved at least as violently to each other as any predecessors had. And they no longer appeared to westerners to have the political solidity which Manuel had had – when the Third Crusade came through in 1189–90, the empire's weaknesses were very apparent. As for the Italian cities, already in 1171 Manuel had confiscated the property of the Venetians; in 1182 Andronikos I actually massacred the Pisans and Genoese. The Venetians benefited from 1182, but did not forget 1171; the other Italian cities never forgave 1182; the turns of Byzantine politics with respect to each in the next two decades alienated both sides. For almost the first time, the instability of central government also allowed provincial leaders to aim for separatism: the Serbs in the north-west, the Armenians in the south-east, a Komnenos in Cyprus, a local magnate in the eastern Aegean, and, most problematic of all because closest to the capital, the revolt of Peter and Asen in 1186 which resulted in the revival of an independent Bulgaria. This was, by any standards, a lot of separatist revolts. One important result was that the capital was starved of money, and the army diminished quickly as well. This meant that, when the crusaders of the Fourth Crusade in 1202–03, in debt to the Venetians and thus in need of money themselves, agreed to deviate from their path to put a claimant on the imperial throne, Alexios IV – which they did by storming the city in 1203 – Alexios could neither pay them what he promised nor resist them. Constantinople had been stormed before; Alexios I had done so in 1081 for example, with notable violence and loss of life; 1203 was less serious than that. But when the crusaders got tired of waiting (Alexios IV was anyway by now dead in another coup) and stormed it again in 1204, that time it was very serious. By now Constantinople was not looked at with any sort of impressedness at all, but just as the over-rich capital of worthless and schismatic Greeks. This made the events of 1204 fatal. The capital's treasures were systematically looted and in large part taken to the west; and the empire was replaced by a dozen small successor states, often heirs of the separatist revolts of the 1180s and 1190s, with the addition of weak Latin rule in the centre.[25]

In a sense, this account decentres 1204 as the key event in Byzantine history; it was only possible because of the previous disintegration of Manuel's state, and because the western powers and the Byzantines had, so to speak, fallen out of love with each other. But it made these possibly temporary developments final. Had the events of 1203–04 never occurred, it would be easy to imagine that a second Alexios I could have reunified the empire again and re-established its centrality as a European power which could have been more culturally integrated with those of the rest of Europe, possibly through the mediation of the Italian cities. The thirteenth century was, after all, a period in which vernaculars were beginning to take off in several western regions, and Greek was no harder for a French or Italian politician or intellectual to grasp than, say,

German; and the thirteenth century was also, as we saw in the last chapter, the century in which an interest in innovative techniques of government became much more developed in the west than in previous centuries. The Byzantine model might have become effective again, and maybe even more effective than it had been previously. But this did not happen; or, rather, when it did, with the rise of the Ottomans, it happened in a way which westerners did not and, given their cultural and religious assumptions, could not, value. We shall conclude this chapter by looking at how that occurred.

*   *   *

The Latin empire of Constantinople was a failure, and it is surprising that it lasted until 1261. But, as I said at the start of this chapter, there was never a period after this that the revived Byzantine empire, now under a new dynasty, the Palaiologoi, gained any sort of substantial territorial base. In the later thirteenth century and early fourteenth, it focused on extending its authority from its north-western Anatolian power-base back into what is now Greece (Bulgaria was beyond its powers), but it was rivalled by an expansionist Serbia, which under Stephen Dušan (1331–55) temporarily took control of the whole of northern Greece, whereas the Byzantine state faced civil war in the 1340s, and the Black Death did particular harm to Constantinople in 1347–48. The Peloponnesos, for its part, was divided between small Greek and Latin principalities; the Venetians, in the islands, co-ran the commercial system with the Genoese. The Aegean world was thus simply a mix of fractious principalities, none of them with any chance of winning out over the others. All that one can say is that the Constantinople-based empire was the richest, with a strong city-based culture which continued that of previous centuries and was still capable of producing ambitious and expensive architecture, like the rebuilding and decoration of the Chora monastery (Kariye Camii) by the senior administrator and intellectual Theodore Metochites in 1315–21, which contains the most impressive surviving mosaic- and fresco-work in the whole of Istanbul, outside Hagia Sophia itself.[26]

What changed this was an unexpected development. This was the break-up of the Anatolian Seljuq state in the 1270s, wrecked once again by Mongol conquest, for this released the random energies of a set of small Muslim Turkish lordships, who could look to the rich Aegean lands of the Greeks as much as they fought their rivals. One of these, that of the Osmanlı (Ottoman) family, originally from the tiny town of Söğüt outside Nicaea, took Nicaea and Bursa in 1326–31. From this still-small base they expanded with dramatic effectiveness. In 1354 they moved into Thrace, and by the late 1360s they reached the

Black Sea, cutting Constantinople off except by ship. From then on, they occupied nearly the whole of the Balkans in twenty-five years, slowing only in 1389, when the Serbs held the Ottomans to a draw on the Kosovo field, celebrated ever after in song. (The Serbs had to recognise Ottoman hegemony not long after, all the same, and in 1439 the Ottomans took them over totally.) On the mainland, only Albania and southern Greece remained in the hands of Latin and Greek powers; Sultan Beyazit I (1389–1402) was already besieging Constantinople. The Byzantines were temporarily saved by the latest central Asian conqueror, Timur, who destroyed Beyazit's army at Ankara in 1402, but by now Byzantium was reduced to hardly more than a single city, plus a fragment of the Peloponnesos around Mistras. Renewed Ottoman expansion in the 1430s picked off all the major Latin and Greek remnants by 1461 except the Venetian islands, with Constantinople itself going to a neatly executed siege by Mehmet II (1451–81) in 1453.[27]

The Ottoman empire in the Balkans was the most innovative political development of the later fifteenth century in the whole of Europe (its territory stretched ever further into Asia too), and the state which ran it was by 1500 the most coherent political and fiscal structure of the continent. If I do not discuss it in detail, it is only because the evidence for its coherence begins to be available only in the last years of the century, and to be substantial only after 1500, too late for this book. But the major question it poses needs at least some discussion: that is to say, how did it happen? How did the Ottomans manage to achieve, from a minuscule initial power-base, something which emperors of Constantinople and aggressive Serbian kings could not manage, the stable reunification of the old Byzantine imperial lands, and then well beyond? They certainly built up an effective army, which seems to have been paid from nearly the start by a land tax, the standard system in the Islamic and Byzantine traditions. By the late fifteenth century, if not earlier, this army was mostly paid through the devolution of blocks of local tax revenues to soldiers who collected them directly, called *timars*; these too had antecedents in both the Islamic world (the *iqta'*) and the Byzantine world (the *pronoia* – which was a more important feature of the late Byzantine state than it had been before). Different historians stress these different origins, but we can at least see considerable linkage between Byzantine and Ottoman fiscal patterns when there is documentation (as in northern Greece) for the succession of political régimes.[28]

Essentially, the political practices which the Ottomans inherited from the Arab-Turkish past – in particular the near-universal assumption that a paid standing army, with its own career structure, was a standard part of any political system – made it necessary for them to adopt and adapt whatever fiscal structures they found when they conquered, which meant, above all, those of the Byzantines. They soon turned this into a centralised system, adding new elements as well. They built on it by rapidly incorporating regional élites into their system, and stabilising the latter's local authority by doing so. Their power was not immune to fragmentation, especially in the troubled years after 1402; but it could be, and was, re-established effectively as well, indeed so effectively that the Ottoman state by the sixteenth century became the best-organised, not only in the whole of contemporary Europe, but in the whole of Islamic history up to the nineteenth. That this solid structure first developed in lands which had once been Byzantine was by no means chance, and Mehmet recognised his Byzantine inheritance, which of course he saw himself as transcending, when he repopulated Constantinople/Istanbul, re-established as his new capital, with so much care.[29] Western European conquerors of ex-Byzantine, and indeed ex-Arab, lands, had seldom been so effective. For example, even though the Norman kingdom of Sicily owed much to Byzantine and Arab example, the Byzantine land tax in Puglia was quickly privatised; and, although taxation survived longer in Sicily, for it was exacted from Muslims there, it too mostly went to private lords, and declined with the Muslim community itself across the twelfth and early thirteenth centuries[30] – the thirteenth-century re-establishment of taxation there was on different bases, and was less well organised. But the Ottomans recognised the importance of these structures, and were better able to make use of them. They were well placed to be the heirs of the Byzantines, and the Romans, in a new Muslim world. But they were much more separated from the other European powers than the Byzantines had ever been or ever could have been; they were an object of hatred and fear (as well as orientalising fascination), not of admiration or emulation, and that tension lasted as long as the Ottomans did themselves.

Actually, the polity which claimed to be the heir of Byzantium with most insistence was Muscovy, the principality of Moscow. After the Mongols conquered Rus' in 1237–40, they established a loose suzerainty, plus tribute-taking, from the various Russian principalities, under one of the Mongol successor states, the Golden Horde. Kiev, the old focus of Russian power, lost any centrality, and the new political centre was by now stably in and around Vladimir in the far north-east. In the interminable carousel of disputing between the Ryurikid princes, which continued after 1240 as much as before, the rulers of Moscow, up to then a tiny town in the territory of Vladimir, emerged as the most influential by the 1320s, largely thanks to the choices of the Mongol khan; the metropolitan bishop of Rus' was most often based there from then onwards too. When, from the 1420s, the power of the Horde began definitively to fade, the grand prince in Moscow became the dominant ruler of the Russian lands; by 1520, with the submission of Ryazan, Ivan III (1462– 1505) and his successor Vasiliy III had taken over every other independent Russian principality.[31]

Until now, Russian metropolitans had always been consecrated in Constantinople, and were often chosen directly by the patriarch there. From 1448, with the Byzantine empire on its last legs, that ceased. But the ideological attachment of the Russian church to the Byzantine tradition remained tight, and so did that of the Ryurikids; Ivan III's wife Sophia, for example, was a Palaiologan. By the sixteenth century, the Russian response to the fall of Constantinople was that Moscow had become its successor. 'Third Rome' imagery developed steadily thereafter, and in 1547 Ivan IV was crowned as tsar. This ideological tradition (expressed architecturally, as well, in the impressive Byzantine-inspired churches of medieval and early modern Russia) was the only Byzantine element that persisted in Moscow's lands, however. The fiscal structure of Muscovy long remained a fairly simple one, of tribute-taking from towns and from a still-largely independent peasantry; this independence was lessening by now, in the face of increased church and aristocratic landowning, but the process was not yet fast. As Muscovy grew larger, and its political infrastructure had to develop, the models it chose in practice were much more similar to those of the Mongols.[32] This is hardly surprising, for Muscovy's centre was even further from the rest of Europe, including Byzantium, than Kiev-ruled Rus' had been: it was separated from the south not only by the steppe corridor, which remained a hostile marcher land until well into the seventeenth century, but also by the expanded grand duchy of Lithuania, now solidly associated with Poland (see below, Chapter 11), which had moved fast when the Horde began initially to lose its grip, and established long-lasting control over Kiev itself by the 1360s. Between an Ottoman empire which ruled the old Byzantine lands from the Byzantine capital in a largely Byzantine way, and a Muscovy which laid claim to a Byzantine succession with an insistence which no sultan would have wanted to match, but which had a wholly unrelated infrastructure and social practice, it is easy to put more weight on the continuities between Byzantium and the Ottomans. But it was all the same significant that the Muscovite church put so much emphasis on its Roman/Byzantine past and orthodox identity, and this would remain impor-tant in the future.

*   *   *

The Byzantine empire was a crucial part of European history until its eclipse in the years leading up to 1204, and, but for the Fourth Crusade, might have been again. No serious account of the middle ages can leave it out. It is curious that so many do; probably this is because they tend to give so much weight to the period from the twelfth century onwards, when Byzantium, although a major player until 1180, was slipping out of the vision of western writers and then vanished as an effective force. The European community of states after that was a very Latin one indeed, apart from the Balkans and the Russian lands, which few outside Hungary and Poland by now (and as yet) paid much attention to. But anyway, until then, the Byzantine empire was the richest and most complex European power, and was widely recognised as such at least into the eleventh century. Choniates, in his bitterness after 1204, claims, apart from the graphic insults which one would expect (they always hated us, we were their prey, etc.), that there was actually nothing in common between west and east at all: 'between us and them [the Latins] the greatest gulf of disagreement has been fixed, and we are separated in purpose and diametrically opposed'.[33] His bitterness is understandable, but we do not have to follow him here.

CHAPTER TEN

Defining society: gender and community in late medieval Europe

When we get into the later middle ages, the information we have about Europeans, particularly western Europeans, increases exponentially. Court records survive from Italian cities in their hundreds of thousands, and financial records from the English government almost to the same extent. Furthermore, the increasing range of lay literacy means that we have writings by ever-wider groups of people, and from ever further down the social scale – sometimes artisans, very occasionally peasants. These texts are increasingly not in Latin, and are thus closer to, although not the same as, the ordinary speech of the laity. The result of all this is that it becomes easier to get a sense of some of the cultural values and practices of the non-élite majority, and to know more about the non-religious values of élites as well. Let us therefore look at how cultural practices actually worked in this period, focusing on gender difference, with particular regard to women, and community solidarity: mostly after 1300, but looking back where possible too. This will be the inescapable underpinning, the cultural base if you like, for the analyses of political superstructures and discourses, and economic change, which will follow in the next two chapters. I will begin with two examples of female religious innovation and reactions to it, which will help to illuminate some of the wider presuppositions of the period as well, above all concerning female gender roles. That in itself will take us into the world of the values of the laity, and we will then look at other aspects of these, using, among other sources, contemporary imaginative literature. Here we will concentrate on the collective identities, of, in turn, aristocrats, townspeople and peasants, and how they were increasingly clearly defined – including the dark side of such definition, the stigmatisation of outsiders.

So let us start with the future saint Catherine of Siena, who died in 1380 at the age of thirty-three, whose success and whose strangeness show what possibilities there were for a certain sort of female protagonism in her time. She was

from a prosperous artisan family, of dyers, who were part of Siena's medium
élite, and included city leaders in the 1360s; she was said by her biographer to
be her mother's twenty-third child, but was one of only five or so to survive
into adulthood. She refused food early, and by 1370 was eating virtually
nothing; it is entirely likely that her decision in 1380 to stop drinking water for
a month as well contributed to her death not long after. Caroline Bynum has
convincingly shown how this decision by Catherine – and its associated physical signs, like sleeplessness, plus more extreme food choices like drinking pus
– cannot simply be seen through the prism of anorexia, but also needs to be
understood inside the complex relationship to food, to the Eucharist and to
Christ's blood which was a characteristic feature of female spirituals. Catherine,
who also refused marriage and withdrew into a single room for some years,
certainly saw her vocation as overwhelmingly spiritual and visionary. This was
recognised early, and she had Dominican advisors in the 1360s (the Dominican
church of Siena towers over the section of the city where she lived); by 1374 she
had become formally attached to the order, had come to the attention of the
pope, and was assigned a senior Dominican as a confessor, who later wrote her
longest biography. All major female spiritual figures had a male confessor, who
very often is our only source for their activities, normalising their lives in a
male narrative framework. We get rather more of a sense of Catherine's own
personality, however, for she authored over 380 surviving letters and a theological work – all in Italian; if she had any Latin it was sketchy – and so emerges
as a figure with her own down-to-earth metaphorical style (for example,
Christ's divine nature is the wine in the opened wine barrel on which one gets
drunk; his double divine and human nature is like a grafted tree). She was
active in Tuscan and papal politics, and began to travel extensively; she was
taken seriously as a political and moral force, urging Pope Gregory XI, then
based in Avignon (see Chapter 11), to return to Rome, which he did in 1377. In
Siena she was taken very seriously indeed, although she by no means always
argued for the interests of the current Senese government; she also developed
an entourage of influential male Senesi, whom she called her *famiglia* (she was
their *mamma* – her family-based political imagery extended to addressing
popes as *babbo*, 'daddy'). Catherine was often viewed with suspicion, as were
other female spirituals, whose prominence outside marriage or the monastery
often seemed problematic, as we shall see. She was tested by panels of ecclesiastics more than once. Like other female religious actors, she did not make it to
sainthood early, and was only canonised in 1461, by a Senese pope. All the
same, in the last six years of her life, this artisan's daughter, with no Latin, the
standard political language, was a significant political figure in Siena and

Florence, Rome and Avignon. Her extreme ascetic acts, plus a personal charisma which is very clear in her letters, were enough for that.[1]

My second example is Margery Kempe (d. after 1439), daughter, wife and mother of merchants of the port of (King's) Lynn in Norfolk. Her father, many times mayor of Lynn and an MP, was particularly successful, and Margery was seldom poor, except when she gave away her money. Almost everything we know about her comes from the autobiographical book that she dictated in the 1430s, when she was in her sixties. This mediated writing does not show she was illiterate in the sense of being unable to read (Catherine of Siena also dictated, until she miraculously learned to write in 1377, as did many male chroniclers); Margery's book is ambiguous as to whether she could read, but a rich merchant's child, even female, is likely to have had some training in it by now, and she was certainly well acquainted with spiritual religious texts. The text depicts her – 'this creature' as she calls herself throughout – as developing a highly personal style of ecstatic Christianity, not based on asceticism (except chastity, which she found hard) but on public weeping and crying out, especially in religious contexts, on self-humiliation, and on intense visions of Christ, with whom she went through a visionary marriage when on pilgrimage in Rome. She had a more-or-less normal marriage for a long time, despite a moment of mental breakdown, including bearing fourteen children, but visions persuaded her in the 1410s to ask her long-suffering husband for a chaste marriage and permission to go on pilgrimage, which he agreed to as long as she paid his debts. Dressed in virginal white, she went to Jerusalem, Rome and Santiago de Compostela. These were the classic pilgrimages for anyone who could afford it, but it was very unusual to do all three; and a lone woman on such long journeys, even though travelling with companions as she always did, was distinctly uncommon. Late in life, she also added religious shrines in the Baltic (she had a German daughter-in-law who, rather unwillingly, took her to Gdańsk). More visibly to her social world, she also travelled around England, creating a certain degree of notoriety for herself, given her garments and her crying and her constant discussions about religion with everyone she met. In 1417, on her return from abroad, she ran into trouble, for that was a time of panic about heretical Lollards (see Chapter 12), and several times she was hauled in to face charges in front of bishops and town officials (the mayor of Leicester said 'thou art come hither to lure away our wives from us', one of the many signs of discomfort which Margery generated, according to her text). Actually, however, bishops were relatively sympathetic to her, as she could respond to all interrogation in a totally orthodox manner, and she got certificates of orthodoxy from both English archbishops; she could also get out of accusations that she was preaching – a potentially heretical act – by saying that she simply talked to people. Margery Kempe was doubtless, on the basis of her book at least, a totally infuriating person, but she managed to create a Margery-sized space for herself and defend it against people of every social level. Modern historians have sometimes hypothesised that she sought sainthood with her book; it does not really seem so to me; but she certainly saw her personal close-ness to Christ as highly special, and it is clear that many others were prepared to go along with that too.[2]

I will come back to the gendered aspects of Catherine's and Margery's activities in a moment; let us start by simply looking at them as members of the laity. These two were obviously wildly atypical figures in their religious commitment, and also atypical in that they both, despite their considerable differences, came from the interior-minded, spiritual wing of Christianity (it is often called 'mysticism', but the term is very vague). What is important for us, however, is not that most ordinary people did not behave like this, but rather that they tolerated, and often admired, these forms of action. Lay religious devotion was normally a matter of regular weekly and yearly rituals, in churches or processing between them, and its outward forms were essentially run by priests, who were also expected to preach to the laity and to confess them annually.[3] The idea that the Christian religion should be mediated by the clergy was fundamental, and much of the anti-heresy activity of the thirteenth century had been aimed at people who did not accept that, as we saw in Chapter 8. So was it later; Margery Kempe was explicitly accused of heresy, and Catherine skirted its edges; they got away with it, and gained protection from the powerful, because their acceptance of the church hierarchy (even if not their respect for its individual members) was, or appeared to be, complete. We will come back to late medieval versions of heresy in the last chapter of this book, for they can be seen best in the framework of wider problems of authority and dissent in this period. Here, however, the important point is that Margery and Catherine were *not* ultimately seen as heretical, but they were nonetheless engaged in innovative ways of acting morally in the world; and religious authorities such as bishops and indeed popes were happy with that. Clearly, then, it is not the case that all lay religious protagonism was seen as wrong by the church, and it never was; it had to be scrutinised before it was accepted, but, once that happened, senior clerics rather welcomed the extra access to the divine which lay commitment could provide. Gregory XI indeed sought Catherine out in part because his previous spiritual interlocutor, Birgitta of Sweden (a similar figure, but aristocratic, rather than of an artisan background, so in a way less exceptional), had recently died. This had already been the case with the impact Francis of Assisi had on Innocent III, and the beguines in Flanders and northern France sometimes gained similar respect. But there does seem to have been more lay spiritual activism, and more acceptance of it, in the later middle ages; a further instance was the influential (and well-studied) Modern Devotion movement in the fifteenth-century Low Countries.[4]

How was that acceptance achieved, and what were the obstacles to it? It is not easy to tell, for our narratives all know that acceptance would come in the end, and how it was arrived at is dominated by cliché. Some patterns are clear, all the same. It is not chance, for a start, that both my examples are of urban-based religiosity; there was more of a social space for self-fashioning in towns (it was one of the reasons why people emigrated to them, not least women, who could, by working for pay, live independently, longer than they could manage in the countryside).[5] Urban communities also often valued having a recluse or other ascetic figure in the town, as a sign that the town was special. Sibylla of Marsal was an earlier instance, a beguine of exceptional religious commitment in a small town in Lorraine, who fasted and had visions and in 1240 began to attract pilgrims to Marsal; the inhabitants had no problems with this at all, and nor did the bishop of Metz, who had come in person to investigate, once he encountered the demon whom Sibylla was fighting. Only more detailed scrutiny revealed, apparently by chance, that Sibylla was faking it, to the extent that she had made her own demon suit and dressed up in it. Had she not been so successful, she might never have been checked on, and Marsal would have continued to benefit.[6] This makes the initial excitement of the Senesi about Catherine's sanctity rather less surprising.

Conversely, it is equally clear that the suspicion of lay 'spiritual athletes' which also existed in this period, as Catherine and Margery both found, was highly gendered. Catherine managed to establish a considerable degree of international respect, as we have seen, but a more common reaction to female spirituality, taken as a whole, was negative, and became still more negative as time went on. This was in large part because women were liminal to the male religious world: they were thought to be spiritually weaker, more prone to demonic possession, which resembled divine spirituality so greatly, and more prone to have a chaotic effect on the male order which circumscribed them. Another, famous, example was Joan of Arc, the peasant girl whose access to saintly voices led Charles VII of France to use her to inspire his armies against the English invaders in 1429–30 and whom the English burned for heresy in 1431: the whole argument of her show trial hung on whether her voices were divine or diabolical – because they were not signed off by the church, that is – as well as on the legitimacy of a woman cross-dressing as a soldier. This sort of worry would strengthen further after the mid-fifteenth century, when some female visionaries began to be assimilated to a newly important category of the spiritually dangerous, witches; Joan was in fact one of the first to be accused of this, as a minor part of the charges against her.[7] But spiritual worries of this kind were spin-offs of patriarchal power relations of a less religious type as well: these were women whose actions were not, as it was believed they should be, mediated or controlled by fathers or husbands, or even, often, their confessors; and they were claiming a public role which many thought they were not entitled to. We need to look at more widely at these power relations, in particular as they concerned women.

It is not news that women were constrained by male power, in this as in every period, but it is worth making it clear all the same. Dante refers in his *Monarchy* to a proverbial curse, 'may you have an equal in your house'; households were regarded as hierarchical by definition. In 1392–94 an anonymous Parisian bourgeois wrote an advice manual for his young wife which takes for granted that it was his responsibility to direct her every action, however unreasonable his demands, with much citation of improving stories from medieval literature of hyper-dutiful and abused wives such as Patient Griselda, who humbly obeyed the intentionally humiliating instructions of her husband (more attractive and more useful is the second part of the book, which contains gardening advice and recipes). Women were weaker, inferior, more lecherous, more prone to evil; they needed controlling, if necessary by force, and their reputation was easily at risk – and, it is important to add, these were assumptions held by women as much as men.[8] Rape was common and was rarely punished; the writer of an early etiquette guide to courtly behaviour, Andreas Capellanus in the 1180s, sees it as a standard and amusing usage of aristocrats when they meet peasant women. And so on. These were widely held norms, against which every literary account of a bold female actor in, for example, Giovanni Boccaccio's *Decameron* of *c.* 1350 needs to be understood (Boccaccio included Griselda among his stories as well, with little irony).[9]

Constraints on women were also in part enforced by law, as in legislation on dowries, which limited the property any married woman could inherit or control directly. Once again urban environments made other female protagonism, particularly in gendered economic activities such as weaving and brewing, less unusual – and we should also not forget that, even in the countryside, women of the peasant majority worked all their lives as part of the family collective, and were often responsible for marketing goods. Nonetheless, the only secular women who had any long-term chance of acting independently were widows; the economic rise of the Fugger family as rich cloth merchants in fifteenth-century Augsburg was quite as much the work of widowed women as of men, for example. The one thing which women did tend to have under their direct control was household management and the household economy – even the Parisian bourgeois assumed that; this is indeed the context for the role Anna Dalassene had in managing Byzantine imperial finances in the 1080s for her son Alexios I, as we saw in the last chapter, in what was in effect a family takeover of the Byzantine state apparatus. Much wider economic activity tended to derive from that household role elsewhere too: weaving, for example, was gendered as a female trade because it was always done by women in a family context, and indeed men often took over larger-scale, more 'public', weaving.[10] Expertise was gendered as well: women always controlled child-birth, and much practical medical knowledge as well, but as soon as medicine became professionalised (this was in most places a late medieval tendency) its career structure became male. Patriarchal control was never complete; personal relationships with acquiescent husbands (like Margery Kempe's), as well as economic necessity, gave a practical space for many women to operate in. Indeed, the Reformation, when it came in the sixteenth century, often regarded the practical autonomy of many wives as something to combat by ever-tighter regulation.[11] But the control was still there, usable if anyone wanted it.

It is not surprising that when historians want to study female protagonism, they very often find themselves studying queens and senior aristocratic women, who could exercise considerable power, either by inheritance (in the absence of brothers) or, most commonly, as regents for children after their husband's deaths; women had these roles in non-élite families as well, but aris-tocracies are far better-documented. That power was real, but it too was circumscribed. Female rulers tended to find a rather more hostile and critical political environment, or else bolstered up their authority by marriage, or indeed both, from Urraca of Castile (1109–26), through Joan and Margaret, successive countesses of Flanders (1206–78) and Joanna I of Naples (1343–82), to Margaret I of Denmark (1375–1412) and Isabella I of Castile (1474–1504), the last two of whom were the most successful of this set. Margaret of Denmark, even though she inherited her kingdom as her father's heir, in fact almost always ruled through young males, her son and then a handpicked nephew, like queens-regent did elsewhere. It is true that Margaret is also notable, not only for overcoming opposition almost completely, but also for actually extending her power-base: it was during the only period in which she ruled on her own, 1387–89, that she unified the three kingdoms of Denmark, Norway and Sweden, by force in the Swedish case.[12] There were tough matriarchs else-where, too – on the Welsh Marches, for example; and Isabella of France, wife of

Edward II of England, was even capable of overthrowing her husband, with the help of her lover Roger Mortimer, in 1327.[13] All the same, other female rulers found that the fragility of all political authority particularly applied to them. And so did the policing of behaviours. With the development of 'courtly love' and Arthurian-inspired rules of etiquette (see below), a king's or lord's wife could easily find herself surrounded by young knightly admirers, but woe betide any lady who was thought to have fallen for that; even royal figures could be brought down by accusations of illicit sex with such admirers, from the daughters-in-law of Philip IV of France in 1314 to Anne Boleyn in England in 1536. The survival of the Arthurian Guinevere and Isolde in the face of such accusations was simply the fiction of romances.

There was thus no secure public space for women, unless nunneries count as that (but female monasteries, too, were often more enclosed, and often poorer, than those of men).[14] Female secular power was obtained, when it was obtained at all, only in the context of positions in family life cycles. Every time power was exercised by collectivities, it also moved away from being available to women; Italian city communal government was a male space, for example, so were universities, and so were most craft guilds (although some guilds had female members, particularly widows, and Cologne and Paris, in particular, had specifically female weaving and spinning guilds and wider female guild membership).[15] Gender analysis thus tends to be about the negotiation (by men as well as by women) of expectations, assumptions, boundaries, body-based categories, and it is logical that it should be. It is by such negotiation, too, to come back to Catherine and Margery and also Joan of Arc, that exceptional women could play with gender expectations, including that of female frailty, to create spiritual spaces for themselves which could sometimes have political implications. But this was restricted to the exceptional (and the exceptionally pious), and it, too, was hedged around with constraint and risk.

Did anything change in this across the middle ages as a whole? There is disagreement. Some have argued that the early middle ages gave more space to female property-holding and power, whereas from roughly 1100 onwards the growing patrilinearity of aristocratic family structures in the west, and the exclusion of daughters from inheritance if there were sons, cut them out from political protagonism as well, constraining them inside family and marriage patterns made by men.[16] It is certainly true that male-line families are rather more visible in the second half of the middle ages (though they existed before too); it is also true that the marriage-portions women had access to in the later middle ages were, in general, smaller than those of earlier periods, and that women in some cases lost other rights of inheritance (but here the issue is also

how much control they had ever had over their land, which was very variable).[17] The transactional power of political women was however always fragile:
as we saw earlier in this book, the queens-regent of the Merovingian period or
pre-1100 Byzantium were powerful, but faced the same sorts of constraints and
criticisms as those of the twelfth to fifteenth centuries; Carolingian queens
faced accusations of adultery just as the daughters-in-law of Philip IV did, and
for similar reasons. The growth of male-line lineage actually increased the
number of queens- and countesses-regent for male children, who were all the
more essential because there was less choice as to who could be a legitimate
heir. I would rather see women as making the best of varying but always limited
opportunities for personal agency, with success rates which, although low, were
not vanishing in any period, and no major shift around 1100 in this respect.

What seems to me to be different about the late middle ages, however, is
above all the increase in ambiguities. Patrilinearity excluded women from
inheritance, but gave them more authority as widow-mothers. University
education and the professionalisation of knowledge excluded women, but a
steady widening of lay literacy gave more of them access to books (there were
always female authors, and mothers – notably St Anne and the Virgin Mary –
are regularly depicted in late medieval images teaching their children to read[18]).
Towns excluded women from urban government and usually from guild
protection, and often cut them out of artisanal activities they had dominated
before, but gave them opportunities for employment and, sometimes, prosperity which they could not have gained elsewhere. The sharpening of the hierarchy of the church gave more power to celibate men, but lay piety gave a new,
even if restricted, space to female religious sensibility. The basic reason for all
this is that Europe was now more economically complex, as we have seen; with
that complexity came ambiguities of all kinds. And it is in societies where
complexity and ambiguity give space for pragmatic solutions that women have
in general found it most possible to negotiate space for their own protagonism.
Societies with sharper lines, by contrast, like those of the Reformation, and,
later, the French Revolution, have often made that negotiation harder, between
an initial period of innovation and a later period in which the complexities
which are also there are allowed fuller play again.

Hence also the fact that Christine de Pizan (d. c. 1430) became an intellectual figure, after her husband died young in 1390 and she had to raise her
family on her own in Paris, with all the difficulties in securing control over her
husband's property which widows often faced. She made ends meet thereafter,
very unusually, by writing poetry and prose for money. She would hardly have
managed this if she had not been the daughter of the royal astrologer to Charles

V of France and widow of a well-known royal notary, so was well connected, even if in financial trouble. But she would certainly not have managed it had she not been highly educated, including in Latin and Italian, her parents' language, more than almost anyone so far mentioned in this chapter, which is significant in itself (she had access to the royal library too, and was influenced by Ovid, Boethius, Boccaccio and Aquinas). She was also a remarkably gifted poet. In 1404–05 she wrote a long tract against male hostility to women, *The book of the city of ladies*, in which she is called on to build the city by Reason, Rectitude and Justice, who all agree with her that women have been maligned by the lies of men, and that the catalogue of virtuous women in the past (a long list, including Griselda again) shows that women are in reality kind and loyal, whereas men are lustful and violent. This text is interesting for its independence of thought and evident anger, of a type which modern commentators can identify with (and they have); but it has also to be said that, although Christine clearly prefers women to men in moral terms, and thinks that they are fully as intelligent, she accepts the normative medieval female roles outlined above in other respects almost completely: men do naturally rule; women should be modest, and simply endure wicked and violent husbands. She was a woman of her time, then, as were (in very different ways) her partial contemporaries Catherine of Siena and Margery Kempe. But she is an intellectually stimulating one to finish with here; and she well shows the possibilities that a virtually self-guided education could produce, towards the end of our period.[19]

*   *   *

I have here cited writers in the vernacular almost exclusively, which is itself, as we have been seeing, a sign of the steady extension of lay literacy. They were of course not the only writers in the later middle ages – in most of the west, Latin remained the standard international, administrative and intellectual language throughout the medieval centuries, and often beyond – but such writers often reflect the cultural attitudes of wider sections of the laity. (It was easier in Byzantium, where everyone still spoke Greek, although, conversely, there were few fully 'vernacular' texts there, for the literary language was by now usually quite far from the spoken one.) These attitudes need to be followed further, if we want to understand how aristocratic, urban and peasant communities defined themselves in the later middle ages; this will be the focus of the rest of the chapter, with vernacular literary representations set against other elements of the sociocultural practices of each in turn.

The first thing to keep in mind is that a French literary culture was usually dominant in this period in western Europe. The twelfth-century French epic

poems about Charlemagne, particularly the *Song of Roland*, were widely translated and adapted, into Old Norse, German, Spanish, English, as well as, and
most influentially of all, Latin prose, as the so-called *Pseudo-Turpin chronicle*.[20]
The late-twelfth- and thirteenth-century French romance tradition, largely
associated with stories about the court of King Arthur in verse and prose,
spread even further across Latin Europe, including back to Wales, where the
first Arthurian material came from. Much literary creation in German consisted
of adaptations of them in the thirteenth century, and, later, English authors
from Geoffrey Chaucer (d. 1400) to Thomas Malory (d. 1471) did the same: in
these countries, a dialogue between French and native literary styles continued
for a long time.[21] In Italy too, although romance itself only came in much later,
French initially had a similar status; the works of Brunetto Latini (d. 1294)
were largely in French, and so in 1298 was the first version of Marco Polo's
Milione, the account of his travels to China. It was not until Dante Alighieri
(d. 1321) made the choice to write the highly literary *Divine comedy* in Italian
that the vernacular really took off there. Dante's complexity fascinated Italians
from the start, in much the same way that James Joyce did for modernists in the
1920s and 1930s, and sections of the *Comedy* circulated even while he was
finishing it in the 1310s, with commentators following on fast as well; but his
impact outside Italy was for some time relatively restricted, except in Spain.[22]
Of Italian texts, Boccaccio's *Decameron* had the greatest early effect beyond the
Alps, thanks to multilingual figures like Chaucer and Christine de Pizan (they
knew Dante too, but used him less).

The problem about vernaculars was of course translation; French was
widely spoken (in England the whole aristocracy spoke it for a long time), but
other languages were not, so their literary achievements were less known. This
was even more the case for Byzantine romance literature, which was unknown
west of the Adriatic; although it predates the first Arthurian romances, it did
not influence them (it is also timeless in a way which much western secular
writing is not; its loving couples are separated by shipwreck and capture by
pirates, then brought back together by coincidence – social context, except
gender of course, is cut out of these texts almost deliberately). Conversely,
French romance, in particular, provided a template for the 'courtly' and 'chivalric' behaviour of the aristocracy of over half of Europe, with rulers and their
courtiers on occasion dressing up as Arthurian figures and the like, from the
late twelfth into the sixteenth century; Edward III of England's Order of the
Garter of 1348, for example, played off Arthurian imagery very explicitly.[23]
This contributed substantially to the self-consciousness of the aristocratic
strata of the period.

Chivalry had other origins than literature. Jousting and the tournament developed out of military training; the bond between a lord and his knights had been strong since the early middle ages, and all lords wished to keep it that way with as much ritual and feasting as possible, as we have seen; the religious imagery of the Grail quest and other Arthurian themes had at its roots the assumption, which military aristocrats had had since the Merovingian period, that they were far more moral than everyone else. French romance was initially successful simply because it represented that aristocratic world in emblematic terms, adding in the *fin'amors* (courtly love) rhetoric of the south French troubadour tradition, and creating attractive plotlines around the trials of individual knights, such as Lancelot, loyal to his lord Arthur but tragically in love with Arthur's wife Guinevere. As we saw earlier, eroticised power games were very risky if they went too far in real life, but as a literary image they were very strong indeed. The rituals of knighthood steadily gained coherence, defining and idealising as they did so the order of 'those who fight', one of the three orders or estates of society (together with 'those who pray' and 'those who work'), which were rapidly gaining currency as a classification from the end of the twelfth century onwards. As they did so, an etiquette for knights at court was ready-made for them, in the works of Chrétien de Troyes, Marie de France, and, in the thirteenth century, the authors of the huge Arthurian prose cycle which Malory would later translate and adapt. This chivalric etiquette gained in elaboration across the rest of the middle ages. The dialectic between literature and self-image was here unusually tight. Of course aristocrats were usually far from chivalric in practice, and they mistreated peasants and townspeople during both war and peace with at least as much commitment as they had done in earlier centuries, but the ideal of the honourable wandering knight, being constantly tested, and fortified by love and religion, had a long future.[24]

Aristocracies also developed a new degree of definition in this period. Being a member of the ruling élite was taken for granted by its members in the early middle ages, and not theorised; there was indeed no word before 1200 or so which accurately translates the words 'aristocrat' or 'élite', which are our words, not theirs. *Nobilis*, which came closest, was a word with many meanings, both narrow and wide. Élite membership was in practice negotiated, for it was based on several different elements, wealth, birth, office, political skills, training, royal favour, not all of which every potential aristocrat had. By 1500, however, at least in the Europe of kingdoms (communal Italy was, for a long time, more flexible), you were either a 'noble' or you were not. The upper aristocracy was thus bounded, even if differently in different countries. The right ancestors by now made one a noble almost automatically, and the policing of heredity became ever more visible. One could rarely become noble by marrying up, even if a few women managed it, like Alice Chaucer (d. 1475), grand-daughter of the poet, who married a knight and then two earls, and died duchess of Suffolk. But kings and other rulers by the fourteenth century could create aristocrats as well, 'ennobling' them, after which, at least in theory, they were the equals of older families. Sometimes (in Germany in particular), this aristocracy defined itself as a 'nobility' (*Adel*) against cities and their rich élites; elsewhere, participation in the upper secular house in parliaments and their equivalents was a key element. As the code of chivalry became ever more explicit as a self-image for such nobles, rulers could play with that too, with new orders of noble knighthood, the Garter in England or the Golden Fleece (1430) in Burgundy. This still often left a wide knightly and quasi-knightly stratum outside the narrower nobility, such as the English gentry or the urban *caballeros villanos* of Castile. Their élite status was certainly real – they too could have chivalric aspirations, for instance – but it remained more informal, and sometimes more transactional, as that of all élites had been in the early middle ages (the gentry were for example sometimes called *nobiles* in texts, without being 'nobles' in a strict sense). All the same, everywhere in Europe the centuries after 1200 brought both clarity and restriction for the aspirant aristocrat.[25]

The concept of urban identity was becoming equally elaborate too, and is increasingly well documented in this period. By 1300, towns had some type of self-government everywhere, in the wholly autonomous city-states of north-central Italy, the imperial cities with their special status in Germany, the towns of Flanders which could defy their ruling count with regularity, and then in every possible form, whether defined or de facto, everywhere else. They expressed their identity publicly, and indeed the latest medieval centuries are the first period in which urban public ritual begins to be really clear in our texts in most of the west. Such ritual was at its base religious in almost every case, and processions on major religious feast days were standard everywhere (not only in towns, indeed), but they acted in many urban centres as the basis for remarkable elaboration. There were sometimes dozens of them every year in large cities. The processional map was very complex and long-standing in places like Rome and Milan, and of course Constantinople, where it went back to the early middle ages; but Florence, Venice, Bruges, Ghent and other Italian and Flemish cities developed similar patterns in later centuries. From 1317, when it was properly established as a universal church feast in the west, Corpus Christi in June became a particularly significant focus for public events: in England, major late medieval towns like York, Chester, Wakefield and Coventry established cycles of 'mystery' plays for performance at Corpus Christi, as did some south-west German towns such as Künzelsau and Freiburg, and there was a playwriting competition on that day in Lille in northern France too. Public events with a more secular element matched them, such as the archery and poetic competitions of the fifteenth-century Low Countries, or the bull-fighting and jousting in Rome on the first Sunday of Lent, regulated in some detail in its communal statutes of 1360. But none of these were events with a purely religious meaning anyway. Rituals are polyvalent, for a start: they regularly take on different meanings for participants from those intended by organisers, often several different meanings at once. One general meaning of all these processions and other events was a celebration of the civic identity of the participants, which was frequently fully explicit, and also marked by dances and jousting in the days before and after the more formal religious ceremonials. They were also, of course, intended to support local power structures and social hierarchies, as with the pope's Easter Monday procession in Rome, which represented (among other things) his local sovereignty, or the particular festivities at Carnival and on St John's day which Lorenzo de' Medici developed around 1490 in Florence to showcase his charismatic authority. Conversely, such rituals were also foci for contestation, as, earlier in Florence, the opposition between urban aristocratic jousting and guild processions. Any procession could be disrupted, indeed, to make a political point: that was how internal civic crises often started. One-off political points were also made processionally, as with the often elaborate and expensive *joyeuses entrées* into towns by Burgundian dukes and French kings, which of course represented external power, but could be manipulated to make their own public arguments by the citizen groups (guilds, confraternities) who had paid for them. Almost all these public events, indeed, were paid for by town-dwellers, and that conveyed a sense of ownership which allowed plenty of different points to be made, if necessary.[26]

Towns were complex places, even after their populations halved in the wake of the Black Death, and they needed to be regulated. Urban statutes survive from the thirteenth century onwards in considerable numbers, and the problems of government were many: not only ensuring that civic taxes were collected and markets and guilds were properly run and violence kept under control, but, more widely, the creation and defence of public space, the disposal of sewage (an almost impossible task), the banning of activities held to be unpleasant (such as tanning, and, more unexpectedly, candle-making) from town centres, or attempts, as in Italy, to prohibit unrestrained grief in funeral processions. That last example shows that secular government in cities often saw itself as having a role in the creation of what it saw as public morality, too. The problem of how good government should be achieved was faced first in Italian cities, as is logical since they were effectively sovereign, but widely thereafter as well. Brunetto Latini's encyclopaedic *The book of the treasure*, written in the 1260s and focused on his experience as an official in Florence, was excerpted and adapted in London in the early fourteenth century by the city chamberlain Andrew Horn, for example, and was also widely available and translated in late medieval Spain.[27] Such government, however, was of course also focused on maintaining the power of urban élites, or of one of their factions, often in the face of considerable opposition; it was coercive as much as administrative. Indeed, the need to bolster up élite power, plus a fear that bad behaviour by the few might menace the town as a collectivity, could and did produce moral panics among urban rulers; these largely depended on the chance crises which hit, whether war, struggles with external powers, or plague, but they often accumulated across time. Marginal groups, who could be thought to have provided that menace, suffered as a result, as we shall see later.

For town-dwellers, there was little aspirational literature to match romance. The expressed aspiration of Italian citizens, for example, was more architectural (squares, civic buildings) and image-based, as with the *Allegory of good and bad government* of Ambrogio Lorenzetti (1338–39) in the Palazzo Pubblico of Siena. Patriotic poetry, urban chronicles, and tracts on city government, in Latin for the most part, were seldom aimed at filling this imaginative gap.[28] In Italy, we have to wait for Boccaccio's *Decameron* to find a vernacular 'civic' text, focused on the elegant storytelling of ten Florentine aristocrats fleeing the Black Death in a country retreat. Much of the content of their stories is not as elegant as their conversation, but instead bawdy and comic (and far more attractive for a modern reader than most other writing mentioned so far in this chapter), but it regularly has an urban and commercial background, and its values and prejudices are those of the urban upper class, made slightly more aspirational by the delicate manners of the storytellers, even when they are telling stories about sex. Chaucer borrowed the format for his *Canterbury tales* of the 1380s and 1390s, although in his case he mixed a very urban (in his case London) consciousness with an intent, visible in a wider cast of storytellers than Boccaccio had, to speak not so much for London, but for society as a whole.[29] Unsurprisingly, articulated urban narratives were mostly restricted to élites who did not work with their hands, including the *ricordanze* tradition, developing out of account books, which allowed prosperous civic figures in Italy from the fourteenth century onwards to recount their lives and those of their families. Only in the fifteenth did this tradition occasionally extend to real workers, like the builder Gaspare Nadi of Bologna (d. 1504), whose diary begins with his record of his birth in 1418 and proceeds, over hundreds of pages of the modern edition, until just before his death; even then Nadi's work tends for the most part to record Bolognese and Italian political events, plus some conflict among fellow-builders, and only occasionally the affairs of his family – it is an oddly impersonal text. But anyway we would look in vain for an urban élite Lancelot, let alone a romance hero who was an artisan, in any of our medieval literary forms.[30]

Some medieval urban literature, indeed, was the opposite of aspirational. The bawdy aspect of the storytelling of Boccaccio and Chaucer is matched, and far exceeded, by the thirteenth- and early-fourteenth-century north French *fabliaux*, relatively short comic poems, certainly with roots in oral storytelling, of sometimes quite startling obscenity. A simple example is *The maiden who felt ill at talk of fucking*, in which the new farm servant finds that, as long as he uses euphemisms, the maiden concerned is only too delighted to have his erect young horse and his two round stable boys drink at the spring in her meadow, as often as they like. It cannot be said that *fabliaux* are representative of urban values only; they largely were, but they will have been popular in all kinds of social environments. They were also, undoubtedly, less shocking to the sensibilities of audiences in 1300 than they would have been in (say) 1950, and indeed would still be to some audiences now. But the naturalism of their contexts allows us to recognise the socioeconomic flexibility of the north French society they deal with (there are plenty of *nouveaux riches*, who generally get their comeuppance in the derisive conservatism of these texts), and the imagery of the marketplace returns often: this is a society involved with towns, even if it is not always an urban society. Anyway, what we can certainly say is that the society, which appreciated poems such as these, did not need to idealise itself, or not exclusively at least: they are about trickery, and, above all, enjoyment. This is sexual enjoyment for the most part, as it might be in any time and place, but food imagery marks the genre just as much; the stews, partridges, pastries, fish, wine, and much else, lovingly listed, are as much part of the texts as the equally carefully described human genitalia.[31] It is worth adding that eating (and sometimes avoiding) good food appears repeatedly in Margery Kempe's (very different) book as well, and also in the Parisian bourgeois's advice manual; if we strip away the idealised world in medieval secular representations (or, at least, do our best to strip it away), food and the pleasure of eating is what we end up with on a very regular basis.[32] This was probably common ground in the whole medieval period, but it is particularly clear from now on.

An imagery of direct peasant origin is more of a problem. The *fabliaux* are not always bourgeois, but they are certainly contemptuous of peasants. An often-cited (because relatively clean) example is *The peasant donkey-herd*, in which the peasant, hauling manure, enters a spice market and faints because of the sophisticated and unfamiliar smell, and only revives when some of his own manure is put under his nose. In this respect these poems do not differ from most other medieval literary traditions. Indeed, the ridiculous vileness and stupidity of the peasant majority was so obvious to the literate social strata that it is not always even stressed – it was so much an axiom that, as with the gender boundary, the gulf between peasants and everyone else could be played with in texts, as for example in the myths that the earliest royal houses of Poland and Bohemia were both descended from peasants, or in the Christ-like if simple virtue of William Langland's Piers Plowman in the late fourteenth-century English poem of the same name. The values of the peasantry themselves, by contrast, were so far from the sensibility of most writers that peasant revolts in the late middle ages often seemed close to meaningless. Steven Justice has clearly shown how English-language texts preaching the Peasants' Revolt of 1381 invoke a concept of 'truth', itself related to usages in Langland, which implies collective just activity, something which was so invisible to élite commentators that they casually preserved the texts in their own chronicles. What peasants thought they were doing is otherwise systematically falsified in most of the narratives that survive for us.[33]

It is true that knowledge about and involvement with literate practices extended quite far into peasant society by the fourteenth century in much of Europe. One result was that peasants sometimes found their way into public debates about the direction of politics; we shall look at this in Chapter 12. What literacy was directly available to them, however, tended to be pragmatic, rather than representing in detail their cultural values. Indicative is Benedetto del Massarizia (d. *c.* 1501), a peasant in the countryside outside Siena, part-proprietor, part-sharecropper, who recorded his rent-payments and buying and selling and credit operations between 1450 and his death in two surviving account books; each deal had to be recorded by others, for he could not write (although he evidently valued writing and could doubtless read). That text is gripping for the complexity of his dealings, not for his views about the world.[34] For the most part, peasant values and presuppositions are only available in detail through their witnessing in court – in civil litigation,[35] criminal prosecutions, and inquisitions about heresy and sanctity – and thus, although often expressed in the first person, are recorded in texts written by people who were not peasants, and often not in the language of the witnessing. But such texts are certainly illuminating, perhaps above all those concerning heresy. We saw in Chapter 8 that what peasants told inquisitors about heresy often (even if not always) simply reflected what inquisitors expected, but at least when they contextualised their statements about meetings with supposed heretics they could provide guides to their assumptions about more secular matters too. Emmanuel Le Roy Ladurie's famous account of a very late (1320s) anti-'Cathar' investigation at Montaillou in the Pyrenees, although it takes a literal approach to the inquisition record which sidesteps not only the distortions of the inquisitor but also the narrative strategies of the peasants themselves, nonetheless constructs a rich picture of peasant attitudes to time, space, the complicated relation between pastoralism and agriculture, household structures, contraception and illicit sex (the philandering village priest used a herb which, if worn around the neck, prevented semen from curdling, thus avoiding pregnancy), and mutual delousing etiquette. It is this sort of external framing, then, which gives us our most detailed, even if distorted, account of peasant thoughtworlds, in all their complexity.[36] Future work – for this is a field which is not as fully ploughed as one would think – will give us guides to difference too, for the Europe of the middle ages held a myriad of different peasant societies, each with distinct value systems, which in the future might be, as so far they have not been, properly compared.

In the late medieval period, all the same, we can say more about the construction of rural communities. Villages gained franchises, as we saw in Chapter 7, and other forms of rural collective identity, in much of the west between (very roughly) 1100 and 1300; these became more organisationally developed as time went on, around the village church and its ritual life (parishioners were generally in charge of church upkeep), and around local political and economic collective structures. In much of England, even though peasants were often legally unfree into the late fourteenth century, manorial court records show that the villagers themselves policed their community, using local customs which had largely been generated by themselves. Such customs, and policing, were normal throughout Europe. Customs were formally recorded from 1300 onwards (sometimes earlier) in England in custumals, in Germany in *Weistümer*, in France and Spain in the franchise documents themselves, in Italy in village statutes, some of which are very complex texts.[37] Villages and their parishes already had their boundaries confirmed ceremonially too, through religious processions (as in towns) or the beating of the village bounds, although accounts of these before 1500 are fairly sketchy. The landscape was itself often numinous, full of sacred spaces of differing importance, as we know because Protestant reformers spent much time in the sixteenth and seventeenth centuries trying to secularise it; communities drew on that too, drawing up (often competitive) networks of collective religious practice.[38] Villages were hardly idyllic; they always had difficulties with their lords, obviously, and were also themselves run by village élites who could be over-bearing – part of the tension in the Montaillou inquisition hearings came from the fact that Catholic villagers were happy to bring down a leading 'Cathar' family, who included the village's badly behaved and domineering priest, already mentioned. They faced newer dangers, too: to village solidarity, when new families who were less interested in it rose in status, like the yeomen of late medieval East Anglia, getting rich through dealing in grain and playing the local land market; or to village coherence itself, when, in Tuscany, late medi-eval settlement steadily became more dispersed into the isolated farms of sharecroppers.[39] But the network of rural communities, which had taken shape across Europe by the end of the middle ages everywhere, usually survived.

The only place in Europe where narratives give us a peasant voice is Iceland, for the 'family saga' tradition of the thirteenth and early fourteenth centuries provides us with very detailed and naturalistic imaginative accounts of the affairs of Icelanders who were, certainly, the island's élite, but were peasants all the same. Iceland's tenth-century Norwegian settlers avoided even the weak kingship they had experienced in Norway (see Chapter 5), and any other form of government except regular assemblies, and for much of its medieval history it is hard to see who could have exercised it. Only in the thirteenth century did it become possible for more than a small number of people not to farm the land directly, and for the decades around 1000, the chronological focus of most family sagas, the narratives assume that even the richest people, the subjects of the texts, worked with their hands. These texts are anonymous, so exactly what sort of person wrote them has been disputed, but Icelandic literature was largely secular, and the sagas relate to a certainly secular oral tradition. Icelandic men in these texts were macho and suspicious, but also often very cautious, as peasants frequently are; they were committed to revenge-killing when their spiky honour was at stake, but their assemblies provided an elaborate network of courts in which grievances could be addressed, before peace was made or men turned again to fighting. As Iceland had no superior authority with effec-tive disciplinary power, such courts had no coercive force on their own (all they could do was outlaw people); they worked because they were public arenas in which other men could see where right and wrong lay, and whether it would be sensible to take part in future violence.

Icelandic saga narrative is nonetheless focused, to a remarkable degree, on the need to feud to preserve honour and on the etiquette of feuding. The social set-up just discussed was the basis for some very subtle accounts of the work-ings-out of feud, with an attention to characterisation and motivation for the principal figures, male and female alike, which is unmatched in any other type of medieval text except a handful of the most thoughtful chronicles. One classic example is Gudrun Osvifsdottir, an extremely strong-minded woman, who, out of jealousy, goads her husband Bolli, with great dramatic tension, into killing his cousin and foster brother, Gudrun's former love Kjartan. When Bolli is killed in return by Kjartan's kin and allies, Gudrun resolutely has them hunted down and killed, but admits to her son in old age that 'I was worst to the one I loved the most', meaning (she does not say, but we have to conclude) Kjartan. The reason for this attention to character was that, in a relatively economically equal society like this one, personal strengths and weaknesses, and reputation, could determine success and failure almost totally. This was a non-aristocratic society whose self-representation was indeed aspirational, but here the aspiration was only in part focused on honour, for honour in such a society was available to nearly everyone if they had the character and skill to maintain it; it was highly transactional. People did, nonetheless, aspire to a more ordinary courage, and an effectiveness in negotiation through careful and targeted violence – plus a literary style of laconic discourse in the face of difficulty and death which has seldom been surpassed.[40]

Historians have sometimes written about the discovery or development of 'the individual' when dealing with later medieval sources; this is a false image, for individual identity exists in all societies – and no-one who knows texts of the Carolingian period could doubt that it existed then. All that we are dealing with, when we consider the widening range of social groups whose voice can be heard in the late medieval centuries, is the steady extension of literate prac-tices, which, as stressed in Chapter 8, by no means changed people's wider perceptions, least of all their perception of 'individuality'. But if there was ever a medieval society in which we know a great deal about individual identity it is Iceland, for particular reasons: because, to repeat, in this peasant environment it was individual character which determined success and failure, more completely than almost anywhere else in medieval Europe.

* * *

The construction and bounding of communities had as its other face the growth of practices of exclusion. These were not new in the later middle ages. We saw in Chapter 8 how the growth in central power, both secular and eccle-siastical, in the thirteenth century was accompanied by an increasing hostility to out-groups, heretics, Jews, lepers, homosexuals: these people, defined as beyond the increasingly rigid boundaries of Christian society, were by now more often seen by élites (in particular) as polluting and viscerally dangerous. This argument gives a context to late medieval developments too. Urban governments had regular moral panics about able-bodied beggars and prostitutes, for example, and municipal legislation about them developed systematically. In London, it is notable that the major panics in the fourteenth century fit well with periods of wider tension: the fear of French invasion in 1338–40 at the start of the Hundred Years' War, the aftermath of the Black Death in the 1350s and 1360s, the aftermath of the Peasants' Revolt of 1381, which had a big effect on London; the phraseology of 'cleanliness' appears in municipal acts, and the image of moral pollution is hard to escape. These clean-up campaigns may have had popular support, but were above all élite-led.[41] So was the fifteenth-century development of witchcraft theory, which was generated above all in the minds of theologians and inquisitors, and was hardly at all a major preoccupation of secular society except in the valleys of the Alps, until the success of the *Hammer of witches*, published by the inquisitor Heinrich Kramer in 1487, which would have a long and dark future in the later sixteenth and seventeenth centuries.[42]

Of these exclusions, however, the key one was in every century the experience of the Jews; for they were a permanent non-Christian presence, often disliked but theologically tolerated, and protected by popes as reluctant witnesses to Christian triumph. Jewish communities in Mediterranean Europe went back to the ancient world, and some, particularly in Spain and southern Italy, were substantial; around 1000 or so they moved into towns in northern France and the Rhineland as well, often as merchants, and then into Norman England (their settlement in eastern Europe came later, as part of the German colonisation movement after 1150). Their achievements in biblical commentary, philosophy and spiritual thought match those of the Christian tradition in the central and later middle ages, even if this had less effect on Christian intellectual life than translated Arabic thought did – although the great Jewish theologian Moses Maimonides (d. 1204) did influence Aquinas. As time went on, Jews increasingly became associated with moneylending, which did not help their popularity with their Christian neighbours; and nor did their use as state agents by kings. But it was rulers and urban élites whose hostility tended to be much more important for the history of Jewish communities. As in Visigothic Spain in the seventh century, another society obsessed with religious unity, in the thirteenth century Jews faced greater state persecution: they were forced to wear special clothing by Innocent III, and the Talmud was burned in France under Louis IX (one of medieval Europe's most anti-Jewish kings) as supposedly containing blasphemous statements. These regulations, and early expulsions of Jews – from England in 1290, from France more than once from 1306 onwards – were essentially royal decisions, made for religious and fiscal reasons, with relatively little popular pressure. Not that popular tolerance was particularly benign. David Nirenberg has shown how the secular acceptance of Jews was a violent one as well, punctuated, that is to say, by regular hostile episodes: either fitting the Christian ritual calendar, as with the systematic violence often undergone by Jews during Easter week, or occurring when crusades came through, for, from their very beginnings in the Rhineland in 1096, those moments of religious fervour were regularly accompanied by massacres.

The tolerance of Jews was incomplete, then; and there was a growing hostility to them from élites. And violent moments, even if still episodic, spiralled in number in the fourteenth century. Excluding crusades, 1321 in France, 1336–38 in the Rhineland, 1348–51 in Spain, France and Germany (there was always less of this violence in Italy), 1391 in Spain again, were particularly important instances of religious hatred and massacre, focused on towns. Jews were accused of poisoning wells in 1321 (together with lepers), and again above all in 1348–51, as part of the attempted explanations of and hysteria following the Black Death; fantasies that Jews ritually sacrificed Christian children, which seem to have begun in England in the twelfth century, or that they desecrated the bread used in the Eucharist, also gained ground. Pogroms were largely conducted by urban leaders, city councillors and the like; in Spain, only the 1391 violence (and its successors in the fifteenth century, by now also focused on converted Jews in royal and urban government) was principally a spin-off of the political grievances of non-élite groups. Either way, however, hostility to this religious minority was much more entrenched at the end of the middle ages than it had been in earlier periods. It was part of the sharpening of collective boundaries which can be traced in other ways too. It culminated in 1492 in the expulsion of Europe's largest community of Jews from the kingdoms of Spain, again by royal decree, but this time with rather more popular support.[43]

*   *   *

In the patterns of late medieval culture, we have looked in this chapter at some clear trends: the contradictory directions in the opportunities available to women, a growing availability of evidence (often in the form of imaginative narrative) about the cultural assumptions and practices of more and more social groups, a growing cohesion of social strata and a greater visibility of community boundaries, a growing edginess about and potential hostility to outsiders. These trends were underpinned by more generalised developments: the still-growing complexity of the economy, which allowed for both expansions and contractions in female protagonism (as also considerable social mobility among the lucky and the unlucky, which itself led to the sharper policing of social boundaries); the steady extension of literacy and literate practices, which both reveal to us an ever-greater range of difference and enabled those differences to be accentuated; and the contradictions and ambiguities involved in the growth of central and local power. Major social and cultural shifts cannot be reduced to single causes in any period, of course, but these three developments do indeed seem to me to mark the late medieval centuries more than any others, and they played off each other. As we shall see in the next chapter, rulers and élites had the force and resources to control more, as time went on; but at the same time local societies and practices, which were themselves more and more complex, escaped every control. This is simply the further working-through of the cellular nature of local power after the eleventh century, discussed in Chapters 6 and 8: if wider political power was built up on the basis of such various foundations, the other side of the deal was, in effect, that it was very difficult to change the nature of the cells themselves, lordships, urban communities, villages, from the outside. These cells did not get weaker in the later middle ages, far from it; as we have just seen, they were ever more clearly delimited, now that not only local power structures but social strata, classes, were gaining clearer boundaries. Rulers sometimes reacted badly, trying to coerce local communities in shrill or violent ways. But those communities were themselves entirely capable of behaving coercively when things were seen as having gone wrong. Socioeconomic change which is ill-understood – and, as we shall see shortly, after 1350 this included the shock of the Black Death, not to speak of the spin-off effects of widespread and serious war – tends to provoke fear in most societies, and bad behaviour resulted from that in the late middle ages too.

But this does not mean that the late middle ages was particularly marked by fear, or anxiety; this argument has often been made, but it seems to me to have almost no force.[44] There are terrors in every period, but for the most part people get on with their lives, for better or worse. What really marks out the late middle ages, in this respect by contrast to earlier medieval centuries, is the extension of political activity, both positive and negative, to a much wider range of people. Another result of the long economic boom, and the continuing development of the European economy after the Black Death as well, was that society was much more diverse, and people who considered themselves protagonists in some way or other, and were thus empowered to try to

16. The Shakespeare Hotel, Stratford-upon-Avon, thirteenth–sixteenth centuries. The plot that the hotel sits on is one of the original plots laid out at the foundation of Stratford around 1200, still visible in the town plan. The building itself, in classic English urban half-timbering, dates to the Tudor period, and has been restored since.

17. Notre Dame cathedral, Paris. This church is the best-known of the wave of large and expensive gothic churches built in northern France in the twelfth and thirteenth centuries – in this case in the 1160s–1260s. The spire is nineteenth-century.

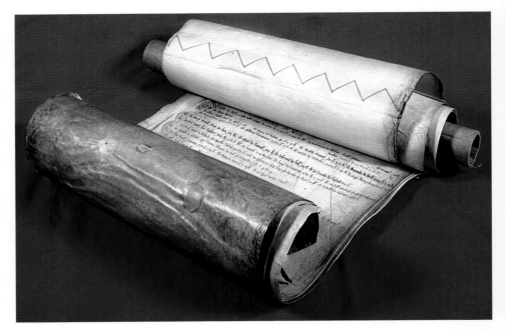

18. A pipe roll, late twelfth century. The English Exchequer (finance department) pioneered systematic copies of government administrative acts; they survive from 1130, and in a near-complete sequence from 1156. Their name comes from the tube shape when the parchments (in sets sewn together) were rolled up.

19. Statues of Ekkehard of Meissen and Uta of Ballenstedt, Naumburg, mid-thirteenth century. These statues are of eleventh-century founders of Naumburg cathedral in north-east Germany, put up two centuries later as part of a group of twelve very high-quality sculptures. They well show the attachment of church communities to lay patrons, which was a feature of every medieval century.

20. The Dream of Innocent III, Assisi, 1290s. This fresco in San Francesco, the first great Franciscan church, plausibly ascribed to Giotto and his school, depicts Innocent dreaming that Francis of Assisi was holding up the Lateran basilica (the cathedral of Rome) on his own. This was part of the early myth-making around Francis and his remarkable political success.

21. The northern (Istanbul) gate of Nicaea, Roman to early thirteenth century. These monumental walls and gate have a Roman base, but were systematically repaired and rebuilt in the Byzantine period, in particular under the emperors of Nicaea (1204–61).

22. The Anastasis, Kariye Camii, Istanbul, *c.* 1320. The Chora (Kariye) monastery was built by the senior Constantinople administrator and intellectual Theodore Metochites in 1315–21. This is its most dramatic fresco, of Christ harrowing hell – here he is lifting up Adam and Eve, to take them to heaven.

23. Rumeli Hisar, Istanbul, 1452. This castle was built in preparation for Mehmet II's siege of Constantinople, to block food supplies coming down the Bosporos in Venetian ships to the city.

24. The church of the Intercession on the Nerl, Vladimir, *c.* 1160. This is a particularly attractive example of the way Russian rulers adopted and adapted Byzantine styles to produce an architecture all their own. It was built outside the town of Vladimir by Prince Andrey Bogolyubskiy (1157–74).

25. St Anne teaching her daughter the Virgin Mary to read, French manuscript, 1430s. This was a common scene in late-medieval illuminated manuscript books, and is a marker of a widespread assumption in the period both that some laywomen could be literate and that, when they were, it was they who taught reading to their children.

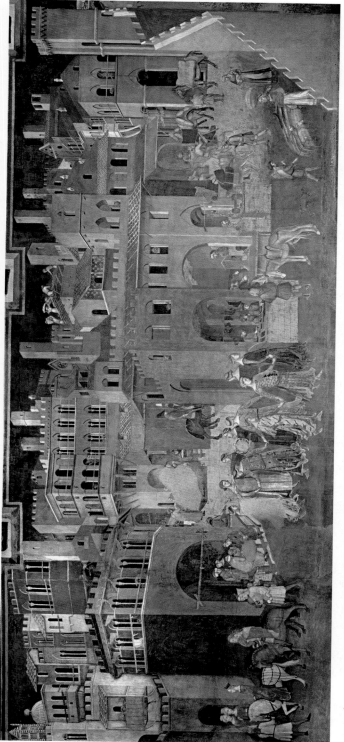

26. Ambrogio Lorenzetti, Effects of good government in the city, Siena, 1338–39. This fresco, appropriately located in Siena's city hall, shows an idealised image of how a well-governed town should look, with a shoe shop, teaching, much movement of goods and (less plausibly) women dancing in the street.

27. Egil Skallagrimsson, Icelandic manuscript, seventeenth century. Egil, a late-tenth-century Icelandic poet of high quality (we have some of his poems), was also a violent and sarcastic troublemaker with a very large skull. This early modern image shows what Icelanders of the time thought a peasant hero should look like.

28. The belfry, Bruges, 1480s. This phallic image of civic pride, topping the covered market in Bruges' main market square, was begun in the thirteenth century in wood, with the octagon at the top being added at the end of the fifteenth.

29. Charles bridge, Prague, late fourteenth century. This bridge, for long the only one over the river Vltava which divides Prague, was rebuilt on a massive scale by the sculptor and architect Peter Parler for the emperor Charles IV. The Old Town bridge tower in the picture is his too, and is a good example of Bohemian secular gothic. The swans are recent.

30. Patio de las Doncellas, Alcazar, Seville, 1360s. After the Castilian conquest of most of al-Andalus, many Muslim Spanish artistic traditions (most visible in the Alhambra in Granada) were taken into the rest of Spain. The Alcazar (the royal palace) of Seville is a particularly good example, using Muslim styles very extensively, mixing them with Christian ones.

31. Enea Silvio Piccolomini sets out for the Council of Basel, 1500s. This is at once a classic 'Renaissance' seascape and a scene in the life of a Senese intellectual who became Pope Pius II (1458–64). The frescoes of Pius's life, by Pinturicchio, were commissioned by a nephew of Enea Silvio who also became pope briefly, as Pius III, in 1503. Enea Silvio made his name at the Council of Basel, which explains the choice of this scene, even if it recalls a defiantly non-papal council.

32. The main square of Pienza, Tuscany, 1459–62. Pius II was born in Corsignano, a small village in southern Tuscany. As pope, he made it a city and renamed it after himself, as Pienza, and had it decorated with large-scale and state-of-the-art 'Renaissance' buildings, as would befit a far larger city – the open countryside can here be seen behind the cathedral.

influence their world, became much more numerous. Landed aristocracies, in their widest definition (that is to say, including the gentry and their equivalents across Europe), had started to become more substantial already in the eleventh and twelfth centuries, with the acceptance of the castellan and knightly strata into different versions of the aristocratic élite; each élite stratum came to have its own separate voice, both locally and nationally. Urban élites, too, who barely existed in 1100 outside Italy, Constantinople and Muslim Spain, were present, often rich, and loud everywhere by 1400, and less privileged urban groups were making their own claims; a few urban women were autonomous protagonists too, as we saw at the start of this chapter. And peasant voices were louder by now as well, in many places; there were, among other things, more peasant revolts after the Black Death. So: this cellular, collective world was one with more players in than before. They were harder to control, and they required different forms of politics to confront, as well as generating different forms of the public sphere themselves. How that political environment worked we shall look at in Chapter 12.

CHAPTER ELEVEN

Money, war and death, 1350–1500

The Black Death of 1347–52 defines the beginning of the late middle ages. But really three sets of events bestride the last century and a half of the medieval millennium; the other two are the network of wars, in particular between England and France, called by historians the Hundred Years' War (notionally 1337–1453), and the Great Schism of the papacy (1378–1417). All three characteristically have capital letters in historical writings. Actually, despite this, none of the three had quite as much effect as they have been often ascribed; but they are important starting points all the same. I will begin with them and the issues they raise, and then move on: first to a sketch of the economic changes of the period, and then to a rapid country-by-country survey of what was going on in the politics of late medieval western Europe, particularly in the fiscal underpinning of state-building. This will act as a framing for the discussions in the next chapter of changes in the nature of political practice in Europe.

The Black Death is first documented in the Crimea in 1346–47, and from there it spread around all the coasts of the Mediterranean (it was very severe in Egypt), and moved steadily northwards from Italy in 1348–49, reaching Scandinavia in 1349–50 and doubling back into Russia from there. Glands swelled up, black pustules appeared, fever was high, and death was usually fast. The death rate was huge, a third to a half of the population; and the successive, lesser, waves of plague which were regular until around 1400 and then steadily less regular for centuries after, resulted in a Europe at the end of the fourteenth century with around half the people it had in 1346. Demographic levels were slow to pick up in the fifteenth too. Not every region was hit in the first wave of plague, but later waves caught them as well. Towns, where people lived cheek by jowl, were particularly affected. Even the powerful caught it (to the particular horror of chroniclers), although only one European king seems to have died of it in the first wave, Alfonso XI of Castile. And if the first wave could be seen as a one-off devastation, by the time of the second (in 1361–63 for many places) people realised that it was going to stay, as an extra new and deadly peril.[1]

The Black Death affected the imagery of mortality for centuries afterwards. But – and this is the first of several buts – this did not, after the terror of the first wave (which resulted in anti-Jewish pogroms, as we have seen), have the devastating effect on people's confidence and emotional states that has sometimes been claimed. Life was too uncertain anyway; the causes of early death were numerous, in the absence of decent medical knowledge, and this just added one more, which, a generation after 1350, was already being taken for granted. We also might have expected the Black Death to interrupt wars, by making army recruitment and also taxation harder; it did not, or only for a short while (the Hundred Years' War resumed in 1355). And, given the close link between demographic growth and the expansion of complex economies in Europe in previous centuries, we might have expected economic crisis after 1350 – indeed, for a long time historians took it for granted that this happened; but recent work on England, the Low Countries and Italy has doubted that too, convincingly. Only economic regions whose prosperity depended on high levels of population suffered systemically, and there were few of these. The Black Death did have an impact on economies, all the same; we shall see how in the next section.

The Hundred Years' War began because Philip VI of France (1328–50) and Edward III of England (1327–77) were in the 1330s on ever-worse terms over the autonomy of English Gascony, around Bordeaux; and the war became hard to end because Edward thought (not wrongly) that he had a good claim to the French throne through his mother Isabella, one of the last two direct heirs of Philip IV. It escalated into intermittent war after 1337, marked above all by numerous English cavalry raids across France, sometimes met by the French in pitched battles, which the French tended to lose. In 1356 the battle of Poitiers resulted in the capture of the French king John II, and the resultant peace gave the English an enormously enlarged Gascony in the south of France. These territorial gains were then eaten away by cavalry raids, now undertaken by the French, and English gains were mostly lost by the 1370s. The war began again in earnest with a new attack by Henry V of England (1413–22) in 1415 which ended in a new victory, at Agincourt, and this time a full-scale war of conquest in northern France, which brought half the country under English hegemony by 1429 – Paris was in English hands in 1420–36, and the child king Henry VI was crowned king of France there in 1431. Partially thanks to Joan of Arc, however, a French fightback had begun by that point; Charles VII of France (1422–61) had already been crowned in the proper coronation site at Reims in

1429. By 1450 the English had lost all their post-1415 conquests, and in 1453 Bordeaux too.[2]

The war was remembered, ever after, as England's greatest European imperial moment, and France's greatest crisis (until 1940, at least). It has parallels with some other examples of adventurism in this period, notably French and Aragonese conquests in southern Italy, as we shall see;[3] but here it menaced, and at times substantially reduced the strength of, Latin Europe's major power. All the same, England, which had tried and failed to conquer Scotland in 1296–1314, was in reality far too small to defeat and occupy France, a country three times its size and population, on any permanent basis; its successes may have begun with battles, but were above all maintained by support from French partners in an intermittent internal civil war, which left the English much more exposed when the French made peace with each other. Also, for large sections of the 'hundred' years of this war there was no fighting in reality (it was indeed punctuated by treaties and marriages); conversely, wars between the French and the English had already begun in 1294, and did not really end until the English lost their last French mainland possession, Calais, in 1558. The particular period of the war can thus easily be deconstructed. But it is important nonetheless, for two different reasons. First, because this semi-permanent state of war became the axis around which much western European politics revolved. Anglo-Scottish wars, the hangover of the English attempt to conquer Scotland, continued throughout the fourteenth century and were swept into the French war through a Franco-Scottish alliance; English and French involvement in wars in Castile and Portugal in the 1360s and 1370s was another spin-off; and imperial princes were regularly part of the war as well, such as King John of Bohemia, who died in battle against the English in 1346.[4] Secondly, because the knowledge that this was an ongoing war led to a fiscalisation of state policy in both countries which was largely new. Wars were by now almost always fought by mercenaries, everywhere in Europe with a few exceptions such as Scotland, Switzerland and Lithuania, so states needed money to pay for them on a considerable scale. Short wars could be sold to cautious taxpayers as one-off expenses; not this one. The implications of this for the way political power worked in both England and France were great, and I will come back to it later.

The third key event was the Great Schism. The popes after the humiliation of Boniface VIII in 1303 were all French-speaking until 1378, and did not base themselves in Rome; in 1309 they settled in Avignon in what is now southern France, a small city which they could control rather better than Rome, and during the century they were based there the sophistication and wealth of the papal administration reached its height, as also its power over the church appointments of Latin Europe. Although the French kings did not actually rule Avignon, this was a very French power; nearly half the funding of the papacy came from church dues in France, and, conversely, the popes by now allowed the French king to tax church land for the English war. But the sense that Rome was the 'proper' place for popes to be never went away, and by the 1370s it had become powerful; as we have seen, Gregory XI moved back in 1377. He died a year later, and in a tense conclave the cardinals elected an Italian archbishop as Urban VI (1378–89). Urban in short order fell out with them, however, and they reunited four months later, announced that they had been coerced to elect him, and replaced him with a French cardinal as Clement VII (1378–94). Clement's lack of support in central Italy resulted in him returning to Avignon again, where he stayed. This was not the first schism in the papacy (1130 has similarities in the parallel legitimacy of each side), but on this occasion the European powers found it hard to agree on who was the legitimate pope: France, Scotland, Castile, Aragón and (initially) Naples went for Clement; England, most of Germany, north-central Italy, Poland, Hungary and Scandinavia went for Urban. Much of that was again Hundred Years' War choices; almost all the rest was geopolitical in other ways. It proved impossible to get either side to back down, even at papal deaths; the Avignon pope was renewed once, and the Roman pope three times, in the next nearly forty years. Embarrassment grew, and cardinals from each side met at Pisa in 1409 to remove both popes and elect a compromise candidate; unfortunately, the two popes did not resign, and now there were three. A second council, at Konstanz in Germany (1414–18), held under the aegis of the emperor Sigismund (1410–37), was more carefully planned, and one pope resigned, one was deposed and one lost almost all his political support and was marginalised. Martin V (1417–31), from an old Roman aristocratic family, was the first universally recognised pope since 1378, which by now few people could remember.[5]

The Great Schism has its comic sides, but it was deeply upsetting at the time, particularly inside the church and the universities, for it undermined the moral legitimacy and international reach of a church hierarchy which was by now taken for granted, particularly because even canon-law experts genuinely could not decide, and soon made the decision not to decide, which pope was the legitimate one – their task was to get the rival popes to agree to step down so that the process could be begun again, which the popes all agreed to do in principle but not, for a long time, in practice. Lay powers were less upset, and could cope pretty well with an uncertain and weakened papacy, although papal division was in the long run inconvenient for the French, and they made most of the efforts to end it. What the Schism did not produce was the deep-seated malaise about papal power which was for a long time part of the Protestant grand narrative of the origins of the Reformation. But it did lessen the ability of popes to determine church appointments across Europe, and it reduced their income very considerably – Martin V had half the income of Gregory XI, although it rose again later;[6] as a direct result, from now on, the national churches gained a degree of autonomy which they had not had since the twelfth century. And the religious theory which had to be developed to justify church councils with the power to depose popes would have a significant effect on the broader theory of politics from now on, as we shall see in the next chapter.

These three framing events were serious enough that they can be seen as giving a flavour to the whole of the late middle ages, one of crisis. Historians have very often done so, indeed. But that would be to misunderstand the period. John Watts, among others, has argued convincingly against much previous work, that this was not an age of systemic crisis for political power. Far from it, in fact; it was a period in which political systems steadily gained territorial coherence and fiscal strength, building on the thirteenth-century consolidation process that we looked at in Chapter 8.[7] The economy of the period fits that picture too, as we are about to see. The second half of this chapter and the one following will then develop the political analysis further; for, if we want to understand how Europe worked at the end of the middle ages, how its politics was constructed seems to me one of the most crucial issues to confront.

*   *   *

The European economy was not devastated by the Black Death, even if losing half the population inevitably had economic results. There was indeed a potentially positive effect on the survivors of the plagues, simply because among peasants fewer people meant more land per person, and among salaried workers a smaller workforce had considerably improved bargaining powers, in theory at least. And the macroeconomic context was not seriously damaged. We saw in Chapter 7 how the centuries up to 1300/1350 saw greater levels of commercialisation, with a newly capillary relationship between towns and the countryside, and also a beginning to peasant demand for urban artisanal products; this did not lessen. Towns were hit hard by the plague, but overall, after a period of shock, immigration began again, and average percentages of urbanisation in the now-smaller population seem to have remained much the same; indeed, urban wealth is evident in the fact that, still today, the most striking medieval secular buildings in major cities such as York, Bruges, Valencia, Venice, Prague are mostly from after 1350. It is true that the sense of bounce which is visible in the European economy between 1150 and 1300 is less visible. There was no long-term economic depression, but economies did not all continue their steady increase in complexity, and shorter-term downswings, for example in the mid-fifteenth century in much of northern Europe, do seem to have been more common.[8] Conversely, however, Europe continued a trend to economic integration. The heavy focus on the Flemish cloth towns which was so strong a feature of the north European economy of the twelfth and thirteenth centuries dropped back, in favour of a wider range of northern urban areas. The Hanse towns of the Baltic and north Germany reached their height in the fourteenth century and early fifteenth, profiting from, among other things, the opening up of the plains of Poland for grain production and export, in return for cloth and salt. England turned from the export of wool to the production and export of woollen cloth, partly cutting out the Flemish producers; and the great south German towns, Ulm, Augsburg, Nürnberg, backed up by a network of smaller towns, began their centuries-long regional dominance of cloth and metal production and increasingly banking too. The Hanse turned itself into an urban league which dominated the politics of weaker Baltic countries such as Sweden, and the strength of both the Hanse and the southern towns had clear effects on German political balances as well.[9]

Flanders faced difficulty as a result of this competition, certainly. All the same, a continuing demand for luxury cloth plus a complex structure of local demand, and also the centrality of Bruges as a port, preserved urban prosperity there until the end of the middle ages, by which time the epicentre of the Low Countries productive economy had moved north, to Antwerp as a trading centre and to what is now the Netherlands as a developing area of intensive agriculture and cheap cloth.[10] The rise of new centres of production and exchange was thus additional to Flanders, not a replacement for it, and Flemish commercial activity was tightly integrated into the Hanse. The major Italian towns did not face the same threats. States in the peninsula by now gave preferential treatment to the key economic activities of their largest cities, which were also regional political capitals, such as Florence, Venice and Milan, and government interventions were important in, for example, the establishment of major silk industries in Milan, Ferrara and Naples; but this was counterbalanced by an increasing density of small-town and rural artisanal activity, which again marked a trend to wider urban-rural exchange. Venice and Genoa, for their part, continued to control the Mediterranean luxury trade, almost as completely as before.[11] In southern Europe, nonetheless, productive foci spread outwards too, to Sicily, Valencia, and Ragusa (now Dubrovnik), plus the great Castilian entrepôt of Seville.[12]

This movement outwards of economic activity would have been impossible if commercialisation had not continued on much the same scale as before. And this is where the Black Death had its most substantial effects. In villages, there was breathing space again, and peasants both had more land at their disposal and could potentially negotiate better terms with landlords. The post-1350 period was, for example, the moment at which serfdom finally disappeared from western Europe, and, in the western kingdoms, in general landlords did less well than peasantries. This did not come without a struggle – as we shall see in the next chapter, this was a period with some notable rural revolts – and in some areas of Europe, in particular east of the Elbe, lords won, resulting in the new subjection of previously freer peasants: this subjection indeed helped the development of Poland as a region of major grain production for export.[13] But in the west agricultural specialisations appeared (dairy farming, market gardening, hops), peasant diet improved (in England and Germany it included more meat, for example), and also, importantly, so did peasant buying power for artisanal goods. In an earlier period, this would not have helped much, for economic complexity had largely been based on the demand of lords, not peasants; but now that capillary local commerce had been established it could continue with a peasant market as well, and did. Furthermore, peasant family members in the Low Countries, England, and parts of northern Italy, increasingly worked for others for salaries, for at least part of their lives, a fact which in itself presupposes an increased level of commercialisation. The next stage in parts of the Low Countries and eastern England would be the rise of peasant élites and middlemen, yeomen, whose accumulated estates were increasingly worked with a salaried labour force, resulting in a substantial change in the basic structures of production.[14] And salaried workers everywhere – particularly in towns, where working for money was overwhelmingly the norm – were able to use their scarcity for 150 years after the plagues to negotiate higher wages, notwithstanding the labour regulations which most rulers enacted as soon as they could after the Black Death (in England, already in 1349) to try to hold down wage levels.[15] Workers and employers fought over this with some commitment in the next century and more, with urban revolts even commoner than those in the countryside. But mass buying-power increased here too, feeding off and feeding into the commercialisation of the period.

This is obviously a very broad-brush sketch, and its implications must not be overstated. Social mobility is very evident in this period, with new rural strata, and the still-constant move of peasant families into towns, a few of whom would prosper greatly; an increasingly dense network of buying and selling is evident too. But its development was relative; economic integration had not got very far, for example (of course it is still, in the twenty-first century, incomplete), salaried workers were in a minority (sometimes a small minority) in most regions, and, even in this period, whether economic complexity depended on peasant (i.e. mass) demand *more* than on élite demand still cannot be said. Overall, what one can see in the fifteenth-century economy is a high-level equilibrium system, with its ups and downs, which included opportunities for an increasing intensity of agricultural and urban production – as also opportunities for new regions to take advantage of the continuing facility of exchange, such as southern Germany and eastern England and the northern Low Countries; more of France would join them after the end of the Hundred Years' War too. This changed the geopolitics of Europe, sometimes substantially. But there were no indications in 1500, or indeed 1600, that this system was anywhere due to change dramatically in its economic structure, despite every attempt by historians who have the Industrial Revolution in the corner of their eye to see its early signs. Europe had certainly developed the infrastructure to take economic advantage of the next, entirely external, change, the opening up by violence of the Indian Ocean by Portugal, and the Atlantic and the Americas by Spain, at the very end of the fifteenth century and into the sixteenth. By then the most active regions of southern Europe were also doing better than the long-standing Mediterranean economic powerhouse, Egypt, which (as it currently seems) had not, as Europe's regions had, recovered from the effects of the plague. But Europe had not by the end of our period become more economically complex than the great Asian regions, the west coast of India, Bengal and east-central China, and no-one would have expected it to.[16]

*   *   *

This is the background for understanding Europe's political histories after 1350, which I want here to set out in order, briefly, so that the reader gets a fuller sense of the variety of Europe, in the period with the best documentation. I will start with France and take a broad anticlockwise sweep, through Britain, Iberia, Italy, up into the German lands, then east to Hungary and Poland and north to Scandinavia (for further east than that, see Chapter 9). The set includes three interesting new arrivals, Switzerland, Burgundy and Lithuania, although several of the others show new configurations too. What I want to bring out here is less the narrative detail of political ups and downs than some basic political structures, above all the changing wealth of rulers. My main underlying focus throughout will indeed be on the nature of the fiscal structure of each polity, as both government and war (war in particular) by now cost much more than they had in, say, 1200, and this had consequences.

Whether kings and other rulers still relied on the wealth coming from their own lands ('the domain', as historians of this period often call it), or could develop taxation on a scale large enough to pay for bigger or more permanent armies and denser infrastructures of government, thus has crucial implications for the comparative history of politics. Put simply, rulers who did not develop strong fiscal systems by now could do less, both inside their polities and outside them, than rulers who did, even though they often tried to behave in the same way – for those without resources had the same ambitions as those with them. This point is not always stressed by historians, but it seems to me essential, so I shall stress it here.[17]

France was in 1300 the most powerful state in Europe, and in 1500 it was again, at least in the west (in south-east Europe, it was by now surpassed by the Ottoman empire); but it had gone through hard times in between. Most of that was the fault of the English invasions, but not all. The madness of its long-lived king Charles VI (1380–1422) meant that the period between the two great English attacks was taken up with squabbles, and sometimes wars, between his immediate relatives, each of whom had a substantial territorial power-base, who sought to control the regency. France, as we saw in previous chapters, had been constructed out of a network of lordships, and some of these themselves became larger and more coherent with time; in periods when the king was ineffective, this partially decentralised structure was more visible, and the troubles of the early fifteenth century were certainly one such period. The major lords were still fighting when Henry V invaded in 1415, and this contributed markedly to his success after Agincourt; for the new duke of Burgundy and count of Flanders, Philip 'the Good' (1419–67), after his father's murder by his French enemies, formally allied with England between 1420 and 1435. The 1420s were the low point for the cohesion of the French state as a result. All the same, what is also striking is its resilience. Charles V (1364–80), while still regent for his imprisoned father John II, easily managed to get the estates-general of France in 1360 to agree a substantial levy to pay his father's ransom, which turned into a regular tax after 1363; this paid both for the first French counterattacks against the English and for adventurism in Spain and southern Italy, as well as for a more developed bureaucracy, which was, importantly, an increasingly active employer of aristocrats, thus binding their interests together with royal power. France's fiscal system was unusually solid from now on. Significantly, although it was eroded substantially under Charles VI and by Henry V's conquests, it could be formally revamped in 1421 by the future Charles VII to pay for the new war, and regularised further from 1435; by Charles' death in 1461, tax, and the standing army it paid for, were a normal part of French royal resources, now no longer dependent on the assent of the estates-general. Whereas royal lands provided half the revenues of Philip VI in the 1330s, by the late fifteenth century that proportion was down to 2 per cent of a far larger budget. Louis XI (1461–83) built on this systematically, and fought off aristocratic anti-tax revolts; after he took over the duchy of Burgundy in 1477–82, the king was hegemonic in his kingdom.[18]

England did not do so well. Of course, it lost the French war in the end; but even while it was going on, successful occupations of French land did not result in dramatically increased fiscal resources, for these were all spent on the war. (Individual aristocrats got rich from the war, however, which provided a push to continue it.)[19] English taxation was more firmly established as a principle when the war began, which helped in its early years – one-off taxes for the start of war in both 1339 and 1415 produced huge sums of money which no other European polity could then match. But so was the granting of money by parliaments, and no late medieval English king ever managed, or even tried, to tax on more than a small scale without parliamentary consent. As I argued in Chapter 8, the English ruling class was already used to seeing its role as one of co-participants in government – unlike in every other European polity outside the Italian city-states, there were no hard-to-touch autonomous lordships, except in colonial Ireland – and that role was more and more exercised through meetings of parliament, which were by now close to annual. The Lords dominated parliamentary politics, but the Commons, representing gentry and urban élites, was vocal by the late fourteenth century too. At times of royal weakness, parliament could intervene directly, attacking the 'corruption' of royal courtiers, as in 1376, 1388 and 1449–50. And kings were personally weak, for a long time, even if the cohesion of the English state in general favoured governmental strength. After 1370, Edward III's old age and the minority of his grandson Richard II (1377–99) allowed, as in France, for the unpopular hegemony of royal relatives, notably Richard's uncle John of Gaunt. Gaunt's son Henry of Lancaster seized the throne from a now-adult Richard, who was trying to reduce aristocratic influence over his government, but Henry IV (1399–1413) was in a difficult position as a usurper, Wales spun out of his control for a decade under a charismatic prince, Owain Glyn Dŵr (d. c. 1415), and he became increasingly ill: a magnate council ruled in his last years. Henry V was quite a different figure, but he only ruled nine years, and Henry VI (1422–61) was a child, again with a regency of relatives. The adult Henry VI was the most inept king in medieval English history, and by the 1440s the war was going very badly; tensions between major aristocrats and between them and parliament ended up in open civil war after 1455, with a rival descendant of Edward III, Richard of York, claiming the throne by 1460. Richard's son Edward IV (1461–83) won the war, but his brother Richard III was killed in battle against an Anglo-Welsh usurper with almost no royal blood, Henry VII Tudor, in 1485. Henry V and Edward IV, neither of them long-lived, were in fact the only effective kings in the century after 1370.[20]

What kept England operative as a cohesive and densely governed community in this period – which it remained throughout, notwithstanding the troubles of the Lancaster – York wars (called the 'Wars of the Roses' in the nineteenth century) after 1455 – was the commitment of the magnate oligarchy, which ran the king's council and interacted constantly with parliament. It fought internally, and its personnel changed as a result, but the oligarchy remained. Conversely, one thing that did not remain at earlier levels was taxation. Apart from in 1339 and 1415, royal resources were usually at levels of about half those of France throughout the period up to 1400, but in the fifteenth century taxation steadily fell, and by the 1480s English royal incomings were under a quarter of those of its larger neighbour, over a third of them being from the royal domain, which had enlarged thanks to confiscations during the civil wars. The international traction of England dropped back as well. When Edward IV invaded France in 1475, Louis XI could simply buy him off, with money Edward badly needed, and English offensive war was henceforth relatively rare for over a century.[21]

Scotland was a much simpler political system. Its army was unpaid, and mostly there to defend against English attack, plus border raiding. Royal land, plus judicial and customs dues, provided almost all the king's revenues, which were very small by English (never mind French) standards; attempts by James I and James III to get the Scots parliament to agree regular taxation in the 1420s and 1470s came to little. The Scottish political system, indeed, resembled that of many early medieval states more than that of most of its contemporaries, and for long its local governing structures were hardly changed from those of the twelfth century. Robert I the Bruce (1306–29), who had fought off the English, created a partly new Scottish aristocracy out of his own followers in the wake of that victory, and his grandson, the first Stewart king Robert II (1371–90), put his own family members into many lordships too. But this did not increase royal power much, for it was never conceivable that a king with such limited resources and infrastructure could directly control what happened in the localities, and even his sheriffs were hereditary lords. The ever-present English threat (although weaker in the fifteenth century) allowed a community of the realm to persist here, with king and magnates generally collaborating and intermarrying, except at occasional moments of crisis – both James I and

James III were assassinated, in 1437 and 1488. James IV (1488–1513) achieved more by moving systematically around his kingdom, again early-medieval-style. But Scotland remained highly decentralised.[22]

Moving south into the Iberian peninsula, Scotland's need for defence against a stronger neighbour also fits Portugal, the minor player out of the three main kingdoms here. Portugal was under constant threat from Castile, particularly in the fourteenth century, and when there was a succession dispute there in 1383–85 the Castilians tried to conquer it; but they failed (partly thanks to English troops), and John I of Avis (1385–1433) and his fifteenth-century successors ruled a stable country, with borders which did not change after 1297 (and, except for one village, have not changed since). The kings took advantage of the political aggregation which was necessary for Portugal's survival to create a coherent legal system and a permanent sales tax; after peace was finalised with Castile in 1411 they also looked to the only area for adven-turism which was available to them, Africa. Attempts to conquer Morocco were always a costly failure, but the coast of west Africa brought more: Madeira in 1419–21, which soon became a valuable sugar producer, and from the 1420s onwards incursions ever further south along the African mainland, in voyages funded by royal princes and port towns. This steady extension of economic and military commitment southwards explains why the Portuguese ended up invading the Indian Ocean in the 1490s, but up till then the scale of their ambi-tion was rather less, as also was the profit they got from it. The Portuguese kings taxed, but they maintained a prosperous domain-based state above all, thanks to their wide lands, even if a rather stronger one than Scotland.[23]

Castile was much larger and more of a player. The king here potentially had an ideological centrality as the frontline fighter against the Muslims, although after the mid-fourteenth century the small remaining Arab amirate of Granada was not a threat, and not very often threatened either. A civil war in the 1360s saw Peter I replaced by his illegitimate elder brother Henry II of Trastámara in 1369. Civil wars tended to produce fiscal cessions to wavering aristocrats and towns but at the same time a contradictory need to find money for armies, and so it was here; all the same, the kings, as in Portugal, kept control of a sales tax, and the Castilian *cortes* were also prepared to vote direct taxation for Aragonese and English wars for Henry and his son John I (1379–90). The figures we have for royal revenues in Castile in the later fourteenth century are substantial, matching those for England. This gives a political context for the anti-Jewish pogroms of 1391, when the new king Henry III was a minor, for they were part of a violent popular reaction against a royal power which was by now at its height.[24]

That power slipped back in the fifteenth century, though. There was then a sequence of weak reigns in Castile, and also a civil war in the 1440s between ruling magnates which paralleled that in England a decade later. Royal claims to power remained ambitious, but royal revenues steadily declined in the middle decades of the century through cessions to aristocrats, and were half those of England – which were themselves by now lower, as we have seen – by the 1470s. Isabella I (1474–1504), who was married to the heir to Aragón Ferdinand II (1479–1516), seized power from her niece, the rightful heiress Joanna, in a moment for the Castilian state which was, overall, quite negative. But it is significant that she managed to turn it around. Hers was not the first dynastic link with Aragón, but it held, and was intended to from early on; she and her husband managed to reassert their fiscal powers again, establish a much greater degree of order, and regain a measure of direct control over the *cortes*, the towns and even some lordships which had not been seen since 1400. The political collectivity created by Isabella in Castile reached a high intensity with less attractive measures, the decision to conquer Granada (1487–92), the expulsion of the Jews in the latter year, and a campaign against Jewish converts. But the fact was that a sense of what late medieval Europeans frequently called the 'public good' had not vanished in the troubles of recent decades, and in Castile, as in France and England, the aristocracy was by now deeply involved in a royal government which they gained financial benefit from, so could see the advantage in its renewed strength.[25]

Aragón had a similar political structure to Castile, with *cortes* or *corts* as parliaments (here several, representing the kingdom's greater decentralisation) which agreed taxation; but here they offered less money, and on much more conditional terms, than in Castile. Its major towns, in particular, were stronger and far from easy to control. The Catalonia and Valencia *corts*, central to Aragonese authority, developed a contractual political theory of limited royal government based on consent, as expressed for example in the influential political-religious tract, *The twelfth of the Christian*, by Francesc Eiximenis (d. 1409), which had parallels in English political practice, and they used this to get concessions from the kings. But Aragón was also on the Mediterranean coast, and Barcelona and Valencia were major trading centres, meaning that the kingdom did have resources, however conditionally available. It thus looked outwards too, and both Sardinia and Sicily were regularly in its range – Aragonese kings, usually from junior lines, ruled Sicily after 1282, plus Naples after 1442, and Ferdinand II definitively conquered both again in 1503. These effectively colonial conquests, in the case of Sicily of a rich island, meant that Aragón punched above its weight, much as England did at times.[26]

Naples (i.e. continental southern Italy) and Sicily had been a single kingdom until 1282, ruled by the Normans and then the Staufen as we have seen. As a spin-off of papal wars against Frederick II, Charles of Anjou, Louis IX's brother, conquered the kingdom in 1266; but Sicily revolted in 1282 and chose an Aragonese king instead. Charles I, when he had secure control of the whole Staufen kingdom, was the richest monarch in Europe in financial terms, with a strong tax base; the resources of his grandson Robert (1309–43), who only ruled Naples, were still at the level of contemporary England.[27] But the two southern kingdoms spent much of their incomings in the fourteenth century fighting each other, and in both cases magnates gained more autonomy as a result. Charles III of Naples (1381–86) did not help this when he also invaded Hungary in 1385, a piece of adventurism which gained an extra throne for a year but resulted in his assassination; the Hungarian claim persisted until 1414, although Naples was by now fighting off equally adventurist attacks from France again. Fifteenth-century Sicily was more prosperous, under external Aragonese rule. Naples was less so until the Aragonese conquered here as well; Alfonso V of Aragón (1416–58, 1442–58 in Naples) based himself there at the end of his life, and he and his son Ferrante (d. 1494) made use of a much more peaceful period to establish coherent government, with a strong fiscal base unconstrained by parliament, which Ferdinand II of Aragón would then retake a decade later. Both kingdoms were, evidently, always rich enough for outsiders to be interested in taking them over, but weak enough to find it hard to resist them, not a fortunate combination.[28]

The numerous north Italian city-states present particular problems of synthesis, but at least have in common two developments in this period, a move away from 'republican' rule and a steady move to larger political units. The permanent effervescence of political systems in the thirteenth-century communes, which were continuously changing to try to calm factional rivalry and to accommodate the claims of new social strata, began to make way for the longer-term rule of single rulers, who tended to gain power as head of a faction and then grab it permanently for themselves and their heirs. In English they are often termed 'despots'; the Italians call them, more neutrally, signori, 'lords'. They were very various. The Visconti in Milan (1277–1447) and the Este in Ferrara (from as early as 1240 onwards) were old aristocratic families which had been important since the eleventh century or before; the Della Scala in Verona (1263–1404) and the Medici in Florence (1434 onwards) were from the commercial élite, in the latter case the largest-scale bankers of their time; the Sforza in Milan (1450–1500) were initially mercenary leaders. In almost all cases, however, they gained power by promising to respect and better defend republican institutions, which by and large they did, while filling them with their own men and cutting out rivals, in ways made famous by the Florentine Niccolò Machiavelli's highly pragmatic masterpiece, *The prince*, of 1513–14. Only Venice, Genoa, Siena and, after a period of signorial government, Lucca stood out against this trend, and they mostly did so by establishing tight and closed oligarchies of leading families who split urban offices between them – a system which was indeed often less open than the still fairly meritocratic governing systems in the *signorie*.

The second development was one of conquest. Italian cities had systematically fought wars against each other since the twelfth century, but in the fourteenth century, in particular, stronger cities began to take over the whole territory of their rivals. Florence and Milan began this, and Venice followed after 1404; by 1454, when the powers of Italy made the Peace of Lodi and established relative stability for a generation, these three were by far the dominant cities in the north. It is worth adding that the trend to larger states was unconnected to the trend to signorial rule; of these three only Milan had a *signore* at the time of its conquests, and it had a particularly strong communal tradition of aggression to build on. It is, conversely, important to recognise that conquered cities, Pisa under the Florentines or Verona under the Venetians, kept their previous political structures, which were simply from now on conditioned by the rule of others; there was here a parallel with the wider continuities of government under the *signori*. In most cases, indeed, rulers of Italian cities were well aware of and respected the concerns of the ruled, and if they were not they could face revolt: both Milan and Florence, for example, re-established full republics briefly, in 1447–50 and 1494–1512 respectively, and so did Pisa in 1494–1509. Notwithstanding that, Italian cities were tightly governed, and also very used to paying taxes; cities in northern Italy – and, still more, their rural territories – were almost certainly more highly taxed than anywhere else in Latin Europe in the later middle ages. Indeed, tax assessment by the fifteenth century was more elaborate than it had ever been, as with the Florentine *catasto* of 1427–30, in which every field possessed by potential contributors was valued. Here, the officers of the state (themselves paid for by this taxation) had to deal directly with every householder in the Florentine republic, in far more detail than had been the case for the English Domesday Book, the cutting-edge assessment tool of three centuries before. The money produced by these means was for long needed to pay for mercenary armies, despite the risks which these could bring to small-scale political systems; everyone in Italy knew well that Francesco Sforza was only the tip of an iceberg of potentially ambitious war-leaders. After the Peace of Lodi it was still collected, however, and Italian wealth – still visible in the expensive fifteenth-century buildings of nearly every Italian city – would attract new sequences of invasion, from France and Germany, in the decades after 1494.[29]

Halfway through this survey of Europe, it is worth setting out an interim report. All the kingdoms and city-states we have looked at so far, in western and southern Europe, had some form of systematic tax-raising powers, except Scotland. In eastern and northern Europe, which we are about to come to, for the most part they did not – the major exceptions being Burgundy, which was on the edge of France and shared in the latter's fiscal complexity, and the stand-out eastern European state, Hungary. A line running, roughly, from Venice north-west to Antwerp thus marked a real difference in political cohesion and political heft in the late middle ages – and also political influence, for the eastern and northern polities of Latin Europe looked to France, the principal western and southern European power, and to a lesser extent Italy and England, far more than the French (or the Italians or English) looked to them. We saw in Chapter 5 how the north–south boundary in Europe, which was so visible in 800, had become considerably attenuated by 1100; but even in the late middle ages, with exceptions, it still marked a rough opposition, by now not so much of culture, but one of economic and thus political power. All the same, the eastern and northern polities were at least as interesting as their western and southern neighbours, so we must now turn to them for a closer, if still brief, look.

*   *   *

If Italy is hard to generalise about, Germany is by now impossible. The German empire continued (the 'Holy Roman Empire of the German Nation' as it was called from 1474), but its direct power had gone. In fact, the emperors for the most part had powerful local bases, coming as they did from the Luxemburg kingdom of Bohemia (1346–1400, 1410–37) and then the Habsburg duchy of Austria, for Bohemia was a large and relatively coherent principality and Austria, although less coherent, was at least large. But their presence in the rest of the empire was largely ceremonial. That is not a small thing, and the force of the imperial ideal, including the practical appreciation of the emperor as a neutral arbiter, increased rather than decreased. But Charles IV (1346–78) mortgaged away imperial lands and rights very extensively, to support immediate political needs, and by the mid-fifteenth century there was close to nothing of these left. It is striking that at the end of that century there was an attempt to revive the imperial role, particularly under the active Habsburg emperor Maximilian I (1493–1519), with legislation in imperial assemblies and in 1495–99, for the first time, a general empire-wide tax, but even then the estates of the large duchy of Bavaria refused to ratify it, and it was not renewed. Instead, the empire was a carapace for hundreds of principalities and imperial cities, occupying land-areas large and small. The cities, headed by Nürnberg, Augsburg, Lübeck and Cologne, were the richest and most influential polities in the south and north of the country; the largest territorial states were, by contrast, in the east, Brandenburg, Saxony, Bohemia, Austria, Bavaria, plus, over in the far west, the lands of the duchy of Burgundy, which in the fifteenth century were expanding out from France. The imperial cities had quite elaborate fiscal and governmental systems, parallel to, although simpler than, those of Italy. The larger principalities by and large did not, and, even after tax-raising became more common in the fifteenth century, princely revenues were above all based on domain lands there. The very great differences across the German lands, set against an increasing sense of common German identity, produced a constant shimmer of discussion and an awareness of alternative possibilities which was greater than in many places in Europe.[30] That awareness would increase further after Martin Luther circulated his ninety-five theses in Wittenberg in 1517, and after many German principalities adopted versions of Roman law in the decades after 1500. But for now we simply need to register it; let us instead look at three local examples, all of them unusual, to get a sense of the potential of political action in the empire: Bohemia, the Swiss lands and Burgundy.

Bohemia was the only Slavic-speaking polity to become part of the German empire, and wooded mountains around three sides of it gave it an unusually solid territorial integrity, even if there was substantial German immigration around its edges and in its towns. Its native Czech dynasty of Přemyslids ended in 1306, and by 1310 its ruling kings were from the western German Luxemburg family; Charles IV was not only emperor but the dominant prince of his time. He made Prague a real capital, with a newly founded university, and the city still preserves his stamp. Charles ruled in Bohemia largely on the basis of domain lands and the profits from the great Kutná Hora silver mines; he took over several other principalities, at least temporarily, but he spent imperial mortgages on that. Charles's son Wenceslas/Václav IV (1378–1419) had less presence; he was emperor too, but was deprived of the title by half the electors in 1400, and in Bohemia itself he was forced to cede much authority to a collectivity of aristocrats in 1405. By his death in 1419, this had become swept up into the Hussite revolt, a religious movement inspired by the teachings of Jan Hus, who was executed for heresy in 1415 at the Council of Konstanz. We will look at Hus and his successors in the next chapter; what is relevant here is simply that the movement took over the Czech lands, fighting off a sequence of

Catholic armies. Between 1419 and 1436 the Czechs did not even recognise a king, but instead ruled by councils, which were intercut by conflicts between a radical Hussite wing of lesser aristocrats, townsmen and peasants and a moderate wing of nobles and university masters; its armies were volunteer, and the state's fiscal resources became much weaker, even after the moderate wing won in the late 1430s. The next effective king, George of Poděbrady (1458–71) was an aristocratic Hussite, and he too had to ward off papal-sponsored attacks against him. He resisted them, and did his best to re-establish a national community; his power was further underpinned by the revival of dues from silver mining, which continued under absentee Jagiełłonian and then Habsburg kings thereafter.[31]

The Swiss confederation is claimed to have begun with a peace agreement between three rural communities of the western Habsburg lands around Lake Luzern, in 1291. In 1351, more concretely, they agreed a pact of mutual defence with the nearby city of Zürich, which was backed up with similar pacts with Bern, Luzern and other centres. These were not the only pacts which cities and small territories in southern Germany entered into to establish a measure of mutual security in the fragmented empire, but most of these particular territories were also subject to the Habsburgs, and they had to fight off an army sent against them to restore Austrian rule in 1386. The fact that the Habsburg duke Leopold III was then defeated and killed gave the Swiss confederation a measure of confidence that allowed it to extend its range significantly. Habsburg power never returned, and was formally renounced in 1474. Instead, the confederation developed a skilled peasant-based infantry army whose members were used as mercenary forces by other powers, and established a very loose autonomous government, extending slowly to more and more principalities and cities across the fifteenth century and early sixteenth. It needs to be stressed that the Swiss had a confederation (they still do), not a unitary state. Each member had a separate identity and fiscal structure, and indeed they sometimes fought each other. The interests of towns, nobles and peasant communities were also structurally in conflict. But, unusually (and, in particular, unlike in Bohemia), the losing social stratum was for the most part the rural aristocracy; the main conflictual relationship became that between cities and strong peasant communities. Small wonder that 'turning Swiss' was a threat with revolutionary overtones in the early sixteenth century.[32]

The dukes of Burgundy were a junior branch of the ruling house of France, who in 1384 inherited the immensely rich county of Flanders, also part of the kingdom of France. But both of these principalities were on the borders of the kingdom, and had close links with lands in the empire too. Of imperial territories, in 1384 they gained Franche-Comté, in 1404–30 Brabant, in 1428 Hainaut and Holland; by the mid-fifteenth century they had expanded outwards and controlled almost the whole of the Low Countries, the first time that a single regional power ever had – nationalist history in both Belgium and the Netherlands traces its lineage back to them. The Burgundian dukes were often a key support for England in the second phase of the Hundred Years' War, as we have seen, and Philip the Good began to think in terms of a newly configured territorial state, with a very ambitious court culture. The dukes were certainly wealthy enough for it; the figures we have put their revenues after their expansion at the level of those of England, above all from taxation. Most of that was from the Low Countries, however, and with that came the need to deal with the Flemish and Brabançon towns, a relationship which was always fraught. The other key problem for the Burgundian dukes was that their lands were not fully contiguous, interspersed as they were with those of several imperial powers, and were never fiscally unified. Philip's son Charles 'the Rash' (1467–77) tried to remedy this by conquest, but this brought him firm opposition from the German lands, and he was defeated by the Swiss in 1476 and killed in battle in 1477. The Burgundian realm in its strict sense ended here, for Louis XI regained Burgundy itself soon after. But the dukes had at least united the Low Countries, and Charles' daughter Mary (1477–82), who continued to rule them, was married to Maximilian of Habsburg. Maximilian took them over as a block after her death, in wars against both the French and the Flemish towns between 1482 and 1492.[33] The Habsburgs, from their insecure Austrian and imperial base, thus inherited the main centre of Burgundian wealth and power. And that would become, by chance, the basis for still more. Mary and Maximilian's son Philip married the heiress of Castile and Aragón, Joanna; Philip died young and Joanna was excluded for insanity; so between 1517 and 1519 Philip's son Charles V inherited the imperial title, Austria, the whole of the Low Countries, the whole of Spain, and the whole of southern Italy. Mexico and Peru would come later. Charles, with almost no need for war this time, thus reaped the benefit of all the military adventurism of the Burgundians and the Aragonese, and European history would shift as a result in the new century.

These three examples show what divergent results could develop inside the imperial lands. The political players in the empire could also be active well outside it: the last Luxemburg emperor, Wenceslas's brother Sigismund, was indeed for the most part based not in his family kingdom of Bohemia (until a treaty with the Hussites in the last year of his life), but in Hungary, which he ruled for fifty years, from 1387. And, for all that Bohemia could be a strong power base at times, Hungary was a much stronger one. The weakening of royal power there in the thirteenth century (see Chapter 8) had been reversed by two forceful kings from a new dynasty, yet another inheritance for the house of Anjou, Charles-Robert and Louis I (1309–82), who, on the back of dues from silver and then (from the 1320s) gold mines, and, soon, a land tax, regained half the castles of the kingdom and ruled with little hindrance from the old aristocracy. Louis, in particular, fought abroad, expanding southwards, and inherited the crown of Poland too, in 1370. His daughters divided Poland and Hungary between them, and after a confused period, marked as we have seen by invasion from Naples, Sigismund succeeded in Hungary as husband of Louis's daughter Mary. But aristocratic revolts against a German/Czech king continued until after 1400, and, subsequently, Sigismund's imperial activities kept him out of Hungary half the time, too. It is not surprising that royal wealth lessened and the internal structure of the kingdom weakened in this period, one reason being that the gold mines, and the profits from them, were by now less remunerative. But mining and taxation continued, and the infrastructure of the kingdom, with paid officials, was solid enough to cope with Sigismund's absences, the new need to defend the southern frontier against the Ottomans, and a sequence of short-lived rulers after his death. Matthias Corvinus, son of the aristocratic general and regent John Hunyadi, was chosen as king in 1458 and ruled effectively until 1490, reviving royal power, and taxing heavily enough to maintain a standing army and a rich court at Buda, his capital. It is true that weaker kings and greater aristocratic influence succeeded him, and most of the Hungarian kingdom was conquered by the Ottomans after their great victory of Mohács in 1526. Largely because of this, Hungarian historians have a very negative view of aristocratic power in medieval Hungary. But the key point that must be stressed here is that a strong and lucky king was always able to bounce back. Charles-Robert and Matthias both show it; so does Sigismund to a lesser extent. A lot of royal land, a tradition of taxation, and – not least – royal-dominated mining allowed the kings to have access to at least some resources even when they were weak, and resources on the level of English and Castilian kings when they were strong. Both in royal wealth and in political infrastructure, Hungary was the most powerful kingdom north of Rome and east of France for the whole of the later middle ages.[34]

Exactly the opposite was the case of Poland, Hungary's neighbour to the north. The early kingdom of Poland, divided between heirs in 1138 as we saw in Chapter 5, was reunited in part and with great difficulty by Władisław I Łoketiek (king 1320–33); thereafter, he and his son Kazimierz III (d. 1370) still had to contend with a very decentralised kingdom, with dukes who were semi-independent, a legal system intercut with autonomous German-law towns, and an increasingly forceful community of aristocrats. Next door to Poland was the grand duchy of Lithuania, the only major polity in Europe which had not become Christian; it stabilised as a power under Gediminas (1315–42) and steadily expanded eastwards, mostly at the expense of warring Russian principalities (see Chapter 9). Poland and Lithuania were tactically linked by common opposition to the German crusader state of the Teutonic knights, based on the Baltic coast, which was seeking to conquer the eastern Baltic and which reached the height of its own power in this period. After the deaths of Kazimierz and then his successor Louis of Hungary in 1382, in the jockeying for power that followed, Jogaila of Lithuania (1377–1434) married Louis's other daughter Jadwiga, and converted to Christianity in 1386, taking the Polish throne a year later as Władisław II Jagiełło. His cousin Vytautas took over Lithuania in a family deal in 1392, and ruled as grand duke until 1430, taking Lithuanian hegemony south-eastwards to the Black Sea, as well as crushing the Teutonic knights at Tannenberg in 1410. Vytautas's reign marked the height of Lithuanian rule in the Russian lands, and its eastern borders began slowly to contract from then on in the face of the rulers of Moscow. All the same, the combined Poland–Lithuania – by now the basic political structure of the region, even if different descendants of Władisław Jagiełło sometimes ruled each half – was in geographical terms the largest polity in the whole of Europe in the fifteenth century. But it was not the strongest, by any means. Although the Lithuanian army was an effective attacking force, the grand duchy had almost no political infrastructure, and had to recognise considerable autonomy in the major subdivisions of what had been Kievan Rus'. And Poland, although more coherent, crystallised in the later fifteenth century, under Kazimierz IV (1446–92) and his successors, as a polity dominated as much by a collectivity of aristocrats, united in the *sejm* assemblies, as by a king. Only the most forceful kings, as Kazimierz was himself, could counter that. Poland lacked a structured fiscal system (assemblies often refused royal tax requests), and the kings usually ruled on the basis of the resources of their domain lands almost alone except in times of war, for which taxation grants did become more frequent. The often-tense relation between kings and powerful local lords, which usually resolved itself in favour of the king in Hungary and sometimes also in Bohemia, thus went the other way in Poland, in particular from the 1490s on. Complicated family interrelationships between these three kingdoms – which resulted, indeed, in Jagiełłonians ruling every one of them after 1490 – did not change this basic structural difference.[35]

Similar dynastic games marked the three Scandinavian kingdoms of Denmark, Norway and Sweden – Denmark being always by far the strongest in its infrastructure, and Sweden the weakest. We saw in the last chapter that Margaret I (d. 1412), heiress to Valdemar IV of Denmark after 1375 and widow of Håkon VI of Norway after 1380, united all three by force in 1387–89. Her nephew and designated heir Erik of Pomerania (1389–1439) was crowned king of all three kingdoms at the Union of Kalmar in 1397, an act far more formal than the de facto dynastic unifications of the Jagiełłonians, and one which survived Erik's own deposition in 1439–40. It did not last, all the same. Denmark and Norway stayed together until 1815, but Sweden was less keen, and elected as its own king the aristocrat Karl Knutsson in 1448. Christian I of Denmark (1448–81) reconquered it in 1457, but renewed Swedish independence was only a matter of time, and was complete by 1523, under the new Vasa dynasty. There was a temporary trend towards elective monarchy in the three Scandinavian kingdoms, and a resultant prominent role for aristocratic councils in each of the three, with aristocrats as local administrators as well; in all this they resembled Poland in its noble-dominated 'constitutionalism', and the political structure of each was often as weak. But in Scandinavia the aristocracy was much less locally hegemonic. In many regions, the peasantry had not been uprooted and disenfranchised, and in practice often dominated the local legal and political assemblies, *thingar*, inherited from the early middle ages (see Chapter 5). Peasant revolts began in 1433–34 in Sweden and Denmark and 1436 in Norway, and marked the move to Swedish independence in particular. Although kings did tax in Scandinavia, this was usually on a small scale, and insufficient to establish armies which were separate from aristocratic and indeed peasant political protagonism – to which we must add the autonomous political input of major towns, and the transnational (but German-dominated) Hanseatic league which linked them. When the Swedish *riksdag* or parliament was formalised in the sixteenth century, indeed, it had a fourth estate of peasants, almost uniquely in Europe. The inability of kings to dominate political society in Scandinavia (even, to an extent, in Denmark) brackets them above all, apart from Poland, with Scotland; and so does a political system which, although showing plenty of late medieval attributes such as charters of legal and political liberties (in Sweden in 1319 and Denmark in 1360), resembled rather more the assembly politics of the early middle ages in its basic structure.[36]

* * *

This rapid survey of the political history of Latin Europe after 1350 shows up some common themes. One was the game of dynastic inheritance of thrones which could claim more than one kingdom at once: an Anjou-based branch of the French royal family in Naples, Hungary and Poland, Castilian kings in Aragón, Aragonese kings in Sicily and Naples, German and then Polish kings in Bohemia and Hungary, Austrian kings in almost all of these at the end of the middle ages and after; plus occasional German kings in the Scandinavian kingdoms, and the brief English kingship in France and, earlier, Scotland. Political boundaries did not change very greatly except in parts of eastern Europe, and nor did the internal political structures of kingdoms which were united in this way, but the plate tectonics of dynastic alliance did, constantly. A second theme, linked tightly to the first, was the possibility of some quite ambitious adventurism abroad, often overseas; it was usually ephemeral (even if, as with the English in France, it could cause a lot of damage), but sometimes led to more permanent control, as with the Aragonese in Sicily. What links almost all the rulers we have looked at, in fact, is their preparedness, as soon as they had enough money to get an army together (and sometimes even before that), to attack not only their neighbours but also on occasion realms quite some way away, for military glory and hoped-for permanent territorial control. Hardgained resources were spent above all on displays of power, the rich courts and ambitious buildings which mark the post-1350 period, but an army was the biggest – and most expensive – display of power of all, and using it to fight someone was the logical next step. The military machine underlying early modern political and fiscal development has its beginnings in this period, and shows clearly that the state-building of the thirteenth century was built on thereafter, systematically, nearly everywhere in Latin Europe. As was argued at the start of the chapter, although many realms faced crises of different types, this was not an age of systemic crisis for political power: it was quite the opposite, indeed, as we can now see in more detail.[37]

When we come to fiscal systems themselves, all the same, what needs to be stressed is difference. The polities of late medieval Europe were not all alike fiscally, at all; they had different forms of taxation (direct versus indirect taxes), different pacings for it (some taxes were annual and regular, but many were only collected during wars), different weights of taxation, and different balances between domain and tax revenues. All these meant that different styles of royal exactions had different sorts of effect on their subjects, a set of contrasts that has not yet been studied systematically by anyone. But they also had a global weight. The more resources rulers had, of whatever type, the more they could do; the level of those resources had a direct effect on the internal infrastructure and political coherence of the different European powers.

By the end of the fifteenth century, the strongest and richest state in Europe, with the most remunerative taxation system, was certainly the Ottoman empire, which was based on fiscal patterns inherited from the Byzantine empire and the caliphate alike (see Chapter 9). It had a density of assessment and exaction which was not paralleled by any western polities except the most effective of the Italian city-states – for, as we have seen, Roman and Islamic fiscal expertise had been lost in the west, and the western states, in their re-invention of taxation, created less efficient structures, and failed to learn from their more sophisticated neighbours. In the west, by far the richest kingdom was France, in every period after the late thirteenth century except during the troughs of the Hundred Years' War; the extent of its fiscal control was less great than that of the Italian cities, as just implied, but the latter were far smaller and thus weaker. At a third level, there were England and Castile, and the Burgundian Low Countries of the fifteenth century, although the first two of these were more successful in this respect in the fourteenth century than until very late in the fifteenth. Not far behind came Hungary, Naples/Sicily and Aragón, and some German cities. Next, but rather further down, Bohemia and Portugal. Every other polity in Europe had a far simpler political structure, and its rulers, in Poland–Lithuania and the rest of eastern Europe, Scotland, Scandinavia and much of the German lands, although they had the same sort of political style and motivations as the rulers of richer territories, could do less with it. Their wars were more difficult to pursue in the long term, their control over their aristocracies was less great, their judicial role was also, very often, less developed. Here fiscal coherence linked very tightly to political coherence.

It must be stressed that this is a structural conclusion, not a moral judgement. The view that a rich and autocratic king, who extracts a lot of money from his subjects, is somehow 'better' (even worse, more 'modern') than a king who has to face a powerful aristocracy cannot be justified in any sensible way. But it is worth adding that political coherence could also derive from a very well-organised internal decision-making and legal structure. Here England stands out, plus the Italian city-states. The latter could again do so more easily because they were small, but English internal organisation continued to benefit here from an oligarchic involvement in policy-making and a tradition of justice based on assemblies which went back to the early middle ages without a break, the only example of this among the more powerful polities of the period – for other kingdoms which maintained an early medieval tradition of assembly politics, notably in Scandinavia, were the opposite of powerful.

This very rough league table of political-fiscal coherence and basic wealth in most cases was a league table of military effectiveness as well – with some exceptions, notably an Italy whose numerous rich polities mostly punched below their weight militarily, and a Lithuania and a Switzerland which punched well above. It is the basic framework which this account leaves us with. It must be borne in mind as we look, in the next chapter, at political organisation and protagonism: at the way parliaments of different types worked, at problem-solving, at the intellectualisation of political decision-making, and at dissent. These show common themes as well, as we shall see; but the differences just sketched mean that the way these themes inflected locally remained distinct.

CHAPTER TWELVE

Rethinking politics, 1350–1500

We have now seen how the states of Europe were organised and resourced in the late middle ages; but that was only one part of the politics of the period. Equally important was what people – both élites and non-élites – thought their rulers should do with their resources, and, more widely, how government should be run. The late middle ages was, indeed, a period of considerable debate about these questions. It marked the widening of a public sphere for politics, which characterises this period in particular; the aim of this chapter is to characterise some of its social and political context.

In the miserable years of Henry VI's reign in England, especially in the decades of the king's nominal adult rule (1437–61), when the country increasingly lost political direction and the war in France was failing, there was a notable array of political discussion inside the literate strata of society, and indeed sometimes beyond them. This discussion extended into the 1460s and 1470s under Henry's Yorkist supplanter Edward IV as well. It was marked by a series of suggestions about which were the best political actions to take, which were often contradictory, but also greatly varying in content and focus. The *Libel* [booklet] *of English policy*, a xenophobic but well-informed pamphlet in verse dating from around 1436–37, proposed that England's foreign policy would best be served by controlling the trade routes of the Channel very aggressively, which would force the dreadful Flemings and Italians to support English political interests. The *Dream of the vigilant*, an anti-Yorkist tract of 1459, argued sharply and cogently that rebellion against the realm to support the 'common wealth' is self-contradictory, for it means setting oneself unjustifiably above the law; the Yorkists were a rotten tooth in the mouth, and should not be pardoned. The *Active policy of a prince*, of around 1463, an often banal poem by the imprisoned Lancastrian official George Ashby, which blamed the greed of counsellors for their disloyalty to Henry VI (in itself far from a new idea), had some quite targeted suggestions too: Henry's son Edward, if he became king, should never trust his courtiers; Edward should regularly make himself visible to the common people, but never trust them either. This sort of intervention reached its most developed expression with John Fortescue (d. *c.* 1477), chief justice of England after 1442 and another Lancastrian loyalist, who changed sides in 1471 and presented his revised *The governance of England* to Edward IV shortly after: here he advised the king to accumulate as much land as possible, removing it from its recent beneficiaries, so as to be able to outspend his richest subjects, who might otherwise rebel, as they recently had so often – as well as keeping the poor prosperous, again to avoid conflict (for the English poor are less cowardly than the French, so are more likely to rebel).[1]

We cannot show that any of these pieces of advice were followed; even if Edward IV certainly did his best to become rich, it would be hard to say that he did so because of Fortescue's suggestions. But what they together demonstrate is that political actors of this period, including non-aristocratic ones, were thinking about what was going wrong politically and trying to figure out the best way to deal with it. These literate interventions – significantly, mostly in English, not Latin – were backed up by a wider array of actors still, for the sailors in 1450 who summarily beheaded the duke of Suffolk (since 1443 effectively the regent of the kingdom) at sea did so in the name of the community of the realm, which they saw as being above the king. That action was followed by Jack Cade's Kent-based peasant revolt of the same year, which was rather more loyalist than its predecessor of 1381 (see below), and simply sought a better government than that on offer in those decades ('we blame not all the lords, nor all that be about the king's person . . . but such who may be found guilty by a just and true enquiry by the law'). However cynical the actual manoeuvring of political leaders in this period, the latter had to do so in an environment of a continual and urgent discussion about what constituted good government and how to improve it, which they could not be seen too blatantly to ignore.[2]

This debate was not restricted to England; far from it. Hussite collective debates were one example. Northern Italy was another: Italians argued in every city council (including under signorial régimes) about how best to organise their government, deliberations which in many cases survive. These in their turn interrelated with the works of theorists, like the Roman lawyer Bartolo of Sassoferrato (d. 1357), who discussed, in his sharp-eyed tract on (and against) tyrants, i.e. those who rule unjustly, the need for cities sometimes to expel someone 'powerful, troublesome and seditious' if a 'just judge' thought it necessary. Such arguments then underlay the sensible but not quite so anti-tyrannical suggestions about how to rule effectively in Niccolò Machiavelli's *The prince* (for example: kill people if you really have to, but 'above all else, abstain from the property of others; for men forget the death of their father more quickly than the loss of their patrimony'); and these in turn are themselves sometimes only crisper versions of what Fortescue had been writing over a thousand kilometres away.[3] All across Europe, the detail of political action was being analysed and critiqued in the fifteenth century. This was new; or, at least, its intensity was new.

It is important to be clear about the nature of the novelty I am trying to describe here. It is of course true that educated Europeans had been debating the moral and legal underpinnings of appropriate political action, that is to say 'political theory', since the Carolingian period and before. In the late eleventh century, such debates were enriched by the intense polemics of the pope vs. emperor disputes of Gregory VII and his successors; in the twelfth, this was developed, thanks to canon and Roman law, newly elaborated; in the thirteenth, a now-translated Aristotle was further added to the mix. In succession, and among many others, John of Salisbury in the twelfth century, Thomas Aquinas and Giles of Rome in the thirteenth, Dante Alighieri, Marsilio of Padua, Bartolo of Sassoferrato and John Wyclif in the fourteenth, Leonardo Bruni, Christine de Pizan and Nicholas of Cusa in the fifteenth, all added their views, many of them very sophisticated indeed (we shall come back to some of them); medieval political thought is a rich sub-field as a result. But these luminaries tended, for the most part, to be quite unspecific when they came to practical political suggestions. They were laying down theory, not relating it closely to daily political practice. The 'mirror of princes' genre of advice manuals for rulers, again one with Carolingian, as also Byzantine, roots but reaching its height with Giles of Rome's On the rule of princes of 1277–80, written for the future Philip IV of France, also tended to be quite generic moral tracts.[4] Even when they were more concrete, such writers tended simply to present invective in favour of or against wider political structures (the power of the emperor in Italy, for example, or the relation between the ruler and the law) which were often being constructed on rather different principles in the real world. And that was so even when some of them, Bruni for example, who was chancellor of Florence in 1427–44, exercised political power themselves. The political interventions in the England of the mid-fifteenth century which I started with were, however, quite different. They were not, except for Fortescue, the work of intellectuals (he had read several of the authors just cited, but the others show no signs of it); and they were concerned with specifics of policy, far more than abstract principles. If we go back into the thirteenth century and even the twelfth, we do find some debate about policy; I discussed some of it in Chapter 8. But there was less of it. By the late fourteenth century, something had changed; the process of public political discussion had become much more substantial and easier to document, and also more influential.

One basic reason for this was certainly the greater importance of parliaments after 1350, linked to a greater need for taxation, and as a result a more elaborate field for state action, above all in the stronger political/fiscal systems in the league table outlined at the end of the last chapter. But that was not all that was involved; another reason is the notable activity of international church councils, particularly in the early fifteenth century; we can add a growing role for elaborate legal systems, and, of course, the underpinning increase of literacy, or at least of activities linked with writing, among the laity. Let us look at how these interrelated.

The word 'parliament' was used in this period to mean 'deliberative assembly' only in England and Scotland. (France had its own *parlements*, but they were above all courts of law.) In France, such assemblies were called *états-généraux*, estates-general (there were important provincial estates too), in Spain *cortes* or *corts*, in Poland *sejm*, in the German lands and Bohemia very often *dieta*, diet (in German *Landtag* or *Reichstag*), in Scandinavia *thing* (although *riksdag* came in later, following German usage). They were in nearly every case divided into estates, with greater aristocrats sitting and deliberating separately from lesser landed élites and urban leaders, in many cases a separate clerical estate too (though not in England), and in a very few cases (Sweden, as we have seen; also, in the German empire, some territories in the Alps) an estate of peasants. They were often representative bodies – that is to say, men (they were all men) were chosen to speak for others who were not there – except for aristocratic and church leaders, who mostly served in person.[5] They have therefore always had a lot of attention from historians who see them as the origins of modern representative democracy. This is unhelpful; their presuppositions were different, and there are very few cases in which there is even a genealogical relationship with modern democratic structures (England and Scandinavia are the clearest here). More interesting in my view is to determine how far they were the heirs of the political assemblies of the early middle ages, which had legitimated royal rule as meetings of the free men of the kingdom, as we saw in earlier chapters, and here only Scandinavia seems to me to be able to make that claim in full. In England, again the only other possible candidate, the clearest surviving heirs of the assemblies of the Anglo-Saxon period were shire and hundred courts, as we have seen. Twelfth-century royal assemblies, even if late Old English texts still refer to them with pre-1066 terminology, were – given that the aristocracy was itself created by William I after the Norman Conquest – most of all collections of aristocratic counsellors called by the king, and legitimised by his authority, not the other way round; the post-1230s English parliaments descended from them, rather than from Anglo-Saxon precedents.[6] Everywhere outside Scandinavia, in fact, parliaments (as I shall call them all for convenience) developed out of royal councils, that is to say of members of the king's court who were called by the ruler to advise him, rather than to legitimate him.

But they became legitimating bodies again, for different reasons from those of the early medieval past. As we have seen, parliaments were powerful (when they were) because of the steady development of royal fiscal needs, particularly in the strongest states; in much of Europe, only parliaments were authoritative enough collective bodies to be able to sign off large-scale taxation. This was usually why urban representatives were added to assemblies, too, in Aragón already in the 1210s, in England stably by the 1290s: because taxing towns was remunerative, and towns were also coherent enough bodies to resist if they had not consented.[7] But once collective bodies were recognised as necessary to agree taxation, it is unsurprising that they would come to think that they needed to discuss what that taxation was for, as well; and this meant that, in most parliamentary environments, debate about national policy could (re-)emerge. By the end of the fourteenth century, legislation was in much of Europe signed off – in some places, initiated – by parliaments as well. By then, too, the thirteenth-century concept of the 'community of the realm' had become generalised, as the 'public thing' (res publica, chose publique) or the 'common good/profit/wealth' (bonum commune, bien commun), as images of a kingdom-based collective good which was important for wide sectors of society. And, increasingly, these included those who were involved in any way in political activity, including, sometimes, non-élites like the sailors who beheaded the duke of Suffolk.[8]

There are two aspects to this which need stressing. One is simply the range of political discussion which was coming to be a recognisable part of the public sphere. Popular reactions began to be expressed in songs and sayings; they were often subversive, but they did not have to be. We find petitions to the English parliament by the fourteenth century that show that non-élites – urban communities, in particular, but the occasional peasant too – both respected the role (particularly the judicial/legislative role) of parliament and thought that they could influence it.[9] Propaganda begins to be visible for the first time: writings deliberatedly circulated by political powers to shore up support, first in politically active (and literate) circles, but also by public proclamation.[10] When printing became more common at the very end of the middle ages, such actions were of course still easier, but the world of manuscripts already had a place for it.

The other aspect, however, is that this world was very parcellised. We are not talking here about the existence of single communities that covered whole realms: or at least, if and when we are, that was the world of the real political élite, of royal officials, and aristocratic or episcopal collectives. For everyone else the initially relevant world was that of a local community, the often quite sharply bounded social groupings which gained coherence in the eleventh century in much of Europe and were ever more clearly delimited in the late middle ages, as we have seen: the lordship, the town; or, at a lower level, the kindred, the guild or confraternity, the village.[11] These overlapping groupings were often themselves opposed to each other, and much of the evidence that we have for late medieval conflict is for disputes between them.[12] Such communities were often by now, however, much more aware of their wider role in a larger political structure and culture – 'national' identity can indeed usefully be discussed for many late medieval polities. And, in return, in the fifteenth century as much as in the thirteenth (see Chapter 8), the rulers of kingdoms themselves related, not to everyone in the kingdom at once (or even to every prosperous adult male, a more likely grouping), but to these cellular networks of communities. In France, even taxation was agreed by towns and local assemblies (*états*), as much as, or more than, by the estates-general, and its exaction was sometimes devolved back down to them (it was often differently run from place to place as well); fifteenth-century kings also devolved justice to regional *parlements*, which became foci for local political communities.[13] In Castile from the late thirteenth century to the early sixteenth, leagues of towns called 'brotherhoods' formed spontaneously to confront royal power or inadequacy, and sometimes wielded considerable authority in the kingdom.[14] The expanded territories of Venice, Milan, Florence, and also of the fifteenth-century dukes of Burgundy, were all made up of networks of self-governing communities, mostly towns in these urbanised areas, plus, in the inland Low Countries, rural lordships; the ruling cities or dukes hegemonised them, certainly, and taxed them, but left them alone for much of the time. Switzerland was nothing other than a confederation of such communities; so was the Hanse. The cellular configuration of politics which, as I have stressed, owed its form to the local reconstructions after the 'feudal revolution', still marked the basic patterns of late medieval political life, however shot through the cells were by now with structures which linked them to royal power and kingdom-level relationships. Any successful ruler had to and did negotiate with the different types of community which made up his or her realm.

The importance of collective politics received a brief fillip during the period of the Council of Basel, 1431–49, an unexpected direction in many ways and a failure, but important all the same. The Council of Konstanz of 1414–18, which had deposed popes (see Chapter 11), established the legitimacy of councils of prelates to decide on the fate of the western church, and was always intended to have successors. Basel was the next to run effectively (there was one failed council in between), and it was very well supported by the secular rulers of Europe, who did not wish for a return to the untrammelled papal power of the thirteenth and fourteenth centuries, and who rested their hopes for church reform on conciliar decisions; they also thought, here more accurately, that a church council might be more effective than a pope in coming to terms with the scariest political development of the period, the Hussite takeover of Bohemia. Basel had a full complement of bishops and abbots – larger than Konstanz in fact – and also, significantly, many university masters and lesser clergy. But it did not have the pope; Eugenius IV (1431–47) not only never attended it, but sought at every stage to undermine it. Indeed, at its beginning he had tried to cancel it; the attendees ignored him, and at once responded with a decree stating that only the council could end itself.

The stage was thus set for the most principled trial of strength between monarchy and community of the whole late medieval period. Basel suspended Eugenius (most of his own cardinals deserted him), and made its own deals with the Hussites, rather effectively in fact, as well as brokering a treaty between France and Burgundy. It also addressed several of the most serious church abuses as they appeared to contemporaries, focusing on papal choices for ecclesiastical offices. But Eugenius's attempts to undermine the council became more adept as the 1430s wore on, and matters became more tense as a result, culminating in the council deposing the pope in 1439 and electing in his stead, weirdly, the recently retired duke of Savoy, Amedeo VIII, as Felix V. The secular powers maintained a studied neutrality, but this was too radical for many, and support slowly leached back to Eugenius, and, after his death, his successor Nicholas V; in 1449 the council finally recognised defeat and wound itself up. Eugenius and Nicholas had to recognise much de facto secular power over regional churches in return for lay support, all the same, even more than had happened during the Great Schism. The interest of Basel here lies, above all, in its role as a hothouse for new thinking about political practice. Many of the conciliarists did indeed believe that a properly constituted council should be the supreme authority in the church, and not popes, or even bishops. Nicholas of Cusa (d. 1464), probably the council's most innovative thinker, wrote *On Catholic concordance* in 1433 to argue strongly for the supremacy of consensus and law over the authority of popes, and prelates in general. And Basel's failure did not stop the men trained in nearly twenty years of discussion in the council from going their separate ways across Europe with these ideas in mind; much like the League of Nations in the 1920s and 1930s, a similarly interesting failure, it had bred a new generation of transnational experts in the principles and practice of collective government – and also of strong but self-proclaimed constitutionalist monarchies, which were in fact the dominant powers of the next period.[15]

Law is the other element that needs stress here, because there was steadily more of it. First, theory. Justinian's Roman-law corpus was often in the twelfth and thirteenth centuries treated as a text with quasi-religious authority, and commentators on it could be remarkably unhelpful contributors to current political understanding. One could cite here Jacques de Révigny (d. 1296), who wrote 'that France is subject to the empire you can find in [the code of Justinian]. If the king of France does not recognise this, I do not care': an attractively forceful view, but one that wilfully ignored actual political realities. By two generations later, however, there were some very sophisticated Roman-law thinkers, notably Bartolo of Sassoferrato, already mentioned, and his pupil Baldo degli Ubaldi (d. 1400), who in their most influential works showed for the first time how Romanist ideas could cope with the medieval world as it was, rather than as it ought ideally to be. They discussed, for example, the nature of the divided sovereignty of their time in notably neutral terms, which was certainly more helpful than de Révigny. As one would expect from Italians of the period, this Bartolist adaptation worked especially well when concerning itself with signorial rule and popular consent at the level of cities, but their sovereignty arguments went further too; these two had a growing impact in Spain, France and Germany at the end of the middle ages, and indeed after.[16]

It was in particular legal practice, however, which imposed itself in this period. More law was written down, and more new law was made; and, above all, more people went to public courts, and far more court decisions were recorded. Nor did people go to court only when they were in conflict; local courts were often the public locations for credit agreements and other accords as well. Early court records are associated above all with Italy and England, as we have seen, but by the late middle ages they were everywhere, and not only at the level of cities and kingdoms: the proceedings of public courts even at the village level survive from Catalonia to Poland by the fifteenth century, and rural Poland was by no means at the vanguard of processes like this.[17] That is to say, peasants as much as townspeople and élites were coming to be involved in the arena of written law, everywhere, which in itself tied them into the political networks we have been looking at. Even if this participation was not always willing, and took place in contexts of greater or lesser subjection, the literate world was touching everyone by now: not changing people's modes of thinking (to repeat, literacy never did that), but making them aware of regularities elsewhere. Public forms of the legal process were thus pervasive in nearly every local environment, and its rules, although never perfect (and also far from just), became familiar to an ever-higher percentage of Europeans. Trained lawyers were more numerous (in southern Europe, they had often read Bartolo), and legal expertise, both trained and practice-based, was even more widespread. We saw in Chapters 8 and 10 that lay religious activity was wider-based by 1200, and onwards from there, and that this could result in innovative interpretations of religion which church authorities found (whether rightly or not) threatening. The same was true for legal expertise, in the secular world, a century or so later. Much of the sophistication of the late medieval public sphere at both the élite level and the local level came from legal practice, and the discourse that it generated.

*   *   *

To sum up so far, based on the discussions in both this chapter and the previous one: late medieval politics was more expensive than it had been, largely because paid armies were now normal nearly everywhere (and artillery after 1400 or so would only add to that expense);[18] taxation was thus by now much more normal too, at least in the most coherent polities of the period, France, England, Burgundy, the Iberian and Italian states, Hungary and the Ottoman empire. State power was by now taken for granted; its presuppositions were only resisted at the edges of Europe, such as Scotland and Sweden. Public debate assumed it nearly everywhere else; disagreement focused on its direction and its cost, not its legitimacy. And, thanks to the existence of political discussion in parliaments and city councils, and to legal discussion in towns and villages, the parameters of public debate were extending ever deeper into the still-separate cells of society, which, more and more, were coming to understand the nature of their relationships with the 'public good' and the way that 'good' could and should be directed. Conscious political problem-solving is by now better-documented too, and seems to have been rather more common than it had been in previous centuries. We must not overgeneralise here; the different European kingdoms and polities in 1350–1500 were very far from completely coherent, particularly in the fiscally weaker realms of the north and east. The large majority of peasants were also, in practice, excluded from real participation in most political processes, even if such processes impinged heavily on them (as with all taxation, and of course in any war), and even if they sometimes demonstrably had views about how such processes should be managed.

But we cannot by now ignore the public sphere. Here, I want to build on this in two directions: by looking at the role of intellectuals in this environment; and then by looking at the space that it gave people for dissent, both in words and in deeds. These were two different trends, but they meet, as we shall see, in the figure of the Czech intellectual, Jan Hus, whose dissent changed the politics of a part of Europe.

Public intellectuals in Europe, that is to say people who gained a wide hearing for their views because of their personal expertise and authority, rather than because of their political or social standing, did not begin in the late middle ages. In their different and opposing ways, both Peter Abelard and Bernard of Clairvaux in the early twelfth century were examples, as was Michael Psellos in Constantinople in the eleventh; people already wanted to know what they would do and say next. But there were many more of them after 1300 or so, and also more of them were laymen than had been the case before. When Dante, in exile for twenty years after 1302 from a position in Florentine government because of the defeat of his city faction, wrote his highly ambitious allegorical poem *Divine comedy*, people paid attention, as we have seen; but so did they when he wrote *Monarchy*, a tract on the superior legitimacy of the secular rule of the emperor to that of the pope, and, by implication, to that of the autonomous cities of Italy as well. This second work, not surprisingly, was of no real use to most politically active figures in those cities, but it was still seriously engaged with, because of the authority of its author.[19] Half a century later, Francesco Petrarca (Petrarch, d. 1374) emerged around 1340 from a standard career as a client of Avignonese prelates into a more (to him) attractive one as guest of several Italian cities in succession, by becoming a famous poet (in both Latin and Italian), Ciceronian letter-writer, and writer of highly literary tracts – as well as being the first known person to claim to have climbed a mountain for the aesthetic or spiritual pleasure of it (Cézanne's Mont Ventoux in Provence, in 1336). Petrarch was useful to cities as a speechwriter, but his real use was as a cultural icon, based on his wide reading and remarkable literary skills.[20]

As Italian city élites came to value similarly wide reading, particularly in classical literature, and (above all) elegant classicising rhetorical skills and prose, the ranks of such intellectuals became ever denser across the late fourteenth and especially fifteenth centuries. The ability to argue and write in a 'humanist' manner became a passport to patronage and prosperity. This movement has traditionally been attached above all to Florence, but in fact nearly every Italian city – and courts across northern Europe too, from England to Poland – caught onto this century-long fashion for intellectual debate and

complex Latin (later, Greek as well), which extended in many different directions, to science, to textual criticism, to architecture.[21] This latter included the
architectural writings of Leon Battista Alberti (d. 1472), intellectual client as
usual of several city courts but also designer of some of the most expensive and
best-loved buildings in Italy in the new classical (called now, but not then,
'Renaissance') style, from Rimini to Rome – plus, via his protégé Bernardo
Rossellino, a dramatic piazza built for the Senese pope Pius II (1458–64) in the
tiny Tuscan hill village of Pienza, a medieval Italian Portmeirion.[22]

Alberti, unlike Dante and Petrarch, became a cleric, and public intellectuals
could be clerics elsewhere too, particularly in northern Europe. Jean Gerson
(d. 1429) is a good example: a rare case of a peasant boy rising to the élite by
education, he became chancellor of the university of Paris, so had a recognised
official role; but his writing of tracts in both Latin and French, once again on
every conceivable subject, from monastic vegetarianism, through popular
'superstition', to nocturnal emissions, far extended his presence. He came into
his own during the council of Konstanz, for which he was one of the principal
theorists, and he was writing tracts to the end of his life (one just before his
death on the virtues of Joan of Arc stands out for its topicality – as well as its
political commitment, for Paris was by then controlled by the English, and
other university masters from there would be Joan's trial judges). Gerson's
tracts survive in larger numbers of manuscripts than the works of any other
late medieval intellectual except Dante. He shows well how university masters
by now could achieve a wide audience, this time for a theologically derived
intellectualism, rather than the classical culture just mentioned – reminding
us, indeed, that theology remained the dominant partner in the intellectual life
of the period.[23] And this brings us to the last two public intellectuals we need
to look at here, for they had something of the ambition and public success of
Gerson, and in an equally theological mould, but in each case a very different
and more dissenting direction: John Wyclif (d. 1384) and Jan Hus (d. 1415).

Wyclif had the more complex theology of the two. He was a master of the
university of Oxford, who in the 1360s and 1370s published a series of philo-
sophical and then theological works of considerable subtlety; by the mid-
1370s, however, his thought had evolved, rapidly, in the direction of a
theological critique of papal wealth, and the need for the disendowment of the
church. He also had critical ideas on the presence of Christ in the Eucharist.
These views, which he expressed with characteristic sharpness, were enough to
get him a papal condemnation in 1377 and expulsion from Oxford in 1382. But
it is significant that Wyclif, for a long time, had defenders too; the king's son
and regent John of Gaunt was his patron in the 1370s, and he had a popular

following as well. It was only after the Peasants' Revolt of 1381, which he was claimed to have helped foment though his preaching – a claim which in itself shows how much support he was believed to have had – that the establishment turned against him.[24] Wyclif had followers afterwards as well, the Lollards, who were regarded as heretics by the church hierarchy; one prominent Lollard, Sir John Oldcastle, staged a half-hearted revolt in 1414, which led to a clampdown on Lollards generally, and an increasing marginalisation of them in England across the rest of the century. By now, however, Wycliffite views had gone well beyond the university, and sometimes changed as a result; Lollards were often self-educated preachers, the sort of people who had been 'good men' in the 'Cathar' period in southern Europe. Not unlike earlier lay heretics, they regarded the authority of scripture, which they had by now in English, as superior to that of the church, rejected the latter's temporal power (here they were at their most Wycliffite), and for the most part rejected transubstantiation.[25] But this heresy was different from most of its predecessors, in that it had highly complex theological roots; Wyclif, although he took his ideas further than most, was far from out of place in the normal run of university debates. Had he not also had a public role, he might have survived papal hostility; the Great Schism was starting, after all, and popes were busy.

Hus, in Bohemia a generation later, had read Wyclif, whose writings had come to Prague, and was highly influenced by him. He was a master of the university of Prague, and from 1409 its rector; as or more important, he was also the main preacher at the influential Bethlehem chapel in the town. He used this base not only to write but to preach along largely Wycliffite lines, especially on church wealth and temporal power, on the Bible in the vernacular (he translated much of it into Czech), and on authority in the church: popes and priests should only be followed if they were personally holy. As the Schism was moving to its close, it has to be said that this last view was less controversial than it had been, and it had direct links to the principles of the councils of Konstanz and Basel (it also had parallels in the earlier, and not-then-heretical, Pataria in Milan). So it is not as surprising that it might be that Hus took the risk of going to Konstanz in 1414–15 to defend his views, protected as he also was by an imperial safe-conduct. He was tried and burned for heresy for all that; he would not recant his adherence to Wyclif, who was by now fully accepted as a heretic, and, by resisting, he rejected the authority of the council too. This time, however, Hus's lay support was far greater than that of Wyclif: it extended to King Václav IV to an extent, and to a large sector of the aristocracy, as well as to Czech-speaking clerics, townsmen and peasants. The Hussite revolt, which involved the majority of Bohemia's inhabitants and represented far and away the most energetic 'heresy' of the middle ages, was a direct result of his death. Not all of its principles were strictly those of Hus; the clearest distinguishing mark of subsequent Hussites, the insistence on the right to drink wine at the Eucharist, was only taken up by Hus himself very late, in 1414, and he would, beyond doubt, have been opposed to the activities of his most radical followers, to whom we will come in a moment. But Hus was the one public intellectual of the middle ages whose words and actions – even if only activated by his martyrdom – really did have an effect on the political life of the continent.[26]

Apart from Hus, none of these figures had a major influence on the development of the public sphere in itself. By its very nature, the discourse of the many is seldom determined directly by the writings of the few, and not many public intellectuals, operating outside the formal structures of power that is to say, have ever been really effective; Luther, Marx (but again mostly after his death), Gandhi stand out precisely because of their rarity. What these medieval writers show, all the same, is the complexity of public discourse by now and the acceptability of quite elaborate intellectual arguments as part of it, even if the more policy-directed versions of such discourse – debate over the tax-raising rights of kings, or the problem-solving discussed at the start of this chapter – were also linked to more practical concerns. This was a real development of the later middle ages, thanks to the steadily greater ease of communications, and to the greater availability of writing among the laity, which both made the reception of written communication easier and facilitated the dissemination of complex ideas. It does not, it must be stressed, point directly towards the Reformation, even though that movement claimed both Wyclif and Hus as precursors, a view still frequently held by modern historians too. Neither of them moved in the direction of sixteenth-century Reform theorists, to oppose the sacrality of the clergy or to insist on a thoroughgoing predestination; rather, they were reformers in a framework of Latin revival movements going back to at least the eleventh century, with the added twist by now of a university background in disputation. But the communications and writing-based culture of the late medieval period (both soon further developed thanks to the rapid expansion of printing after 1450) made the next set of moves by intellectuals and laity to change the church, which were indeed those of Luther and his contemporaries, that much more quickly effective.

*   *   *

Religious dissent was only one type of oppositional movement in the later middle ages, and not the most common. The Hussites are the only large-scale example of it, so we shall start with them, although we need also to recognise that the Hussites were quite exceptional in their organisation among more secular-minded dissenting movements too. It is not possible to attach an overarching social identity onto the various Hussite factions in Bohemia, which ranged from the highest aristocrats (and even bishops) to the peasantry, but it is at least striking that the death of Hus in 1415 led at once to an outburst of indignation right across Bohemia, which took on more and more radical elements in the immediately following years. Preaching in towns and villages led to the spontaneous formation of religious communities, which then chose their own doctrinal paths. In 1419 an insurrection in Prague led to the lynching of the city's ruling councillors; in 1419–20 a group of radicals founded the new town of Tábor and held their property in common; in May 1420 radicals and moderates approved the Four Articles of Prague, which became the mantra on which the different Hussite factions could agree: their main themes being the drinking of wine at the Eucharist, the freedom to preach, and the need for the church to be poor. In 1420 a Hussite peasant army, led by the remarkable general Jan Žižka (d. 1424), won the first of a series of romantically successful defensive battles against crusades sent against them by the papacy and Sigismund of Hungary, now heir to his brother Wenceslas/Václav in Bohemia as well. These victories continued until 1434, and, as long as they did, the radical wing of Hussitism was dominant; but even after that an aristocratic version, with similar core beliefs, dominated in the region for nearly two centuries more.[27]

Hussitism was not ever really a movement that had the interests of peasants in the forefront. Tábor's leadership, however religiously radical, took rents from the peasantry in its territory just as local lords had done before, and the only real social change which resulted from the radical Hussite period (even if it was a major one) was a sharp reduction in church landholding and overall wealth. The most significant feature of the movement, particularly in its early years, 1415–20, was, rather, the speed with which excited reaction to Hus's death brought in more and more social strata and ever-larger areas of both city and countryside in at least Czech-speaking Bohemia. This simple fact shows how fast ideas could by now spread in Europe, and how rapidly involved the peasant majority could by now become in some quite recondite theological issues, which in Bohemia led temporarily to a peasant presence in national politics too. That fits popular involvement in political discussion elsewhere in Europe, even if nowhere else in this period went as far as the Czechs in their preparedness, on religious grounds, to rethink political questions which extended as far as the legitimacy of royal power.

Oppositional movements apart from the Hussites had more secular aims, social and political reform above all. There were more of them than historians have often thought. Using a wide definition, Samuel Cohn has recently identified over a thousand popular movements and revolts, in towns and villages, in Italy, France and the Low Countries alone between 1200 and 1425. Of these, nearly 60 per cent postdated the Black Death; that is to say, the second half of the fourteenth century saw a sharp increase in them.[28] They continued throughout the fifteenth century too, and indeed into the sixteenth, up to the Castilian *comuneros* of 1520–21, the south German Peasants' War of 1525, and the Norfolk Rising in England in 1549. One of the most successful was one of the latest in the middle ages, the uprising in Catalonia of the Remences, servile peasants, against the seigneurial dues which marked their subjection, in 1462–86. The case is unusual, because the peasants here had the support of a succession of Aragonese kings, from the 1380s onwards, who had their own reasons to want to reduce the rights of their aristocracy. But the coherence of peasant demands steadily increased from then onwards, which led to one-off uprisings, and then generalised war in the 1460s as a royal succession dispute engulfed Aragón. In part because of peasant armed support for his father in the war, Ferdinand II formally abolished serfdom in 1486. The Remença revolt shows quite clearly that a common narrative of peasant rebellion, that each one was tragically drowned in blood, is not always accurate. Many uprisings in Cohn's earlier data-set also went unpunished, even if few were as successful as the Remences; so did, outside his area of study, the peasants of Dithmarschen in the far north of Germany, who held off both local lords and the kings of Denmark throughout the fifteenth century, the legally informed peasants of the Croatian islands in the same period, who could negotiate with the doge of Venice in person, and, not least, the peasants of the Swiss mountain communities, whose independence had been definitively established by the end of the fourteenth century.[29]

The Remença uprising was however atypical in one crucial respect: that it was focused on landlords. Most revolts were not against landowners (or, in towns, against employers); they were not against working conditions, or only partially so. What links most of the popular oppositional movements of the later middle ages is their resistance to the exactions and injustices less of landlords than of the state, including to the new oppression of fiscality. The great Peasants' Revolt in eastern England in 1381, already cited, was set off by the poll tax of that and previous years, and when the rebels attacked London they targeted royal officials quite carefully, such as John of Gaunt (whose palace they burned down) and the chancellor, Archbishop Sudbury (whom they beheaded). They did, certainly, seek the abolition of serfdom, as well as the lowering of rents, but their demands otherwise focused on taxation, law and good government, and their demand for freedom from serfdom was as much a demand for a generalised, community-based, political liberty.[30] The equally large-scale Jacquerie in the countryside around Paris in 1358 (this revolt, at least, was repressed very bloodily) was against the aristocracy, not a tax revolt against the state, but its main context was still political: in the chaos of the Hundred Years' War, peasant self-help developed into an attack on the aristocracy who had failed to protect the peasantry, as aristocratic rhetoric claimed it was supposed to. The rural revolts against the city of Florence in the 1400s were set off because tax was not only high, but unfair, in that it was higher in some parts of the Florentine territory than in others, which the peasants were fully aware of. This was even more clearly the case in the very numerous uprisings in towns throughout continental Europe, in the Low Countries, France, Spain, Italy, or the German lands, which were aimed at reducing taxes, or asserting local political rights for citizens who felt excluded (although these were not often the poorest urban strata), or simply to make the exercise of such rights real in the maze of overlapping jurisdictions which marked most cities. Revolts of this kind were very rare in the early middle ages, when state power was relatively weak or distant. The fact that they became more common after 1250 and much more common after 1350 was a result, above all, of the fact that states (including city-states) taxed more heavily and ruled more intensively than they had before; they were a reaction to a more intrusive state power, that is to say, and were also more frequent where that power was strongest. The explicit imagery of liberty marked a large number of them; so did justice, and truth, as again in England in 1381. Communities here asserted themselves, not just against outsiders, as we saw in Chapter 10, but against rulers as well.[31]

And that brings these oppositional movements and revolts back to the arena of the public sphere. We have seen that discussion about the direction of politics had by now extended to ever-wider strata of society. This sort of discussion could turn to direct, violent, interventions, as, in the England of 1450, the death of the duke of Suffolk and Jack Cade's rebellion both show; and the speed in Bohemia in the 1410s by which animated religious dissent led to direct action is another example of the same process. In 1381, too, even if the English rebels had not been inspired by Wyclif (which remains unproven), they understood much of what was going on in English politics and could target its leaders – as well as being very conscious indeed of the power of writing, as the strategic burning of public legal records in London and of manorial records in the villages of much of eastern England both show. So, in the generations after the Black Death, a sense that political discussion and protagonism did not belong only to traditional élites became much more generalised in much of Europe; conversely, given that there were in most countries no legitimate outlets for non-élite protagonism, either urban or rural, it is not surprising that it could turn to violence. But, although this violence was sometimes so far-reaching that one can see it as genuinely revolutionary, it could easily be trans-actional as well, aimed at more immediate political goals, which were sometimes achieved. It thus belonged on the same spectrum as the more institutionalised, but equally active and protagonistic (and sometimes itself violent), public arena of parliaments, law courts, and political tracts. There was a socio-economic background to these patterns of non-élite direct action as well, of course. It may well be that the shock of the Black Death and the rising pros-perity of its survivors allowed at least some of the great majority of disenfran-chised Europeans to think more widely about their place in the world; and the regions with the greatest fiscal pressure were also often regions with relatively great internal economic complexity and social mobility too, which helped the development of new ideas. But it is also the case that the ease of communica-tions and the widening of literacy made not only political debate but also organised opposition a more possible process. In this respect the English Peasants' Revolt was not at all the one-off and fantasy-based failure which it has often been painted as being, but, rather, a model for the political protago-nism of the later middle ages as a whole.[32]

CHAPTER THIRTEEN

Conclusion

What really changed in Europe in the medieval millennium? I listed what I see as the most important single moments of change at the start of Chapter 1, and we have followed them across the whole of this book. Now, however, we need to step back a little, and get a sense of Europe as a whole, with some wider generalisations, ending up with the late medieval world we have been looking at in the last three chapters. One thing which remained constant throughout the middle ages was the importance of the old Roman imperial frontier. It is true that, as we have seen, the broad configuration of the political map of most of twenty-first-century Europe was very roughly established by 1500; this is important in itself, and was a real consequence of medieval European social and political change as a whole. But we can also by now see that, if we look underneath that map, at the infrastructure of the kingdoms and polities of the fifteenth century, the old Rhine–Danube border kept its relevance: nearly all the strong states lay south of that border, and north of it, political coherence was rather more intermittent, as we saw in Chapter 11. It is true that, south of the border, some regions had had a relatively difficult history, with severe structural breaks at different times – much of the Balkans, for example; to the north, too, Hungary and some other polities had gained considerable strength. But the infrastructures of the Roman world, roads and the city network in particular, still mattered; in France, in Spain, in Italy, and not least in the Ottoman empire (whose territories hardly, except after 1500 for Iraq and Hungary, extended outside the old imperial provinces), the continuities with the past remained. The Roman frontier indeed only finally lost its force from the eighteenth century onwards.

That was a marker of structural continuities, then, across the agrarian world of the middle ages. But there were plenty of structural changes too. As we saw in Chapters 7 and 11, the population of Europe went through some sharp shifts; after a decrease in the early middle ages, it picked up again around 900, and tripled in size between then and 1300, after which the Black Death halved it again. This had an effect on agricultural production, which, by and large, followed these developments quite closely, the central middle ages being a period of intensification and land clearance, and the late middle ages being a period in which agrarian specialisation became more widespread, as there was a less intense demand for grain as the basic staple for human life. The long boom also produced a commercial complexity, focused on Flanders and northern Italy, which was sufficiently well based that it could survive the Black Death, and indeed increase its geographical range in the later middle ages. Economic activity was much more broadly based at the end of the middle ages than it had been at the beginning, then, and it was beginning to lessen even the long-standing economic differences between north and south.

As to cultural change: the Christianisation of most of Europe, spreading outwards from the ex-Roman provinces to the north and east of the continent in the second quarter of the middle ages in particular, was one major shift, even if, as I argued in Chapter 5, its effects were very regionally diverse. It brought the structures of the church with it, which meant that from the twelfth century onwards there was a single ecclesiastical hierarchy which covered the whole of Latin Europe, although not the more decentralised Orthodox east. Church leaders tried to use that structure to impose consistent patterns of belief, or at least observance, across over half the continent. They failed – Europe never became culturally homogeneous, a point I will come back to – but it is at least significant that they tried. Perhaps more important than this, however, was the slow extension of literate practices across more and more of Europe, and also, from the thirteenth century onwards, to a greater range of social strata: from lay élites to townspeople, then even, occasionally, to a few sectors of the peasant majority. The effect that this had on the way people behaved we have explored in Chapters 4, 8, 10 and 12. It means that we know more, about more sectors of society, but it also meant that they did themselves too; information exchange was much more widely based at the end of the middle ages than it had been at the beginning. But, if the structures of the church tended towards attempted religious and thus cultural homogeneity, the extension of literate practices reinforced difference; local societies were just as likely to reach varying conclusions about how they should deal with the world if they had independent access to the texts which discussed it, and sometimes would become more obstinate about their views as well. This was all the more the case because local societies tended more and more to be constructed as bounded communities with distinct social structures and identities, which was one key element of the sociopolitical changes across the medieval millennium.

If we focus on these sociopolitical changes, in fact, we can see a particularly clear division between the first half of the medieval millennium and the second. The political developments in Latin Europe after the Black Death which we have looked at in the last two chapters had earlier roots, but these went back, above all, to the eleventh century. The eleventh century indeed marked more of a break in the history of medieval western Europe than any century after the fifth, in several crucial respects. Before then, despite the dramatic regionalisation of the post-Roman world, which led to the loss of wealth and power of most rulers and élites (except in part in Francia), the larger early medieval kingdoms, Spain, Francia and Italy, had inherited from the Roman empire a political practice and a sense of a public power which lasted for centuries. This public world led to some very ambitious politics indeed under the Carolingians, when kings, lay aristocrats and clerics worked more tightly together to further political 'reform' than in any other period of the middle ages. The centrality of the royal-focused public sphere for political players was inherited straight from the Roman past, and was augmented by a widespread sense across the early medieval centuries that the politics of assemblies, which were also held in public, was a key to political legitimacy. Even if that centrality was no longer made definitive by the continuity of the wealth derived from taxation, it was still crucial, for power at the local level was ill-developed and was seldom considered legitimate on its own: aristocrats, in particular, were regarded – not inaccurately – as losers if they focused on local power, and avoided the royal patronage which remained so honourable and lucrative. The tenth century marked the continuation of that world, particularly in Germany and Italy, and by now in England too, and also the beginnings of its extension northwards and eastwards into the Scandinavian and Slavic lands; but across a long eleventh century it ended nearly everywhere. These western polities were surpassed by a Byzantine empire, where the loss of its eastern provinces to the Arabs in the seventh century did not result in the breakdown of traditional political and fiscal structures; for a shorter period, essentially the tenth century, the Byzantine example was matched by the brilliance and coherence of the Umayyad caliphate in al-Andalus as well. The Byzantines remained Roman in their style of ruling until the permanent destruction of imperial unity with separatist revolts in the late twelfth century and the fall of Constantinople to the crusaders in 1204; in the east, in fact, the late-twelfth-century break matches that of the eleventh in the west, and was even sharper.

In the west, the political practice of the eleventh century onwards was however very different. We have seen in the last half of this book how it initially depended on three underlying changes. First, the breakdown of Carolingian political structures in much of western Europe, into a network of counties, lordships and local urban and rural communities, in the so-called 'feudal revolution', at different moments between 950 and 1100 or so. Second, the reconstruction of political power in the twelfth and thirteenth centuries, which was henceforth, however, set against the cellular network of these partly autonomous communities. Third, the long economic boom of the tenth to thirteenth centuries, just mentioned, which left a Europe with considerable economic prosperity and flexibility, continuing into the later middle ages. The second and third of these, put together, allowed the development of more complex forms of taxation by some rulers, which in their turn allowed for the expansion of new strata of paid officials, who were more often trained, in universities and other schools, institutions by now themselves made possible because a more complex economy could sustain them. Most of these developments can soon be found, in slightly different forms, in the Ottoman empire as well; but there the processes of development were more continuous, after the decentralisation of the period 1200–1400 in south-eastern Europe, for the Ottomans inherited so much from Byzantium – notwithstanding sharp changes, of course, in their religion and political language.

And this brings us back to the late middle ages. By 1350 in the west, legal expertise was sufficiently widely spread that written law could become more visible in localities, a process that would extend literate practices further and further into the different communities of Europe. And after 1350 the steady extension of tax-raising powers itself contributed in much of Europe to the development of communities of taxpayers, whether cities or newly appearing collective kingdom-wide bodies, that is to say parliaments. But a greater access to writing, and a reaction to a growing intrusiveness of central power, themselves contributed to the coherence of local communities, and to their capacity to react against outsiders, whether rival communities, out-groups, or the state. Rulers were thus stronger, but so were the communities of the ruled. In this environment, the need to consent to taxation, and often legislation, created a public sphere which after 1350/1400 was stronger than it had ever been before in the middle ages, except in the high days of Carolingian assembly politics. The protagonism of all levels of society, from aristocrats to peasants, which we looked at in the last chapter, derived from that. So did a newfound attention to political problem-solving, which was another product of this developing public sphere – as also of the training of the official strata and an attention to their accountability, which started in the twelfth century and which extended thereafter. From this derived a new capacity for organised dissent, the signs of which are present in nearly every country of Latin Europe. In this way the world of the English Peasants' Revolt, the Hussites, and the late medieval public sphere as a whole, can be tracked back, through these multiple channels, to the social and political changes unleashed by the 'feudal revolution'. This process in a sense simply marked the reinvention of the public world of the Carolingian period; but this time it was reinforced, strongly, by local community politics, just as much as by the assemblies ratified and called by kings.

To repeat, however: this apparently Europe-wide politics was not homogeneous. European cultures, it is true, had moved closer together in some ways, as communications, and indeed commerce, linked nearly everywhere, at least at a couple of removes – and that again included the Ottoman world too, and even Muscovy, where Italian architects were building churches and secular buildings in the Moscow Kremlin from the 1470s.[1] The fact that Scandinavian kings in their dealings with their parliaments sometimes look as if they are trying to imitate the immensely richer and more powerful kings of France is a sign that some practices did indeed cover almost the whole of Europe. Perhaps only Lithuania and Muscovy at one edge of Europe, and the Irish princes at the other, had by now presuppositions about political action which would have been really unfamiliar to other Europeans. Some form of parliamentary politics was close to universal, at least in Latin Europe, and intellectuals moved about in it everywhere, including to (and from) Poland, Sweden and Scotland. But, once again, this was a far from complete process. The growth of vernaculars, which reintroduced problems of translation, actively impeded it; so did the revival of nationally focused churches in the fifteenth century, and the increasing antagonism between the Ottomans and the Latin polities. We have seen that similarities in political practices covered up major differences in political resources. And other aspects of local society and culture travelled much less well than the patterns of politics. Venetian ambassadors, whose frank reports on the countries they were serving in begin to survive from the end of the fifteenth century, were highly critical at some of the things they saw: the surprising tendency of Parisians to praise the childish behaviour of King Charles VIII in 1492, or the extreme hostility to foreigners and the weird custom of wives inheriting from husbands in England in 1497.[2] Venice would, of course, not have been any less strange to northern Europeans.

But these divergences do not detract from the basic argument of the second half of this book. Which is that the strength of local, cellular, politics, plus the extension of literate practices to ever-wider social groups, plus a continuing high-equilibrium economic system, plus a newly intrusive state, made possible by taxation, communications and, once again, literacy, helped to create political systems across Europe which allowed *engagement*, nearly everywhere. *This* marks the last century of the middle ages, not the supposedly late medieval features which mark so many textbooks: crisis, or anxiety, or the Renaissance, or a sense that the continent was, somehow, waiting for the Reformation and European global conquest. And it is one of the main elements that the medieval period handed on to future generations.

Notes

1. A new look at the middle ages

1. The best textbook, for me (it is in fact more than a textbook), is B. Rosenwein, *A short history of the middle ages* (2009). Other key interpretative works include G. Tabacco and G.G. Merlo, *Medioevo* (1981); J.H. Arnold, *What is medieval history?* (2008); and two better-than-average collective volumes, *Storia medievale* (1998), and C. Lansing and E.D. English, *A companion to the medieval world* (2009). For shorter periods, M. Innes, *Introduction to early medieval western Europe, 300–900* (2007) and J.M.H. Smith, *Europe after Rome* (2005) for the early middle ages; R. Bartlett, *The making of Europe* (1993) and M. Barber, *The two cities* (2004) for the central period; J. Watts, *The making of polities* (2009) for the late middle ages. C. Wickham, *The inheritance of Rome* (2009) also covers the first half of the middle ages, in rather more detail than I do here. This fits with the fact that the second half of the medieval period makes up more than 60 per cent of this book; for more on the early middle ages, see Wickham, *The inheritance.*
    An additional note: my aim throughout this book is to refer to authoritative bibliography, in whatever language; but when I cite overviews, which is quite often, I will use English-language ones by preference.
2. For the history of the word 'medieval', see e.g. W.A. Green, 'Periodisation in European and world history' (1992).
3. For critiques of nationalist imagery, see e.g. P.J. Geary, *The myth of nations* (2002), 1–40; C. Wickham, 'The early middle ages and national identity' (2006). For the very long back history to serious work on the early middle ages, I. Wood, *The modern origins of the early middle ages* (2013).
4. See e.g. C. Holmes and N. Standen, *The global middle ages* (forthcoming).
5. See above all V. Lieberman, *Strange parallels* (2003–09), vol. 1 for Southeast Asia, vol. 2 for comparisons.
6. See for a long-term survey D. Abulafia, *The great sea* (2011).
7. K.J. Leyser, 'Concepts of Europe in the early and high middle ages' (1992). For later periods, D. Hay, *Europe: The emergence of an idea* (1968), 37–55, 73–95; and above all, now, K. Oschema, *Bilder von Europa im Mittelalter* (2013), esp. 195–315, 429–50.
8. K. Marx, *The eighteenth Brumaire of Louis Bonaparte* (1973), 146.
9. I.S. Robinson, *Henry IV of Germany, 1056–1106* (1999), 73–4, 140–50. One result was that neither Henry nor Gregory had any clear idea what the other's real political positions and value systems were: see H. Vollrath, 'Sutri 1046 – Canossa 1077 – Rome 1111' (2012), 147–9.
10. J.E. Kanter, 'Peripatetic and sedentary kingship' (2011), 12–15.
11. See above all J. Martindale, '"An unfinished business"' (2003), with some differences of interpretation. Quotes from Robert of Torigni, *Chronica* (1889), 203; William fitz Stephen, *Vita Sancti Thomae* (1877), c. 22. Note that Raymond did homage to Henry

later, in 1173, and recognised his overlordship, which was an eventual face-saver for the English king, although it did not have much political commitment behind it.

12. S. Reynolds, *Fiefs and vassals* (1994), esp. (for this period) 266, 272–3. Against feudalism, e.g. E.A.R. Brown, 'The tyranny of a construct' (1974); D. Crouch, *The birth of nobility* (2005), 261–78. Recent good-quality and historiographically aware surveys of it (especially its 'feudo-vassalic' variant) are S. Patzold, *Das Lehnswesen* (2012); G. Albertoni, *Vassalli, feudi, feudalesimo* (2015). For its different core meanings, C. Wickham, 'Le forme del feudalesimo' (2000).

13. J. France, *Western warfare in the age of the Crusades, 1000–1300* (1999), 59–62, 68–75.

14. M. Bloch, *La société féodale* (1940), vol. 2, 249 for the quote (the English trans., *Feudal society*, 446, is not exact).

15. Major recent instances include J. Fried, 'Gens und regnum' (1994), 73–104 (but see, e.g., S. Airlie et al., *Staat im frühen Mittelalter* (2006)); R. Davies, 'The medieval state' (2003), (but see e.g. S. Reynolds, 'There were states in medieval Europe' (2003)).

16. J.A. Green, 'The last century of Danegeld' (1981).

17. For the games-playing, see above all G. Althoff, *Spielregeln der Politik im Mittelalter* (1997). For Henry's own court etiquette and games-playing, W. Map, *De nugis curialium* (1983), is the classic contemporary guide.

18. T.N. Bisson, *Tormented voices* (1998), gives a clear account of peasant views of such extortions, as seen in legal pleas against lords from the twelfth century in Catalonia, a type-example of a region in which lords were then extending the range of dues they demanded from peasants in the framework of the 'seigneurie banale' (see Ch. 6). For the generalised contempt for peasants felt by the landowning classes, see P. Freedman, *Images of the medieval peasant* (1999).

19. See for the early middle ages e.g. C. Wickham, *Framing the early middle ages* (2005), 259–65, 558–66; A. Rio, *Slavery after Rome, 500–1100* (2016). For post-1000 (the date is a very rough one), e.g. F. Panero, *Schiavi servi e villani nell'Italia medievale* (1999); D. Barthélemy, *La mutation de l'an mil a-t-elle eu lieu?* (1997), 57–171; and above all P. Freedman and M. Bourin, *Forms of servitude in northern and central Europe* (2005). For Catalonia, P. Freedman, *The origins of peasant servitude in medieval Catalonia* (1991).

20. See e.g. T.B. Lambert, 'Theft, homicide and crime in late Anglo-Saxon law' (2012); T. Fenster and D.L. Smail, *Fama* (2003). For honour in an early medieval context, Smith, *Europe after Rome*, 100–14.

21. T.R. Gurr, 'Historical trends in violent crime' (1981). For strategic violence in court contexts, see e.g. C. Wickham, *Courts and conflict in twelfth-century Tuscany* (1998), 85–8, 199–222. For the normality of violence see, as a case study of France around 1300, H. Skoda, *Medieval violence* (2013).

22. W.I. Miller, *Bloodtaking and peacemaking* (1990), for Iceland; Gregory of Tours, *Decem libri historiarum* (1951), 9.19, cf. 7.47; C. Lansing, *The Florentine magnates* (1991), 166–8, for Buondelmonte di Buondelmonti. For the vagueness in common definitions of 'feud', G. Halsall, 'Violence and society in the early medieval west' (1998); for how it shades into private war, see the late medieval evidence presented in H. Kaminsky, 'The noble feud in the middle ages' (2002); the bibliography here is however substantial.

23. K.W. Nicholls, *Gaelic and Gaelicized Ireland in the middle ages* (1993), 98–100.

24. Einhard, *Vita Karoli Magni* (1911), c. 24; for the obligations of drinking, see e.g. the imagery which runs throughout the early medieval Welsh *Y Gododdin* poem. For the trope of killing at dinner, see e.g. Gregory of Tours, *Decem libri historiarum*, 10.27, a clearly written-up account.

25. P. Skinner, *Women in medieval Italian society, 500–1200* (2001), 35–47 for Italy; F. Kelly, *A guide to early Irish law* (1988), 104–5. See in general for the early middle ages Smith, *Europe after Rome*, 115–47; L. Brubaker and J.M.H. Smith, *Gender in the early medieval world* (2004); L.M. Bitel, *Women in early medieval Europe, 400–1000* (2002). For the second half of the middle ages (but with important contributions for earlier too), the fundamental starting point is now J.M. Bennett and R.M. Karras, *The Oxford handbook*

of women and gender in medieval Europe (2013). For women at assemblies in late Anglo-Saxon England, A.J. Robertson, *Anglo-Saxon charters* (1939), nn. 66, 78; J. Crick, *Charters of St Albans* (2007), n. 7. For the cliché in China, Li Bozhong, *Agricultural development in Jiangnan, 1620–1850* (1998), 143.

26. See in general C.A. Lees, *Medieval masculinities* (1994); D.M. Hadley, *Masculinity in medieval Europe* (1999). For the physical toughness required for battlefield fighting in the early middle ages, see G. Halsall, *Warfare and society in the barbarian west, 450–900* (2003), 177–214.

27. See Ch. 8 n. 55 for a range of sceptical local reactions to basic Christian rituals and dogma; but scepticism is not the same as complete unbelief, which was, as it appears, rare: see J.H. Arnold, *Belief and unbelief in medieval Europe* (2005), 225–30.

28. See Ch. 8 n. 50 for preaching.

2. Rome and its western successors, 500–750

1. A. Demandt, *Der Fall Roms* (2014), 719 with 638–9, lists 227 reasons which have been proposed for Rome's 'fall', up from 210 in the first edition.

2. For slavery see K. Harper, *Slavery in the late Roman world, AD 275–425* (2011). Gregory of Nyssa (d. *c.* 395) was the only major religious theorist to criticise slavery as an institution: ibid., 345–6. For basic studies of the later Roman empire, A.H.M. Jones, *The later Roman empire* (1964), is still essential; A. Cameron, *The Mediterranean world in late antiquity, AD 395–600* (1993), is the best short survey; A. Demandt, *Die Spätantike* (2014), is a large-scale synthesis; P. Brown, *Through the eye of a needle* (2012), is a remarkable summation of a life's work on late antique Christian culture and society.

3. C.R. Whittaker, *Frontiers of the Roman empire* (1994).

4. See for surveys covering this paragraph and the following, among many, G. Halsall, *Barbarian migrations and the Roman west, 376–568* (2007); P. Heather, *The fall of the Roman empire* (2005) (accounts which vary considerably in emphasis); Wickham, *The inheritance*, all of which cite other bibliography. The arguments in *The inheritance*, which cover the early middle ages as a whole, underly this whole chapter and the next three; the book will not often be cited again, but its presence can be assumed. Chur: see R. Kaiser, *Churrätien im frühen Mittelalter* (1998).

5. P. Heather, 'The Huns and the end of the Roman empire in western Europe' (1995), 27–8, defends Aetius, to me not fully convincingly.

6. P. MacGeorge, *Late Roman warlords* (2002), 167–268.

7. For guides to these debates, see the very different pictures in W. Goffart, *Barbarians and Romans, A.D. 418–584* (1980); Halsall, *Barbarian migrations*; P.J. Geary, 'Ethnic identity as a situational construct in the early middle ages' (1983); H. Reimitz, *History, Frankish identity and the framing of Western ethnicity, 550–850* (2015); W. Pohl and F.W. Heydemann, *Strategies of identification* (2013); H. Wolfram and W. Pohl, *Typen der Ethnogenese* (1990); P. Heather, *The Goths* (1996). T.F.X. Noble, *From Roman province to medieval kingdoms* (2006), republishes key chapters and articles in the debate. For the debates at their most uncivil, see A. Gillett, *On barbarian identity* (2002).

8. A. Demandt, 'The osmosis of late Roman and Germanic aristocracies' (1989), 75–86.

9. Sidonius Apollinaris, *Carmina* and *Epistolae* (1936–65), *Epistolae*, 1.2.

10. A. Merrills and R. Miles, *The Vandals* (2014), 177–203; J. Conant, *Staying Roman* (2012), 159–86; R. Whelan, *Being Christian in Vandal Africa* (in press); these books are now basic starting points for Vandal Africa.

11. See e.g. Heather, *The fall*, 415–25; and, for Africa, the previous note.

12. E.g. *Anonymus Valesianus, pars posterior,* c. 60. For the Ostrogoths, see J. Moorhead, *Theodoric in Italy* (1992); P. Heather, 'Theoderic, king of the Goths' (1995); and the stimulating revisionist account in P. Amory, *People and identity in Ostrogothic Italy, 489–554* (1997). For a comparative analysis of what did happen in fifth-century Italy, even without much invasion, see P. Delogu and S. Gasparri, *Le trasformazioni del V secolo* (2010).

13. See for a survey J. Moorhead, *Justinian* (1994), 63–88, 101–9.
14. See for a detailed survey H.-W. Goetz, *Regna and gentes* (2003); for Francia, Reimitz, *History, Frankish identity*; see further E. Buchberger, *Shifting ethnic identities in Spain and Gaul, 500–700* (2016).
15. See in general G. Ripoll and J.M. Gurt, *Sedes regiae (ann. 400–800)* (2000).
16. See Wickham, *Framing*, 62–124 for a survey; for focused studies of Roman taxation and administration, see e.g. Jones, *The Later Roman empire*, 450–69; C. Kelly, *Ruling the later Roman empire* (2004), 107–231, two very different takes; for the Ostrogoths, S. Barnish, 'Taxation, land and barbarian settlement in the western empire' (1986).
17. Wickham, *Framing*, 711–59, 805–14 and passim; B. Ward-Perkins, *The fall of Rome and the end of civilization* (2005); Halsall, *Barbarian migrations*, 320–70; A.S. Esmonde Cleary, *The Roman west, AD 200–500* (2013), 303–482. For Britain, see A.S. Esmonde Cleary, *The ending of Roman Britain* (1989); R. Fleming, 'Recycling in Britain after the fall of Rome's metal economy' (2012).
18. For general surveys of all of these, see *NCMH*, vol. 1; P. Sarris, *Empires of faith, 500–700* (2011); Innes, *Introduction*, 214–313.
19. Wickham, *Framing*, 635–81.
20. Wickham, *The inheritance*, 170–7; see further, from a different perspective, V.I.J. Flint, *The rise of magic in early medieval Europe* (1991). The key overview is P. Brown, *The rise of western Christendom* (1997).
21. See, for Gaul, e.g. R. Van Dam, *Leadership and community in late antique Gaul* (1985), 202–29; for the late Roman background, P. Brown, *Power and persuasion in late antiquity* (1992); C. Rapp, *Holy bishops in late antiquity* (2005); for relics, above all P. Brown, *The cult of the saints* (1981). Western rulers took advantage of the control of relics later too: see J.M.H. Smith, 'Rulers and relics *c.* 750–950' (2010).
22. Gregory of Tours, *Decem libri historiarum* (5.18 for 577); idem, *De virtutibus sancti Martini episcopi* (1885). For Gregory see W. Goffart, *The narrators of barbarian history (A.D. 550–800)* (1980); M. Heinzelmann, *Gregory of Tours* (2004); I. Wood, *Gregory of Tours* (1994); K. Mitchell and I. Wood, *The world of Gregory of Tours* (2002); Reimitz, *History, Frankish identity*, 27–123. For the later role of bishops in warfare, F. Prinz, *Klerus und Krieg im früheren Mittelalter* (1971).
23. This is discussed in greater detail in C. Wickham, 'Consensus and assemblies in the Romano-Germanic kingdoms' (2016). Quote: Liutprand, prologue to law 1, in *Leges Langobardorum 643–866* (1962). Assemblies were weaker in the very Roman-style Visigothic kingdom.
24. Basic for the Merovingians is I. Wood, *The Merovingian kingdoms, 450–751* (1994).
25. J.L. Nelson, *Politics and ritual in early medieval Europe* (1986), 1–48; quote from Gregory of Tours, *Decem libri historiarum*, 6.5.
26. For Gertrude, see the *Vita sanctae Geretrudis* (1888). For aristocrats in general, see R. Le Jan, *Famille et pouvoir dans le monde franc (Vlle–Xe siècle)* (1995), esp. 387–401 for the Merovingian period; P. Depreux, *Les sociétés occidentales du milieu du VIᵉ à la fin du IXᵉ siècle* (2002), 115–24, 131–41; F. Irsigler, *Untersuchungen zur Geschichte des frühfränkischen Adels* (1969); H.-W. Goetz, '"Nobilis"' (1983); Wickham, *Framing*, 168–203; and above all, for the whole early medieval period, the series of volumes on *Les élites*, in R. Le Jan's *Collection haut moyen âge* series – they are listed under *Collection* in the bibliography. For aristocrats and the control of monasteries, see in general S. Wood, *The proprietary church in the medieval West* (2006).
27. For the seventh century, Wood, *The Merovingian kingdoms*, 140–272; P. Fouracre, *Frankish history* (2013); thereafter, P. Fouracre, *The age of Charles Martel* (2000).
28. I. Wood, 'Administration, law and culture in Merovingian Gaul' (1990), 63–81; P.S. Barnwell, *Kings, courtiers and imperium* (1997), 23–40; Wickham, *The inheritance*, 120–9.
29. See n. 26 above for the aristocracy. For case studies of individual Frankish aristocratic families, see A. Bergengruen, *Adel und Grundherrschaft im Merowingerreich* (1958),

65–80; J. Jarnut, *Agilolfingerstudien* (1986); M. Werner, *Der Lütticher Raum in frühkaro-lingischer Zeit* (1980), esp. 216–27, 341–475; P.J. Geary, *Aristocracy in Provence* (1985).

30. Gregory of Tours, *Decem libri historiarum*, 8.9; *Passio prima Leudegarii* (1910), c. 5.

31. General surveys: D. Claude, *Adel, Kirche und Königtum im Westgotenreich* (1974); R. Collins, *Visigothic Spain 409–711* (2004). Citations: *Leges Visigothorum* (1902), 12. 2 and 3 (Jewish laws), 9.1.21 (Egica); for the Third Council, see *Concilios visigóticos* (1963); for Ervig, ibid, 413.

32. For the archaeology, see most recently the surveys and bibliography in S. Gelichi and R. Hodges, *New directions in early medieval European archaeology* (2015).

33. See e.g. S. Castellanos, 'The political nature of taxation in Visigothic Spain' (2003). For the army, see D. Pérez Sanchez, *El ejército en la sociedad visigoda* (1989).

34. General surveys: C. Wickham, *Early medieval Italy* (1981); C. La Rocca, *Italy in the early middle ages* (2002); P. Delogu, 'Il regno longobardo' (1980); P. Cammarosano and S. Gasparri, *Langobardia* (1990); W. Pohl and P. Erhart, *Die Langobarden* (2005); and G. Ausenda et al., *The Langobards before the Frankish conquest* (2009). For the Lombards at the end of their rule, see S. Gasparri, *774* (2008). For the Roman areas of Italy, T.S. Brown, *Gentlemen and officers* (1984); E. Zanini, *Le Italie bizantine* (1998).

35. P. Cammarosano, *Nobili e re* (1998), 74–83; C. Wickham, 'Social structures in Lombard Italy' (2009); Liutprand, law 135, in *Leges Langobardorum*. For case studies of local societies, see M. Costambeys, *Power and patronage in early medieval Italy* (2007); S. Gasparri and C. La Rocca, *Carte di famiglia* (2005). For the archaeology/economy, see most recently N. Christie, *From Constantine to Charlemagne* (2006); G.P. Brogiolo and A. Chavarría Arnau, *Aristocrazie e campagne nell'Occidente da Costantino a Carlo Magno* (2005), a general survey of the west but paying particular attention to Italy.

36. Ratchis, law 13, in *Leges Langobardorum*; for context, see W. Pohl, 'Frontiers in Lombard Italy' (2001).

3. Crisis and transformation in the east, 500–850/1000

1. See for Syrian churches, A. Naccache, *Le décor des églises des villages d'Antiochène du IVe au VIIe siècle* (1992); for irrigation and general agricultural expansion, M. Decker, *Tilling the hateful earth* (2009), esp. 174–203; for Hagia Sophia, R.J. Mainstone, *Hagia Sophia* (1988).

2. For surveys and bibliography, see C. Panella, 'Merci e scambi nel Mediterraneo in età tardoantica' (1993); Wickham, *Framing*, 713–20.

3. See in general L.K. Little, *Plague and the end of antiquity* (2007); for the plague pathogen, among others D.M. Wagner et al., '*Yersinia pestis* and the plague of Justinian 541–543 AD: a genomic analysis' (2014); for its relative lack of effect, J. Durliat, 'La peste du VIe siècle' (1989), an article which survives its critics.

4. See in general Moorhead, *Justinian*; M. Maas, *The Cambridge companion to the age of Justinian* (2005); P. Sarris, *Economy and society in the age of Justinian* (2006), 200–27; for John Lydos, Kelly, *Ruling*, 11–104; for John the Cappadocian, John Lydos, *On powers* (1983) 2.21, 3.57–71.

5. See for example P.T.R. Gray, *The defence of Chalcedon* (1979).

6. P. Brown, 'The rise and function of the holy man in late antiquity' (1971); for Simeon and Theodore, M. Kaplan, *Les hommes et la terre à Byzance du VIe au XIe siècle* (1992), 199–202, 224–7; V. Déroche, 'La forme de l'informe' (2004); M. Dal Santo, *Debating the saints' cult in the age of Gregory the Great* (2012), 195–216; for the demons, *Vie de Théodore*, cc. 43, 114–18.

7. G. Greatrex and S.N.C. Lieu, *The Roman eastern frontier and the Persian wars, part II* (2002), W.E. Kaegi, *Heraclius* (2003), and J. Howard-Johnston, *Witnesses to a world crisis* (2010), give sources, narratives and bibliography.

8. See J.F. Haldon, *Byzantium in the seventh century* (1997), for the period as a whole; for pseudo-Methodios and its reception, see J.T. Palmer, *The Apocalypse in the early middle*

ages (2014), 107–29; for Christian views of Islam, R. Hoyland, *Seeing Islam as others saw it* (1997), 484–9, 535–44. An important guide to imperial theology is G. Dagron, *Emperor and priest* (2003), esp. 158–91.

9. For the land and resources figures, M.F. Hendy, *Studies in the Byzantine monetary economy, c. 300–1450* (1985), 620. For the Byzantine empire as still fully Roman, A. Kaldellis, *The Byzantine republic* (2015).

10. Haldon, *Byzantium in the seventh century*, 208–54.

11. W. Brandes, *Finanzverwaltung in Krisenzeiten* (2002), 116–238; for the aristocracy, see F. Winkelmann, *Quellenstudien zur herrschenden Klasse von Byzanz im 8. und 9. Jahrhundert* (1987) for this period, and, for later, Ch. 9, n. 6.

12. F. Curta, *Southeastern Europe in the middle ages, 500–1250* (2006), 39–84. For cities see e.g. L. Zavagno, *Cities in transition* (2009).

13. For Italian exchange, see F. Ardizzone, 'Rapporti commerciali tra la Sicilia occidentale ed il Tirreno centro-meridionale alla luce del rinvenimento di alcuni contenitori di trasporto' (2000), A. Nef and V. Prigent, *La Sicile de Byzance à l'Islam* (2010), and C. Negrelli, 'Towards a definition of early medieval pottery' (2012); but a wider synthesis is needed here.

14. R.A. Markus, *Gregory the Great and his world* (1997), e.g. 87–91, 104–5; A.J. Ekonomou, *Byzantine Rome* (2007), 199–243; J.M. Sansterre, *Les moines grecs* (1983), 3–127.

15. H. Ahrweiler, *Byzance et la mer* (1966), 17–92; for the route, M. McCormick, *Origins of the European economy* (2001), 502–8.

16. The very highly contested date of the construction of the Qur'an (at least among non-Muslim scholars) may have been made easier to resolve by the discovery of a very early Qur'an fragment in the university of Birmingham (MS Mingana 1572a); a careful survey of the current situation of scholarship concerning this new discovery is 'Birmingham Quran manuscript', https://en.wikipedia.org/wiki/Birmingham_Quran_manuscript, accessed 25 October 2015 (this citation is particularly likely to change). A palimpsest of up to eighty folios of an almost certainly pre-660 MS of the Qur'an found in Sana'a in Yemen also shows only minor changes from the standard version: B. Sadeghi and M. Goudarzi, 'Ṣanʿāʾ 1 and the origins of the Qurʾān' (2012). Earlier, F. Donner, *Narratives of Islamic origins* (1998), 35–63, had already given arguments for a date around 650 which convinced me. For the variety in lived Islams in the early period see e.g. T. Sizgorich, 'Narrative and community in Islamic late antiquity' (2004).

17. H. Kennedy, *The armies of the caliphs* (2001), 2–7.

18. G.-R. Puin, *Der Dīwān von 'Umar ibn al-Ḥaṭṭāb* (1970); Kennedy, *The armies of the caliphs*, 59–78.

19. See the surveys in M.J.L. Young et al., *Religion, learning and science in the 'Abbasid period* (1990); J. Ashtiany et al., *'Abbasid belles-lettres* (1990); P. Crone, *Medieval Islamic political thought* (2004); C.F. Robinson, *Islamic historiography* (2003).

20. See for example A. Walmsley, *Early Islamic Syria* (2007).

21. Surveys of this long period are many, but H. Kennedy, *The prophet and the age of the caliphates* (2004), and P. Crone, *Slaves on horses* (1980), still stand out. For the 'Alids, T. Bernheimer, *The 'Alids* (2014).

22. Y. Lev, *State and society in Fatimid Egypt* (1991); P. Sanders, *Ritual, politics and the city in Fatimid Cairo* (1994); for the Fatimid world from the standpoint of its large Jewish minority, M. Rustow, *Heresy and the politics of community* (2008).

23. E. Manzano Moreno, *Conquistadores, emires y califas* (2006), 34–195.

24. H. Pirenne, *Mohammed and Charlemagne* (1939); idem, *Histoire de Belgique*, vol. 1 (1929), 34–41, 177ff.

25. See J. Goldberg, *Trade and institutions in the medieval Mediterranean* (2012); for the Spanish end, O.R. Constable, *Trade and traders in Muslim Spain* (1994). 1–51.

26. See for this whole section L. Brubaker and J. Haldon, *Byzantium in the iconoclast era, c. 680–850* (2011).

27. For Theophilos, J. Signes Codoñer, J., *The emperor Theophilos and the east, 829–842* (2014).

28. Brubaker and Haldon, *Byzantium in the iconoclast era*, 9–68, summarised neatly also by L. Brubaker, *Inventing Byzantine iconoclasm* (2012). For the acts of the council, see G. Nedungatt and M. Featherstone, *The Council in Trullo revisited* (1995).
29. Brubaker and Haldon, *Byzantium in the iconoclast era*, 69–286; for theology see also C. Barber, *Figure and likeness* (2002). For the surviving sections of the *Peuseis*, copied so as to be attacked, see Nicéphore, *Discours contre les Iconoclastes* (1989).
30. L. James, *Empresses and power in early Byzantium* (2001).
31. For the Christian kingdoms, see A. Isla Frez, *La alta edad media* (2002); W. Davies, *Acts of giving* (2007); S. Castellanos and I. Martín Viso, 'The local articulation of central power in the north of the Iberian peninsula (500–1000)' (2005); R. Portass, 'All quiet on the western front?' (2013); J.A. García de Cortázar, 'La formación de la sociedad feudal' (1999).
32. See in general Manzano, *Conquistadores*; H. Kennedy, *Muslim Spain and Portugal* (1996).
33. Manzano, *Conquistadores*, 363–491; M. Acién Almansa, *Entre el feudalismo y el Islam* (1997); idem, 'El final de los elementos feudales en al-Andalus' (1998). For Madinat al-Zahra', see A. Vallejo Triano, *Madinat al-Zahra* (2004).
34. A.T. Tibi, *The Tibyān* (1986): 87–92 for Alfonso, 111–12 for advice, 124–55 for 'Abd Allah's fall, 152–3 for Granada. For the Taifas in general, M.J. Viguera Molins, *Los reinos de Taifas* (1994); D. Wasserstein, *The rise and fall of the party-kings* (1985).
35. See most recently P. Cressier et al., *Los Almohades* (2005), a large collective volume.

4. The Carolingian experiment, 750–1000

1. The best guide to the Carolingians is now M. Costambeys et al., *The Carolingian world* (2011). The previous classic is R. McKitterick, *The Frankish kingdoms under the Carolingians, 751–987* (1983), with the collection of articles in *NCMH*, vol. 2. For an overview of historiography, see M. de Jong, 'The empire that was always decaying' (2015); for key approaches, S. Airlie, *Power and its problems in Carolingian Europe* (2012). For Charlemagne's reign in general, J. Story, *Charlemagne* (2005). See all these for the political outline that follows.
2. See in general M. Becher and J. Jarnut, *Der Dynastiewechsel von 751* (2004).
3. See e.g. Costambeys et al., *The Carolingian world*, 160–70.
4. For the army, F.L. Ganshof, *The Carolingians and the Frankish monarchy* (1971), 267. For Aachen, see J.L. Nelson, 'Aachen as a place of power' (2001), and J.R. Davis, *Charlemagne's practice of empire* (2015), 322–35; I prefer them to the scepticism of R. McKitterick, *Charlemagne* (2008), 157–71.
5. For Charles the Fat, see S. MacLean, *Kingship and politics in the late ninth century* (2003), a convincingly upbeat reading.
6. Italy: G. Tabacco, *The struggle for power in medieval Italy* (1989) (the basic synthesis of Italian medieval history), 109–36; G. Albertoni, *L'Italia carolingia* (1997); F. Bougard, 'La cour et le gouvernement de Louis II (840–875)' (1998). East Francia: E.J. Goldberg, *Struggle for empire* (2006). Charles the Bald: J.L. Nelson, *Charles the Bald* (1992).
7. *MGH, Epistolae*, vol. 7 (1928), 386–94, at 388–9.
8. T. Reuter, *Medieval polities and modern mentalities* (2006), 251–67, for the problems of the post-expansion empire; R. McKitterick, *Perceptions of the past in the early middle ages* (2008), 63–89, and Davis, *Charlemagne's practice of empire*, 135–57, for 780s–790s rebellions.
9. Widonids: Le Jan, *Famille et pouvoir*, 95–6, 250–1. For Carolingian aristocrats in general, G. Tellenbach, *Königtum und Stämme in der Werdezeit des Deutschen Reiches* (1939), 42–55; K.F. Werner, 'Important noble families in the kingdom of Charlemagne' (1975); Goetz, ' "Nobilis" '; Le Jan, *Famille et pouvoir*, 401–13; S. Airlie, 'The aristocracy' (1995); Costambeys et al., *The Carolingian world*, 271–323. See Ch. 2 n. 26 for wider bibliography on aristocracies/élites.
10. See above all J.-P. Devroey, *Puissants et misérables* (2006); idem, *Économie rurale et société dans l'Europe franque (VIe–IXe siècles)* (2003) (267–96 for aristocratic wealth);

P. Toubert, *L'Europe dans sa première croissance* (2004), 27–115, 145–217; O. Bruand, *Voyageurs et marchandises aux temps carolingiens* (2002); McCormick, *Origins*, 639–69; A. Verhulst, *The Carolingian economy* (2002). The classic, G. Duby, *The early growth of the European economy* (1974), was too pessimistic.

11. Mainz: E. Wamers, *Die frühmittelalterlichen Lesefunde aus der Löhrstrasse (Baustelle Hilton II) in Mainz* (1994); M. Innes, *State and society in the early middle ages* (2000), 96–9, focused on the Rhineland. Ports: H. Clarke and B. Ambrosiani, *Towns in the Viking age* (1995), gives a survey; for a wider context, see now above all C. Loveluck, *Northwest Europe in the early middle ages, c. AD 600–1150* (2013); the classics are R. Hodges, *Dark age economics* (2012); R. Hodges and D. Whitehouse, *Mohammed, Charlemagne and the origins of Europe* (1983).

12. See in general G. Tellenbach, 'Die geistigen und politischen Grundlagen der karolingischen Thronfolge' (1979), esp. 249–53; J.L. Nelson, 'How the Carolingians created consensus' (2009); P. Depreux, 'Lieux de rencontre, temps de négotiation' (1998), 213–31; T. Reuter, 'Assembly politics in western Europe from the eighth century to the twelfth' (2001); S. Airlie, 'Talking heads' (2003), 29–46; R. Le Jan, 'Les cérémonies carolingiennes' (2015). For horses, J.L. Nelson, 'The settings of the gift in the reign of Charlemagne' (2010), 143; for Attigny and public penance, M. de Jong, 'What was *public* about public penance?' (1997), esp. 887–93.

13. For the 'public' see e.g. H.-W. Goetz, 'Die Wahrnehmung von "Staat" und "Herrschaft" im frühen Mittelalter' (2006); Y. Sassier, 'L'utilisation d'un concept romain aux temps carolingiens' (1988), discusses the early medieval usage of *res publica*. For Agobard, M. de Jong, *The penitential state* (2009), 142–3.

14. B. Schneidmüller, *Die Welfen* (2000), 58–72.

15. C. West, 'Lordship in ninth-century Francia' (2015), for Hincmar of Laon – and see, in general, the nuanced account in idem, *Reframing the feudal revolution* (2013), 19–105. For 802 (*MGH, Capitularia* (1883–97), n. 33, cc. 2–9) and oaths in general, M. Becher, *Eid und Herrschaft* (1993).

16. Einhard, *Epistolae*, n. 42, in *MGH, Epistolae*, vol. 5 (1889), 131; see Innes, *State and society*, 129–30, 146–7. The best account of a local medium family, located in central Italy, is L. Feller et al., *La fortune de Karol* (2005).

17. See for rare peasant victories C. Wickham, 'Space and society in early medieval peasant conflicts' (2003), 560, and (for royal interventions) *MGH, Formulae* (1886), 293, 324–5; for the latter, see Costambeys et al., *The Carolingian world*, 267. For an important account of a peasant-based society and legal system in the Carolingian world, located on the edge of Brittany, see W. Davies, *Small worlds* (1988).

18. In addition to the works cited in nn. 11, 15, 16, 17, see e.g. P. Bonnassie, *La Catalogne du milieu du Xe à la fin du XIe siècle* (1975–76); J. Jarrett, *Rulers and ruled in frontier Catalonia, 880–1010* (2010); T. Kohl, *Lokale Gesellschaften* (2010); Costambeys, *Power and patronage*; P. Toubert, *Les structures du Latium médiéval* (1973); L. Feller, *Les Abruzzes médiévales* (1998); Gasparri and La Rocca, *Carte di famiglia*.

19. Wickham, *Framing*, 573–88; E. Müller-Mertens, *Karl der Grosse, Ludwig der Fromme, und die Freien* (1963), 97–111. Costambeys et al., *The Carolingian world*, 263–8, seems to me too upbeat.

20. E.J. Goldberg, 'Popular revolt, dynastic politics and aristocratic factionalism in the early middle ages' (1995).

21. *MGH, Poetae*, vol. 2 (1884), 120–4; see W. Brown, *Unjust seizure* (2001), 1–5, 206–9 (I use his translation).

22. K.F. Werner, 'Missus-marchio-comes' (1980); Davis, *Charlemagne's practice of empire*, esp. 47–127, 293–8; P. Fouracre, 'Carolingian justice' (1995), a pragmatic look at judicial abuses; Bullough, ' "Baiuli" in the Carolingian "regnum Langobardorum" and the career of Abbot Waldo (+813)' (1962), 630–1, for *missi* investigating their predecessors; A. Krah, *Absetzungsverfahren als Spieglbild von Königsmacht* (1987), 7–88, for the few cases of the dismissal of counts up to 840 (nearly half of them were in the troubles of the early

830s). *MGH, Capitularia*, n. 58 for Charlemagne's replies; Paschasius Radbert, *Epitaphium Arsenii* (1900), 1.26, for the imagery of collusion; *MGH, Epistolae*, vol. 5, 277–8, and Einhard, *Epistolae*, nn. 20–1, in ibid., 120–1, for one-off tasks under Louis the Pious.

23. R. McKitterick, *The Carolingians and the written word* (1989); eadem, *Charlemagne*, 214–91; Davis, *Charlemagne's practice of empire*, 311–22; J.L. Nelson, 'Literacy in Carolingian government' (1990); for the ad hoc nature of many capitularies, C. Pössel, 'Authors and recipients of Carolingian capitularies, 779–829' (2006). For personal collections, McKitterick, *The Carolingians and the written word*, 46–60; eadem, *Charlemagne*, 263–6; P. Wormald, *The making of English law* (1999), 53–70. For the Paris assembly: *MGH, Capitularia*, n. 39.

24. *MGH, Capitularia*, n. 22; see e.g. McKitterick, *Charlemagne*, 237–45, 306–20.

25. For Paschal, see C. Goodson, *The Rome of Pope Paschal I* (2010), esp. 257–73; for the popes up to 825, see T.F.X. Noble, *The Republic of St. Peter* (1984), esp. 277–324. For ninth-century popes as a whole, who have not had many overall analyses, see the survey in S. Scholz, *Politik – Selbstverständnis – Selbstdarstellung* (2000), 147–245.

26. Education in general: J.J. Contreni, 'The Carolingian renaissance' (1995); P. Riché, *Écoles et enseignement dans le haut moyen âge* (1989). For 784, *MGH, Capitularia*, n. 29. For admonition, see e.g. de Jong, *The penitential state*, 112–41; R. Stone, *Morality and masculinity in the Carolingian empire* (2011), e.g. 42–6, 116–58. For predestination, D. Ganz, 'The debate on predestination' (1990); M.B. Gillis, 'Heresy in the flesh' (2015). For the many-faceted activities of Hincmar, see now R. Stone and C. West, *Hincmar of Rheims* (2015).

27. Dhuoda, *Liber manualis* (1975). See in general P. Wormald, *Lay intellectuals in the Carolingian world* (2007). For Einhard, S. Patzold, *Ich und Karl der Grosse* (2013); J.M.H. Smith, 'Einhard: the sinner and the saints' (2003). For Eccard, e.g. McKitterick, *The Carolingians and the written word*, 248–50. For the use made of documents by the laity (not just in the Carolingian period), see W. Brown et al., *Documentary culture and the laity in the early middle ages* (2013).

28. De Jong, *The penitential state*, 148–84; see also P.E. Dutton, *The politics of dreaming in the Carolingian empire* (1994), 92–101, for Einhard. For the imagery of hunting, E.J. Goldberg, 'Louis the Pious and the hunt' (2013). On the importance of Biblical texts, M. de Jong, 'Carolingian political discourse' (2015), sums up her recent work.

29. De Jong, *The penitential state*, 188–205; eadem, 'Bride shows revisited' (2004), for Judith. See in general G. Bührer-Thierry, 'La reine adultère' (1992); S. Airlie, 'Private bodies and the body politic' (1998).

30. De Jong, *The penitential state*, 214–62, 271–9.

31. Notker, *Gesta Karoli magni imperatoris* (1959), 1.30, and, for *vigilantissimus*, 1.10, 2.12; see S. Airlie, 'The palace of memory' (2000), 5; and, in general for Notker's political context, MacLean, *Kingship and politics*, 199–229.

32. For the history of each of the kingdoms, see the surveys in *NCMH*, vol. 3. A case study is B. Rosenwein, 'The family politics of Berengar I, king of Italy (888–924)' (1996). For *reguli*, *Annales Fuldenses* (1891), s.a. 888.

33. K.F. Werner, *Les origines avant l'an mil* (1984), 487–561; J. Dunbabin, *France in the making, 843–1180* (2000), 17–123; G. Koziol, *The politics of memory and identity in Carolingian royal diplomas* (2012), an important rethinking, especially (459–533) of Charles the Simple.

34. See T. Reuter, *Germany in the early middle ages* (1991); G. Althoff and H. Keller, *Heinrich I. und Otto der Grosse* (1994); J. Fried, *Die Ursprünge Deutschlands* (1984). Queens: P. Stafford, *Queens, concubines and dowagers* (1983), 149–52 and passim; Le Jan, *Famille et pouvoir*, 372–9.

35. Reuter, 'Assembly politics'; K. Leyser, *Rule and conflict in early medieval society* (1979); idem, 'Ottonian government' (1982); for royal movements, C.R. Brühl, *Fodrum, gistum servitium regis* (1968), 116–28, with important contextualisation in S. MacLean, 'Palaces, itineraries and political order in the post Carolingian kingdoms' (2014), 291–320.

36. P. Riché, *Gerbert d'Aurillac* (1987); P. Dronke, *Women writers of the middle ages* (1984), 55–83.

37. H. Fichtenau, *Living in the tenth century* (1991), 3–77; Althoff, *Spielregeln*, esp. 21–56, 157–84, 229–57; G. Althoff, *Family, friends and followers* (2004), 136–59; for methodological warnings, P. Buc, *The dangers of ritual* (2001). Such choreography could also be subverted by equally formalised acts of critique, as Althoff stresses.

38. P.J. Geary, *Phantoms of remembrance* (1994), esp. 23–9, 115–57. For the debate about the year 1000, see Ch. 6 n. 10.

39. West, *Reframing the feudal revolution*, esp. 72–7, 98–105, 259–63.

5. The expansion of Christian Europe, 500–1100

1. See L. Abrams, 'Germanic Christianities' (2008), for their range; I. Wood, *The missionary life* (2001), for missionary self-images. What actually happened to people when they converted can never be said; every convert has a story of seeing the light of truth which is only constructed afterwards (see K.F. Morrison, *Understanding conversion* (1992), xii, 23, focused on conversion to a more rigorist faith inside medieval Christianity, but with wider application).

2. A good guide to history-writing is S. Foot and C.F. Robinson, *The Oxford history of historical writing* (2012).

3. See R. Fletcher, *The conversion of Europe* (1997), for a good standard account; N. Berend, *Christianization and the rise of Christian monarchy* (2007), for the north and east of Europe.

4. There is no adequate account of northern paganism(s), but see for some good specific examples J.-H. Clay, *In the shadow of death* (2010), 132–7, 279–331; S. Semple, 'Sacred spaces and places in pre-Christian and conversion period Anglo-Saxon England' (2011); Jón Hnefill Aðalsteinsson, *Under the cloak* (1999), 37–43, 109–23; and, more generally, R. Bartlett, 'From paganism to Christianity' (2007), 47–72. J. Palmer, 'Defining paganism in the Carolingian world' (2007), has sensible warnings.

5. Rimbert, *Vita Anskarii* (1884) cc. 26–7 (Sweden); Snorri Sturluson, *Heimskringla* (1941–51), *Hákona saga goða*, cc. 15–19 (Norway); J. Byock, *Viking age Iceland* (2001), esp. 170–84; Thietmar of Merseburg, *Chronicon* (1935), 6.24–5 (Liutizi).

6. See in general Wickham, *Framing*, 303–79, 519–88. For the substantial presence of a landowning peasantry in sixteenth-century Scandinavia, J.R. Myking and C. Porskrog Rasmussen, 'Scandinavia, 1000–1750' (2010), 290–1; see S. Bagge, *From Viking stronghold to Christian kingdom* (2010), 111–21, for ideas about how to read these figures back into the middle ages.

7. Kelly, *A guide to early Irish law*, 29–33; R. Faith, *The English peasantry and the growth of lordship* (1997), 1–14 and passim.

8. Byock, *Viking age Iceland*, 121–2, 252–62, 326–9, for a variety of small-scale, but cumulative, élite emoluments; N. Berend et al., *Central Europe in the high middle ages* (2013), 282–3; J. Martin, *Medieval Russia, 980–1584* (2007), 13–19, 64–8, 139, etc.

9. C. Stancliffe, 'Religion and society in Ireland' (2005), for conversion. For Wales, W. Davies, *Wales in the early middle ages* (1982) and T.M. Charles-Edwards, *Wales and the Britons, 350–1064* (2013); for fifth-century breakdown in Britain, see Ch. 2 n. 17.

10. See in general F.J. Byrne, *Irish kings and high-kings* (1973); T.M. Charles-Edwards, *Early Christian Ireland* (2000); D. Ó Corráin, *Ireland before the Normans* (1972); M. Herbert, *Iona, Kells and Derry* (1998).

11. For Máel Sechnaill and Brian, Byrne, *Irish kings and high-kings*, 256–66; M. Ní Mhaonaigh, *Brian Boru* (2007).

12. See in general A. Cosgrove, *A new history of Ireland*, vol. 2 (2008); K. Simms, *From kings to warlords* (1987).

13. See S. Bassett, *The origins of Anglo-Saxon kingdoms* (1989), for the scale of kingdoms; B. Yorke, *The conversion of Britain, 600–800* (2006); for the complexities of the post-conversion world, J. Blair, *The Church in Anglo-Saxon society* (2005).

14. J. Campbell, *The Anglo-Saxons* (1982), 53–68; for assemblies, A. Pantos, '*In medle oððe an þinge*' (2004); for ports, C. Scull, 'Urban centres in pre-Viking England?' (1997) and

R. Fleming, *Britain after Rome* (2010), 183–212: this whole book is an essential starting point for the history of Britain seen through its material culture.

15. See in general N. Brooks, *Communities and warfare, 700–1400* (2000); D. Hill and M. Worthington, *Æthelbald and Offa* (2005); J. Story, *Carolingian connections* (2003), 167–211; for towns, S. Bassett, 'Divide and rule?' (2007); for the dyke, P. Squatriti, 'Digging ditches in early medieval Europe' (2002); for royal resources and coins, R. Naismith, *Money and power in Anglo-Saxon England* (2012), esp. 23–46, 96–106; for the councils, C. Cubitt, *Anglo-Saxon church councils, c. 650–c. 850* (1995).

16. Faith, *The English peasantry*, 56–125, 153–77; Wickham, *Framing*, 347–51.

17. See in general for the late Anglo-Saxon kingdom P. Stafford, *Unification and conquest* (1989).

18. A. Williams, *Kingship and government in pre-conquest England, c. 500–1066* (1999), 73–122; R. Fleming, *Kings and lords in conquest England* (1991), 21–52; J. Campbell, 'The late Anglo-Saxon state: a maximum view' (1994); Wormald, *The making of English law*, 277–85, 306, 311, 344–5, 417–26, 444–65, for the Carolingians; L. Roach, *Kingship and consent in Anglo-Saxon England, 871–978* (2013); P. Stafford, *Queen Emma and Queen Edith* (1997), 199–206; G. Molyneaux, *The formation of the English kingdom in the tenth century* (2015); for Louis the Pious and monastic reform, R. Deshman, *The benedictional of Æthelwold* (1995), 209–14.

19. Gudme and early political aggregations: see P. Mortensen and B. Rasmussen, *Fra stam til stat i Danmark* (1988–91); P.O. Nielsen et al., *The archaeology of Gudme and Lundeborg* (1994). Godofrid's kingdom: P. Sawyer, 'Kings and royal power' (1991); K. Randsborg, *The Viking age in Denmark* (1980); M. Axboe, 'Danish kings and dendrochronology' (1995).

20. For the Vikings, a good overview is P. Sawyer, *The Oxford illustrated history of the Vikings* (1997); for the diaspora, L. Abrams, 'Diaspora and identity in the Viking age' (2012).

21. See in general I. Skovgaard-Petersen, 'The making of the Danish kingdom' (1978); for the military camps, E. Roesdahl, *The Vikings* (1987), 136–41.

22. For how estates worked and their relationship to peasant owning, see N. Hybel and B. Poulsen, *Danish resources c. 1000–1550* (2007), 165–95, 385–90; and the detailed studies in B. Poulsen and S.M. Sindbaek, *Settlement and lordship in Viking and early medieval Scandinavia* (2011).

23. For archaeology, see e.g. B. Myhre, 'Chieftains' graves and chiefdom territories in south Norway and in the migration period' (1987). For post-900, C. Krag, 'The early unification of Norway' (2003); Bagge, *From Viking stronghold*, 25–37; A. Winroth, *The conversion of Scandinavia* (2012), 115–44; S. Bagge and S.W. Nordeide, 'The kingdom of Norway' (2007). For caution about the poems in early narratives, S. Ghosh, *Kings' sagas and Norwegian history* (2011). For the Olafs and the *thingar*, and Stiklarstaðir, see Snorri Sturluson, *Heimskringla, Óláfs saga Tryggvasonar*, cc. 55–8, 65–9; *Óláfs saga ins Helga*, cc. 40, 181, 205, 215–35.

24. H.J. Orning, *Unpredictability and presence* (2008), 125–53, 257–310; K. Helle, 'The Norwegian kingdom' (2003); Bagge, *From Viking stronghold*, 38–63, 229–32, 292–4; S. Bagge, 'Borgerkrig og statsutvikling i Norge i middelalderen' (1986). For the army, *Sverris saga* (2007), cc. 8, 11, etc.

25. For an argument parallel to this one, see S. Bagge, 'The Europeanization of Europe' (2012).

26. P.M. Barford, *The early Slavs* (2001), 47–88, 113–23, 131–3; for slaves, McCormick, *Origins*, 733–77; for the slave trade in the tenth century, see M. Jankowiak, 'Two systems of trade in the western Slavic lands in the 10th century' (2013), the first publication of a substantial research project, which Marek Jankowiak has kindly discussed with me.

27. Barford, *The early Slavs*, 251–67; A. Buko, 'Unknown revolution' (2005); P. Urbańczyk and S. Rosik, 'Poland' (2007); Berend et al., *Central Europe*, 97–102, 118–24, 144–7, 282–3 – this latter being now the most up-to-date survey in English.

28. Berend et al., *Central Europe*, 161–3, 330–2.

29. Berend et al., *Central Europe*, 172–6, 198–201, 267–73, 282–6, 374–80; for how estates worked, particularly in the early thirteenth century, see P. Górecki, *Economy, society, and lordship in medieval Poland, 1100–1250* (1992), esp. 67–192.

30. For Scotland in the central middle ages, see above all A. Taylor, *The shape of the state in medieval Scotland* (2016); for later, see Ch. 11.

31. M. Bogucki, 'On Wulfstan's right hand' (2013), is a good recent survey of the Polish ports up to *c.* 1000. For England and the continent, see Loveluck, *Northwest Europe*, esp. 302–60.

32. Bartlett, *The making of Europe*, esp. 269–91.

6. Reshaping western Europe, 1000–1150

1. The text is most recently edited by G. Beech et al., *Le conventum (vers 1030)* (1995); a prior edition with good commentary is in J. Martindale, *Status, authority and regional power* (1997), studies VIIa, VIIb, VIII. There has been much recent analysis of this text; see for example S.D. White, *Re-thinking kinship and feudalism in early medieval Europe* (2005), studies VII, VIII, X, XIII; D. Barthélemy, *L'an mil et la paix de Dieu* (1999), 339–54.

2. S. Kay, *Raoul de Cambrai* (1992), lines 1284–1352, 1459–1549.

3. R.E. Barton, *Lordship in the county of Maine, c. 890–1160* (2004), is a good discussion of the continuities in lordship. For the debates here, see below, nn. 10 and 11.

4. 'France' was simply the French for 'Francia'; as for Germany, it was not until late in the eleventh century that the term *regnum Teutonic(or)um* began to appear, still intermittently: for its terminology, E. Müller-Mertens, *Regnum Teutonicum* (1970), 87–144, 328ff. For an excellent recent collective guide to the complexities of social change in the period of this chapter, and also of Ch. 8 (the book is focused on a long twelfth century), see T.F.X. Noble and J. Van Engen, *European transformations* (2012).

5. See Reuter, *Germany* and H. Keller, *Zwischen regionaler Begrenzung und universalem Horizont* (1986) for general surveys of this and what follows.

6. For the late eleventh century, Robinson, *Henry IV*. For *ministeriales*, B. Arnold, *German knighthood, 1050–1300* (1985), 23–75; T. Zotz, 'Die Formierung der Ministerialität' (1992).

7. Dunbabin, *France in the making*, is a good survey; D. Barthélemy, *Nouvelle histoire des Capetians* (2012), is stimulating.

8. See for a survey Stafford, *Unification and conquest*, 69–100; for the aristocracy, A. Williams, *The world before Domesday* (2008).

9. See for surveys, among many, M. Chibnall, *Anglo-Norman England, 1066–1166* (1986); M.T. Clanchy, *England and its rulers, 1066–1307* (2006), 23–137; R. Bartlett, *England under the Norman and Angevin kings, 1075–1225* (2000); J.A. Green, *The government of England under Henry I* (1986). For Domesday, S. Harvey, *Domesday* (2014) is now the basic starting point.

10. For major contributions to this debate, see J.-P. Poly and É. Bournazel, *The feudal transformation, 900–1200* (1991); Barthélemy, *La mutation de l'an mil*, esp. 15–28; T.N. Bisson, 'The "feudal revolution"' (1994), and the debate which followed it in *Past and present*; Barton, *Lordship*; T.N. Bisson, *The crisis of the twelfth century* (2009); West, *Reframing the feudal revolution*. R.I. Moore, *The first European revolution, c. 970–1215* (2000), a stimulating overview of the eleventh and twelfth centuries, generalises the 'revolution' model very widely indeed.

11. G. Duby, *La société aux XIe et XIIe siècles dans la région mâconnaise* (1971), 173–90, 245–62, first set out the model of the *seigneurie banale*; R. Fossier, *Enfance de l'Europe, Xe–XIIe siècles* (1982), 288–601, called the division into formalised *seigneuries* a process of *encellulement*, an image I have picked up when I talk about 'cellular' structures in this book. For an updated international survey of *seigneuries* of different types, see M. Bourin and P. Martínez Sopena, *Pour une anthropologie du prélèvement seigneurial*

dans les campagnes médiévales (XIe–XIVe siècles) (2004–07). For how life worked in the world 'without states', see e.g. P.J. Geary, *Living with the dead in the middle ages* (1994), 95–160, as well as S.D. White, *Feuding and peace-making in eleventh-century France* (2005), although he would not agree with this picture. For early, low-key, peasant resistance see B. Gowers, '996 and all that' (2013).

12. For Bloch, see Ch. 1 n. 14. One might add England to the taxing states by now, but its land tax was not a dominant part of royal resources (10 per cent in 1130), and after the 1130s was probably not taken annually; it was last exacted under Henry II in 1162 – see Green, 'The last century of Danegeld'.

13. Loveluck, *Northwest Europe*, 215–48; G. Fournier, *Le château dans la France médiévale* (1978), 35–79, 100–14; G.P. Fehring, *The archaeology of medieval Germany* (1991), 98–135; R. Francovich and M. Ginatempo, *Castelli* (2000) with the back history in M. Valenti, *L'insediamento altomedievale nelle campagne toscane* (2004); P. Grimm, *Tilleda* (1968–90).

14. J. Hudson, *The Oxford history of the laws of England: 871–1216* (2012), 273–84, 537–62, 751–68; see Ch. 7 n. 14 for the free–unfree boundary, and Ch. 8 n. 35 for Castile.

15. B. Arnold, *Princes and territories in medieval Germany* (1991), esp. 61–76, 196–201.

16. T. Meyer, 'The state of the dukes of Zähringen' (1938); Keller, *Zwischen regionaler Begrenzung*, 347–9.

17. West, *Reframing the feudal revolution*, esp. 232–54. The same is true of Germany and Italy, although this comparison is even less often made; but see J. Eldevik, *Episcopal power and ecclesiastical reform in the German empire* (2012).

18. Tabacco, *The struggle for power*, 191–208; H. Keller, *Signori e vassalli* (1995), esp. 118–36; F. Menant, *Campagnes lombardes au moyen âge* (1993), 395–477, 728–35, 757–65; L. Provero, *L'Italia dei poteri locali* (1998); A. Fiore, 'From the diploma to the pact' (in press); Wickham, 'The "feudal revolution"'. For case studies, S. Collavini, '*Honorabilis domus et spetiosissimus comitatus*' (1998); M.E. Cortese, *Signori, castelli, città* (2007).

19. See C. Wickham, *Sleepwalking into a new world* (2015); G. Milani, *I comuni italiani, secoli XII–XIV* (2005); J.-C. Maire Vigueur and E. Faini, *Il sistema politico dei comuni italiani (secoli XII–XIV)* (2010).

20. D. Bates, *Normandy before 1066* (1982), 162–82.

21. See C. Leyser, 'The memory of Gregory the Great and the making of Latin Europe, 600–1000' (2016), 197–201.

22. See the synthesis in C. Cubitt, 'The tenth-century Benedictine reform in England' (1997). For England and Louis, see above, Ch. 5 n. 18.

23. See among many B. Rosenwein, *Rhinoceros bound* (1982); G. Constable, 'Cluny in the monastic world of the tenth century' (1991); D. Iogna-Prat et al., *Cluny* (2013), a collection of wide-ranging articles.

24. See *Die Touler Vita Leos IX.* (2007), 1.1, 3, 8–14; for a rapid biography, M. Parisse, 'Leone IX, papa, santo' (2005).

25. See in general T. Head and R. Landes, *The Peace of God* (1992); Barthélemy, *L'an mil*; good critical commentary in K.G. Cushing, *Reform and the papacy in the eleventh century* (2005), 39–54.

26. C. Violante, 'I laici nel movimento patarino' (1968); R.I. Moore, 'Family, community and cult on the eve of the Gregorian reform' (1980), 65–9. I am grateful here to insights from James Norrie's Oxford doctoral thesis, in course of completion. Lay moral panics were not just Italian; in Denmark, there was a lay revolt against clerical marriage in Roskilde in 1124: F. Pedersen, 'A good and sincere man . . . even though he looked like a Slav' (2010), 152–3.

27. See most recently R.I. Moore, *The war on heresy* (2012), 63–83.

28. R.W. Southern, *The making of the middle ages* (1953), 125–7 tells the story best. For me, the best introductions to this whole period, out of huge numbers, are G. Tellenbach, *The church in western Europe from the tenth to the early twelfth century* (1993), and Cushing, *Reform and the papacy*; see further S.C. Hamilton, *Church and people in the medieval*

west, 900–1200 (2013), and the acute overall critique in M.C. Miller, 'The crisis in the Investiture Crisis narrative' (2009).

29. For Pier Damiani, see D. Elliott, *Fallen bodies* (1999), 95–106; Cushing, *Reform and the papacy*, 120–4. For simony as a moral panic, see T. Reuter, 'Gifts and simony' (2000). For Humbert see C. West, 'Competing for the Holy Spirit' (2015).

30. Here I follow R. Schieffer, *Die Entstehung des päpstlichen Investiturverbots für den deutschen König* (1981).

31. C. Wickham, *Medieval Rome* (2015), 423–5.

32. For Urban in general, A. Becker, *Papst Urban II. (1088–1099)* (1964–2012). For Clermont, ibid., vol. 1, 220–5, vol. 2, 374–413; *Le concile de Clermont* (1997), 1–140.

33. J. Barrow, *The clergy in the medieval world* (2015), 135–47.

34. For Verona, M.C. Miller, *The formation of a medieval church* (1993), esp. 50–60, 71–80; for continuities across the period, see Hamilton, *Church and people*, 60–118.

35. L. Melve, *Inventing the public sphere* (2007), esp. 45–119, is now the basic text, but he sees the audience for eleventh-century polemic as a 'public sphere'; I would see it as more restricted than that, and, in particular, except in some Italian cities, more restricted than in either the Carolingian period or the period after 1350 or so.

36. For useful approaches to Bernard, see A. Bredero, *Bernard of Clairvaux* (1996); for the Cistercians, another autonomous international monastic order, see E. Jamroziak, *The Cistercian order in medieval Europe, 1090–1500* (2013).

37. G. Loud, *The age of Robert Guiscard* (2000), is a good political analysis with a good survey of earlier bibliography. On lordships, the fundamental study is S. Carocci, *Signorie di Mezzogiorno* (2014). For Puglia in the heel of Italy, J.-M. Martin, *La Pouille du VIᵉ au XIIᵉ siècle* (1993). For Sicily, see above all J. Johns, *Arabic administration in Norman Sicily* (2002).

38. Bartlett, *The making of Europe*, 85–90.

39. C. Tyerman, *God's war* (2006), a non-triumphalist analysis, can stand well for any number of other more fervent writers. For recruitment, see M. Bull, *Knightly piety and the lay response to the First Crusade* (1993).

40. One instance is S. Runciman, *A history of the Crusades* (1951–54), vol. 3, 469–80. For a neutral view, good recent examples are C. Hillenbrand, *The Crusades: Islamic perspectives* (1999); C. Kostick, *The social structure of the First Crusade* (2008), esp. 287–300.

41. See the recent narrative account in M. Barber, *The Crusader states* (2012).

42. For arguments in this direction, see Bisson, *The crisis*, 573–82, summing up the second half of his book.

7. The long economic boom, 950–1300

1. Some basic surveys are: *The Cambridge economic history* of Europe (1963–87), vols. 1 and 2; G. Duby, *Rural economy and country life in the medieval west* (1968) (the most intelligent); Fossier, *Enfance*; and the textbook P. Contamine, *L'économie médiévale* (1993). All these are showing their age very seriously.

2. As J. Masschaele, 'Economic takeoff and the rise of markets' (2009), remarks (he does have a view, however: he would prefer to see demographic rise as a consequence rather than a cause of commercialisation).

3. P. Grillo, *Milano in età comunale (1183–1276)* (2001), 209–34.

4. Names are invidious here; but it is necessary to say that British economic history is an exception. For recent surveys, see C. Dyer, *Standards of living in the later middle ages* (1989); idem, *Making a living in the middle ages* (2002); R. Britnell, *The commercialisation of English society, 1100–1500* (1996); idem, *Britain and Ireland, 1050–1530: Economy and society* (2004); J. Masschaele, *Peasants, merchants, and markets* (1997); J. Langdon and J. Masschaele, 'Commercial activity and population growth in medieval England' (2006).

5. Exceptions are W. Kula, *An economic theory of the feudal system* (1976) and G. Bois, *The crisis of feudalism* (1984), neither of them focused empirically on the pre-1350 period.

6. For the city of Paris to 1223, A. Lombard-Jourdan, *Paris: genèse de la 'ville'* (1976), 35–154, is the fullest analysis, if incomplete; see also J.W. Baldwin, *The government of Philip Augustus* (1986), 342–51. For John's and Philip's resources, the most recent study is N. Barratt, 'The revenues of John and Philip Augustus revisited' (1999). In the thirteenth century, the problem becomes easier, as Parisian documentation expands and so did the city, hugely: from up to 50,000 inhabitants in 1200 to over 200,000 by 1328, making it by then equal to Milan (and perhaps ahead) as the largest city in Europe: see É. Carpentier and M. Le Mené, *La France du XIe au XVe siècle* (1996), 296–306; R. Cazelles, *Nouvelle histoire de Paris de la fin du règne de Philippe Auguste à la mort de Charles V (1223–1380)* (1972), 131–49.

7. See J. Hatcher, *Plague, population and the English economy, 1348–1530* (1977), 68–71, Langdon and Masschaele, 'Commercial activity and population growth', 54–68, and S. Broadberry et al., *British economic growth, 1270–1870* (2015), 10–13, for the diversity of calculations even for England (my own figures are compromises, and are simply offered to give a sense of growth rates); for Francia in the ninth century, Devroey, *Économie rurale*, 65–75.

8. For irrigation, T.F. Glick, *From Muslim fortress to Christian castle* (1995), 64–91; Menant, *Campagnes lombardes*, 182–203.

9. A survey of clearance of all kinds is Fossier, *Enfance*, 126–247.

10. The most cogent guide to this is Bartlett, *The making of Europe*, 111–66.

11. See for example M. Montanari, *L'alimentazione contadina nell'alto medioevo* (1979), esp. 211–18, 469–76.

12. J. Chapelot and R. Fossier, *The village and house in the middle ages* (1985), 251–82; Dyer, *Standards*, 160–6; A. Molinari, 'Mondi rurali d'Italia' (2010).

13. Verhulst, *The Carolingian economy*; Devroey, *Puissants et misérables*.

14. See in general Duby, *Rural economy*, 186–278; R.H. Hilton, 'Freedom and villeinage in England' (1965), for the increase in English unfreedom after 1180 or so; and Ch. 1 n. 19.

15. Duby, *Rural economy*, 186–93, 224–31, 239–52; see now the regional analyses in Freedman and Bourin, *Forms of servitude*.

16. B.M.S. Campbell, 'The agrarian problem in the early fourteenth century' (2005).

17. O. Redon, 'Seigneurs et communautés rurales dans le contado de Sienne au XIIIe siècle' (1979), 158, for the quote; for franchises as a whole, see for surveys C. Wickham, *Community and clientele in twelfth-century Tuscany* (2003), 192–219; Bourin and Martínez Sopena, *Pour une anthropologie*, vol. 2, 115–267.

18. S. Reynolds, *Kingdoms and communities in western Europe, 900–1300* (1984), 122–54.

19. See in general M. Bourin and R. Durand, *Vivre au village au moyen âge* (1984); for English customs, J. Birrell, 'Manorial custumals reconsidered' (2014).

20. P. Spufford, *Money and its use in medieval Europe* (1988), 74–131, 339–62.

21. See for England C. Briggs, *Credit and village society in fourteenth-century England* (2009). For the sheep price, D.L. Farmer, 'Prices and wages' (1988), 754.

22. Basic guides to towns: D.M. Palliser, *The Cambridge urban history of Britain* (2008); C. Dyer, 'How urbanized was medieval England?' (1995); R.H. Hilton, *English and French towns in feudal society* (1995); F. Menant, *L'Italie des communes (1100–1350)* (2005); D. Nicholas, *The growth of the medieval city* (1997); D. Keene, 'Towns and the growth of trade' (2004). For Constantinople, see Ch. 9 n. 1. Italian town sizes: M. Ginatempo and L. Sandri, *L'Italia delle città* (1990); I have extrapolated from their data.

23. M. Postan, *The medieval economy and society* (1972), 212.

24. See in general Wickham, *Sleepwalking*, 67–117; for archaeology, F. Cantini, 'Ritmi e forme della grande espansione economica dei secoli XI–XIII nei contesti ceramici della Toscana settentrionale' (2010); for the treaties, see G. Müller, *Documenti sulle relazioni delle città toscane coll'Oriente cristiano e coi Turchi* (1879), 40–58; M. Amari, *I diplomi arabi del R. Archivio fiorentino* (1863), nn. 2–6. D. Abulafia, *The two Italies* (1977), discusses twelfth-century trade for Genoa and Pisa.

25. Walls, houses: G. Garzella, *Pisa com'era* (1990). 1228: E. Salvatori, *La popolazione pisana nel Duecento* (1994). For Pisa after 1200, see A. Poloni, *Trasformazioni della società e mutamenti delle forme politiche in un Comune italiano* (2004).
26. For Ghent up to 1200, see A. Verhulst, *The rise of cities in north-west Europe* (1999), 12–13, 38–9, 54–6, 61–5, 75–9, 123–40; M.C. Laleman and P. Raveschot, 'Maisons patriciennes médiévales à Gand (Gent), Belgique' (1994). For post-1200, D. Nicholas, *Medieval Flanders* (1992), 110–23, 130–8, 164–79, 217–30 conveniently sums up his own work and that of others.
27. W.H. TeBrake, *A plague of insurrection* (1993); J. Dumolyn and J. Haemers, 'Patterns of urban rebellion in medieval Flanders' (2005); see in general S.K. Cohn, *Lust for liberty* (2006), 32–3, 54–7, and below, Ch. 12.
28. Britnell, *Britain and Ireland*, 140 with 153; J. Blair, 'Small towns 600–1270' (2008), 258–70.
29. See E.M. Carus-Wilson, 'The first half-century of the borough of Stratford-upon-Avon' (1965), and C. Dyer, 'Medieval Stratford' (1997), for what follows.
30. Dyer, *Making a living*, 163–74; Britnell, *The commercialisation*. For the fraternity, G. Rosser, *The art of solidarity in the middle ages* (2015), 80–1, 114–15, 204–5.
31. B.M.S. Campbell et al., *A medieval capital and its grain supply* (1993), esp. map at 61; for Sicily, see S.R. Epstein, *An island for itself* (1992), 163ff., 270ff., for a critical analysis.
32. Wickham, *Framing*, 712–18, 794–819.
33. P. Spufford, *Power and profit* (2002), is a good recent survey. For Italy, P.J. Jones, *The Italian city-state* (1997), 152–332.
34. E.B. Fryde and M.M. Fryde, 'Public credit, with special reference to north-western Europe' (1963), 455–61; the Bardi and Peruzzi also fell because of internal Florentine difficulties, however: A. Sapori, *La crisi delle Compagnie mercantili dei Bardi e dei Peruzzi* (1926), 50–86, 140–82, 204–6, with the critical comments of E.S. Hunt, 'A new look at the dealings of the Bardi and Peruzzi with Edward III' (1990).
35. J.L. Abu Lughod, *Before European hegemony* (1989), is a good general guide to the global economy in the period 1250–1350; 212–47 for Egypt.
36. For the *geniza* and economic history, see S.D. Goitein, *A Mediterranean society* (1967–93), esp. vol. 1; Goldberg, *Trade*. For European Jews, see Ch. 10.
37. L.A. Kotel'nikova, *Mondo contadino e città dal XI al XIV secolo* (1975), 26–141.
38. Duby, *Rural economy*, 126–52, is still a good general guide; this set of developments has not been studied much recently. Stockfish: see B. Sawyer and P. Sawyer, *Medieval Scandinavia* (1993), 157–9.
39. W.C. Jordan, *The great famine* (1996).
40. B.M.S. Campbell, *Before the Black Death* (1991) (a nuanced picture for England); S.R. Epstein, *Freedom and growth* (2000), 38–55; M. Bourin et al., 'Les campagnes européennes avant la peste' (2014).
41. For masons moving around Europe, P. du Colombier, *Les chantiers des cathédrales* (1973), 47–8; R. Recht, *Les batisseurs des cathédrales gothiques* (1989), 113–77, gives some good case studies of cathedral construction. For social mobility, see the multi-regional studies in S. Carocci, *La mobilità sociale nel medioevo* (2010).

8. The ambiguities of political reconstruction, 1150–1300

1. R.W. Southern, *Saint Anselm* (1990), 191, 232ff., 274–304.
2. For the canons, see N.P. Tanner, *Decrees of the ecumenical councils* (1990), vol. 1, 230–71. Context: see e.g. C. Morris, *The papal monarchy* (1989), esp. 417–38. For lack of effect, e.g. P.B. Pixton, *The German episcopacy and the implementation of the decrees of the Fourth Lateran Council, 1216–1245* (1995), esp. 437–59. For effect, see e.g. R. Bartlett, *Trial by fire and water* (1986), 98–102, 127–35, for the relative speed by which ordeal was abandoned, country by country, in the decades after the council condemned it.
3. See among many Baldwin, *The government of Philip Augustus*, esp. 152–75, 220–58; W.C. Jordan, *Louis IX and the challenge of the Crusade* (1979), 45–64, 159–71; cf. J. Le

274 NOTES to pp. 143–150

Goff, *Saint Louis* (2009), 45–64, 159–71, an idiosyncratic book (and one not so interested in the points made here) but one which cannot be excluded; for Philip IV, J.R. Strayer, *The reign of Philip the fair* (1980), esp. 36–99.

4. See e.g. Clanchy, *England and its rulers*, 181–283; Bartlett, *England*; M. Prestwich, *Plantagenet England 1225–1360* (2005), 81–187; J.R. Maddicott, *The origins of the English parliament, 924–1327* (2010), 157–331; D.A. Carpenter, *The reign of Henry III* (1996), 75–106, 183–97, 381–408; and P. Coss, *The origins of the English gentry* (2003), for the relationship between these processes and the structures of the aristocracy.

5. S. Barton, 'Spain in the eleventh century' (2004) and P. Linehan, 'Spain in the twelfth century' (2004) give rapid political outlines; S. Barton, *The aristocracy in twelfth-century León and Castile* (1997), 104–47, and I. Álvarez Borge, *La plena edad media* (2003), 247–84, give more developed sociopolitical surveys. A.J. Kosto, 'Reconquest, Renaissance and the histories of Iberia, ca. 1000–1200' (2012) is an effective argument against the *reconquista* straitjacket. For crusading imagery, W.J. Purkis, *Crusading spirituality in the Holy Land and Iberia, c.1095–c.1187* (2008), 120–78. For early *merinos* see I. Álvarez Borge, *Clientelismo regio y acción política* (2014); C. Jular, *Los adelantados y merinos mayores de León (siglos XIII–XV)* (1990), 56–159; cf. eadem, 'The king's face on the territory' (2004).

6. A. Rodríguez López, *La consolidación territorial de la monarquía feudal castellana* (1994), for Ferdinand III; M. González Jiménez, *Alfonso X el Sabio* (2004), very upbeat; for the complexities of the 1270s revolts, I. Alfonso, 'Desheredamiento y desafuero, o la pretendida justificación de una revuelta nobiliaria' (2002). For the fiscal structure, see above all M.A. Ladero Quesada, *Fiscalidad y poder real en Castilla (1252–1369)* (1993); E.S. Prater, *Curia and Cortes in León and Castille* (1980), 186–202; and, for the beginnings of taxation, I. Álvarez, 'Soldadas, situados y fisco regio en el reinado de Alfonso VIII de Castilla (1158–1214)' (2015).

7. P. Engel, *The realm of St Stephen* (2001), 37–107; Berend et al., *Central Europe*, 147–60, 176–81, 189–94, 208–11, 226–36, 244–9, 286–8, 425–32; for taxation, W.M. Ormrod and J. Barta, 'The feudal structure and the beginnings of state finance' (1995), 76–9, and G. Barta and J. Barta, 'Royal finance in medieval Hungary' (1999).

8. For good introductions see H. Takayama, *The administration of the Norman kingdom of Sicily* (1993); D. Abulafia, *Frederick II* (1988), esp. 321–39; J. Dunbabin, *Charles I of Anjou* (1998), esp. 55–76; Carocci, *Signorie di Mezzogiorno*.

9. Key introductions are D. Waley and T. Dean, *The Italian city-republics* (2010); Menant, *L'Italie des communes*; Milani, *I comuni italiani*; Jones, *The Italian city-state*; with the important monographic study of J.C. Maire Vigueur, *Cavaliers et citoyens* (2003). For the war against Barbarossa, see G. Raccagni, *The Lombard league, 1167–1225* (2010); P. Grillo, *Legnano 1176* (2010). Compare for the cities of southern Italy P. Oldfield, *City and community in Norman Italy* (2009); P. Skinner, *Medieval Amalfi and its diaspora, 800–1250* (2013).

10. R.W. Southern, *Western society and the church in the middle ages* (1970), 105–21, 184–5, is an excellent introduction; for the development of papal justice before Innocent III, see e.g. I.S. Robinson, *The papacy 1073–1198* (1990), 179–208. For the political uses of the papal control over marriage law, D.L. d'Avray, *Papacy, monarchy and marriage, 860–1600* (2015).

11. For the thirteenth century see Southern, *Western society*, 122–33, 188–213; R. Brentano, *Two churches* (1968); A. Paravicini Bagliani, *Il trono di Pietro* (1996); J. Sayers, *Innocent III* (1994).

12. A sensible overview of these developments is Keller, *Zwischen regionaler Begrenzung*, 375–500.

13. Important guides to this paragraph are Arnold, *Princes and territories*, and L. Scales, *The shaping of German identity* (2012).

14. P. Moraw, *Von offener Verfassung zu gestalteter Verdichtung* (1985), 175. For cities, see T. Scott, *The city-state in Europe, 1000–1600* (2012), 56–63, 129–64.

15. H. Helbig, *Der wettinische Ständestaat* (1955), 1–53, for Meissen; O. Brunner, *Land and lordship* (1992), esp. 36–94, 139–99, 296–324.

16. For a survey, see C. Wickham, 'Lineages of western European taxation, 1000–1200' (1997).

17. France, *Western warfare*, 70–5, 131–4; for figures for the relative wealth of kings, see J. Pryor, 'Foreign policy and economic policy' (1980), 45–6. See in general M. Ginatempo, 'Esisteva una fiscalità a finanziamento delle guerre del primo "200?"' (2011), who warns against the assumption that taxation paid for more than a minority of wars before 1250 or so.

18. Jordan, *Louis IX*, 78–104; Strayer, *The reign*, 250–60.

19. G.H. Martin, 'Merton, Walter of (c.1205–1277)' (2004).

20. L. Thomas, 'La vie privée de Guillaume de Nogaret' (1904); Strayer, *The reign*, esp. 52–62.

21. M.T. Clanchy, *From memory to written record* (2013), 61–4, and see more generally 46–82.

22. *Libri dell'entrata e dell'uscita della republica di Siena* (1904ff.) collect the early Biccherna registers in Siena; for Bologna and Perugia and their successors, see A. Zorzi, 'Giustizia criminale e criminalità nell'Italia del tardo medioevo' (1989), 942–5. For recent work on the uses of writing in Italian communes, see H. Keller, 'Die italienische Kommune als Laboratorium administrativen Schriftgebrauchs' (2014).

23. See Ch. 4 n. 23.

24. Lupus of Ferrières, *Epistolae* (1925), nn. 121, 124 (nn. 118, 123 of the translation); Map, *De nugis curialium*, 470–2, for Henry I. For the politics of oral communication, see M. Billoré and M. Soria, *La rumeur au moyen âge* (2011).

25. J. Sabapathy, *Officers and accountability in medieval England 1170–1300* (2014), 47–52, 86–91, 113–20, is now the best starting point for England; for France, Jordan, *Louis IX*, 51–64, 236–45; M. Dejoux, 'Mener une enquête générale, pratiques et méthodes' (2010). See in general C. Gauvard, *L'enquête au moyen âge* (2005); T. Pécout, *Quand gouverner c'est enquêter* (2010). For Carolingian inquests, see Davis, *Charlemagne's practice of empire*, 260–78.

26. *Dialogus de Scaccario* (2007), 1.1, 5 (p. 10 for quote); Jean sire de Joinville, *Histoire de Saint Louis* (1868), c. 140; V. Crescenzi, 'Il sindacato degli ufficiali nei comuni medievali italiani' (1981), 406–51. Basic here are Sabapathy, *Officers and accountability*, passim (91–110 for Richard fitzNigel); idem, 'Accountable *rectores* in comparative perspective' (2012); and, more generally, Bisson, *The crisis*, 316–49, who shows how accounting preceded and was a prerequisite for accountability, across western Europe in the later twelfth century.

27. C.E. Bosworth, 'Muṣādara' (2002).

28. Surprisingly, there is no decent comparative analysis of central medieval European law codes as texts. A. Padoa-Schioppa, *Il diritto nella storia d'Europa* (1995), is better than most; for Scandinavia, a good brief introduction can be found in R.M. Karras, *Slavery and society in medieval Scandinavia* (1988), 167–78.

29. For Oberto, see M.G. di Renzo Villata, 'La formazione dei «Libri Feudorum»' (2000); Reynolds, *Fiefs and vassals*, 215–30. See in general A. Watson, *The evolution of law* (1985), 66–97. For Roman law and legal procedures in practice, an excellent study of northern Italy is M. Vallerani, *Medieval public justice* (2012).

30. See in general Wickham, *Sleepwalking*.

31. See Clanchy, *From memory*, 65 and *Dialogus de Scaccario*, 2.2 (p. 112) for Richard of Ilchester and the summons rolls in the 1160s; T.F. Tout, *Chapters in the administrative history of mediaeval England* (1920), vol. 2, 258–67 for Walter Stapledon's administrative reforms in the 1320s. The *Dialogus*, it can be added, is an explanation of the running of English government written in a question-and-answer format; simply the need to give explanations for government procedures is halfway to thinking about how to do them better. But see also U. Kypta, *Die Autonomie der Routine* (2014), esp. 208–22, 245–50, a

reference which I owe to John Sabapathy, on how the habitus of English government clerks favoured unintended innovation above all; that remained the background to all more conscious change.

32. *Annali genovesi di Caffaro e de' suoi continuatori*, vol. 2 (1901), 36; Wickham, *Medieval Rome*, 442–5; P. Vignoli, *I costituti della legge e dell'uso di Pisa (sec. XII)* (2003).

33. See above all Bisson, *The crisis*. This paragraph and the next are indebted to the insights of Bisson, *The crisis*, Reynolds, *Kingdoms and communities*, and Watts, *The making of polities* – in disagreement although they surely are.

34. Freedman, *The origins of peasant servitude*, 89–118; Bisson, *The crisis*, 508–12. Basic for Aragón more generally is T.N. Bisson, *The medieval crown of Aragon* (1991).

35. For the lordships, see above all C. Estepa Díez, *Las behetrías castellanas* (2003), esp. vol. 1, 39–87, 181–229.

36. For the community of the realm, Reynolds, *Kingdoms and communities*, 268–87.

37. J.E.A. Jolliffe, *Angevin kingship* (1955), 96–109, and G. Althoff, '*Ira regis*' (1998), for royal anger; Map, *De nugis curialium*, 2–24, 498–512; see Althoff, *Spielregeln*, for political choreography under the Ottonians and onwards.

38. G. Klaniczay, *Holy rulers and blessed princesses* (2002), 96–9, 123–55, 158–61, 171–3, 296–8. Cnut III of Denmark, Erik IX of Sweden and Olaf Haraldsson of Norway, among others, were similar royal saints.

39. C. Valente, 'The deposition and abdication of Edward II' (1998), quote at 880.

40. For early schools moving towards universities, see C.S. Jaeger, *The envy of angels* (1994); for the poor scholar, it is hard not to cite H. Waddell, *The wandering scholars* (1932), esp. 156–8, for her evocative imagery. For contemporary Greek parallels, see Ch. 9 n. 21.

41. See in general S.C. Ferruolo, *The origins of the university* (1985), esp. 11–66; R.W. Southern, *Scholastic humanism and the making of Europe* (1995–2001). For Bologna, E. Cortese, *Il diritto nella storia medievale* (1995), vol. 2, 57–214, and R.G. Witt, *The two Latin cultures and the foundation of Renaissance humanism in medieval Italy* (2012), 235–59 – this book being now the basic starting point for looking at north Italian intellectual culture, 900–1250. For Abelard, see among many M.T. Clanchy, *Abelard* (1997), and D. Luscombe, *The letter collection of Peter Abelard and Heloise* (2013); cf. M. Colish, *Peter Lombard* (1994), esp. 96–131, 254–63.

42. See Ferruolo, *The origins*, 279–315; I.P. Wei, *Intellectual culture in medieval Paris* (2012), esp. 87–124, for this and what follows. (Note that, by contrast, the *universitates* of Bologna were guilds not of the masters, but of the students.)

43. B. Stock, *The implications of literacy* (1983), 90–2.

44. M. Rubellin, *Eglise et société chrétienne d'Agobard à Valdès* (2003), 455–500; see for later periods P. Biller, 'Goodbye to Waldensianism?' (2006), a defence of the relative coherence of the sect. Much the same happened to a north Italian lay preaching group known as the Humiliati, but most of them came back into the fold as quasi-friars in 1199–1201: F. Andrews, *The early Humiliati* (1999), 38–98. For a case study of a new monastic movement, the Gilbertines, see K. Sykes, *Inventing Sempringham* (2011).

45. See above all W. Simons, *Cities of ladies* (2001), and also D. Elliott, *Proving woman* (2004), 47–84.

46. See most recently A. Vauchez, *Francis of Assisi* (2012). For the continuing liminality of the Franciscans and other friars, see G. Geltner, *The making of medieval antifraternalism* (2012).

47. Here the debate is very extensive. Among recent works, differing considerably in their views but all textually aware, are M. Zerner, *Inventer l'hérésie?* (1998); C. Bruschi and P. Biller, *Texts and the repression of heresy* (2003); J.H. Arnold, *Inquisition and power* (2001); C. Bruschi, *The wandering heretics of Languedoc* (2009); L. Sackville, *Heresy and heretics in the thirteenth century* (2011); C. Taylor, *Heresy, crusade and inquisition in medieval Quercy* (2011); G. Zanella, *Hereticalia* (1995), esp. 127–43; C. Lansing, *Power and purity* (1998); M.G. Pegg, *The corruption of angels* (2001); Moore, *The war on heresy* (see also the review by Biller, and Moore's reply, in *Reviews in history* (2014)).

J.H. Arnold, 'The Cathar middle ages as an historiographical problem' (in press), sums up the debate neatly. They collectively underlie the next paragraphs.

48. Lansing, *Power and purity*, 92–6; J.L. Peterson, 'Holy heretics in later medieval Italy' (2009).

49. For a recent, and angry, account of the crusade, see M.G. Pegg, *A most holy war* (2008).

50. See D.L. d'Avray, *The preaching of the friars* (1985), esp. 15–28; A. Vauchez, 'The Church and the laity' (1999), 183–94; for previous centuries, Hamilton, *Church and people*, 10–15, 172–7.

51. For 1233, A. Thompson, *Revival preachers and politics in thirteenth-century Italy* (1992).

52. See Rosser, *The art of solidarity*.

53. R.I. Moore, *The formation of a persecuting society* (2007) is the classic text, although C. Rawcliffe, *Leprosy in medieval England* (2006), shows how attitudes to leprosy were notably complex throughout the middle ages, and that segregation was only relative. For homosexuals in this period (I use the modern term even though sexual characterisations were then rather different), J. Boswell, *Christianity, social tolerance and homosexuality* (1981), 269–302 (an odd mixture of careful textual work and over-the-top hypothesis).

54. See the examples in C. Bruschi, '*Familia inquisitionis*' (2013).

55. See in general Arnold, *Belief and unbelief*; and, for good examples of complex microcultural beliefs from inquisitors' records across the period 1240–1330, Pegg, *The corruption of angels*; E. Le Roy Ladurie, *Montaillou* (1978); plus, for later periods, J. Edwards, 'Religious faith and doubt in late medieval Spain' (1988); C. Ginzburg, *The night battles* (1983).

9. 1204: the failure of alternatives

1. P. Magdalino, *Constantinople médiévale* (1996), 55–7, is inclined to accept Geoffroy de Villehardouin's estimate of 400,000 inhabitants in 1204; but even if one does not, Constantinople surely outmatched its main rivals, thirteenth-century Paris and Milan, for which around 200,000 has been canvassed (see Ch. 7).

2. See C. Wickham, 'Ninth-century Byzantium through western eyes' (1998), for the Carolingians; A. von Euw and P. Schreiner, *Kaiserin Theophanu* (1991), and A. Davids, *The empress Theophano* (1995), for the Ottonians. A sensible initial guide to the period of this chapter is J. Shepard, *The Cambridge history of the Byzantine empire, c. 500–1492* (2008).

3. M. Whittow, *The making of Orthodox Byzantium, 600–1025* (1996), 310–91; C. Holmes, *Basil II and the governance of empire (976–1025)* (2005), 448–543.

4. J. Haldon, *Warfare, state and society in the Byzantine world, 565–1204* (1999), 112–20, 217–25; A. Dain, 'Les stratégistes byzantins' (1967); J. Haldon, *A critical commentary on the Taktika of Leo VI* (2014), 3–87.

5. M. Psellos, *Chronographia*, trans. Sewter (1966), 45–6. For the fiscal system in this period see, still, F. Dölger, *Beiträge zur Geschichte der byzantinischen Finanzverwaltung, besonders des 10. und 11. Jahrhunderts* (1927), 9–112; Hendy, *Studies*, 157–242 (covering more than this period); V. Prigent, 'The mobilisation of fiscal resources in the Byzantine empire (eighth to eleventh centuries)' (2014).

6. M. Angold, *The Byzantine aristocracy, IX to XII centuries* (1984); Kaplan, *Les hommes et la terre*, 331–73; J.-C. Cheynet, *Pouvoir et contestation à Byzance (963–1210)* (1996), 207–48; J.-C. Cheynet, 'Les Phocas' (1986). For the provincial world, L. Neville, *Authority in Byzantine provincial society, 950–1100* (2004).

7. *To eparchikon biblion* (1970).

8. Liutprand of Cremona, *Opera* (1998), *Antapodosis*, 6.10 (trans. Squatriti, 200–2); Constantin VII Porphyrogénète, *Le livre des cérémonies* (1935–39); A. Cameron, 'The construction of court ritual' (1987), 106–36; M. McCormick, *Eternal victory* (2001), 144; Dagron, *Emperor and priest*, 84–124, 204–19.

9. For Nikephoros, see *Le traité sur la guérilla*; Kekaumenos, *Consilia et narrationes* (2013); for Boilas, P. Lemerle, *Cinq études sur le XIe siècle byzantin* (1977), 15–63 (24–5 for the textual reference to books), vol. 1, 2.

10. Constantin VII Porphyrogénète, *Le livre des cérémonies*, vol. 1, 2; for what Constantine probably did write, see I. Ševčenko, 'Re-reading Constantine Porphyrogenitus' (1992).

11. See e.g. P. Lemerle, *Byzantine humanism* (1986); H. Maguire, *Byzantine court culture from 829 to 1204* (1997); M.T. Fögen, 'Reanimation of Roman law in the ninth century' (1998).

12. A. Kaldellis, *The argument of Psellos' Chronographia* (1999); S. Papaioannou, *Michael Psellos* (2013).

13. See in general Curta, *Southeastern Europe*, 119–24, 147–79, 213–47; J. Shepard, 'Bulgaria' (1999); P. Stephenson, *Byzantium's Balkan frontier* (2000), 18–23.

14. For this and the next two paragraphs see above all J. Shepard and S. Franklin, *The emergence of Rus, 750–1200* (1996), and Martin, *Medieval Russia*.

15. S. Franklin, *Writing, society and culture in early Rus, c.950–1300* (2002).

16. J. Haldon, 'Approaches to an alternative military history of the period ca. 1025–1071' (2003); see in general M. Angold, *The Byzantine empire, 1025–1204* (1984), 12–91, but a recent overall analysis of the period is lacking.

17. P. Frankopan, *The First Crusade: the call from the east* (2011), 57–172; P. Magdalino, *The empire of Manuel I Komnenos, 1143–1180* (1993), 95–8, 123–32.

18. *Digenis Akritis* (1998) (the actual texts we have are late medieval).

19. Magdalino, *The empire of Manuel I*, 180–266; for *pronoia*, M.C. Bartusis, *Land and privilege in Byzantium* (2012), 64–111, 165–70; Niketas Choniates, *Historia*, trans. in H.J. Magoulias, *O city of Byzantium* (1984), 118–19 (cc. 208–9).

20. A. Harvey, *Economic expansion in the Byzantine empire, 900–1200* (1989); Magdalino, *The empire of Manuel I*, 140–71; A.E. Laiou and C. Morrisson, *The Byzantine economy* (2007), 90–165 (which synthesises the monumental A.E. Laiou, *The economic history of Byzantium from the seventh through the fifteenth century* (2002)); M. Whittow, 'The Byzantine economy (600–1204)' (2008), for caution; G.D.R. Sanders, 'Corinth' (2002); *To eparchikon biblion*.

21. R. Beaton, 'The rhetoric of poverty' (1987); for Nikephoros, L. Neville, *Heroes and Romans in twelfth-century Byzantium* (2012); for Anna, a more significant figure than her husband, T. Gouma-Peterson, *Anna Komnene and her times* (2000).

22. Magdalino, *The empire of Manuel I*, 56–108.

23. T.M. Kolbaba, *The Byzantine lists* (2000), 35ff.

24. Liutprand of Cremona, *Antapodosis*, bk. 6; *Relatio*, passim (trans. Squatriti, 195–202, 238–82). For the city of wonders: I. Seidel, *Byzanz im Spiegel der literarischen Entwicklung Frankreichs im 12. Jahrhundert* (1977), 49–54, 95–9; B. Ebels-Hoving, *Byzantium in westerse ogen, 1096–1204* (1971), 119–23, 170–81, 253–4, 263–9; M. Angold, *The fourth crusade* (2003), 58–74.

25. C.M. Brand, *Byzantium confronts the West* (1968); Angold, *The fourth crusade*; J. Phillips, *The Fourth Crusade and the sack of Constantinople* (2005).

26. For the political history see, still, D.M. Nicol, *The last centuries of Byzantium, 1261–1453* (1993); for the Chora, R. Ousterhout, *The art of the Kariye Camii* (2002), sums up current knowledge. For a narrative account of Serbs and Bulgarians, J.V.A. Fine, *The late medieval Balkans* (1987).

27. See C. Imber, *The Ottoman empire, 1300–1650* (2002), 7–37 for a survey.

28. Bartusis, *Land and privilege*, 579–96, is very sensible here. For the Ottoman army, Gy. Káldy-Nagy, 'The first centuries of the Ottoman military organization' (1977). C. Kafadar, *Between two worlds* (1995), esp. 118–50, and H.W. Lowry, *The nature of the early Ottoman state* (2006), give an important framing.

29. H. İnalcık, 'The policy of Mehmed II towards the Greek population of Istanbul and the Byzantine buildings of the city' (1969–70); for the limits of Mehmet's recognition and

Byzantine responses, K. Moustakas, 'Byzantine "visions" of the Ottoman empire' (2011). Post-1402 fragmentation: D.J. Kastritsis, *The sons of Beyazid* (2007).
30. Johns, *Arabic administration*, esp. 38.
31. R.O. Crummey, *The formation of Muscovy, 1304–1613* (1987), 29–93; Martin, *Medieval Russia*, 174–254.
32. D. Ostrowski, *Muscovy and the Mongols* (1998), 36–63, 177–80, 219–43.
33. Choniates, *Historia*, trans. Magoulias, 167 (c. 301).

10. Defining society: gender and community in late medieval Europe

1. E. Dupré Theseider, 'Caterina da Siena, santa' (1979); C.W. Bynum, *Holy feast and holy fast* (1987), 165–80, 204–7; and the very valuable F.T. Luongo, *The saintly politics of Catherine of Siena* (2006) – 97, 109 for the wine barrel (he also points up the sexual imagery invoked by Catherine in the opening of the barrel, here made of the cross of the Crucifixion, with a spike); for the grafted tree, *Epistolario di Santa Catarina da Siena* (1940), n. 41.
2. *The Book of Margery Kempe* (2004) (cc. 48 for Leicester, 52 for not preaching); I have found particularly useful J.H. Arnold and K.J. Lewis, *A companion to the book of Margery Kempe* (2004) and A. Goodman, *Margery Kempe and her world* (2002).
3. See for a survey R.N. Swanson, *Religion and devotion in Europe, c.1215–c.1515* (1995).
4. See esp. J.H. Van Engen, *Sisters and brothers of the common life* (2008).
5. For England, P.J.P. Goldberg, *Women, work and life cycle in a medieval economy* (1992), esp. 324–61; contrast J.M. Bennett, *History matters* (2006), 82–107; eadem, *Ale, beer, and brewsters in England* (1996), e.g. 37–43, 58–9; her more pessimistic view does not affect the general point. See for a Europe-wide survey K. Reyerson, 'Urban economies' (2013), 295–310.
6. N. Caciola, *Discerning spirits* (2003), 87–98.
7. For the patterns and problems of female sanctity, see C.W. Bynum, 'Women's stories, women's symbols' (1992); Caciola, *Discerning spirits*, 309–19 and passim; Elliott, *Proving woman*; A. Vauchez, *The laity in the middle ages* (1993), 171–264. For anxieties about the demonic and about (particularly female) sexuality, Elliott, *Fallen bodies*, esp. 35–60. For Joan, H. Castor, *Joan of Arc* (2014), sums up an extensive bibliography (largely in English, perhaps surprisingly); Cr. Taylor, *Joan of Arc: la Pucelle* (2006), is more than a good collection of texts. For witches, see n. 42 below.
8. Dante, *Monarchia* (1995), 1.5.5; *Le ménagier de Paris* (1846). There are many guides to medieval gender and women's history, but Bennett and Karras, *The Oxford handbook of women and gender*, is now by far the best collective introduction to the whole of this section and cites earlier work. For the fragility of female reputation, see e.g. the case study of scolding accusations in late medieval England, S. Bardsley, *Venomous tongues* (2006). For patriarchy in a family context, R.E. Moss, *Fatherhood and its representations in Middle English texts* (2013).
9. Andreas aulae regiae capellanus, *De amore* (2006), 1.11.3; see in general K. Gravdal, *Ravishing maidens* (1991), 104–21 and passim; G. Boccaccio, *Decamerone* (1993), 10.10 for Griselda.
10. D. Herlihy, *Opera muliebria* (1990), 75–102. Bennett, *Ale, beer, and brewsters*, 51–76, shows that late medieval men took over large-scale brewing too. D. Cardon, *La draperie au moyen âge* (1999) shows that the late medieval male–female balance in large-scale weaving in continental Europe was fairly even. For the Fuggers, M. Häberlein, *The Fuggers of Augsburg* (2012), 12–20 (who were not exceptional here: see E. Ennen, *The medieval woman* (1989), 165–84, 201, 209–10); by contrast, in the sixteenth century women were excluded from directive roles in the Fugger trading company: Häberlein, *The Fuggers*, 34–5, 204.
11. For medicine, e.g. M.H. Green, 'Women's medical practice and health care in medieval Europe' (1989); H. Skoda, 'La Vierge et la vieille' (2012). For the Reformation, L. Roper,

The holy household (1989) (who stresses that regulation affected husbands too); eadem, *Oedipus and the Devil* (1994). 37–52.

12. For Margaret, see for a rapid survey J.E. Olesen, 'Inter-Scandinavian relations' (2003), 720–9; for queens in general, see T. Earenfight, *Queenship in medieval Europe* (2013); A. Rodríguez, *La estirpe de Leonor de Aquitania* (2014).

13. E. Cavell, 'Intelligence and intrigue in the March of Wales' (2015); J.C. Parsons, 'Isabella (1295–1358)', *Oxford dictionary of national biography* (2004). (Isabella's public liaison with Mortimer was very unusual; they were both exiles in France when they began their relationship, however – Isabella could never have got away with it in her husband's court.)

14. R. Gilchrist, *Gender and material culture* (1994).

15. Ennen, *The medieval woman*, 170, 180–7, 230.

16. See e.g. J.A. McNamara and S. Wemple, 'The power of women through the family in medieval Europe: 500–1100' (1973); G. Duby, 'Women and power' (1995). I prefer to follow the more continuitist reading of J. Bennett, *Medieval women in modern perspective* (2000).

17. See S.M. Stuard, 'Brideprice, dowry, and other marital assigns' (2012), and M.C. Howell, *The marriage exchange* (1998), 196–228, for general overviews of dowries and marriage contracts; Howell's case study, Douai, shows that the control by women over property could be more complex and in some respects longer-lasting than many previous studies assume.

18. M.T. Clanchy, 'Did mothers teach teach their children to read?' (2011), 139–53.

19. Christine de Pizan, *Le livre de la cité des dames* (1997), esp. 1.11, 27, 2.50, 3.9; see for commentary, among many, R. Brown-Grant, *Christine de Pizan and the moral defence of women* (2000), 128–74.

20. For the complex meanings of *Pseudo-Turpin* in France (in particular in its later retranslations back into French), see above all G.M. Spiegel, *Romancing the past* (1993), 69–98.

21. For Germany, e.g. M.H. Jones and R. Wisbey, *Chrétien de Troyes and the German middle ages* (1993); for England, W.R.J. Barron, *The Arthur of the English* (2001); for Wales, R. Bromwich et al., *The Arthur of the Welsh* (1991).

22. G. Petrocchi, 'Biografia' (1978), 45–9, for early citations; M. Caesar, *Dante: the critical heritage* (1989), 15–18 for Dante abroad.

23. For courts and their social dramas, see e.g. M. Vale, *The princely court* (2001), esp. 179–246; S. Gunn and A. Janse, *The court as a stage* (2006). For Byzantine romances, E. Jeffreys, *Four Byzantine novels* (2012).

24. For a rapid guide to all medieval French literature, see F. Lestringant and M. Zink, *Histoire de la France littéraire*, vol. 1 (2006); for the three orders, G. Duby, *The three orders* (1980), 271–353. For knighthood, J. Flori, *L'essor de la chevalerie* (1986), with correctives in D. Barthélemy, *The serf, the knight and the historian* (2009), 137–53. For the complexities of chivalry in practice, see e.g. M. Keen, *Chivalry* (1984). For the religious virtue of aristocrats (and their continued fast track to sanctity), see A. Murray, *Reason and society in the middle ages* (1978), 331–82.

25. See in general Coss, *The origins*; Crouch, *The birth of nobility*; K.B. McFarlane, *The nobility of later medieval England* (1973); J. Morsel, *L'aristocratie médiévale* (2004), who gives a Europe-wide analysis. For early medieval uses of *nobilis*, Goetz, '"Nobilis"'. For Alice Chaucer, see R.E. Archer, 'Chaucer, Alice, duchess of Suffolk (c.1404–1475)' (2004).

26. R.C. Trexler, *Public life in Renaissance Florence* (1980), 218–23, 450–2; J.-C. Maire Vigueur, *L'autre Rome* (2010), 178–84; M. Rubin, *Corpus Christi* (1991), 164–84, 271–87. For entry ceremonies, A. Brown and G. Small, *Court and civic society in the Burgundian Low Countries c. 1420–1530* (2007), 23–8, 165–209 for texts; P. Arnade, *Realms of ritual* (1996), esp. 127–58; E. Lecuppre-Desjardin, *La ville des cérémonies* (2004), esp. 103–97, 259–302.

27. J. Catto, 'Andrew Horn' (1981), 387–91; cf. Q. Skinner, *The foundations of modern political thought* (1978), vol. 1, 27–48, and B. Latini, *Li livres dou tresor* (2003), (xxxii for Spain); for grief, see C. Lansing, *Passion and order* (2008); for candles, e.g. *Statuta sive leges municipales Arelatis* (1846), 221, c. 93, for Arles.

28. Jones, *The Italian city-state*, 440–76, gives a good survey.

29. Boccaccio, *Decamerone*; for Chaucer, e.g. P. Strohm, *Social Chaucer* (1989), 84–91; for London's absence, D. Wallace, *Chaucerian polity* (1997), 156–81.

30. *Diario bolognese di Gaspare Nadi* (1886); for *ricordanze* see e.g. P.J. Jones, 'Florentine families and Florentine diaries in the fourteenth century' (1956). Boccaccio, *Decamerone*, 5.8, 9, 10.1, comes half-way to the values of chivalric literature as attached to civic élites, but only half-way; note also the quasi-epic poem on a football match attributed to the fifteenth-century Florentine merchant and diplomat Giovanni Frescobaldi, in L. Avellini, 'Artigianato in versi del secondo Quattrocento fiorentino' (1980), 178–81, 213–29.

31. See N.E. Dubin, *The fabliaux* (2013) for a recent parallel text of nearly half the corpus, although his decision to match the French verse forms creates imaginative rather than literal translations; 872–85 for *La damoisele qui n'oït parler de fotre qui n'aüst mal au cuer*. I have gained insights about the social context of the *fabliaux* above all from P. Ménard, *Les fabliaux* (1983) (65–72 for food); C. Muscatine, *The Old French fabliaux* (1986) (73–83 for food) and N.J. Lacy, *Reading fabliaux* (1993).

32. For the spiritual context of Margery's eating, see M. Raine, '"Fals flesch"' (2005). For peasant attitudes to good food, see e.g. J. Birrell, 'Peasants eating and drinking' (2015).

33. *Le vilain asnier* (in Dubin, *The fabliaux*, 176–80); see in general, above all Freedman, *Images of the medieval peasant*, 133–56. For 1381, S. Justice, *Writing and rebellion* (1994), 102–39, 181–90; and below, Ch. 12.

34. D. Balestracci, *La zappa e la retorica* (1984).

35. See the rural witnessing in Wickham, *Courts and conflict*, and G. Brucker, *Giovanni and Lusanna* (1986), 21–5. For a classic example not long after 1500, even if further mediated by commentators, see N.Z. Davis, *The return of Martin Guerre* (1983).

36. Le Roy Ladurie, *Montaillou*; key critiques are L.E. Boyle, 'Montaillou revisited' (1981), and N.Z. Davis, 'Les conteurs de Montaillou' (1979). For later examples, see Ch. 8 n. 55.

37. Birrell, 'Manorial custumals'; G. Algazi, 'Lords ask, peasants answer' (1997); S. Teuscher, *Lords' rights and peasant stories* (2012); G. Brunel and O. Guillotjeannin, 'Les préambules des chartes de franchises' (2007) provides a comparative survey with bibliography. For a list of medieval Italian village statutes, see A. Rizzi, *Statuta de ludo* (2012), 29–76; one of the few analytical studies of them is P. Toubert, 'Les statuts communaux et l'histoire des campagnes lombardes au XIVe siècle' (1960).

38. See A. Walsham, *The Reformation of the landscape* (2011); B. Kümin, *The shaping of a community* (1996); A. Torre, *Il consumo di devozioni* (1995); W.A. Christian Jr., *Local religion in sixteenth-century Spain* (1981), for important case studies focused on the post-1500 period.

39. J. Whittle, *The development of agrarian capitalism* (2000); G. Cherubini and R. Francovich, 'Forme e vicende degli insediamenti nella campagna toscana dei secoli XIII–XV' (1973).

40. For Iceland see above all Miller, *Bloodtaking and peacemaking*; Byock, *Viking age Iceland*; Jón Viðar Sigurðsson, *Chieftains and power in the Icelandic commonwealth* (1999); for the historicity of the family sagas, a point of reference is C. Callow, 'Reconstructing the past in medieval Iceland' (2006). The classic texts are *Brennu-Njáls saga* (1954), for which see W.I. Miller, *'Why is your axe bloody?'* (2014), and *Laxdœla saga* (1934) (quote from c. 78).

41. London: see above all F. Rexroth, *Deviance and power in late medieval London* (2007), 27–187; for prostitutes in general, R.M. Karras, *Common women* (1996). Cf. also B. Geremek, *The margins of society in late medieval Paris* (1987), 199–215, for Paris (repression of beggars but not prostitutes), and the Europe-wide citations in T. Dean, *Crime in medieval Europe* (2001), 47–72.

42. See L. Stokes, *Demons of urban reform* (2011), for the fifteenth-century starting points of the witch craze.
43. For the contradictions of papal policy, R. Rist, *Popes and Jews, 1095–1291* (2016). For the fourteenth century, D. Nirenberg, *Communities of violence* (1996) (200–30 for the stability of Easter week violence); S.K. Cohn, 'The Black Death and the burning of Jews' (2007); P. Wolff, 'The 1391 pogrom in Spain' (1971); A. MacKay, 'Popular movements and pogroms in fifteenth-century Castile' (1972). For the desecration myth, M. Rubin, *Gentile tales* (1999). For an overall view, R. Chazan, *The Jews of medieval western Christendom, 1000–1500* (2006). J.M. Elukin, *Living together, living apart* (2007), stresses the relative peacefulness of Jewish–Christian relations, more than I would.
44. Sensible remarks in S.K. Cohn, *The Black Death transformed* (2002), 223–46.

11. Money, war and death, 1350–1500

1. Cohn, *The Black Death transformed*, is the best current survey. He does not believe the plague was bubonic (*Yersinia pestis*), but more recent bioarchaeological work gives strong reasons for thinking it was (see M.H. Green, *Pandemic disease in the medieval world* (2014), for recent bibliography); all the same, the course and transmission of the Black Death did not closely resemble that of modern bubonic plague. A model study of one town, Orvieto, is É. Carpentier, *Une ville devant la peste* (1962). See also the critical points in D.C. Mengel, 'A plague on Bohemia?' (2011).
2. See for a recent survey C. Allmand, *The Hundred Years War* (2001); the very detailed narrative in J. Sumption, *The Hundred Years War* (1990–2015), has reached 1422 so far. For the internal structure (and strikingly small size) of English armies, see A.R. Bell et al., *The soldier in later medieval England* (2013).
3. See in general D. Abulafia, *The western Mediterranean kingdoms, 1200–1500* (1997).
4. See L.J.A. Villalon and D.J. Kagay, *The Hundred Years War: a wider focus* (2005), for the European dimension to the war.
5. Basic sensible accounts are H. Kaminsky, 'The Great Schism' (2000), and, for the university response, R.N. Swanson, *Universities, academics and the Great Schism* (1989); for some new directions, J. Rollo-Koster and T.M. Izbicki, *A companion to the great western schism (1378–1417)* (2009).
6. P. Partner, 'The "budget" of the Roman church in the Renaissance period' (1960).
7. Watts, *The making of polities*, with previous bibliography.
8. For England, Britnell, *The commercialisation*, 155–203; idem, *Britain and Ireland*, 320–506; Dyer, *Making a living*, 265–362; idem, *An age of transition?* (2005); idem, 'England's economy in the fifteenth century' (2014). Classic surveys which assume the economic depression model are *The Cambridge economic history*, vol. 2; Contamine, *L'économie médiévale*, 329–405.
9. For the Hanse, P. Dollinger, *The German Hansa* (1964), is still essential; updatings in E. Isenmann, *Die deutsche Stadt im Spätmittelalter 1250–1500* (1988), 341–402, which covers south Germany too. For recent work on English cloth, see e.g. Britnell, *Britain and Ireland*, 326–31, 351–4.
10. See in general B. van Bavel, *Manors and markets* (2010), 242–371; for Flanders, Nicholas, *Medieval Flanders*, 273–85, 378–91.
11. Two significant monographic studies using Italian evidence are R.A. Goldthwaite, *The economy of Renaissance Florence* (2009), and Epstein, *Freedom and growth*; for effective short syntheses of current work on Italy as a whole, see F. Franceschi and L. Molà, 'L'economia del Rinascimento' (2006); iidem, 'Regional states and economic development' (2012), 444–66; T. Scott, 'The economic policies of the regional city-states of Renaissance Italy' (2014).
12. See e.g. for Valencia, A. Furió, *Història del país valencià* (1995), 204–10; for Sicily, Epstein, *An island for itself*, 162–313; for Ragusa, S.M. Stuard, *A state of deference* (1992), 171–202.

13. R. Brenner, 'Agrarian class structure and economic development in pre-industrial Europe' (1976).
14. See as varying examples Dyer, *An age of transition?* 194–229 (who stresses that wage labour in England was older than that); Whittle, *The development*; Brenner, 'Agrarian class structure', 61–75; van Bavel, *Manors and markets*, 242–6; Bois, *The crisis of feudalism*, 300–68.
15. For England as a case study for this development, see e.g. Dyer, *Standards*, 211–33.
16. Egypt: see most recently S.J. Borsch, *The Black Death in Egypt and England* (2005), 23–54; earlier, M.W. Dols, *The Black Death in the Middle East* (1977), 255–80. India and China: P. Parthasarathi, *Why Europe grew rich and Asia did not* (2011); K. Pomeranz, *The great divergence* (2000) (which has in this respect survived its critics) – both of them focused on later centuries, but with observations which fit the period before 1500 too.
17. As general guides to all late medieval polities, see *NCMH*, vols 6 and 7, for fairly traditional, usually good-quality, political surveys. Watts, *The making of polities*, offers a fresh and explicitly comparative approach. For fiscal structures, R. Bonney, *Economic systems and state finance* (1995) and idem, *The rise of the fiscal state in Europe, c. 1200–1815* (1999) are the key starting point, plus the critical analysis in S. Carocci and S.M. Collavini, 'Il costo degli stati' (2011), 20–48. By contrast, some of the local bibliography on taxation which I cite later is much less good.
18. See M.-T. Caron, *Noblesse et pouvoir royal en France, XIIIe–XVIe siècle* (1994), for the late middle ages as a whole; P.S. Lewis, *Later medieval France* (1968), a pioneering socio-political study; G. Small, *Late medieval France* (2009); for taxation, J.B. Henneman, 'France in the middle ages' (1999); W.M. Ormrod, 'The west European monarchies in the later middle ages' (1995), esp. 136–55. C. Fletcher et al., *Government and political life in England and France, c.1300–c.1500* (2015), is an important comparative study of France and England.
19. McFarlane, *The nobility*, 19–40 is a succinct analysis.
20. See in general (among many) G. Harriss, *Shaping the nation* (2005); J. Watts, *Henry VI and the politics of kingship* (1996); C. Carpenter, *The Wars of the Roses* (1997); R. Davies, *The revolt of Owain Glyn Dŵr* (1995).
21. For taxation, see Ormrod, 'England in the middle ages' (1999); Ormrod, 'The west European monarchies', esp. 136–55.
22. A. Grant, *Independence and nationhood* (1984); J. Wormald, 'Scotland: 1406–1513' (1998); K. Stevenson, *Power and propaganda* (2014); at their back is the narrative in R. Nicholson, *Scotland: the later middle ages* (1974). For the politics of taxation, R. Tanner, *The late medieval Scottish parliament* (2001), 7–30, 51–4, 197–222. For comparisons with England, M. Brown, *Disunited kingdoms* (2013).
23. See above all A.H. de Oliveira Marques, *Portugal na crise dos séculos XIV e XV* (1987), esp. 81–6 (land), 298–316 (justice and taxation).
24. See in general, still, A. MacKay, *Spain in the middle ages* (1977), 133–59 (also for the period after 1400); more specifically, Ladero, *Fiscalidad*, 331–44; idem, 'Castile in the middle ages' (1999); Ormrod, 'The west European monarchies', esp. 144–55; cf. J.F. O'Callaghan, *The cortes of Castile-León, 1188–1350* (1989), 130–51, for the preceding period, and Wolff, 'The 1391 pogrom in Spain'.
25. See e.g. J. Edwards, *The Spain of the Catholic monarchs, 1474–1520* (2000), esp. 38–141. For taxation, M.A. Ladero Quesada, *El siglo XV en Castilla* (1982), 58–113; and, for a long fifteenth century, the focused studies in D. Menjot and M. Sánchez Martínez, *Fiscalidad de estado y fiscalidad municipal en los reinos hispánicos medievales* (2006), which also cover Aragón.
26. See in general Bisson, *The medieval crown of Aragon*; for Eiximenis, Ll. Brines i Garcia, *La filosofia social i política de Francesc Eiximenis* (2004), esp. 130–5, 143–58.
27. Pryor, 'Foreign policy and economic policy', esp. 45–6.
28. Abulafia, *The western Mediterranean kingdoms*, gives a political account; convenient recent structural surveys which cite the Italian bibliography are F. Titone, 'The kingdom

of Sicily', (2012) and F. Senatore, 'The kingdom of Naples' (2012). For taxation, S. Morelli, 'Note sulla fiscalità diretta e indiretta nel regno angioino' (2011).

29. See now the remarkable collection of articles in A. Gamberini and I. Lazzarini, *The Italian Renaissance state* (2012), which cites all earlier material; earlier, the comparative articles in F. Salvestrini, *L'Italia alla fine del medioevo*, vol. 1 (2006), and the shorter surveys in J.M. Najemy, *Italy in the age of the Renaissance: 1300–1550* (2004), still stand out. For a monographic account, see I. Lazzarini, *L'Italia degli stati territoriali, secoli XIII–XV* (2003). For taxation, see P. Mainoni, *Politiche finanziarie e fiscali nell'Italia settentrionale (secoli XIII–XV)* (2001); M. Ginatempo, 'Finanze e fiscalità' (2006). For the Florentine *catasto*, D. Herlihy and C. Klapisch-Zuber, *Tuscans and their families* (1985), esp. 10–27.

30. See in general Scales, *The shaping of German identity*; Moraw, *Von offener Verfassung*, esp. 183–94; Isenmann, *Die deutsche Stadt im Spätmittelalter*; idem, 'The Holy Roman Empire in the middle ages' (1999) for taxes. I have learned much here from unpublished work by Duncan Hardy. For the name of the empire in 1474, J. Whaley, *Germany and the Holy Roman Empire*, vol. 1 (2012), 17.

31. For a general guide to Bohemian history, see the ageing F. Seibt, 'Die Zeit der Luxemburger und der hussitischen Revolution' (1967). For the Hussites to 1436, see Ch. 12 n. 27.

32. R. Sablonier, 'The Swiss confederation' (1998); Scott, *The city-state*, 164–92; G.P. Marchal, *Sempach 1386* (1986) (a local study of Luzern); idem, 'Die Antwort der Bauern' (1987); for the effect of the Swiss on others, T.A. Brady, *Turning Swiss* (1985).

33. See in general the able synthesis of W. Blockmans and W. Prevenier, *The promised lands* (1999); for finances, M. Mollat, 'Recherches sur les finances des ducs valois de Bourgogne' (1958) and W. Blockmans, 'The Low Countries in the middle ages' (1999).

34. Engel, *The realm of St Stephen*, provides a convenient recent narrative account. For taxation, Ormrod and Barta, 'The feudal structure', 76–9; Barta and Barta, 'Royal finance'.

35. For Lithuania to 1345, S.C. Rowell, *Lithuania ascending* (1994); for the rapidity of its fifteenth-century conversion, D. Baronas and S.C. Rowell, *The conversion of Lithuania* (2015). For Poland, N. Nowakowska, *Church, state and dynasty in Renaissance Poland* (2007), 11–36, 65–7, discusses Kazimierz IV; for a narrative, R. Frost, *The making of the Polish–Lithuanian union, 1385–1569* (2015), 267–76, 286–90, 354–73 – this book is now also an initial guide to fifteenth-century Lithuanian politics. For taxation, e.g. J. Bardach, 'La formation des Assemblées polonaises au XVe siècle et la taxation' (1977).

36. See as a good recent guide to this the articles in Helle, *Cambridge history of Scandinavia*, vol. 1, 581–770; for peasant uprisings, K. Katajala, 'Against tithes and taxes, for king and province' (2004), 39–49.

37. This again follows Watts, *The making of polities*, to whose insights this chapter has owed much.

12. Rethinking politics, 1350–1500

1. Respectively, T. Wright, *Political poems and songs relating to English history, composed during the period from the accession of EDW. III to that of RIC. III* (1861), vol. 2, 157–205 (this collection contains many similar vernacular texts reacting to specific events or arguing for specific political changes); J.P. Gilson, 'A defence of the proscription of the Yorkists in 1459' (1911); M. Bateson, *George Ashby's poems* (1899), 12–41 (at 19, 24–6, 33, 40); Sir John Fortescue, *On the laws and governance of England* (1997), 92–3, 100–14. Cf. G.A. Holmes, 'The "libel of English policy"' (1961), for the first; M. Kekewich, 'The attainder of the Yorkists in 1459' (1982), for the second. See Watts, *Henry VI*, esp. 39–51, idem, 'The pressure of the public on later medieval politics' (2004), and idem, 'Ideas, principles and politics' (1995); and A. Pollard, 'The people, politics and the constitution in the fifteenth century' (2013), for the general issues.

2. Watts, 'Ideas, principles', 110 (and 92–3 for Suffolk's death); for Cade, I.M.W. Harvey, *Jack Cade's rebellion of 1450* (1991) (quote from 190). Suffolk's death was acclaimed in a sharply ironical vernacular poem: Wright, *Political poems*, vol. 2, 232–4. For popular bill-posting, see W. Scase, ' "Strange and wonderful bills" ' (1998).

3. F. Šmahel, *Die hussitische Revolution* (2002), e.g. 1735–81; Bartolo, *Tractatus de tyranno*, in D. Quaglioni, *Politica e diritto nel Trecento Italiano* (1983), 175–213, quote at 199; N. Machiavelli, *De principatibus* (1994), c. 17.

4. Giles: see M.S. Kempshall, *The common good in late medieval political thought* (1999), 130–55. For the others, J.H. Burns, *The Cambridge history of medieval political thought, c. 350–c. 1450* (1988), and A. Black, *Political thought in Europe, 1250–1450* (1992), provide introductions. J. Dunbabin, 'Government', in Burns, op. cit., 477–519, is the closest to the argument here.

5. For a survey of their structural differences, see W.P. Blockmans, 'A typology of representative institutions in late medieval Europe' (1978); see also idem, 'Representation (since the thirteenth century)' (1998); for France and England, C. Fletcher, 'Political representation' (2015), 217–39. For an important comparative analysis of the habitus of parliaments in western Europe, see M. Hébert, *Parlementer* (2014).

6. See Bartlett, *England*, 143–59. In more detail, Maddicott, *The origins*, is the best guide to kingdom-level assemblies, although more continuist than the argument here; for shire and hundred, F. Pollock and F.W. Maitland, *The history of English law before the time of Edward I* (1898), vol. 1, 532–60.

7. Bisson, *The medieval crown of Aragon*, 76–81; Maddicott, *The origins*, 204–5, 299–300, 316–20, for England; and, more generally, Hébert, *Parlementer*, 175–84.

8. See in general e.g. H.R. Oliva Herrer et al., *La comunidad medieval como esfera pública* (2014); A. Gamberini et al., *The languages of political society* (2011). For the Burgundian lands, J. Dumolyn, 'Justice, equity and the common good' (2006). It should be added that the image of the collective power of the people, at least of Constantinople, in the *res publica* or *politeia* had already been a feature of the eleventh-century (and earlier) Byzantine empire: Kaldellis, *The Byzantine republic*, esp. 89–164.

9. G. Dodd, *Justice and grace* (2007), 207–11 (peasants), 266–78 (towns). Most such petitions were made by the relatively prosperous, however.

10. Cr. Taylor, 'War, propaganda and diplomacy in medieval France and England' (2000) (for texts with a restricted circulation); J.A. Doig, 'Political propaganda and royal proclamations in late medieval England' (1998); and, for Italy (starting there already in the thirteenth century), P. Cammarosano, *Le forme della propaganda politica nel Due e nel Trecento* (1994), even if not all the examples studied here were really for a wider public of any kind.

11. See Reynolds, *Kingdoms and communities*, for the interrelationship between them, at least up to 1300.

12. See for example P. Lantschner, *The logic of political conflict in medieval cities* (2015).

13. See, traditionally, F. Lot and R. Fawtier, *Histoire des institutions françaises au moyen âge*, (1958), vol. 2, 201–85, 472–508; see further Lewis, *Later medieval France*, 245–64, 328–74 and idem, 'The failure of the French medieval estates' (1962), for towns and assemblies.

14. J. Valdeón Baruque, *Los conflictos sociales en el reino de Castilla en los siglos XIV y XV* (1975), 65–81, 192–200; E. Fuentes Ganzo, 'Pactismo, cortes y hermandades en Léon y Castilla' (2008): their high point was the early fourteenth century, but the idea of the brotherhood inspired and structured peasant and urban revolts from then onwards (see, for fifteenth-century Galicia, C. Barros, *Mentalidad justiciera de los irmandiños, siglo XV* (1990)).

15. See in general for Basel, A. Black, *Council and commune* (1979); for Nicholas of Cusa, M. Watanabe, *The political ideas of Nicholas of Cusa* (1963). For the stronger monarchies of the next period, see Watts, *The making of polities*, 339–419.

16. M. Ryan, 'Bartolus of Sassoferrato and free cities' (2000); J. Canning, *The political thought of Baldus de Ubaldis* (1987). For the quote, Jacques de Révigny, *Lectura in digestum vetus in proemio*, cited in E.M. Meijers, *Études d'histoire du droit* (1959), vol. 3, 9 (cf. 59–80 for the author's writings in general).

17. For Catalonia and Poland, see Ll. Sales i Favà, 'Suing in a local jurisdictional court in late medieval Catalonia' (2014), and P. Guzowski, 'Village court records and peasant credit in fifteenth- and sixteenth-century Poland' (2014). Other major studies include C. Gauvard, '*De grace especial*' (1991); Vallerani, *Medieval public justice*. Credit: Briggs, *Credit*.

18. P. Contamine, *War in the middle ages* (1984), 137–72.

19. Dante, *Monarchia*. See for example J. Canning, *Ideas of power in the late middle ages, 1296–1417* (2011), 60–80.

20. For a brief but dense account, see N. Mann, *Petrarch* (1984). V. Kirkham, 'Petrarch the courtier' (2009) is a good discussion of his political role, in a book which gives an equally good survey of his range.

21. Out of the vast bibliography, books I find particularly helpful include L. Martines, *The social world of the Florentine humanists, 1390–1460* (1963); J. Hankins, *Renaissance civic humanism* (2000); G. Ruggiero, *The Renaissance in Italy* (2015); N.S. Baker and B.J. Maxson, *After civic humanism* (2015); O. Margolis, *The politics of culture in Quattrocento Europe* (2016). A guide to the often rather enclosed Anglo-American historiography is M. Jurdjevic, 'Hedgehogs and foxes' (2007).

22. See as a still-useful basic account J. Gadol, *Leon Battista Alberti* (1969); for Pienza, C.R. Mack, *Pienza* (1987).

23. D. Hobbins, *Authorship and publicity before print* (2009); idem, 'The schoolman as public intellectual' (2003).

24. S.E. Lahey, *John Wyclif* (2009); A. Hudson and A. Kenny, 'Wyclif, John (d. 1384)' (2004).

25. For Lollards, see in general A. Hudson, *The premature Reformation* (1980). J.P. Hornbeck, *What is a Lollard?* (2010), clearly shows the range of Lollard views; for the later Lollards, S. McSheffrey, 'Heresy, orthodoxy and English vernacular religion, 1480–1525' (2005) is important. For reactions to them, I. Forrest, *The detection of heresy in late medieval England* (2005).

26. For a recent English-language biography, see T.A. Fudge, *Jan Hus* (2010).

27. H. Kaminsky, *A history of the Hussite revolution* (1967), T.A. Fudge, *The magnificent ride* (1998), J. Klassen, 'Hus, the Hussites and Bohemia' (1998), and above all the enormous Šmahel, *Die hussitische Revolution*, sum up the Czech historiography at the back of this paragraph and the next.

28. Cohn, *Lust for liberty* (228 for the figures).

29. Freedman, *The origins of peasant servitude*, 179–202, for the Remences; idem, *Images of the medieval peasant*, 190–203 (and above, Ch. 11) for Dithmarschen and Switzerland; O.J. Schmitt, 'Les hommes et le pouvoir' (2011), for Korčula in Croatia.

30. There is a huge bibliography here too. Some classics are R.H. Hilton, *Bond men made free* (1973); R.H. Hilton and T.H. Aston, *The English rising of 1381* (1984); Justice, *Writing and rebellion*; and, for peasant organisation, N.P. Brooks, 'The organization and achievements of the peasants of Kent and Essex in 1381' (1985).

31. See in general Cohn, *Lust for liberty*, supplemented by his *Creating the Florentine state* (1999), for the Florentine revolts around 1400, and his source-book, *Popular protest in late medieval Europe* (2004). For the Jacquerie, J. Firnhaber-Baker, 'The eponymous Jacquerie' (2016). For Flanders, Dumolyn and Haemers, 'Patterns of urban rebellion'; iidem, '"A bad chicken was brooding"' (2012). For France and England, V. Challet and I. Forrest, 'The masses' (2015). For revolts as transactional elements in urban politics in Flanders and Italy, Lantschner, *The logic of political conflict*. For early medieval revolts, Wickham, 'Space and society'. The new starting point is J. Firnhaber-Baker, *The Routledge history handbook of medieval revolt* (2016).

32. As is stressed in the recent work cited in the previous note, and Pollard, 'The people'.

13. Conclusion

1. See e.g. C. Anderson, *Renaissance architecture* (2013), 106–8; E. Karpova Fasce, 'Gli architetti italiani a Mosca nei secoli XIV–XV' (2004).
2. E. Albèri, *Le relazioni degli ambasciatori veneti al senato* (1839), 3–26, at 16; C.V. Malfatti, *Two Italian accounts of Tudor England* (1953), 36, 40 (Malfatti did not know that the author, Andrea de' Franceschi, was a standard Venetian ambassador). Thanks to Isabella Lazzarini for these references.

Bibliography

Abbreviations

EME *Early medieval Europe*
MGH *Monumenta Germaniae historica* (note that all the *MGH* series are available online at www.dmgh.de)
NCMH *The new Cambridge medieval history*, 7 vols (Cambridge, 1995–2005)

Abrams, L., 'Diaspora and identity in the Viking age', *EME*, 20 (2012), 17–38
—— 'Germanic Christianities', in T.F.X. Noble and J.M.H. Smith (eds), *The Cambridge history of Christianity*, vol. 3 (Cambridge, 2008), 107–29
Abu Lughod, J.L., *Before European hegemony* (Oxford, 1989)
Abulafia, D., *Frederick II* (London, 1988)
—— *The great sea* (London, 2011)
—— *The two Italies* (Cambridge, 1977)
—— *The western Mediterranean kingdoms, 1200–1500* (Harlow, 1997)
Acién Almansa, M., 'El final de los elementos feudales en al-Andalus', in M. Barceló and P. Toubert (eds), *L'incastellamento* (Rome, 1998), 291–305
—— *Entre el feudalismo y el Islam*, 2nd edn (Jaén, 1997)
Ahrweiler, H., *Byzance et la mer* (Paris, 1966)
Airlie, S., *Power and its problems in Carolingian Europe* (Farnham, 2012)
—— 'Private bodies and the body politic in the divorce case of Lothar II', *Past and present*, 161 (1998), 3–38
—— 'Talking heads', in P.S. Barnwell and M. Mostert (eds), *Political assemblies in the earlier middle ages* (Turnhout, 2003), 29–46
—— 'The aristocracy', *NCMH*, vol. 2 (1995), 431–50
—— 'The palace of memory', in S. Rees Jones et al. (eds), *Courts and regions in medieval Europe* (York, 2000), 1–19
Airlie, S. et al. (eds), *Staat im frühen Mittelalter* (Vienna, 2006)
Albèri, E., *Le relazioni degli ambasciatori veneti al senato* (Florence, 1839)
Albertoni, G., *L'Italia carolingia* (Rome, 1997)
—— *Vassalli, feudi, feudalesimo* (Rome, 2015)
Alfonso, I., 'Desheredamiento y desafuero, o la pretendida justificación de una revuelta nobiliaria', *Cahiers de linguistique et de civilisation hispaniques médiévales*, 25 (2002), 99–129
Algazi, G., 'Lords ask, peasants answer', in G. Sider and G. Smith (eds), *Between history and histories* (Toronto, 1997), 199–229
Allmand, C., *The Hundred Years War*, revised edn (Cambridge, 2001)
Althoff, G., *Family, friends and followers* (Cambridge, 2004)
Althoff, G., 'Ira regis', in B.H. Rosenwein (ed.), *Anger's past* (Ithaca, NY, 1998), 59–74

—— *Spielregeln der Politik im Mittelalter* (Darmstadt, 1997)

Althoff, G. and H. Keller, *Heinrich I. und Otto der Grosse*, 2 vols (Göttingen, 1994)

Álvarez Borge, I., *Clientelismo regio y acción política* (Murcia, 2014)

—— *La plena edad media: siglos XII–XIII* (Madrid, 2003)

—— 'Soldadas, situados y fisco regio en el reinado de Alfonso VIII de Castilla (1158–1214)', *Journal of Medieval Iberian Studies*, 7 (2015), 57–86

Amari, M. (ed.), *I diplomi arabi del R. Archivio fiorentino* (Florence, 1863)

Amory, P., *People and identity in Ostrogothic Italy, 489–554* (Cambridge, 1997)

Anderson, C., *Renaissance architecture* (Oxford, 2013)

Andreas aulae regiae capellanus, *De amore*, ed. E. Trojel (Berlin, 2006); trans. J.J. Parry, *The art of courtly love by Andreas Capellanus* (New York, 1941)

Andrews, F., 'Living like the laity?', *Transactions of the Royal Historical Society*, 6 ser. 20 (2010), 27–55

—— *The early Humiliati* (Cambridge, 1999)

Angold, M., *The Byzantine empire, 1025–1204* (London, 1984)

—— *The Fourth Crusade* (Harlow, 2003)

—— (ed.), *The Byzantine aristocracy, IX to XIII centuries* (Oxford, 1984)

Annales Fuldenses, ed. F. Kurze, *MGH, Scriptores rerum Germanicarum*, vol. 7 (Hannover, 1891), trans. T. Reuter, *The Annals of Fulda* (Manchester, 1992)

Annali genovesi di Caffaro e de' suoi continuatori, vol. 2, ed. L.T. Belgrano and C. Imperiale di Sant'Angelo (Rome, 1901)

Anonymus Valesianus, pars posterior, ed. and trans. in J.C. Rolfe, *Ammianus Marcellinus*, vol. 3 (Cambridge, MA, 1964), 530–69

Archer, R.E., 'Chaucer, Alice, duchess of Suffolk (c.1404–1475)', *Oxford dictionary of national biography* (Oxford, 2004)

Ardizzone, F., 'Rapporti commerciali tra la Sicilia occidentale ed il Tirreno centro-meridionale alla luce del rinvenimento di alcuni contenitori di trasporto', in G.P. Brogiolo (ed.), *II Congresso nazionale di archeologia medievale* (Florence, 2000), 402–7

Arnade, P., *Realms of ritual* (Ithaca, NY, 1996)

Arnold, B., *German knighthood, 1050–1300* (Oxford, 1985)

—— *Princes and territories in medieval Germany* (Cambridge, 1991)

Arnold, J.H., *Belief and unbelief in medieval Europe* (London, 2005)

—— *Inquisition and power* (Philadelphia, 2001)

—— 'The Cathar middle ages as an historiographical problem', in D. d'Avray and A. Sennis (eds), *Catharism* (in press)

—— *What is medieval history?* (Cambridge, 2008)

Arnold, J.H. and K.J. Lewis, *A companion to the book of Margery Kempe* (Cambridge, 2004)

Ashtiany, J. et al. (eds), *'Abbasid belles-lettres* (Cambridge, 1990)

Ausenda, G. et al. (eds), *The Langobards before the Frankish conquest* (Woodbridge, 2009)

Avellini, L., 'Artigianato in versi del secondo Quattrocento fiorentino', in G.-M. Anselmi et al., *La 'memoria' dei mercatores* (Bologna, 1980), 153–229

Axboe, M., 'Danish kings and dendrochronology', in G. Ausenda (ed.), *After empire* (Woodbridge, 1995), 217–51

Bagge, S., 'Borgerkrig og statsutvikling i Norge i middelalderen', *Historisk Tidsskrift* (Oslo), 2 (1986), 145–97

—— *From Viking stronghold to Christian kingdom* (Copenhagen, 2010)

—— 'The Europeanization of Europe', in Noble and Van Engen, *European transformations*, 171–93

Bagge, S. and S.W. Nordeide, 'The kingdom of Norway', in Berend, *Christianization*, 121–66

Baker, N.S. and B.J. Maxson (eds), *After civic humanism* (Toronto, 2015)

Baldwin, J.W., *The government of Philip Augustus* (Berkeley, 1986)

Balestracci. D., *La zappa e la retorica* (Florence, 1984)

Barber, C., *Figure and likeness* (Princeton, 2002)

Barber, M., *The Crusader states* (New Haven, 2012)
—— *The two cities*, 2nd edn (London, 2004)
Bardach, J., 'La formation des Assemblées polonaises au XVe siècle et la taxation', *Anciens pays et assemblées d'états: Standen en landen*, 70 (1977), 251–96
Bardsley, S., *Venomous tongues* (Philadelphia, 2006)
Barford, P.M., *The early Slavs* (London, 2001)
Barnish, S., 'Taxation, land and barbarian settlement in the western empire', *Papers of the British School at Rome*, 54 (1986), 170–95
Barnwell, P.S., *Kings, courtiers and imperium* (London, 1997)
Baronas, D. and S.C. Rowell, *The conversion of Lithuania* (Vilnius, 2015)
Barratt, N., 'The revenues of John and Philip Augustus revisited', in S.D. Church (ed.), *King John: new interpretations* (Woodbridge, 1999), 75–99
Barron, W.R.J. (ed.), *The Arthur of the English* (Cardiff, 2001)
Barros, C., *Mentalidad justiciera de los irmandiños, siglo XV* (Madrid, 1990)
Barrow, J., *The clergy in the medieval world* (Cambridge, 2015)
Barta, G. and J. Barta, 'Royal finance in medieval Hungary', in W.M. Ormrod et al. (eds), *Crises, revolutions and self-sustained growth* (Stamford, 1999), 22–37
Barthélemy, D., *La mutation de l'an mil a-t-elle eu lieu?* (Paris, 1997)
—— *L'an mil et la paix de Dieu* (Paris, 1999)
—— *Nouvelle histoire des Capétiens, 987–1214* (Paris, 2012)
—— *The serf, the knight, and the historian* (Ithaca, NY, 2009)
Bartlett, R., *England under the Norman and Angevin kings, 1075–1225* (Oxford, 2000)
—— 'From paganism to Christianity', in Berend, *Christianization*, 47–72
—— *The making of Europe* (London, 1993)
—— *Trial by fire and water* (Oxford, 1986)
Barton, R.E., *Lordship in the county of Maine, c.890–1160* (Woodbridge, 2004)
Barton, S., 'Spain in the eleventh century', *NCMH*, vol. 4.2 (2004), 154–90
—— *The aristocracy in twelfth-century León and Castile* (Cambridge, 1997)
Bartoš, F.M., *The Hussite revolution, 1424–1437* (Boulder, CO, 1986)
Bartusis, M.C., *Land and privilege in Byzantium* (Cambridge, 2012)
Bassett, S., 'Divide and rule?', *EME*, 15 (2007), 53–85
—— (ed.), *The origins of Anglo-Saxon kingdoms* (Leicester, 1989)
Bates, D., *Normandy before 1066* (London, 1982)
Bateson, M., *George Ashby's poems* (London, 1899)
Beaton, R., 'The rhetoric of poverty', *Byzantine and Modern Greek studies*, 11 (1987), 1–28
Becher, M., *Eid und Herrschaft* (Sigmaringen, 1993)
Becher, M. and Jarnut, J. (eds), *Der Dynastiewechsel von 751* (Münster, 2004)
Becker, A., *Papst Urban II. (1088–1099)*, 3 vols (Stuttgart-Hannover, 1964–2012)
Beech, G. et al. (eds), *Le Conventum (vers 1030)* (Geneva, 1995)
Bell, A.R. et al., *The soldier in later medieval England* (Oxford, 2013)
Bennett, J M., *Ale, beer, and brewsters in England* (Oxford, 1996)
—— *History matters* (Manchester, 2006)
Bennett, J., *Medieval women in modern perspective* (Washington, DC, 2000)
Bennett, J.M. and R.M. Karras (eds), *The Oxford handbook of women and gender in medieval Europe* (Oxford, 2013)
Berend, N. (ed.), *Christianization and the rise of Christian monarchy* (Cambridge, 2007)
Berend, N., P. Urbańczyk and P. Wiszewski, *Central Europe in the high middle ages* (Cambridge, 2013)
Bergengruen, A., *Adel und Grundherrschaft im Merowingerreich* (Wiesbaden, 1958)
Bernheimer, T., *The 'Alids* (Edinburgh, 2014)
Biller, P., 'Goodbye to Waldensianism?', *Past and present*, 192 (2006), 3–33
—— review of R.I. Moore, *The war on heresy: faith and power in medieval Europe*, with Moore's reply, *Reviews in history*, review no. 1546 (2014), http://www.history.ac.uk/reviews/review/1546, accessed 4 January 2015

Billoré, M. and M. Soria (eds), *La rumeur au moyen âge* (Rennes, 2011)

'Birmingham Quran manuscript', https://en.wikipedia.org/wiki/Birmingham_Quran_manuscript, accessed 25 October 2015

Birrell, J., 'Manorial custumals reconsidered', *Past and present*, 224 (2014), 3–37

—— 'Peasants eating and drinking', *The agricultural history review*, 63 (2015), 1–18

Bisson, T.N., *The crisis of the twelfth century* (Princeton, 2009)

—— 'The "feudal revolution"', *Past and present*, 142 (1994), 6–42; with the debate which followed it in *Past and present*, 152 (1996), 196–223; 155 (1997), 177–225

—— *The medieval crown of Aragon* (Oxford, 1991)

—— *Tormented voices* (Cambridge, MA, 1998)

Bitel, L.M., *Women in early medieval Europe, 400–1000* (Cambridge, 2002)

Black, A., *Council and commune* (London, 1979)

—— *Political thought in Europe, 1250–1450* (Cambridge, 1992)

Blair, J., 'Small towns 600–1270', in Palliser, *The Cambridge urban history*, 245–70

—— *The Church in Anglo-Saxon society* (Oxford, 2005)

Bloch, M., *La société féodale*, 2 vols (Paris, 1940), trans. L.A. Manyon, *Feudal society* (London, 1961)

Blockmans, W. P., 'A typology of representative institutions in late medieval Europe', *Journal of medieval history*, 4 (1978), 189–215

—— 'Representation (since the thirteenth century)', *NCMH*, vol. 7 (1998), 29–64

—— 'The Low Countries in the middle ages', in Bonney, *The rise of the fiscal state*, 281–308

Blockmans, W. and W. Prevenier, *The promised lands* (Philadelphia, 1999)

Boccaccio, G., *Decamerone*, ed. V. Branca, *Tutte le opere di Giovanni Boccaccio*, vol. 4 (Milan, 1976), trans. G. Waldman, *The Decameron* (Oxford, 1993)

Bogucki, M., 'On Wulfstan's right hand', in S. Gelichi and R. Hodges (eds), *From one sea to another* (Turnhout, 2013), 81–110

Bois, G., *The crisis of feudalism* (Cambridge, 1984)

Bonnassie, P., *La Catalogne du milieu du Xᵉ à la fin du XIᵉ siècle* (Toulouse, 1975–76)

Bonney, R. (ed.), *Economic systems and state finance* (Oxford, 1995)

—— (ed.), *The rise of the fiscal state in Europe, c.1200–1815* (Oxford, 1999)

Borsch, S.J., *The Black Death in Egypt and England* (Austin, TX, 2005)

Boswell, J., *Christianity, social tolerance and homosexuality* (Chicago, 1981)

Bosworth, C.E., 'Muṣādara', in P.J. Bearman et al. (eds), *Encyclopedia of Islam*, 2nd electronic edn (Leiden, 2002–), http://referenceworks.brillonline.com/entries/encyclopaedia-of-islam-2/mus-a-dara-COM_0804?s.num=0&s.f.s2_parent=s.f.book.encyclopaedia-of-islam-2&s.q—usadara, accessed 2 January 2015

Bouchard, C.B., *'Those of my blood': constructing noble families in medieval Francia* (Philadelphia, 2001)

Bougard, F., 'La cour et le gouvernement de Louis II (840–875)', in R. Le Jan (ed.), *Le royauté et les élites dans l'Europe carolingienne* (Lille, 1998), 249–67

Bourin, M. and R. Durand, *Vivre au village au moyen âge* (Paris, 1984)

Bourin, M. and P. Martínez Sopena (eds), *Pour une anthropologie du prélèvement seigneurial dans les campagnes médiévales (XIe–XIVe siècles)*, 2 vols (Paris, 2004–07)

Bourin, M., F. Menant and L. To Figueras, 'Les campagnes européennes avant la peste', in iidem (eds), *Dynamiques du monde rural dans la conjoncture de 1300* (Rome, 2014), 9–101

Boyle, L.E., 'Montaillou revisited', in J.A. Raftis (ed.), *Pathways to medieval peasants* (Toronto, 1981), 119–40

Brady, T.A., *Turning Swiss* (Cambridge, 1985)

Brand, C.M., *Byzantium confronts the west, 1180–1204* (Cambridge, MA, 1968)

Brandes, W., *Finanzverwaltung in Krisenzeiten* (Frankfurt, 2002)

Bredero, A., *Bernard of Clairvaux* (Edinburgh, 1996)

Brenner, R., 'Agrarian class structure and economic development in pre-industrial Europe', *Past and present*, 70 (1976), 30–75

Brennu-Njáls saga, ed. Einar Ó. Sveinsson, *Íslenzk Fornrit*, vol. 12 (Reykjavík, 1954), trans. Magnús Magnússon and Hermann Pálsson, *Njal's saga* (London, 1960)

Brentano, R., *Two churches* (Berkeley, 1968)

Briggs, C., *Credit and village society in fourteenth-century England* (Oxford, 2009)

Brines i Garcia, Ll., *La filosofia social i política de Francesc Eiximenis* (Seville, 2004)

Britnell, R., *Britain and Ireland, 1050–1530: economy and society* (Oxford, 2004)

—— *The commercialisation of English society, 1100–1500*, 2nd edn (Manchester, 1996)

Broadberry, S. et al., *British economic growth, 1270–1870* (Cambridge, 2015)

Brogiolo, G.P. and A. Chavarría Arnau, *Aristocrazie e campagne nell'Occidente da Costantino a Carlo Magno* (Florence, 2005)

Bromwich, R. et al. (eds), *The Arthur of the Welsh* (Cardiff, 1991)

Brooks, N., *Communities and warfare, 700–1400* (London, 2000)

—— 'The organization and achievements of the peasants of Kent and Essex in 1381', in R.I. Moore and H. Mayr-Harting (eds), *Studies in medieval history presented to R.H.C. Davis* (London, 1985), 247–70

Brown, A. and G. Small, *Court and civic society in the Burgundian Low Countries c. 1420–1530* (Manchester, 2007)

Brown, E.A.R., 'The tyranny of a construct', *american historical review*, 79 (1974), 1063–88

Brown, M., *Disunited kingdoms* (Harlow, 2013)

Brown, P., *Power and persuasion in late antiquity* (Madison, WI, 1992)

—— *The cult of the saints* (Chicago, 1981)

—— 'The rise and function of the holy man in late antiquity', *Journal of Roman studies*, 61 (1971), 80–101

—— *The rise of western Christendom* (2nd edn, Oxford, 1997)

—— *Through the eye of a needle* (Princeton, 2012)

Brown, T.S., *Gentlemen and officers* (Rome, 1984)

Brown, W., *Unjust seizure* (Ithaca, NY, 2001)

Brown, W. et al. (eds), *Documentary culture and the laity in the early middle ages* (Cambridge, 2013)

Brown-Grant, R., *Christine de Pizan and the moral defence of women* (Cambridge, 2000)

Bruand, O., *Voyageurs et marchandises aux temps carolingiens* (Brussels, 2002)

Brubaker, L., *Inventing Byzantine iconoclasm* (London, 2012)

Brubaker, L. and J. Haldon, *Byzantium in the iconoclast era, c. 680–850* (Cambridge, 2011)

Brubaker, L. and J.M.H. Smith (eds), *Gender in the early medieval world* (Cambridge, 2004)

Brucker, G., *Giovanni and Lusanna* (London, 1986)

Brühl, C.R., *Fodrum, gistum, servitium regis* (Cologne, 1968)

Brunel, G. and O. Guillotjeannin (eds), 'Les préambules des chartes de franchises', in Bourin and Martínez Sopena, *Pour une anthropologie*, vol. 2, 161–309

Brunner, O., *Land and lordship* (Philadelphia, 1992)

Bruschi, C., 'Familia inquisitionis', *Mélanges de l'École française de Rome. Moyen âge*, 125 (2013), https://mefrm.revues.org/1519, accessed 15 November 2015

—— *The wandering heretics of Languedoc* (Cambridge, 2009)

Bruschi, C. and P. Biller (eds), *Texts and the repression of heresy* (Woodbridge, 2003)

Buc, P., *The dangers of ritual* (Princeton, 2001)

Buchberger, E., *Shifting ethnic identities in Spain and Gaul, 500–700* (Amsterdam, 2016)

Bührer-Thierry, G., 'La reine adultère', *Cahiers de civilisation médiévale*, 35 (1992), 299–312

Buko, A., 'Unknown revolution', in F. Curta (ed.), *East central and eastern Europe in the early middle ages* (Ann Arbor, MI, 2005), 162–78

Bull, M., *Knightly piety and the lay response to the First Crusade* (Oxford, 1993)

Bullough, D.A., '"Baiuli" in the Carolingian "regnum Langobardorum" and the career of Abbot Waldo (+813)', *English Historical Review*, 77 (1962), 625–37

Burns, J.H. (ed.), *The Cambridge history of medieval political thought, c. 350–c. 1450* (Cambridge, 1988)

Bynum, C.W., *Holy feast and holy fast* (Berkeley, 1987)

—— 'Women's stories, women's symbols', in eadem, *Fragmentation and redemption* (New York, 1992), 27–51

Byock, J., *Viking age Iceland* (London, 2001)

Byrne, F.J., *Irish kings and high-kings* (London, 1973)

Caciola, N., *Discerning spirits* (Ithaca, NY, 2003)

Caesar, M., *Dante: the critical heritage* (London, 1989)

Callow, C., 'Reconstructing the past in medieval Iceland', *EME*, 14 (2006), 297–324

Cameron, A., 'The construction of court ritual', in D. Cannadine and S. Price (eds), *Rituals of royalty* (Cambridge, 1987), 106–36

—— *The Mediterranean world in late antiquity, AD 395–600* (London, 1993)

Cammarosano, P., *Nobili e re* (Bari, 1998)

—— (ed.), *Le forme della propaganda politica nel Due e nel Trecento* (Rome, 1994)

Cammarosano, P. and S. Gasparri (eds), *Langobardia* (Udine, 1990)

Campbell, B.M.S., 'The agrarian problem in the early fourteenth century', *Past and present*, 188 (2005), 3–70

—— (ed.), *Before the Black Death* (Manchester, 1991)

Campbell, B.M.S. et al., *A medieval capital and its grain supply* (n. p., 1993)

Campbell, J., 'The late Anglo-Saxon state: a maximum view', *Proceedings of the British Academy*, 87 (1994), 39–65

—— (ed.), *The Anglo-Saxons* (Oxford, 1982)

Canning, J., *Ideas of power in the late middle ages, 1296–1417* (Cambridge, 2011)

—— *The political thought of Baldus de Ubaldis* (Cambridge, 1987)

Cantini, F., 'Ritmi e forme della grande espansione economica dei secoli XI–XIII nei contesti ceramici della Toscana settentrionale', *Archeologia medievale*, 37 (2010), 113–27

Cardon, D., *La draperie au moyen âge* (Paris, 1999)

Carocci, S., *Signorie di Mezzogiorno* (Rome, 2014)

—— (ed.), *La mobilità sociale nel medioevo* (Rome, 2010)

Carocci, S. and S.M. Collavini, 'Il costo degli stati', *Storica*, 52 (2011), 7–48; in English as 'The cost of states', in J. Hudson and A. Rodríguez (eds), *Diverging paths* (Leiden, 2014), 125–58

Caron, M.-T., *Noblesse et pouvoir royal en France, XIIIe–XVIe siècle* (Paris, 1994)

Carpenter, C., *The Wars of the Roses* (Cambridge, 1997)

Carpenter, D.A., *The reign of Henry III* (London, 1996)

Carpentier, É., *Une ville devant la peste* (Paris, 1962)

Carpentier, É. and M. Le Mené, *La France du XIe au XVe siècle* (Paris, 1996)

Carruthers, M., *The book of memory* (Cambridge, 1990)

Carus-Wilson, E.M., 'The first half-century of the borough of Stratford-upon-Avon', *Economic history review*, 18 (1965), 46–63

Castellanos, S., 'The political nature of taxation in Visigothic Spain', *EME*, 12 (2003), 201–28

Castellanos, S. and I. Martín Viso, 'The local articulation of central power in the north of the Iberian peninsula (500–1000)', *EME*, 13 (2005), 1–42

Castor, H., *Joan of Arc* (London, 2014)

Catto, J., 'Andrew Horn', in R.H.C. Davis and J.M. Wallace-Hadrill (eds), *The writing of history in the middle ages* (Oxford, 1981), 367–91

Cavell, E., 'Intelligence and intrigue in the March of Wales', *Historical research*, 88 (2015), 1–19

Cazelles, R., *Nouvelle histoire de Paris de la fin du règne de Philippe Auguste à la mort de Charles V (1223–1380)* (Paris, 1972)

Challet, V. and I. Forrest, 'The masses', in Fletcher et al. (eds), *Government*, 279–316

Chapelot, J. and R. Fossier, *The village and house in the middle ages*, trans. H. Cleere (Berkeley, 1985)

Charles-Edwards, T.M., *Early Christian Ireland* (Cambridge, 2000)

—— *Wales and the Britons, 350–1064* (Oxford, 2013)

Chazan, R., *The Jews of medieval western Christendom, 1000–1500* (Cambridge, 2006)
Cherubini, G. and R. Francovich, 'Forme e vicende degli insediamenti nella campagna toscana dei secoli XIII–XV', *Quaderni storici*, 24 (1973), 877–904
Cheynet, J.-C., 'Les Phocas', in *Le traité sur la guérilla*, 289–315
—— *Pouvoir et contestations à Byzance (963–1210)* (Paris, 1996)
Chibnall, M., *Anglo-Norman England, 1066–1166* (Oxford, 1986)
Chittolini, G. (ed.), *La crisi degli ordinamenti comunali e le origini dello stato del Rinascimento* (Bologna, 1979)
Choniates, N., *Historia*, trans. in H.J. Magoulias, *O city of Byzantium: annals of Niketas Choniates* (Detroit, 1984)
Christian, W.A., Jr., *Local religion in sixteenth-century Spain* (Princeton, 1981)
Christie, N., *From Constantine to Charlemagne* (Aldershot, 2006)
Christine de Pizan, *Le livre de la cité des dames*, ed. E.J. Richards, *La città delle dame* (Milan, 1997), trans. R. Brown-Grant, *The book of the city of ladies* (London, 1999)
Clanchy, M.T., *Abelard* (Oxford, 1997)
—— 'Did mothers teach their children to read?', in C. Leyser and L. Smith (eds), *Motherhood, religion and society in medieval Europe, 400–1400* (Farnham, 2011), 129–53
—— *England and its rulers, 1066–1307*, 3rd edn (Oxford, 2006)
—— *From memory to written record*, 3rd edn (Chichester, 2013)
Clarke, H., and B. Ambrosiani, *Towns in the Viking age*, 2nd edn (Leicester, 1995)
Claude, D., *Adel, Kirche und Königtum im Westgotenreich* (Sigmaringen, 1971)
Clay, J.-H., *In the shadow of death* (Turnhout, 2010),
Cohn, S.K., *Creating the Florentine state* (Cambridge, 1999)
—— *Lust for liberty* (Cambridge, MA, 2006)
—— *Popular protest in late medieval Europe* (Manchester, 2004)
—— 'The Black Death and the burning of Jews', *Past and present*, 196 (2007), 3–36
—— *The Black Death transformed* (London, 2002)
Colish, M., *Peter Lombard* (Leiden, 1994)
Collavini, S., '*Honorabilis domus et spetiosissimus comitatus*' (Pisa, 1998)
Collection haut moyen âge, directed by R. Le Jan (Turnhout, 2006–11): vol. 1, F. Bougard et al. (eds), *Les élites au haut moyen âge*; vol. 5, P. Depreux et al. (eds), *Les élites et leurs espaces*; vol. 6, F. Bougard et al. (eds), *Hiérarchie et stratification sociale dans l'Occident médiéval (400–1100)*; vol. 7, F. Bougard et al. (eds), *La culture au haut moyen âge*; vol. 10, J.-P. Devroey et al. (eds), *Les élites et la richesse au haut moyen âge*; vol. 13, F. Bougard et al. (eds), *Théories et pratiques des élites au haut moyen âge*
Collins, R., *Visigothic Spain 409–711* (Oxford, 2004)
Conant, J., *Staying Roman* (Cambridge, 2012)
Concilios visigóticos e hispano-romanos, ed. J. Vives (Barcelona, 1963)
Constable, G., 'Cluny in the monastic world of the tenth century', *Settimane di studio*, 38 (1991), 391–448
Constable, O.R., *Trade and traders in Muslim Spain* (Cambridge, 1994)
Constantin VII Porphyrogénète, *Le livre des cérémonies*, ed. and trans. A. Vogt (Paris, 1935–39)
Contamine, P., *War in the middle ages* (Oxford, 1984)
—— (ed.), *L'économie médiévale* (Paris, 1993)
Contreni, J.J., 'The Carolingian renaissance', *NCMH*, vol. 2 (1995), 709–57
Cortese, E., *Il diritto nella storia medievale*, 2 vols (Rome, 1995)
Cortese, M.E., *Signori, castelli, città* (Florence, 2007)
Cosgrove, A. (ed.), *A new history of Ireland*, vol. 2 (Oxford, 2008)
Coss, P., *The origins of the English gentry* (Cambridge, 2003)
Costambeys, M., *Power and patronage in early medieval Italy* (Cambridge, 2007)
Costambeys, M., M. Innes and S. MacLean, *The Carolingian world* (Cambridge, 2011)
Crescenzi, V., 'Il sindacato degli ufficiali nei comuni medievali italiani', in A. Giuliani and N. Picardi (eds), *L'educazione giuridica*, vol. 4.1 (Perugia, 1981), 383–529

Cressier, P. et al. (eds), *Los Almohades: problemas y perspectivas* (Madrid, 2005)
Crick, J. (ed.), *Charters of St Albans*, Anglo-Saxon charters, vol. 12 (Oxford. 2007)
Crone, P., *Medieval Islamic political thought* (Edinburgh, 2004)
—— *Slaves on horses* (Cambridge, 1980)
Crouch, D., *The birth of nobility* (London, 2005)
Crummey, R.O., *The formation of Muscovy, 1304–1613* (Harlow, 1987)
Cubitt, C., *Anglo-Saxon church councils, c.650–c.850* (Leicester, 1995)
—— 'The tenth-century Benedictine reform in England', *EME*, 6 (1997), 77–94
Curta, F., *Southeastern Europe in the middle ages, 500–1250* (Cambridge, 2006)
Cushing, K.G., *Reform and the papacy in the eleventh century* (Manchester, 2005)
d'Avray, D.L., *Papacy, monarchy and marriage, 860–1600* (Cambridge, 2015)
—— *The preaching of the friars* (Oxford, 1985)
Dagron, G., *Emperor and priest* (Cambridge, 2003)
Dain, A., 'Les stratégistes byzantins', *Travaux et mémoires*, 2 (1967), 317–92
Dal Santo, M., *Debating the saints' cult in the age of Gregory the Great* (Oxford, 2012)
Dante, *Monarchia*, ed. and trans. P. Shaw (Cambridge, 1995)
Davids, A. (ed.), *The empress Theophano* (Cambridge, 1995)
Davies, R., 'The medieval state', *Journal of historical sociology*, 16 (2003), 280–300
—— *The revolt of Owain Glyn Dŵr* (Oxford, 1995)
Davies, W., *Acts of giving* (Oxford, 2007)
—— *Small worlds* (London, 1988)
—— *Wales in the early middle ages* (Leicester, 1982)
Davis, J.R., *Charlemagne's practice of empire* (Cambridge, 2015)
Davis, N.Z., 'Les conteurs de Montaillou', *Annales ESC*, 34 (1979), 61–73
—— *The return of Martin Guerre* (Cambridge, MA, 1983)
de Jong, M., 'Bride shows revisited', in Brubaker and Smith, *Gender*, 257–77
—— 'Carolingian political discourse and the biblical past', in C. Gantner et al. (eds), *The resources of the past in early medieval Europe* (Cambridge, 2015), 87–102
—— 'The empire that was always decaying', *Medieval worlds*, 2015, no. 2, 6–25
—— *The penitential state* (Cambridge, 2009)
—— 'What was *public* about public penance?', *Settimane di studio*, 45 (1997), 863–904
de Oliveira Marques, A.H., *Portugal na crise dos séculos XIV e XV* (Lisbon, 1987)
Dean, T., *Crime in medieval Europe* (Harlow, 2001)
Decker, M., *Tilling the hateful earth* (Oxford, 2009)
Dejoux, M., 'Mener une enquête générale, pratiques et méthodes', in Pécout, *Quand gouverner c'est enquêter*, 133–55
Delogu, P., 'Il regno longobardo', in G. Galasso (ed.), *Storia d'Italia*, vol. 1 (Turin, 1980), 3–216
Delogu, P. and Gasparri, S. (eds), *Le trasformazioni del V secolo* (Turnhout, 2010)
Demandt, A., *Der Fall Roms*, 2nd edn (Munich, 2014)
—— *Die Spätantike* (Munich, 1989)
—— 'The osmosis of late Roman and Germanic aristocracies', in E.K. Chrysos and A. Schwarcz (eds), *Das Reich und die Barbaren* (Vienna, 1989), 75–86
Depreux, P., *Les sociétés occidentales du milieu du VIᵉ à la fin du IXᵉ siècle* (Rennes, 2002)
—— 'Lieux de rencontre, temps de négotiation', in R. Le Jan (ed.), *La royauté et les élites dans l'Europe carolingienne (début IXe siècle aux environs de 920)* (Lille 1998), 213–31
Déroche, V., 'La forme de l'informe', in P. Odorico and P. Agapitos (eds), *Les vies des saints à Byzance* (Paris, 2004), 367–85
Deshman, R., *The benedictional of Æthelwold* (Princeton, 1995)
Devroey, J.-P., *Économie rurale et société dans l'Europe franque (VIe–IXe siècles)* (Paris, 2003)
—— *Puissants et misérables* (Brussels, 2006)
Dhuoda, *Liber manualis*, ed. P. Riché, *Dhuoda: Manuel pour mon fils* (Paris, 1975), trans. C. Neel, *Handbook for William* (Lincoln, NE, 1999)

di Renzo Villata, M.G., 'La formazione dei «*Libri Feudorum*»', *Settimane di studio*, 47 (2000), 651–721

Dialogus de Scaccario, ed. and trans. E. Amt, *Constitutio domus regis*, ed. and trans. S.D. Church (Oxford, 2007)

Diario bolognese di Gaspare Nadi, ed. C. Ricci and A. Bacchi della Lega (Bologna, 1886)

Die Touler Vita Leos IX., ed. H.-G. Krause, *MGH, Scriptores rerum Germanicarum*, vol. 70 (Hannover, 2007), trans. I.S. Robinson, *The papal reform of the eleventh century* (Manchester, 2004), 97–157

Digenis Akritis, ed. and trans. E. Jeffreys (Cambridge, 1998)

Dodd, G., *Justice and grace* (Oxford, 2007)

Doig, J.A., 'Political propaganda and royal proclamations in late medieval England', *Historical research*, 71 (1998), 253–80.

Dölger, F., *Beiträge zur Geschichte der byzantinischen Finanzverwaltung, besonders des 10. und 11. Jahrhunderts* (Leipzig, 1927)

Dollinger, P., *The German Hansa* (London, 1964)

Dols, M.W., *The Black Death in the Middle East* (Princeton, 1977)

Donner, F., *Narratives of Islamic origins* (Princeton, 1998)

Dora Spadaro, M., *Raccomandazioni e consigli di un galantuomo* (Alessandria, 1998)

Dronke, P., *Women writers of the middle ages* (Cambridge, 1984)

du Colombier, P., *Les chantiers des cathédrales*, 2nd edn (Paris, 1973)

Dubin, N.E., *The fabliaux* (New York, 2013)

Duby, G., *La société aux XIe et XIIe siècles dans la région mâconnaise*, 2nd edn (Paris, 1971)

—— *Rural economy and country life in the medieval west* (Columbia, SC, 1968)

—— *The chivalrous society* (London, 1977)

—— *The early growth of the European economy* (London, 1974)

—— *The three orders* (Chicago, 1980)

—— 'Women and power', in T.N. Bisson (ed.), *Cultures of power* (Philadelphia, 1995), 68–85

Dumolyn, J., 'Justice, equity and the common good', in D'A.J.D. Boulton and J.R. Feenstra (eds), *The ideology of Burgundy* (Leiden, 2006), 1–20

Dumolyn, J. and J. Haemers, ' "A bad chicken was brooding" ', *Past and present*, 214 (2012), 45–86

—— 'Patterns of urban rebellion in medieval Flanders', *Journal of medieval history*, 31 (2005), 369–93

Dunbabin, J., *Charles I of Anjou* (Harlow, 1998)

—— *France in the making, 843–1180*, 2nd edn (Oxford, 2000)

Dupré Theseider, E., 'Caterina da Siena, santa', in *Dizionario biografico degli Italiani*, vol. 22 (Rome, 1979), 361–79

Durliat, J., 'La peste du VIᵉ siècle', in *Hommes et richesses dans l'empire byzantin*, vol. 1 (Paris, 1989), 107–19

Dutton, P.E., *The politics of dreaming in the Carolingian empire* (Lincoln, NE, 1994)

Dyer, C., *An age of transition?* (Oxford, 2005)

—— 'England's economy in the fifteenth century', *The fifteenth century*, 13 (2014), 201–25

—— 'How urbanized was medieval England?', in J.-M. Duvosquel and E. Thoen (eds), *Peasants and townsmen in medieval Europe* (Ghent, 1995), 169–83

—— *Making a living in the middle ages* (London, 2002)

—— 'Medieval Stratford', in R. Bearman (ed.), *The history of an English borough* (Stratford, 1997), 43–61, 181–5

—— *Standards of living in the later middle ages* (Cambridge, 1989)

Earenfight, T., *Queenship in medieval Europe* (Basingstoke, 2013)

Ebels-Hoving, B., *Byzantium in westerse ogen, 1096–1204* (Assen, 1971)

Edwards, J., 'Religious faith and doubt in late medieval Spain', *Past and present*, 120 (1988), 3–25

—— *The Spain of the Catholic monarchs, 1474–1520* (Oxford, 2000)

Einhard, *Vita Karoli Magni*, ed. G. Waitz, *MGH, Scriptores rerum Germanicarum*, vol. 25 (Hannover, 1911), trans. P.E. Duttom, *Charlemagne's courtier* (Peterborough, ON, 1998), 15–39

Ekonomou, A.J., *Byzantine Rome and the Greek popes* (Lanham, MD, 2007)

Eldevik, J., *Episcopal power and ecclesiastical reform in the German empire* (Cambridge, 2012)

Elliott, D., *Fallen bodies* (Philadelphia, 1999)

—— *Proving woman* (Princeton, 2004)

Elukin, J.M., *Living together, living apart* (Princeton, 2007)

Engel, P., *The realm of St Stephen* (London, 2001)

Ennen, E., *The medieval woman* (Oxford, 1989)

Epistolario di Santa Catarina da Siena, ed. E. Dupré Theseider, vol. 1 (Rome, 1940), trans. S. Noffke, *The letters of St. Catherine of Siena*, vol. 1 (Binghampton, NY, 1988)

Epstein, S.R., *An island for itself* (Cambridge, 1992)

—— *Freedom and growth* (London, 2000)

Esmonde Cleary, A.S., *The ending of Roman Britain* (London, 1989)

—— *The Roman west, AD 200–500* (Cambridge, 2013)

Estepa Díez, C., *Las behetrías castellanas*, 2 vols (Valladolid, 2003)

Faith, R., *The English peasantry and the growth of lordship* (Leicester, 1997)

Farmer, D.L., 'Prices and wages', in *The agrarian history of England and Wales*, vol. 2, ed. H.E. Hallam (Cambridge, 1988), 715–817

Fehring, G.P., *The archaeology of medieval Germany* (London, 1991)

Feller, L., *Les Abruzzes médiévales* (Rome, 1998)

—— *Paysans et seigneurs au Moyen Âge, VIIIᵉ–XVᵉ siècles* (Paris, 2007)

Feller, L. et al., *La fortune de Karol* (Rome, 2005)

Fenster, T. and D.L. Smail (eds), *Fama* (Ithaca, NY, 2003)

Ferruolo, S.C., *The origins of the university* (Stanford, 1985)

Fichtenau, H., *Living in the tenth century* (Chicago, 1991)

Fine, J.V.A., *The late medieval Balkans* (Ann Arbor, MI, 1987)

Fiore, A., 'From the diploma to the pact' (in press)

Firnhaber-Baker, J., 'The eponymous Jacquerie', in eadem, *The Routledge history handbook of medieval revolt*

—— (ed.), *The Routledge history handbook of medieval revolt* (London, 2016)

Fleckenstein, J., 'Über die Herkunft der Welfen und ihre Anfänge in Süddeutschland', in G. Tellenbach (ed.), *Studien und Vorarbeiten zur Geschichte des grossfränkischen und frühdeutschen Adels* (Freiburg, 1957), 71–136

Fleming, R., *Britain after Rome* (London, 2010)

—— *Kings and lords in conquest England* (Cambridge, 1991)

—— 'Recycling in Britain after the fall of Rome's metal economy', *Past and present*, 217 (2012), 3–45

Fletcher, C., 'Political representation', in idem et al., *Government*, 217–39

Fletcher, C. et al. (eds), *Government and political life in England and France, c.1300–c.1500* (Cambridge, 2015)

Fletcher, R., *The conversion of Europe* (London, 1997)

Flint, V.I.J., *The rise of magic in early medieval Europe* (Oxford, 1991)

Flori, J., *L'essor de la chevalerie, XIe–XIIe siècles* (Geneva, 1986)

Fögen, M.T., 'Reanimation of Roman law in the ninth century', in L. Brubaker (ed.), *Ninth-century Byzantium: dead or alive?* (Aldershot, 1998), 11–22

Foot, S. and C.F. Robinson (eds), *The Oxford history of historical writing*, vol. 2 (Oxford, 2012)

Forrest, I., *The detection of heresy in late medieval England* (Oxford, 2005)

Fortescue, Sir John, *On the laws and governance of England*, ed. S. Lockwood (Cambridge, 1997)

Fossier, R., *Enfance de l'Europe, Xe–XIIe siècles* (Paris, 1982)

Fouracre, P., 'Carolingian justice', *Settimane di studio*, 42 (1995), 771–803
—— *Frankish history* (Farnham, 2013)
—— 'Space, culture and kingdoms in early medieval Europe', in P. Linehan and J.L. Nelson (eds), *The medieval world* (London, 2001), 366–80
—— *The age of Charles Martel* (London, 2000)
Fournier, G., *Le château dans la France médiévale* (Paris, 1978)
France, J., *Western warfare in the age of the Crusades, 1000–1300* (Ithaca, NY, 1999)
Franceschi, F. and L. Molà, 'L'economia del Rinascimento', in M. Fantoni (ed.), *Il Rinascimento italiano e l'Europa*, vol. 1 (Treviso-Vicenza, 2006), 185–200
—— 'Regional states and economic development', in Gamberini and Lazzarini, *The Italian Renaissance state*, 444–66
Francovich, R. and M. Ginatempo (eds), *Castelli*, vol. 1 (Florence, 2000)
Franklin, S., *Writing, society and culture in early Rus, c.950–1300* (Cambridge, 2002)
Franklin, S. and J. Shepherd, *The emergence of Rus, 750–1200* (London, 1996)
Frankopan, P., *The First Crusade: the call from the east* (London, 2011)
Freedman, P., *Images of the medieval peasant* (Stanford, 1999)
—— *The origins of peasant servitude in medieval Catalonia* (Cambridge, 1991)
Freedman, P. and M. Bourin (eds), *Forms of servitude in northern and central Europe* (Turnhout, 2005)
Fried, J., *Die Ursprünge Deutschlands bis 1024* (Berlin, 1994)
—— '*Gens* und *regnum*', in J. Miethke and K. Schreiner (eds), *Sozialer Wandel im Mittelalter* (Sigmaringen, 1994), 73–104
Frost, R., *The making of the Polish-Lithuanian union, 1385–1569* (Oxford, 2015)
Fryde, E.B. and M.M. Fryde, 'Public credit, with special reference to north-western Europe', *The Cambridge economic history*, vol. 3, 430–553
Fudge, T.A., *Jan Hus* (London, 2010)
—— *The magnificent ride* (Aldershot, 1998)
Fuentes Ganzo, E., 'Pactismo, cortes y hermandades en Léon y Castilla: siglos XIII–XV', in F. Foronda and A.I. Carrasco Manchado (eds), *El contrato político en la Corona de Castilla* (Madrid, 2008), 415–52
Furió, A., *Història del país valencià* (Valencia, 1995)
Gadol, J., *Leon Battista Alberti* (Chicago, 1969)
Gamberini, A. and I. Lazzarini, *The Italian Renaissance state* (Cambridge, 2012)
Gamberini, A. et al. (eds), *The languages of political society* (Rome, 2011)
Ganshof, F.L., *The Carolingians and the Frankish monarchy* (London, 1971)
Ganz, D., 'The debate on predestination', in M.T. Gibson and J.L. Nelson, *Charles the Bald*, 2nd edn (Aldershot, 1990), 283–302
—— 'Theology and the organisation of thought', *NCMH*, vol. 2 (1995), 758–85
García de Cortázar, J.A., 'La formación de la sociedad feudal en el cuadrante noroccidental de la Península Ibérica en los siglos VIII a XIII', *Initium*, IV (1999), 57–121
Garzella, G., *Pisa com'era* (Naples, 1990)
Gasparri, S. (ed.), *774* (Turnhout, 2008)
Gasparri, S. and C. La Rocca (eds), *Carte di famiglia* (Rome, 2005)
Gauvard, C., '*De grace especial*': crime, état et société en France à la fin du Moyen Âge (Paris, 1991)
—— (ed.), *L'Enquête au moyen âge* (Rome, 2009)
Geary, P.J., *Aristocracy in Provence* (Stuttgart, 1985)
—— 'Ethnic identity as a situational construct in the early middle ages', *Mitteilungen des anthropologischen Gesellschaft in Wien*, 113 (1983), 15–26
—— *Living with the dead in the middle ages* (Ithaca, NY, 1994)
—— *Phantoms of remembrance* (Princeton, 1994)
—— *The myth of nations* (Princeton, 2002)
Gelichi, S. and R. Hodges (eds), *New directions in early medieval European archaeology* (Turnhout, 2015)

Geltner, G., *The making of medieval antifraternalism* (Oxford, 2012)

Geremek, B., *The margins of society in late medieval Paris* (Cambridge, 1987)

Ghosh, S., *Kings' sagas and Norwegian history* (Leiden, 2011)

Gilchrist, R., *Gender and material culture* (London, 1994)

Gillett, A. (ed.), *On barbarian identity* (Turnhout, 2002)

Gillis, M.B., 'Heresy in the flesh', in Stone and West, *Hincmar of Rheims*, 247–67

Gilson, J.P., 'A defence of the proscription of the Yorkists in 1459', *English historical review*, 26 (1911), 512–25

Ginatempo, M., 'Esisteva una fiscalità a finanziamento delle guerre del primo "200?"', in *XXXVII semana de estudios medievales* (Pamplona, 2011), 279–342

—— 'Finanze e fiscalità', in Salvestrini, *L'Italia*, vol. 1, 241–94

Ginatempo, M. and L. Sandri, *L'Italia delle città* (Florence, 1990)

Ginzburg, C., *The night battles* (London, 1983)

Glick, T.F., *From Muslim fortress to Christian castle* (Manchester, 1995)

Goetz, H.-W., 'Die Wahrnehmung von "Staat" und "Herrschaft" im frühen Mittelalter', in S. Airlie et al. (eds), *Staat im frühen Mittelalter* (Vienna, 2006), 39–58

—— '"Nobilis": der Adel im Selbstverständnis der Karolingerzeit', *Vierteljahrschrift für Sozial- und Wirtschaftsgeschichte*, 60 (1983), 153–91

Goetz, H.-W. et al. (eds), *Regna and gentes* (Leiden, 2003)

Goffart, W., *Barbarians and Romans, A.D. 418–584* (Princeton, 1980)

—— *The narrators of barbarian history (A.D. 550–800)* (Princeton, 1988)

Goitein, S.D., *A Mediterranean society* (Berkeley, 1967–93)

Goldberg, E.J., 'Louis the Pious and the hunt', *Speculum*, 88 (2013), 613–43

—— 'Popular revolt, dynastic politics and aristocratic factionalism in the early middle ages', *Speculum*, 70 (1995), 467–501

—— *Struggle for empire* (Cambridge, 2006)

Goldberg, J., *Trade and institutions in the medieval Mediterranean* (Cambridge, 2012)

Goldberg, P.J.P., *Women, work and life cycle in a medieval economy* (Oxford, 1992)

Goldthwaite, R.A., *The economy of Renaissance Florence* (Baltimore, 2009)

Göller, K.H., *König Arthur in der englischen Literatur des späten Mittelalters* (Göttingen, 1963)

Gonnet, G., 'Le cheminement des vaudois vers le schisme et l'hérésie (1174–1218)', *Cahiers de civilisation médiévale*, 19 (1976), 309–45

González Jiménez, M., *Alfonso X el Sabio* (Barcelona, 2004)

Goodman, A., *Margery Kempe and her world* (Harlow, 2002)

Goodson, C., *The Rome of Pope Paschal I* (Cambridge, 2010)

Górecki, P., *Economy, society, and lordship in medieval Poland, 1100–1250* (New York, 1992)

Gouma-Peterson, T. (ed.), *Anna Komnene and her times* (New York, 2000)

Gowers, B., '996 and all that', *EME*, 21 (2013), 71–98

Grant, A., *Independence and nationhood* (Edinburgh, 1984)

Gravdal, K., *Ravishing maidens* (Philadelphia, 1991)

Gray, P.T.R., *The defence of Chalcedon* (Leiden, 1979)

Greatrex, G. and S.N.C. Lieu, *The Roman eastern frontier and the Persian wars, part II* (London, 2002)

Green, J.A., *The government of England under Henry I* (Cambridge, 1986)

—— 'The last century of Danegeld', *English historical review*, 96 (1981), 241–58

Green, M.H., 'Women's medical practice and health care in medieval Europe', *Signs*, 14 (1989), 434–73

—— (ed.), *Pandemic disease in the medieval world*, 1 (2014), http://scholarworks.wmich.edu/medieval_globe/1/, accessed 7 April 2015

Green, W.A., 'Periodisation in European and world history', *Journal of world history*, 3 (1992), 13–53

Gregory of Tours, *Decem libri historiarum*, ed. B. Krusch and W. Levison, *MGH, Scriptores rerum Merovingicarum*, vol.1.1, 2nd edn (Hannover, 1951), trans. L. Thorpe, *The history of the Franks* (Harmondsworth, 1974)
—— *De virtutibus sancti Martini episcopi*, ed. B. Krusch, *MGH, Scriptores rerum Merovingicarum*, vol. 1.2 (Hannover, 1885), 584–661, trans. R. Van Dam, *Saints and their miracles in late antique Gaul* (Princeton, 1993), 200–303
Grillo, P., *Legnano 1176* (Bari, 2010)
—— *Milano in età comunale (1183–1276)* (Spoleto, 2001)
Grimm, P., *Tilleda*, 2 vols (Berlin, 1968–90)
Gunn, S. and A. Janse (eds), *The court as a stage* (Woodbridge, 2006)
Gurr, T.R., 'Historical trends in violent crime', *Crime and justice*, 3 (1981), 295–353
Guzowski, P., 'Village court records and peasant credit in fifteenth- and sixteenth-century Poland', *Continuity and change* 29 (2014), 115–42
Häberlein, M., *The Fuggers of Augsburg* (Charlottesville, VA, 2012)
Hadley, D.M. (ed.), *Masculinity in medieval Europe* (London, 1999)
Haldon, J., *A critical commentary on the Taktika of Leo VI* (Washington, DC, 2014)
—— 'Approaches to an alternative military history of the period ca. 1025–1071', in *Ē autokratoria se krisē* (Athens, 2003), 45–74
—— *Byzantium in the seventh century*, 2nd edn (Cambridge, 1997)
—— *Warfare, state and society in the Byzantine world, 565–1204* (London, 1999)
Halsall, G., *Barbarian migrations and the Roman west, 376–568* (Cambridge, 2007)
—— *Settlement and social organisation* (Cambridge, 1995)
—— 'Violence and society in the early medieval west', in idem (ed.), *Violence and society in the early medieval west* (Woodbridge, 1998), 1–45
—— *Warfare and society in the barbarian west, 450–900* (London, 2003)
Hamilton, S., *Church and people in the medieval west, 900–1200* (Harlow, 2013)
Hankins, J. (ed.), *Renaissance civic humanism* (Cambridge, 2000)
Harper, K., *Slavery in the late Roman world, AD 275–425* (Cambridge, 2011)
Harriss, G., *Shaping the nation: England, 1360–1461* (Oxford, 2005)
Harvey, A., *Economic expansion in the Byzantine empire, 900–1200* (Cambridge, 1989)
Harvey, I.M.W., *Jack Cade's rebellion of 1450* (Oxford, 1991)
Harvey, S., *Domesday* (Oxford, 2014)
Hatcher, J., *Plague, population and the English economy, 1348–1530* (London, 1977)
Hay, D., *Europe: The emergence of an idea*, 2nd edn (Edinburgh, 1968)
Head, T. and R. Landes, (eds), *The peace of God* (Ithaca, NY, 1992)
Heather, P., *The fall of the Roman empire* (London, 2005)
—— *The Goths* (Oxford, 1996)
—— 'The Huns and the end of the Roman empire in western Europe', *English historical review*, 110 (1995), 4–41
—— 'Theoderic, king of the Goths', *EME*, 4 (1995), 145–73
Hébert, M., *Parlementer: assemblées représentatives et échanges politiques en Europe occidentale à la fin du moyen âge* (Paris, 2014)
Heinzelmann, M., *Gregory of Tours* (Cambridge, 2001)
Helbig, H., *Der wettinische Ständestaat* (Münster, 1955)
Helle, K. (ed.), *The Cambridge history of Scandinavia*, vol. 1 (Cambridge, 2003)
—— 'The Norwegian kingdom', in idem (ed.), *The Cambridge history of Scandinavia*, vol. 1, 369–91
Hendy, M.F., *Studies in the Byzantine monetary economy, c.300–1450* (Cambridge, 1985)
Henneman, J.B., 'France in the middle ages', in Bonney, *The rise of the fiscal state*, 101–22
Herbert, M., *Iona, Kells and Derry* (Oxford, 1988)
Herlihy, D., *Opera muliebria* (New York, 1990)
Herlihy, D., and C. Klapisch-Zuber, *Tuscans and their families* (New Haven, 1985)
Hill, D. and M. Worthington (eds), *Æthelbald and Offa*, British archaeological reports, B383 (Oxford, 2005)

Hillenbrand, C., *The Crusades: Islamic perspectives* (Edinburgh, 1999)
Hilton, R.H., *English and French towns in feudal society* (Cambridge, 1995)
—— 'Freedom and villeinage in England', *Past and present*, 31 (1965), 3–19
—— *Bond men made free* (London, 1973)
Hilton, R.H. and T.H. Aston (eds), *The English rising of 1381* (Cambridge, 1984)
Hobbins, D., *Authorship and publicity before print* (Philadelphia, 2009)
—— 'The schoolman as public intellectual', *American historical review*, 108 (2003), 1308–35
Hodges, R., *Dark age economics*, 2nd edn (London, 2012)
Hodges, R. and D. Whitehouse, *Mohammed, Charlemagne and the origins of Europe* (London, 1983)
Holmes, C., *Basil II and the governance of empire (976–1025)* (Oxford, 2005)
Holmes, C. and N. Standen (eds) *The global middle ages* (Oxford, forthcoming)
Holmes, G.A., 'The "libel of English policy"', *English historical review*, 76 (1961), 193–216
Hornbeck, J.P., *What is a Lollard?* (Oxford, 2010)
Howard-Johnston, J., *Witnesses to a world crisis* (Oxford, 2010)
Howell, M.C., *The marriage exchange* (Chicago, 1998)
—— 'Women, the family economy, and the structures of market production in cities of northern Europe during the late middle ages', in B.A. Hanawalt (ed.), *Women and work in preindustrial Europe* (Bloomington, IN, 1986), 198–222
Hoyland, R., *Seeing Islam as others saw it* (Princeton, 1997)
Hudson, A., *The premature Reformation* (Oxford, 1988)
Hudson, A. and A. Kenny, 'Wyclif, John (d. 1384)', *Oxford dictionary of national biography* (Oxford, 2004)
Hudson, J., *The Oxford history of the laws of England: 871–1216* (Oxford, 2012)
Hunt, E.S., 'A new look at the dealings of the Bardi and Peruzzi with Edward III', *The journal of economic history*, 50 (1990), 149–62
Hyams, P.R., *King, lords and peasants* (Oxford, 1980)
Hybel, N. and B. Poulsen, *Danish resources c. 1000–1550* (Leiden, 2007)
Imber, C., *The Ottoman empire, 1300–1650* (Basingstoke, 2002)
İnalcık, H., 'The policy of Mehmed II towards the Greek population of Istanbul and the Byzantine buildings of the city', *Dumbarton Oaks papers*, 23/4 (1969–70), 229–49
Innes, M., *Introduction to early medieval western Europe, 300–900* (London, 2007)
—— *State and society in the early middle ages* (Cambridge, 2000)
Iogna-Prat, D. et al. (eds), *Cluny* (Rennes, 2013)
Irsigler, F., *Untersuchungen zur Geschichte des frühfränkischen Adels* (Bonn, 1969)
Isenmann, E., *Die deutsche Stadt im Spätmittelalter 1250–1500* (Stuttgart, 1988)
—— 'The Holy Roman Empire in the middle ages', in Bonney, *The rise of the fiscal state*, 243–80
Isla Frez, A., *La alta edad media* (Madrid, 2002)
Jaeger, C.S., *The envy of angels* (Philadelphia, 1994)
James, L., *Empresses and power in early Byzantium* (Leicester, 2001)
Jamroziak, E., *The Cistercian order in medieval Europe, 1090–1500* (Abingdon, 2013)
Jankowiak, M., 'Two systems of trade in the western Slavic lands in the 10th century', in M. Bogucki and M. Rębkowski (eds), *Economies, monetisation and society in the West Slavic lands, 800–1200 AD* (Szczecin, 2013), 137–48
Jarnut, J., *Agilolfingerstudien* (Stuttgart, 1986)
Jarrett, J., *Rulers and ruled in frontier Catalonia, 880–1010* (Woodbridge, 2010)
Jeffreys, E., *Four Byzantine novels* (Liverpool, 2012)
John Lydos, *On powers*, ed. and trans. A.C. Bandy, *Ioannes Lydus, On powers or The magistracies of the Roman state* (Philadelphia, 1983)
Johns, J., *Arabic administration in Norman Sicily* (Cambridge, 2002)
Joinville, Jean sire de, *Histoire de Saint Louis*, ed. N. de Wailly (Paris, 1868), trans. M.R.B. Shaw, *Joinville and Villehardouin* (London, 1963)
Jolliffe, J.E.A., *Angevin kingship* (London, 1955)

Jón Hnefill Aðalsteinsson, *Under the cloak* (Reykjavík, 1999)
Jón Viðar Sigurðsson, *Chieftains and power in the Icelandic commonwealth* (Odense, 1999)
Jones, A.H.M., *The later Roman empire, 284–602* (Oxford, 1964)
Jones, M.H. and R. Wisbey (eds), *Chrétien de Troyes and the German middle ages* (Woodbridge, 1993)
Jones, P.J., 'Florentine families and Florentine diaries in the fourteenth century', *Papers of the British School at Rome*, 24 (1956), 183–205
—— *The Italian city-state* (Oxford, 1997)
Jordan, W.C., *Louis IX and the challenge of the Crusade* (Princeton, 1979)
—— *The great famine* (Princeton, 1996)
Jular, C., *Los adelantados y merinos mayores de León (siglos XIII–XV)* (León, 1990)
—— 'The king's face on the territory', in I. Alfonso et al. (eds), *Building legitimacy* (Leiden, 2004), 107–37
Jurdjevic, M., 'Hedgehogs and foxes', *Past and present*, 195 (2007), 241–68
Justice, S., *Writing and rebellion* (Berkeley, 1994)
Kaegi, W.E., *Heraclius* (Cambridge, 2003)
Kafadar, C., *Between two worlds* (Berkeley, 1995)
Kaiser, R., *Churrätien im frühen Mittelalter* (Basel, 1998)
Kaldellis, A., *The argument of Psellos' Chronographia* (Leiden, 1999)
—— *The Byzantine republic* (Cambridge, MA, 2015)
Káldy-Nagy, Gy., 'The first centuries of the Ottoman military organization', *Acta Orientalia Academiae Scientiarum Hungaricae*, 31 (1977), 147–83
Kaminsky, H., *A history of the Hussite revolution* (Berkeley, 1967)
—— 'The great schism', *NCMH*, vol. 6 (2000), 674–96
—— 'The noble feud in the middle ages', *Past and present*, 177 (2002), 55–83
Kanter, J.E., 'Peripatetic and sedentary kingship', in J. Burton et al. (eds), *Thirteenth-century England, XIII* (Woodbridge, 2011), 11–26
Kaplan, M., *Les hommes et la terre à Byzance du VIe au XIe siècle* (Paris, 1992)
Karpova Fasce, E., 'Gli architetti italiani a Mosca nei secoli XIV–XV', *Quaderni di scienza della conservazione*, 4 (2004), 157–81
Karras, R.M., *Common women* (New York, 1996)
—— *Slavery and society in medieval Scandinavia* (New Haven, 1988)
Kastritsis, D.J., *The sons of Beyazid* (Leiden, 2007)
Katajala, K., 'Against tithes and taxes, for king and province', in idem (ed.), *Northern revolts* (Helsinki, 2004), 32–52
Kay, S., *Raoul de Cambrai* (Oxford, 1992)
Keen, M., *Chivalry* (New Haven, 1984)
Keene, D., 'Towns and the growth of trade', *NCMH*, vol. 4.1 (2004), 47–85
Kekaumenos, *Consilia et narrationes*, ed. and trans. C. Roueché (2013), online at www.ancientwisdoms.ac.uk/library/kekaumenos-consilia-et-narrationes/, accessed 21 November 2015
Kekewich, M., 'The attainder of the Yorkists in 1459', *Historical research*, 55 (1982), 25–34
Keller, H., 'Die italienische Kommune als Laboratorium administrativen Schriftgebrauchs', in S. Lepsius et al. (eds), *Recht – Geschichte – Geschichtsschreibung* (Berlin, 2014), 67–82
—— *Signori e vassalli nell'Italia delle città (secoli IX–XII)* (Turin, 1995)
—— *Zwischen regionaler Begrenzung und universalem Horizont* (Berlin, 1986)
Kelly, C., *Ruling the later Roman empire* (Cambridge, MA, 2004)
Kelly, F., *A guide to early Irish law* (Dublin, 1988)
Kempshall, M.S., *The common good in late medieval political thought* (Oxford, 1999)
Kennedy, H., *Muslim Spain and Portugal* (London, 1996)
—— *The armies of the caliphs* (London, 2001)
—— *The prophet and the age of the caliphates*, 2nd edn (Harlow, 2004)
Kirkham, V., 'Petrarch the courtier', in eadem and A. Maggi (eds), *Petrarch* (Chicago, 2009), 141–50

Klaniczay, G., *Holy rulers and blessed princesses* (Cambridge, 2002)

Klassen, J., 'Hus, the Hussites and Bohemia', *NCMH*, vol. 7 (1998), 367–91

Kohl, T., *Lokale Gesellschaften* (Ostfildern, 2010)

Kolbaba, T.M., *The Byzantine lists* (Urbana, 2000)

Kostick, C., *The social structure of the First Crusade* (Leiden, 2008)

Kosto, A.J., 'Reconquest, Renaissance and the histories of Iberia, ca. 1000–1200', in Noble and Van Engen, *European transformations*, 93–116

Kotel'nikova, L.A., *Mondo contadino e città dal XI al XIV secolo* (Bologna, 1975)

Koziol, G., *The politics of memory and identity in Carolingian royal diplomas* (Turnhout, 2012)

Krag, C., 'The early unification of Norway', in K. Helle (ed.), *The Cambridge history of Scandinavia*, vol. 1 (Cambridge, 2003), 184–201

Krah, A., *Absetzungsverfahren als Spiegelbild von Königsmacht* (Aalen, 1987)

Kula, W., *An economic theory of the feudal system* (London, 1976)

Kümin, B., *The shaping of a community* (Aldershot, 1996)

Kypta, U., *Die Autonomie der Routine* (Göttingen, 2014)

La Rocca, C. (ed.), *Italy in the early middle ages* (Oxford, 2002)

Lacy, N.J., *Reading fabliaux* (New York, 1993)

Ladero Quesada, M.A., 'Castile in the middle ages', in Bonney, *The rise of the fiscal state*, 177–99

—— *El siglo XV en Castilla* (Barcelona, 1982)

—— *Fiscalidad y poder real en Castilla (1252–1369)* (Madrid, 1993)

Lahey, S.E., *John Wyclif* (Oxford, 2009)

Laiou, A.E. (ed.), *The economic history of Byzantium from the seventh through the fifteenth century* (Washington, DC, 2002)

Laiou, A.E. and C. Morrisson, *The Byzantine economy* (Cambridge, 2007)

Laleman. M.C. and P. Raveschot, 'Maisons patriciennes médiévales à Gand (Gent), Belgique', in P. Demolon et al. (eds), *Archéologie des villes dans le Nord-Ouest de l'Europe (VIIe–XIIIe siècle)* (Douai, 1994), 201–5

Lambert, T.B., 'Theft, homicide and crime in late Anglo-Saxon law', *Past and present*, 214 (2012), 3–43

Langdon, J. and J. Masschaele, 'Commercial activity and population growth in medieval England', *Past and present*, 190 (2006), 35–82

Lansing, C., *Passion and order* (Ithaca, NY, 2008)

—— *Power and purity* (New York, 1998)

—— *The Florentine magnates* (Princeton, 1991)

Lansing, C. and E.D. English, *A companion to the medieval world* (Oxford, 2009)

Lantschner, P., *The logic of political conflict in medieval cities* (Oxford, 2015)

Latini, B., *Li livres dou tresor*, ed. S. Baldwin and P. Barrette (Tempe, AZ, 2003)

Laxdæla saga, ed. Einar Ó. Sveinsson, *Íslenzk fornrit*, vol. 5 (Reykjavík, 1934), trans. Magnús Magnússon and Hermann Pálsson, *Laxdæla saga* (London, 1969)

Lazzarini, I., *L'Italia degli stati territoriali, secoli XIII–XV* (Rome, 2003)

Le concile de Clermont de 1095 et l'appel à la Croisade (Rome, 1997)

Le Goff, J., *Saint Louis* (New York, 2009)

Le Jan, R., *Famille et pouvoir dans le monde franc (VIIe–Xe siècle)* (Paris, 1995)

—— *La société du haut moyen âge* (Paris, 2003)

—— 'Les cérémonies carolingiennes', *Settimane di studio*, 52 (2015), 167–96

Le ménagier de Paris, ed. J. Pichon (Paris, 1846); trans. G.L. Greco and C.M. Rose, *The good wife's guide* (Ithaca, NY, 2009)

Le Roy Ladurie, E., *Montaillou* (London, 1978)

Le traité sur la guérilla de l'empereur Nicéphore Phocas (963–969), ed. and trans. G. Dagron and H. Mihăescu (Paris, 1986)

Lecuppre-Desjardin, E., *La ville des cérémonies* (Turnhout, 2004)

Lees, C.A. (ed.), *Medieval masculinities* (Minneapolis, 1994)

Leges Langobardorum, 643–866, ed. F. Beyerle, 2nd edn (Witzenhausen, 1962), trans. up to
    755 in K.F. Drew, *The Lombard laws* (Philadelphia, 1973)
Leges Visigothorum, ed. K. Zeumer, *MGH, Leges*, vol. 1 (Hannover, 1902)
Lemerle, P., *Byzantine humanism* (Canberra, 1986)
—— *Cinq études sur le XIe siècle byzantin* (Paris, 1977)
Lestringant, F. and M. Zink (eds), *Histoire de la France littéraire*, vol. 1 (Paris, 2006)
Lev, Y., *State and society in Fatimid Egypt* (Leiden, 1991)
Lewis, P.S., *Later medieval France* (London, 1968)
—— 'The failure of the French medieval estates', *Past and present*, 23 (1962), 3–24
Leyser, C., 'The memory of Gregory the Great and the making of Latin Europe, 600–1000',
    in K. Cooper and C. Leyser (eds), *Making early medieval societies* (Cambridge, 2016),
    181–201
Leyser, K., 'Concepts of Europe in the early and high middle ages', *Past and present*, 137
    (1992), 25–47
—— 'Ottonian government', in idem, *Medieval Germany and its neighbours 900–1250*
    (London, 1982), pp. 69–101
—— *Rule and conflict in an early medieval society* (London, 1979)
Li Bozhong, *Agricultural development in Jiangnan, 1620–1850* (Basingstoke, 1998)
*Libri dell'entrata e dell'uscita della repubblica di Siena, detti del camarlingo e dei quattro
    provveditori della Biccherna*, vol. 1 (Siena, 1903) and following
Lieberman, V., *Strange parallels*, 2 vols (Cambridge, 2003–09)
Linehan, P., 'Spain in the twelfth century', *NCMH*, vol. 4.2 (2004), 475–509
Little, L.K. (ed.), *Plague and the end of antiquity* (Cambridge, 2007)
Liutprand of Cremona, *Liudprandi Cremonensis opera*, ed. P. Chiesa (Turnhout, 1998),
    trans. P. Squatriti, *The complete works of Liudprand of Cremona* (Washington, 2007)
Lombard-Jourdan, A., *Paris: genèse de la 'ville'* (Paris, 1976)
Lot, F. and R. Fawtier, *Histoire des institutions françaises au moyen âge*, vol. 2 (Paris, 1958)
Loud, G., *The age of Robert Guiscard* (Harlow, 2000)
Loveluck, C., *Northwest Europe in the early middle ages, c. AD 600–1150* (Cambridge, 2013)
Lowry, H.W., *The nature of the early Ottoman state* (Albany, NY, 2003)
Lukowski, J. and H. Zawadski, *A concise history of Poland*, 2nd edn (Cambridge, 2006)
Luongo, F.T., *The saintly politics of Catherine of Siena* (Ithaca, NY, 2006)
Lupus of Ferrières, *Epistolae*, ed. E. Dümmler, *MGH, Epistolae*, vol. 6 (Berlin, 1925), 1–126,
    trans. G.W. Regenos, *The letters of Lupus of Ferrières* (The Hague, 1966)
Luscombe, D. (ed.), *The letter collection of Peter Abelard and Heloise* (Oxford, 2013)
Maas, M. (ed.), *The Cambridge companion to the age of Justinian* (Cambridge, 2005)
MacGeorge, P., *Late Roman warlords* (Oxford, 2002)
Machiavelli, N., *De principatibus*, ed. G. Inglese (Rome, 1994); trans. P. Bondanella, *The
    prince* (Oxford, 2005)
Mack, C.R., *Pienza* (Ithaca, NY, 1987)
MacKay, A., 'Popular movements and pogroms in fifteenth-century Castile', *Past and present*,
    55 (1972), 33–67
—— *Spain in the middle ages* (London, 1977)
MacLean, S., *Kingship and politics in the late ninth century* (Cambridge, 2003)
—— 'Palaces, itineraries and political order in the post-Carolingian kingdoms', in J. Hudson
    and A. Rodríguez (eds), *Diverging paths* (Leiden, 2014), 291–320
Maddicott, J.R., *The origins of the English parliament, 924–1327* (Oxford, 2010)
Magdalino, P., *Constantinople médiévale* (Paris, 1996)
—— *The empire of Manuel I Komnenos, 1143–1180* (Cambridge 1993)
—— 'The medieval empire (780–1204)', in C.A. Mango (ed.), *The Oxford history of
    Byzantium* (Oxford, 2002), 169–208
Maguire, H. (ed.), *Byzantine court culture from 829 to 1204* (Washington, 1997)
Mainoni, P. (ed.), *Politiche finanziarie e fiscali nell'Italia settentrionale (secoli XIII–XV)*
    (Milan, 2001)

Mainstone, R.J., *Hagia Sophia* (New York, 1988)

Maire Vigueur, J.-C., *Cavaliers et citoyens* (Paris, 2003)

—— *L'autre Rome* (Paris, 2010)

Maire Vigueur, J.-C. and E. Faini, *Il sistema politico dei comuni italiani (secoli XII–XIV)* (Milan, 2010)

Malfatti, C.V. (ed.), *Two Italian accounts of Tudor England* (Barcelona, 1953)

Mann, N., *Petrarch* (Oxford, 1984)

Manzano Moreno, E., *Conquistadores, emires y califas* (Barcelona, 2006)

Map, W., *De nugis curialium*, ed. and trans. M.R. James, 2nd edn (Oxford, 1983)

Marchal, G.P., 'Die Antwort der Bauern', *Vorträge und Forschungen*, 31 (1987), 757–90

—— *Sempach 1386* (Basel, 1986)

Markus, R.A., *Gregory the Great and his world* (Cambridge, 1997)

Margolis, O., *The politics of culture in Quattrocento Europe* (Oxford, 2016)

Martin, G.H., 'Merton, Walter of (*c.*1205–1277)', *Oxford dictionary of national biography* (Oxford, 2004)

Martin, J., *Medieval Russia, 980–1584*, 2nd edn (Cambridge, 2007)

Martin, J.-M., *La Pouille du VIe au XIIe siècle* (Rome, 1993)

Martindale, J., ' "An unfinished business" ', *Anglo-Norman studies*, 23 (2000), 115–54

—— *Status, authority and regional power* (Aldershot, 1997)

Martines, L. *The social world of the Florentine humanists, 1390–1460* (London, 1963)

Marx, K., *The eighteenth Brumaire of Louis Bonaparte*, trans. D. Fernbach, *Surveys from exile* (London, 1973), 143–249

Masschaele, J., 'Economic takeoff and the rise of markets', in C. Lansing and E.D. English (eds), *A companion to the medieval world* (Oxford, 2009), 89–110

—— *Peasants, merchants, and markets* (New York, 1997)

McCormick, M., *Eternal victory* (Cambridge, 1986)

—— *Origins of the European economy* (Cambridge, 2001)

McDonnell, E.W., *The beguines and beghards in medieval culture* (New York, 1954)

McFarlane, K.B., *The nobility of later medieval England* (Oxford, 1973)

McKitterick, R., *Charlemagne* (Cambridge, 2008)

—— *Perceptions of the past in the early middle ages* (Notre Dame, IN, 2006)

—— *The Carolingians and the written word* (Cambridge, 1989)

—— *The Frankish kingdoms under the Carolingians, 751–987* (Harlow, 1983)

McNamara, J.A. and S. Wemple, 'The power of women through the family in medieval Europe: 500–1100', *Feminist studies*, 3/4 (1973), 126–41

McSheffrey, S., 'Heresy, orthodoxy and English vernacular religion, 1480–1525', *Past and present*, 186 (2005), 47–80

Meijers, E.M., *Études d'histoire du droit*, vol. 3 (Leiden, 1959)

Melve, L., *Inventing the public sphere* (Leiden, 2007)

Menant, F., *Campagnes lombardes au moyen âge* (Rome, 1993)

—— *L'Italie des communes (1100–1350)* (Paris, 2005)

Ménard, P., *Les fabliaux* (Paris, 1983)

Mengel, D.C., 'A plague on Bohemia?', *Past and present*, 200 (2011), 3–34

Menjot, D. and M. Sánchez Martínez (eds), *Fiscalidad de estado y fiscalidad municipal en los reinos hispánicos medievales* (Madrid, 2006)

Merrills, A. and R. Miles, *The Vandals* (Oxford, 2014)

Meyer, T., 'The state of the dukes of Zähringen', in G. Barraclough (ed. and trans.), *Medieval Germany, 911–1250*, vol. 2 (Oxford, 1938), 175–202

MGH, Capitularia regum Francorum, ed. A. Boretius and V. Krause, 2 vols (Hannover, 1883–97)

MGH, Epistolae, vol. 5, ed. K. Hampe et al. (Berlin, 1899)

MGH, Epistolae, vol. 7, ed. E. Caspar et al. (Berlin, 1928)

MGH, Formulae Merowingici et Karolini aevi, ed. K. Zeumer (Hannover, 1886)

MGH, Poetae Latini aevi Carolini, vol. 2, ed. E. Dümmler (Berlin, 1884)

Milani, G., *I comuni italiani, secoli XII–XIV* (Bari, 2005)

Miller, M.C., 'The crisis in the Investiture Crisis narrative', *History compass*, 7/6 (2009), 1570–80

—— *The formation of a medieval church* (Ithaca, NY, 1993)

Miller, W.I., *Bloodtaking and peacemaking* (Chicago, 1990)

—— *'Why is your axe bloody?'* (Oxford, 2014)

Mitchell K. and I. Wood (eds), *The world of Gregory of Tours* (Leiden, 2002)

Molinari, A. (ed.), 'Mondi rurali d'Italia', *Archeologia medievale*, 37 (2010), 11–281

Mollat, M., 'Recherches sur les finances des ducs valois de Bourgogne', *Revue historique*, 219 (1958), 285–321

Molyneaux, G., *The formation of the English kingdom in the tenth century* (Oxford, 2015)

Montanari, M., *L'alimentazione contadina nell'alto medioevo* (Naples, 1979)

Moore, R.I., 'Family, community and cult on the eve of the Gregorian reform', *Transactions of the Royal Historical Society*, 5th ser., 30 (1980), 49–69

—— *The first European revolution, c. 970–1215* (Oxford, 2000)

—— *The formation of a persecuting society*, 2nd edn (Oxford, 2007)

—— *The war on heresy* (London, 2012)

Moorhead, J., *Justinian* (London, 1994)

—— *Theoderic in Italy* (Oxford, 1992)

Moraw, P., *Von offener Verfassung zu gestalteter Verdichtung* (Berlin, 1985)

Morelli, S., 'Note sulla fiscalità diretta e indiretta nel Regno angioino', in C. Massaro and L. Petracca (eds), *Territorio, cultura e poteri nel Medioevo e oltre*, vol. 1 (Galatina, 2011), 389–413

Morris, C., *The papal monarchy* (Oxford, 1989)

Morrison, K.F., *Understanding conversion* (Charlottesville, VA, 1992)

Morsel, J., *L'aristocratie médiévale* (Paris, 2004)

Mortensen, P., and B. Rasmussen (eds), *Fra stamme til stat i Danmark*, 2 vols (Højbjerg, 1988–91)

Moss, R.E., *Fatherhood and its representations in Middle English texts* (Woodbridge, 2013)

Moustakas, K., 'Byzantine "visions" of the Ottoman empire', in A. Lymberopoulou (ed.), *Images of the Byzantine world* (Farnham, 2011), 215–29

Müller, G. (ed.), *Documenti sulle relazioni delle città toscane coll'Oriente cristiano e coi Turchi* (Florence, 1879)

Müller-Mertens, E., *Karl der Grosse, Ludwig der Fromme, und die Freien* (Berlin, 1963)

—— *Regnum Teutonicum* (Berlin-Vienna, 1970)

Murray, A., *Reason and society in the middle ages* (Oxford, 1978)

Muscatine, C., *The Old French fabliaux* (New Haven, 1986)

Myhre, B., 'Chieftains' graves and chiefdom territories in south Norway in the migration period', *Studien zur Sachsenforschung*, 6 (1987), 169–87

Myking, J.R. and C. Porskrog Rasmussen, 'Scandinavia, 1000–1750', in B. van Bavel and R. Hoyle (eds), *Social Relations: Property and Power* (Turnhout, 2010)

Naccache, A., *Le décor des églises des villages d'Antiochène du IVe au VIIe siècle* (Paris, 1992)

Naismith, R., *Money and power in Anglo-Saxon England* (Cambridge, 2012)

Najemy, J.M. (ed.), *Italy in the age of the Renaissance: 1300–1550* (Oxford, 2004)

Nedungatt, G., and M. Featherstone (eds), *The Council in Trullo revisited* (Rome, 1995)

Nef, A. and V. Prigent (eds), *La Sicile de Byzance à l'Islam* (Paris, 2010)

Negrelli, C., 'Towards a definition of early medieval pottery', in S. Gelichi and R. Hodges (eds), *From one sea to another* (Turnhout, 2012), 393–416

Nelson, J.L., 'Aachen as a place of power', in M. de Jong et al. (eds), *Topographies of power in the early middle ages* (Leiden, 2001), 217–41

—— *Charles the Bald* (London, 1992)

—— 'How the Carolingians created consensus', in. W. Fałkowski and Y. Sassier (eds), *Le monde carolingien* (Turnhout, 2009), 67–81

—— 'Literacy in Carolingian government', in R. McKitterick (ed.), *The uses of literacy in early medieval Europe* (Cambridge, 1990), 258–96

—— *Politics and ritual in early medieval Europe* (London, 1986)

—— 'The settings of the gift in the reign of Charlemagne', in W. Davies and P. Fouracre (eds), *The languages of gift in the early middle ages* (Cambridge, 2010), 116–48

Neville, L., *Authority in Byzantine provincial society, 950–1100* (Cambridge, 2004)

—— *Heroes and Romans in twelfth-century Byzantium* (Cambridge, 2012)

Ní Mhaonaigh, M., *Brian Boru* (Stroud, 2007)

Nicéphore, *Discours contre les Iconoclastes*, trans. M.-J. Mondzain-Baudinet (Paris, 1989)

Nicholas, D., *Medieval Flanders* (Harlow, 1992)

—— *The growth of the medieval city* (Abingdon, 1997)

Nicholls, K.W., *Gaelic and Gaelicized Ireland in the middle ages*, 2nd edn (Dublin, 2003)

Nicholson, R., *Scotland: the later middle ages* (Edinburgh, 1974)

Nicol, D.M., *The last centuries of Byzantium, 1261–1453*, 2nd edn (Cambridge, 1993)

Nielsen, P.O. et al. (eds), *The archaeology of Gudme and Lundeborg* (Copenhagen, 1994)

Nirenberg, D., *Communities of violence* (Princeton, 1996)

Noble, T.F.X., *The Republic of St. Peter* (Philadelphia, 1984)

—— (ed.), *From Roman province to medieval kingdoms* (London, 2006)

Noble, T.F.X. and J. Van Engen (eds), *European transformations* (Notre Dame, IN, 2012)

Notker, *Gesta Karoli magni imperatoris*, ed. H.F. Häfele, *MGH, Scriptores rerum Germanicarum*, N. S., vol. 12 (Berlin, 1959)

Nowakowska, N., *Church, state and dynasty in Renaissance Poland* (Aldershot, 2007)

Ó Corráin, D., *Ireland before the Normans* (Dublin, 1972)

O'Callaghan, J.F., *The cortes of Castile-León, 1188–1350* (Philadelphia, 1989)

Oldfield, P., *City and community in Norman Italy* (Cambridge, 2009)

Olesen, J.E., 'Inter-Scandinavian relations', in K. Helle (ed.), *The Cambridge history of Scandinavia*, vol. 1 (Cambridge, 2003), 710–70

Oliva Herrer, H.R. et al. (eds), *La comunidad medieval como esfera pública* (Seville, 2014)

Ormrod, W.M., 'England in the middle ages', in Bonney, *The rise of the fiscal state*, 19–52

—— 'The west European monarchies in the later middle ages', in Bonney, *Economic systems*, 123–60

Ormrod, W.M. and J. Barta, 'The feudal structure and the beginnings of state finance', in Bonney, *Economic systems*, 53–79

Orning, H.J., *Unpredictability and presence* (Leiden, 2008)

Oschema, K., *Bilder von Europa im Mittelalter* (Ostfildern, 2013)

Ostrowski, D., *Muscovy and the Mongols* (Cambridge, 1998)

Ousterhout, R., *The art of the Kariye Camii* (London, 2002)

Padoa-Schioppa, A., *Il diritto nella storia d'Europa*, vol. 1 (Padua, 1995)

Palliser, D.M. (ed.), *The Cambridge urban history of Britain*, vol. 1 (Cambridge, 2008)

Palmer, J.T., 'Defining paganism in the Carolingian world', *EME*, 15 (2007), 402–25

—— *The Apocalypse in the early middle ages* (Cambridge, 2014)

Panella, C., 'Merci e scambi nel Mediterraneo in età tardoantica', in A. Carandini et al. (eds), *Storia di Roma*, vol. 3.2 (Turin, 1993), 613–97

Panero, F., *Schiavi servi e villani nell'Italia medievale* (Turin, 1999)

Pantos, A., '*In medle oððe an þinge*', in eadem and S. Semple (eds), *Assembly places and practices in medieval Europe* (Dublin, 2004), 180–201

Papaioannou, S., *Michael Psellos: rhetoric and authorship in Byzantium* (Cambridge, 2013)

Paravicini Bagliani, A., *Il trono di Pietro* (Rome, 1996)

Parisse, M., 'Leone IX, papa, santo', in *Dizionario biografico degli Italiani*, vol. 64 (Rome, 2005), 507–13

Parsons, J.C., 'Isabella (1295–1358)', *Oxford dictionary of national biography* (Oxford, 2004)

Parthasarathi, P., *Why Europe grew rich and Asia did not* (Cambridge, 2011)

Partner, P., 'The "budget" of the Roman church in the Renaissance period', in E.F. Jacob (ed.), *Italian Renaissance studies* (London, 1960), 256–78

Paschasius Radbert, *Epitaphium Arsenii*, ed. E. Dümmler, *Philosophische und historische Abhandlungen der königlichen Akademie der Wissenschaften zu Berlin*, 2 (1900), 1–98, trans. A. Cabaniss, *Charlemagne's cousins* (Syracuse, NY, 1967)

Passio prima Leudegarii episcopi Augustodunensis, ed. B. Krusch, *MGH, Scriptores rerum Merovingicarum*, vol. 5 (Hannover, 1910), 282–322, trans. P. Fouracre and R.A. Gerberding, *Late Merovingian France* (Manchester, 1996), 193–253

Pastor, R., *Resistencias y luchas campesinas en la época de crecimiento y consolidación de la formación feudal* (Madrid, 1980)

Patzold, S., *Das Lehnswesen* (Munich, 2012)

Patzold, S., *Ich und Karl der Grosse* (Stuttgart, 2013)

Pécout, T. (ed.), *Quand gouverner c'est enquêter* (Paris, 2010)

Pedersen, F., 'A good and sincere man ... even though he looked like a Slav', *Mediaeval Scandinavia*, 20 (2010), 141–62

Pegg, M.G., *A most holy war* (Oxford, 2008)

—— *The corruption of angels* (Princeton, 2001)

Pérez Sanchez, D., *El ejército en la sociedad visigoda* (Salamanca, 1989)

Peterson, J.L., 'Holy heretics in later medieval Italy', *Past and present*, 204 (2009), 3–31

Petrocchi, G., 'Biografia', *Enciclopedia dantesca: appendice* (Rome, 1978), 3–53

Phillips, J., *The Fourth Crusade and the sack of Constantinople* (London, 2005)

Pirenne, H., *Histoire de Belgique*, vol. 1, 5th edn (Brussels, 1929)

—— *Mohammed and Charlemagne* (London, 1939)

Pixton, P.B., *The German episcopacy and the implementation of the decrees of the Fourth Lateran Council, 1216–1245* (Leiden, 1995)

Pohl, W., 'Frontiers in Lombard Italy', in idem et al. (eds), *The transformation of frontiers* (Leiden, 2001), 117–41

Pohl, W. and P. Erhart (eds), *Die Langobarden* (Vienna, 2005)

Pohl, W. and G. Heydemann (eds), *Strategies of identification* (Turnhout, 2013)

Pollard, A., 'The people, politics and the constitution in the fifteenth century', in R.W. Kaeuper (ed.), *Law, governance and justice* (Leiden, 2013), 311–28

Pollock, F. and F.W. Maitland, *The history of English law before the time of Edward I*, 2 vols (Cambridge, 1898)

Poloni, A., *Trasformazioni della società e mutamenti delle forme politiche in un Comune italiano* (Pisa, 2004)

Poly, J.-P. and É. Bournazel, *The feudal transformation, 900–1200* (New York, 1991)

Pomeranz, K., *The great divergence* (Princeton, 2000)

Portass, R., 'All quiet on the western front?', *EME*, 21 (2013), 283–306

Pössel, C., 'Authors and recipients of Carolingian capitularies, 779–829', in R. Corradini et al. (eds), *Texts and identities in the early middle ages* (Vienna, 2006), 253–74

Postan, M., *The medieval economy and society* (London, 1972)

Poulsen, B. and S.M. Sindbaek (eds), *Settlement and lordship in Viking and early medieval Scandinavia* (Turnhout, 2011)

Prater, E.S., *Curia and cortes in León and Castile* (Cambridge, 1980)

Prestwich, M., *Plantagenet England 1225–1360* (Oxford, 2005)

Prigent, V., 'The mobilisation of fiscal resources in the Byzantine empire (eighth to eleventh centuries)', in J. Hudson and A. Rodríguez (eds), *Diverging paths* (Leiden, 2014), 182–229

Prinz, F., *Klerus und Krieg im früheren Mittelalter* (Stuttgart, 1971)

Provero, L., *L'Italia dei poteri locali* (Rome, 1998)

Pryor, J., 'Foreign policy and economic policy', in L.O. Frappell (ed.), *Principalities, powers and estates* (Adelaide, 1980), 43–55

Psellos, M., *Chronographia*, trans. E.R.A. Sewter, *Fourteen Byzantine rulers* (London, 1966)

Puin, G.-R., *Der Dīwān von ʿUmar ibn al-Ḫaṭṭāb* (Bonn, 1970)

Purkis, W.J., *Crusading spirituality in the Holy Land and Iberia, c.1095–c.1187* (Woodbridge, 2008)

Quaglioni, D., *Politica e diritto nel Trecento italiano* (Florence, 1983)

Raccagni, G., *The Lombard league, 1167-1225* (Oxford, 2010)

Raine, M., ' "Fals flesch" ', *New Medieval Literatures*, 7 (2005), 101–26

Randsborg, K., *The Viking age in Denmark* (London, 1980)

Rapp, C., *Holy bishops in late antiquity* (Berkeley, 2005)

Rawcliffe, C., *Leprosy in medieval England* (Woodbridge, 2006)

Recht, R. (ed.), *Les batisseurs des cathédrales gothiques* (Strasbourg, 1989)

Redon, O., 'Seigneurs et communautés rurales dans le contado de Sienne au XIIIe siècle', *Mélanges de l'École française de Rome: moyen âge*, 91 (1979), 149–96, 619–57

Reimitz, H., *History, Frankish identity and the framing of Western ethnicity, 550–850* (Cambridge, 2015)

Reuter, T., 'Assembly politics in western Europe from the eighth century to the twelfth', in P. Linehan and J.L. Nelson (eds), *The medieval world* (London, 2001), 432–50

—— *Germany in the early middle ages, c. 800-1056* (London, 1991)

—— 'Gifts and simony', in E. Cohen and M. de Jong (eds), *Medieval transformations* (Leiden, 2000), 157–68

—— *Medieval polities and modern mentalities*, ed. J.L. Nelson (Cambridge, 2006)

Rexroth, F., *Deviance and power in late medieval London* (Cambridge, 2007)

Reyerson, K., 'Urban economies', in Bennett and Karras, *The Oxford handbook of women and gender*, 295–310

Reynolds, S., *Fiefs and vassals* (Oxford, 1994)

—— *Kingdoms and communities in western Europe, 900-1300* (Oxford, 1984)

—— 'There were states in medieval Europe', *Journal of historical sociology*, 16 (2003), 550–5

Riché, P., *Écoles et enseignement dans le haut moyen âge* (Paris, 1989)

—— *Gerbert d'Aurillac* (Paris, 1987)

Rimbert, *Vita Anskarii*, ed. G. Waitz, *MGH, Scriptores rerum Germanicarum*, vol. 55 (Hannover 1884)

Rio, A., *Slavery after Rome, 500-1100* (Oxford, 2016)

Ripoll, G. and J.M. Gurt (eds), *Sedes regiae (ann. 400–800)* (Barcelona, 2000)

Rist, R., *Popes and Jews, 1095-1291* (Oxford, 2016)

Rizzi, A., (ed.), *Statuta de ludo* (Rome, 2012)

Roach, L., *Kingship and consent in Anglo-Saxon England, 871-978* (Cambridge, 2013)

Robert of Torigni, *Chronica*, ed. R. Howlett, *Chronicles of the reigns of Stephen, Henry II and Richard I*, vol. 4 (London, 1889)

Robertson, A.J. (ed.), *Anglo-Saxon charters* (Cambridge 1939)

Robinson, C.F., *Islamic historiography* (Cambridge, 2003)

Robinson, I.S., *Henry IV of Germany, 1056-1106* (Cambridge, 1999)

—— *The papacy 1073-1198* (Cambridge, 1990)

Rodríguez, López, A., *La consolidación territorial de la monarquía feudal castellana* (Madrid, 1994)

—— *La estirpe de Leonor de Aquitania* (Barcelona, 2014)

Roesdahl, E., *The Vikings* (London, 1987)

Rollo-Koster, J. and T.M. Izbicki (eds), *A companion to the great western schism (1378-1417)* (Leiden, 2009)

Roper, L., *Oedipus and the Devil* (London, 1994)

—— *The holy household* (Oxford, 1989)

Rosenwein, B., *A short history of the middle ages*, 3rd edn (Toronto, 2009)

—— *Rhinoceros bound* (Philadelphia, 1982)

—— 'The family politics of Berengar I, king of Italy (888–924)', *Speculum*, 71 (1996), 247–89

Rosser, G., *The art of solidarity in the middle ages* (Oxford, 2015)

Rowell, S.C., *Lithuania ascending* (Cambridge, 1994)

Rubellin, M., *Église et société chrétienne d'Agobard à Valdès* (Lyon, 2003)

Rubin, M., *Corpus Christi* (Cambridge, 1991)

—— *Gentile tales* (Philadelphia, 1999)

—— *The hollow crown* (London, 2005)

Rubin, M. and W. Simons (eds), *The Cambridge history of Christianity*, vol. 4 (Cambridge, 2009)

Ruggiero, G., *The Renaissance in Italy* (Cambridge, 2015)

Runciman, S., *A history of the Crusades*, 3 vols (Cambridge, 1951–54)

Rustow, M., *Heresy and the politics of community* (Ithaca, NY, 2008)

Ryan, M., 'Bartolus of Sassoferrato and free cities', *Transactions of the Royal Historical Society*, 6 ser., 10 (2000), 65–89

Sabapathy, J., 'Accountable *rectores* in comparative perspective', in A. Bérenger and F. Lachaud (eds), *Hiérarchie des pouvoirs, délégation de pouvoir et responsabilité des administrateurs dans l'antiquité et au moyen âge* (Metz, 2012), 201–30

Sabapathy, J., *Officers and accountability in medieval England 1170–1300* (Oxford, 2014)

Sablonier, R., 'The Swiss confederation', *NCMH*, vol. 7 (1998), 645–70

Sackville, L., *Heresy and heretics in the thirteenth century* (York, 2011)

Sadeghi, B. and M. Goudarzi, 'Ṣanʿāʾ 1 and the origins of the Qurʾān', *Der Islam*, 87 (2012), 1–129

Sales i Favà, Ll., 'Suing in a local jurisdictional court in late medieval Catalonia', *Continuity and change*, 29 (2014), 49–81

Salvatori, E., *La popolazione pisana nel Duecento* (Pisa, 1994)

Salvestrini, F., (ed.), *L'Italia alla fine del medioevo*, vol. 1 (Florence, 2006)

Sanders, G.D.R., 'Corinth', in Laiou, *The economic history*, vol. 2, 647–54

Sanders, P., *Ritual, politics and the city in Fatimid Cairo* (Albany, NY, 1994)

Sansterre, J.-M., *Les moines grecs et orientaux à Rome aux époques byzantine et carolingienne* (Brussels, 1983)

Sapori, A., *La crisi delle compagnie mercantili dei Bardi e dei Peruzzi* (Florence, 1926)

Sarris, P., *Economy and society in the age of Justinian* (Cambridge, 2006)

—— *Empires of faith, 500–700* (Oxford, 2011)

Sassier, Y., 'L'utilisation d'un concept romain aux temps carolingiens', *Médiévales*, 15 (1988), 17–29

Sawyer, B. and P. Sawyer, *Medieval Scandinavia* (Minneapolis, 1993)

Sawyer, P., 'Kings and royal power', in Mortensen and Rasmussen, *Fra stamme til stat*, vol. 2, 282–8

—— (ed.), *The Oxford illustrated history of the Vikings* (Oxford, 1997)

Sayers, J., *Innocent III* (London, 1994)

Scales, L., *The shaping of German identity* (Cambridge, 2012)

Scase, W., '"Strange and wonderful bills"', in R. Copeland et al. (eds), *New medieval literatures*, vol. 2 (Oxford, 1998), 225–47

Schieffer, R., *Die Entstehung des päpstlichen Investiturverbots für den deutschen König* (Stuttgart, 1981)

Schmitt, O.J., 'Les hommes et le pouvoir', in idem, *Korčula sous la domination de Venise au XVᵉ siècle: pouvoir, économie et vie quotidienne dans une île dalmate au moyen âge tardif* (Paris, Collège de France, 2011), online edn at http://books.openedition.org/cdf/1511, accessed 12 July 2015

Schneidmüller, B., *Die Welfen* (Stuttgart, 2000)

Scholz, S., *Politik – Selbstverständnis – Selbstdarstellung* (Stuttgart, 2006)

Scott, T., *The city-state in Europe, 1000–1600* (Oxford, 2012)

—— 'The economic policies of the regional city-states of Renaissance Italy', *Quaderni storici*, 49 (2014), 219–63

Scull, C., 'Urban centres in pre-Viking England?', in J. Hines (ed.), *The Anglo-Saxons from the migration period to the eighth century* (Woodbridge, 1997), 269–310

Seibt, F., 'Die Zeit der Luxemburger und der hussitischen Revolution', in K. Bosl (ed.), *Handbuch der Geschichte der böhmischen Länder*, vol. 1 (Stuttgart, 1967), 351–568

Seidel, I., *Byzanz im Spiegel der literarischen Entwicklung Frankreichs im 12. Jahrhundert* (Frankfurt, 1977)

Semple, S., 'Sacred spaces and places in pre-Christian and conversion period Anglo-Saxon England', in H. Hamerow et al. (eds), *The Oxford handbook of Anglo-Saxon archaeology* (Oxford, 2011), 742–63

Senatore, F., 'The kingdom of Naples', in Gamberini and Lazzarini, *The Italian Renaissance state*, 30–49

Ševčenko, I., 'Re-reading Constantine Porphyrogenitus', in J. Shepard and S. Franklin (eds), *Byzantine diplomacy* (Aldershot, 1992), 167–95

Shepard, J., 'Bulgaria', *NCMH*, vol. 3 (1999), 567–85

—— (ed.), *The Cambridge history of the Byzantine empire, c. 500–1492* (Cambridge, 2008)

Shepard, J. and S. Franklin, *The emergence of Rus, 750–1200* (London, 1996)

Sidonius Apollinaris, *Carmina* and *Epistolae*, ed. and trans. W.B. Anderson, *Poems and letters*, 2 vols (Cambridge, MA, 1936–65)

Signes Codoñer, J., *The emperor Theophilos and the east, 829–842* (Farnham, 2014)

Simms, K., *From kings to warlords* (Woodbridge, 1987)

Simons, W., *Cities of ladies* (Philadelphia, 2001)

Sizgorich, T., 'Narrative and community in Islamic late antiquity', *Past and present*, 185 (2004), 9–42

Skinner, P., *Medieval Amalfi and its diaspora, 800–1250* (Oxford, 2013)

—— *Women in medieval Italian society, 500–1200* (Harlow, 2001)

Skinner, Q., *The foundations of modern political thought*, vol. 1 (Cambridge, 1978)

Skoda, H., *Medieval violence* (Oxford, 2013)

—— 'La Vierge et la vieille', in T. Kouamé (ed.), *Experts et expertise au Moyen Âge* (Paris, 2012), 299–311

Skovgaard-Petersen, I., 'The making of the Danish kingdom', in K. Helle (ed.), *The Cambridge history of Scandinavia*, vol. 1 (Cambridge, 2003), 163–83

Šmahel, F., *Die hussitische Revolution*, 3 vols (Hannover, 2002)

Small, G., *Late medieval France* (Basingstoke, 2009)

Smith, J.M.H., 'Einhard: the sinner and the saints', *Transactions of the Royal Historical Society*, 13 (2003), 55–77

—— *Europe after Rome* (Oxford, 2005)

—— 'Rulers and relics c. 750–950', *Past and present*, supplement 5 (2010), 73–96

Snorri Sturluson, *Heimskringla*, ed. Bjarni Aðalbjarnarson, 3 vols, *Íslenzk fornrit*, vols 26–28 (Reykjavík, 1941–51): *Hákona saga goða* (vol. 1, 150–97), *Óláfs saga Tryggvasonar* (vol. 1, 225–372), *Óláfs saga ins Helga* (vol. 2); trans. L.M. Hollander (Austin, TX, 1964)

Southern, R.W., *Saint Anselm* (Cambridge, 1990)

—— *Scholastic humanism and the making of Europe*, 2 vols (Oxford, 1995–2001)

—— *The making of the middle ages* (London, 1953)

—— *Western society and the church in the middle ages* (London, 1970)

Spiegel, G.M., *Romancing the past* (Berkeley, 1993)

Spufford, P., *Money and its use in medieval Europe* (Cambridge, 1988)

—— *Power and profit* (New York, 2002)

Squatriti, P., 'Digging ditches in early medieval Europe', *Past and present*, 176 (2002), 11–65

Stafford, P., *Queen Emma and Queen Edith* (Oxford, 1997)

—— *Queens, concubines and dowagers* (London, 1983)

—— *Unification and conquest* (London, 1989)

Stancliffe, C., 'Religion and society in Ireland', *NCMH*, vol. 1 (2005), 397–425

Statuta sive leges municipales Arelatis, ed. C. Giroud, *Essai sur l'histoire du droit français au Moyen Âge*, vol. 2 (Paris, 1846), 185–245

Stephenson, P., *Byzantium's Balkan frontier* (Cambridge, 2000)

Stevenson, K., *Power and propaganda* (Edinburgh, 2014)

Stock, B., *The implications of literacy* (Princeton, 1983)

Stokes, L., *Demons of urban reform* (Basingstoke, 2011)

Stone, R., *Morality and masculinity in the Carolingian empire* (Cambridge, 2011)

Stone, R. and C. West (eds), *Hincmar of Rheims* (Manchester, 2015)
Storia medievale (Rome, 1998)
Story, J., *Carolingian connections* (Aldershot, 2003)
—— (ed.), *Charlemagne* (Manchester, 2005)
Strayer, J.R., *The reign of Philip the Fair* (Princeton, 1980)
Strohm, P., *Social Chaucer* (Cambridge, MA, 1989)
Stuard, S.M., *A state of deference* (Philadephia, 1992)
—— 'Brideprice, dowry, and other marital assigns', in Bennett and Karras, *The Oxford hand-book of women and gender*, 148–62
Sumption, J., *The Hundred Years War*, 4 vols (London, 1990–2015)
Sverris saga, ed. Thorleifur Hauksson, *Íslenzk fornrit*, vol. 30 (Reykjavík, 2007)
Swanson, R.N., *Religion and devotion in Europe, c.1215–c.1515* (Cambridge, 1995)
—— *Universities, academics and the Great Schism* (Cambridge, 1979)
Sykes, K., *Inventing Sempringham* (Berlin, 2011)
Tabacco, G., *The struggle for power in medieval Italy* (Cambridge, 1989)
Tabacco, G., and G.G. Merlo, *Medioevo* (Bologna, 1981)
Takayama, H., *The administration of the Norman kingdom of Sicily* (Leiden, 1993)
Tanner, N.P. (ed.), *Decrees of the ecumenical councils*, vol. 1 (London, 1990)
Tanner, R., *The late medieval Scottish parliament* (East Linton, 2001)
Taylor, A., *The shape of the state in medieval Scotland* (Oxford, 2016)
Taylor, Cl., *Heresy, crusade and inquisition in medieval Quercy* (Woodbridge, 2011)
Taylor, Cr., *Joan of Arc: la Pucelle* (Manchester, 2006)
—— 'War, propaganda and diplomacy in fifteenth-century France and England', in C. Allmand (ed.), *War, government and power in late medieval France* (Liverpool, 2000), 70–91
TeBrake, W.H., *A plague of insurrection* (Philadelphia, 1993)
Tellenbach, G., 'Die geistigen und politischen Grundlagen der karolingischen Thronfolge', *Frühmittelalteriche Studien*, 13 (1979), 184–302
—— *Königtum und Stamme in der Werdezeit des Deutschen Reiches* (Weimar, 1939)
—— *The church in western Europe from the tenth to the early twelfth century* (Cambridge, 1993)
Teuscher, S., *Lords' rights and peasant stories* (Philadelphia, 2012)
The Book of Margery Kempe, ed. B. Windeatt (Cambridge, 2004); trans. A. Bale (Oxford, 2015)
The Cambridge economic history of Europe, vols 1, 2 (2nd edn) and 3, ed. M.M. Postan et al. (Cambridge, 1963–87)
The new Cambridge medieval history, 7 vols (Cambridge, 1995–2005) [*NCMH*]
Thietmar of Merseburg, *Chronicon*, ed. R. Holtzmann, *MGH, Scriptores rerum Germanicarum*, N. S., vol. 9 (Berlin, 1935), trans. D.A. Warner, *Ottonian Germany* (Manchester, 2001)
Thomas, L., 'La vie privée de Guillaume de Nogaret', *Annales du Midi*, 16 (1904), 161–207
Thompson, A., *Francis of Assisi* (Ithaca, NY, 2012)
—— *Revival preachers and politics in thirteenth-century Italy* (Oxford, 1992)
Tibi, A.T., *The Tibyān: memoirs of 'Abd Allāh b. Buluggīn, last Zīrid amīr of Granada* (Leiden, 1986)
Titone, F., 'The kingdom of Sicily', in Gamberini and Lazzarini, *The Italian Renaissance state*, 9–29
To eparchikon biblion, the Book of the Eparch, le livre du préfet (London, 1970)
Torre, A., *Il consumo di devozioni* (Venice, 1995)
Toubert, P., 'Les statuts communaux et l'histoire des campagnes lombardes au XIVe siècle', *Mélanges d'archéologie et d'histoire*, 72 (1960), 397–508
—— *Les structures du Latium médiéval* (Rome, 1973)
—— *L'Europe dans sa première croissance* (Paris, 2004)
Tout, T.F., *Chapters in the administrative history of mediaeval England*, vol. 2 (Manchester, 1920)

Trexler, R.C., *Public life in Renaissance Florence* (New York, 1980)

Tyerman, C., *God's war* (London, 2006)

Urbańczyk, P. and S. Rosik, 'Poland', in Berend, *Christianization*, 263–318

Valdeón Baruque, J., *Los conflictos sociales en el reino de Castilla en los siglos XIV y XV* (Madrid, 1975)

Vale, M., *The princely court* (Oxford, 2001)

Valente, C., 'The deposition and abdication of Edward II', *English historical review*, 113 (1998), 852–81

Valenti, M., *L'insediamento altomedievale nelle campagne toscane* (Florence, 2004)

Vallejo Triano, A., *Madinat al-Zahra* (Seville, 2004)

Vallerani, M., *Medieval public justice* (Washington, DC, 2012)

van Bavel, B., *Manors and markets* (Oxford, 2010)

Van Dam, R., *Leadership and community in late antique Gaul* (Berkeley, 1985)

Van Engen, J.H., *Sisters and brothers of the common life* (Philadelphia, 2008)

Vauchez, A., *Francis of Assisi* (New Haven, 2012)

—— 'The Church and the laity', *NCMH*, vol. 5 (1999), 182–203

—— *The laity in the middle ages* (Notre Dame, IN, 1993)

Verhulst, A., *The Carolingian economy* (Cambridge, 2002)

—— *The rise of cities in north-west Europe* (Cambridge, 1999)

Vie de Théodore de Sykéôn, ed. A.-J. Festugière, 2 vols (Brussels, 1970)

Vignoli, P. (ed.), *I costituti della legge e dell'uso di Pisa (sec. XII)* (Rome, 2003)

Viguera Molins, M.J. (ed.), *Los reinos de Taifas: Al-Andalus en el siglo XI* (Madrid, 1994)

Villalon, L.J.A. and D.J. Kagay (eds), *The Hundred Years War: a wider focus* (Leiden, 2005)

Violante, C., 'I laici nel movimento patarino' in *I laici nella «societas cristiana» dei secoli XI e XII* (Milan, 1968), 587–687

Vita sanctae Geretrudis, ed. B. Krusch, *MGH, Scriptores rerum Merovingicarum*, vol. 2 (Hannover, 1888), 447–74, trans. P. Fouracre and R.A. Gerberding, *Late Merovingian France* (Manchester, 1996), 301–26

Vollrath, H., 'Sutri 1046 – Canossa 1077 – Rome 1111', in Noble and Van Engen, *European transformations*, 132–70

von Euw, A. and P. Schreiner (eds), *Kaiserin Theophanu* (Cologne, 1991)

Waddell, H., *The wandering scholars of the middle ages* (London, 1932)

Wagner, D.M. et al., '*Yersinia pestis* and the plague of Justinian 541–543 AD: a genomic analysis', *The Lancet infectious diseases*, 14.4 (2014), 319–26

Waley, D. and T. Dean, *The Italian city-republics*, 4th edn (Harlow, 2010)

Wallace, D., *Chaucerian polity* (Stanford, 1997)

Walmsley, A., *Early Islamic Syria* (London, 2007)

Walsham, A., *The Reformation of the landscape* (Oxford, 2011)

Wamers, E., *Die frühmittelalterlichen Lesefunde aus der Löhrstrasse (Baustelle Hilton II) in Mainz* (Mainz, 1994)

Ward-Perkins, B., *The fall of Rome and the end of civilization* (Oxford, 2005)

Wasserstein, D., *The rise and fall of the party-kings* (Princeton, 1985)

Watanabe, M., *The political ideas of Nicholas of Cusa* (Geneva, 1963)

Watson, A., *The evolution of law* (Oxford, 1985)

Watts, J., *Henry VI and the politics of kingship* (Cambridge, 1996)

—— 'Ideas, principles and politics', in A.J. Pollard (ed.), *The Wars of the Roses* (Basingstoke, 1995), 110–33, 234–7

—— *The making of polities* (Cambridge, 2009)

—— 'The pressure of the public on later medieval politics', in L. Clark and C. Carpenter (eds), *Political culture in late medieval Britain* (Woodbridge, 2004), 159–80

Wemple, S. and J.A. McNamara, 'The power of women through the family in medieval Europe, 500–1100', *Feminist studies*, 1 (1973), 126–41

Wei, I. P., *Intellectual culture in medieval Paris* (Cambridge, 2012)

Werner, K.F., 'Important noble families in the kingdom of Charlemagne', in T. Reuter (ed.), *The medieval nobility* (Amsterdam, 1975), 137–202

—— *Les origines avant l'an Mil* (Paris, 1984)

—— 'Missus-marchio-comes', in W. Paravicini and K.F. Werner (eds), *Histoire comparée de l'administration (IVᵉ–XVIIIᵉ siècles)* (Munich, 1980), 191–239

Werner, M., *Der Lütticher Raum in frühkarolingischer Zeit* (Göttingen, 1980)

West, C., 'Competing for the Holy Spirit', in P. Depreux et al. (eds), *Compétition et sacré au haut moyen âge* (Turnhout, 2015), 347–60

—— 'Lordship in ninth-century Francia', *Past and present*, 226 (2015), 3–40

—— *Reframing the feudal revolution* (Cambridge, 2013)

Whaley, J., *Germany and the Holy Roman Empire*, vol. 1 (Oxford, 2012)

Whelan, R., *Being Christian in Vandal Africa* (in press)

White, S.D., *Feuding and peace-making in eleventh-century France* (Aldershot, 2005)

—— *Re-thinking kinship and feudalism in early medieval Europe* (Aldershot, 2005)

Whittaker, C.R., *Frontiers of the Roman empire* (Baltimore, 1994)

Whittle, J., *The development of agrarian capitalism* (Oxford, 2000)

Whittow, M., 'The Byzantine economy (600–1204)', in Shepard, *The Cambridge history of the Byzantine empire*, 465–92

—— *The making of Orthodox Byzantium, 600–1025* (Basingstoke, 1996)

Wickham, C., *Community and clientele in twelfth-century Tuscany* (Oxford, 1998)

—— 'Consensus and assemblies in the Romano-Germanic kingdoms', *Vorträge und Forschungen*, 82 (2016, in press)

—— *Courts and conflict in twelfth-century Tuscany* (Oxford, 2003)

—— *Early medieval Italy* (London, 1981)

—— *Framing the early middle ages* (Oxford, 2005)

—— 'Le forme del feudalesimo', *Settimane di studio*, 47 (2000), 15–51

—— 'Lineages of western European taxation, 1000–1200', in M. Sánchez and A. Furió (eds), *Actes, Col·loqui Corona, municipis i fiscalitat a la baixa Edat Mitjana* (Lleida, 1997), 25–42

—— *Medieval Rome* (Oxford, 2015)

—— 'Ninth-century Byzantium through western eyes', in L. Brubaker (ed.), *Ninth-century Byzantium: dead or alive?* (Aldershot, 1998), 245–56

—— *Sleepwalking into a new world* (Princeton, 2015)

—— 'Social structures in Lombard Italy', in Ausenda et al., *The Langobards*, 118–48

—— 'Space and society in early medieval peasant conflicts', *Settimane di studio*, 50 (2003), 551–87

—— 'The early middle ages and national identity', in N. Fryde et al. (eds), *Die Deutung der mittelalterlichen Gesellschaft in der Moderne* (Göttingen, 2006), 107–22

—— 'The "feudal revolution" and the origins of Italian city communes', *Transactions of the Royal Historical Society*, 6th ser., 24 (2014), 29–55

—— *The inheritance of Rome* (London, 2009)

William fitz Stephen, *Vita Sancti Thomae*, ed. J. C. Robertson, *Materials for the history of Thomas Becket*, vol. 3 (London, 1877), 1–154

Williams, A., *Kingship and government in pre-conquest England, c.500–1066* (Basingstoke, 1999)

—— *The world before Domesday* (London, 2008)

Winkelmann, F., *Quellenstudien zur herrschenden Klasse von Byzanz im 8. und 9. Jahrhundert* (Berlin, 1987)

Winroth, A., *The conversion of Scandinavia* (New Haven, 2012)

Witt, R.G., *The two Latin cultures and the foundation of Renaissance humanism in medieval Italy* (Cambridge, 2012)

Wolff, P., 'The 1391 pogrom in Spain', *Past and present*, 50 (1971), 4–18

Wolfram, H., and W. Pohl (eds), *Typen der Ethnogenese*, 2 vols (Vienna, 1990)

Wood, I., 'Administration, law and culture in Merovingian Gaul', in R. McKitterick (ed.), *The uses of literacy in early medieval Europe* (Cambridge, 1990), 63–81
—— *Gregory of Tours* (Oxford, 1994)
—— *The Merovingian kingdoms, 450–751* (Harlow, 1994)
—— *The missionary life* (Harlow, 2001)
—— *The modern origins of the early middle ages* (Oxford, 2013)
Wood, S., *The proprietary church in the medieval west* (Oxford, 2006)
Wormald, J., 'Scotland: 1406–1513', *NCMH*, vol. 7 (1998), 513–41
Wormald, P., *The making of English law*, vol. 1 (Oxford, 1999)
—— (ed.), *Lay intellectuals in the Carolingian world* (Cambridge, 2007)
Wright, T. (ed.), *Political poems and songs relating to English history, composed during the period from the accession of EDW. III to that of RIC. III*, vol. 2 (London, 1861)
Y *Gododdin*, in I. Williams (ed.), *Canu Aneirin* (Cardiff, 1938), trans. K. Jackson, *The Gododdin* (Edinburgh, 1969)
Yorke, B., *The conversion of Britain, 600–800* (Harlow, 2006)
Young, M.J.L. et al. (eds), *Religion, learning and science in the 'Abbasid period* (Cambridge, 1990)
Zanella, G., *Hereticalia* (Spoleto, 1995)
Zanini, E., *Le Italie bizantine* (Bari, 1998)
Zavagno, L., *Cities in transition* (Oxford, 2009)
Zerner, M. (ed.), *Inventer l'hérésie?* (Nice, 1998)
Zorzi, A., 'Giustizia criminale e criminalità nell'Italia del tardo medioevo', *Società e storia*, 46 (1989), 923–65
Zotz, T., 'Die Formierung der Ministerialität', in S. Weinfurter (ed.), *Die Salier und das Reich*, vol. 3 (Sigmaringen, 1992), 3–50

Index

Geographical locations are in every case in modern countries.